THE RISE OF MERCHANT EMPIRES

Studies in
Comparative Early Modern History

Center for Early Modern History
University of Minnesota

Cambridge University Press

THE RISE OF MERCHANT EMPIRES

LONG-DISTANCE TRADE IN THE
EARLY MODERN WORLD, 1350–1750

Edited by
JAMES D. TRACY
University of Minnesota

CAMBRIDGE
UNIVERSITY PRESS

Published by the Press Syndicate of the University of Cambridge
The Pitt Building, Trumpington Street, Cambridge CB2 1RP
40 West 20th Street, New York, NY 10011-4211, USA
10 Stamford Road, Oakleigh, Melbourne 3166, Australia

First published 1990
Reprinted 1991
First paperback edition 1993

Printed in the United States of America

Library of Congress Cataloging-in-Publication Data available.

A catalogue record for this book is available from the British Library.

ISBN 0-521-38210-6 hardback
ISBN 0-521-45735-1 paperback

Contents

Preface

THE essays appearing in this volume were originally prepared for distribution and discussion at a conference on "The Rise of Merchant Empires" sponsored by the Center for Early Modern History at the University of Minnesota in October 1987. I wish to record here our gratitude for the funding support we received from the National Endowment for the Humanities, the Bigelow Foundation of St. Paul, and the University of Minnesota College of Liberal Arts.

As we began planning for the conference in the spring of 1984, we were conscious that the topics we wanted to address are truly universal in scope. In recent years there have been some notable attempts at universal synthesis, such as Fernand Braudel's three volumes on *Commerce and Civilization* and Immanuel Wallerstein's *The Modern World System*. But as critics have noted, it is uncommonly difficult for matters of such complexity to be filtered through the prism of a single mind or framed in the assumptions of a single ideological perspective. Hence we directed our attention toward a group effort at intermediate-level syntheses, each limited to a given region but informed by an awareness of larger questions. Even as our planning proceeded, a number of important works characterized by this kind of intellectual ambition issued from the presses: K. N. Chaudhuri's *Trade and Civilization in the Indian Ocean;* John McCusker and Russell Menard's *The Economy of British America; India, and the Indian Ocean, 1500–1800,* a collection of essays on trade edited by Ashin Das Gupta and M. N. Pearson; and Ralph Austen's *African Economic History.* The success of these works encouraged us in the belief that it would indeed be useful to bring scholars of this caliber together to address questions that are too wide-ranging for any single individual. Happily, a number of leading scholars accepted our invitation to reach beyond their customary areas of expertise and use secondary literature in other fields to make comparative judgments.

The authors represented here are not united by a common perspective, and the careful reader will find them disagreeing with one another on significant points. It is fair to say, however, that Niels Steensgaard's *The Asian Trade Revolution of the Seventeenth Century* had

vii

a substantial influence on the organization of the conference and also on our subsequent decision to publish the essays in two separate volumes, each devoted to a single broad theme. In effect, Professor Steensgaard separates descriptive issues from questions of explanation; one must first determine what can be said about the growth and composition of trade over time and the activities of different groups of merchants before one can attempt to explain why it was that European traders (especially the Dutch and the English) won the prize in the end. In like manner, *The Rise of Merchant Empires* will be concerned with the growth and composition of European overseas trade and with participation of indigenous merchant networks in long-distance trade. A subsequent volume, *The Political Economy of Merchant Empires,* will consider whether the eventual triumph of the Europeans can better be understood in terms of superior forms of business organization or superior weaponry. There is necessarily some overlap between such broad themes, especially as regards the scholarly works that are likely to be cited, and for this reason there will be a common bibliography, printed at the end of the second volume. Along the way, some of the questions raised will have a familiar ring to those who know Steensgaard's arguments – for example, the essays in this volume by Professors Austen and Rossabi, which show that the traditional caravan trades of West Africa and central Asia were not discontinued because of competition from European maritime commerce. Even where the conclusions do not agree with Professor Steensgaard's, as in those essays, the influence of his manner of conceptualizing the problem may still be discerned.

Finally, I would like to record some personal debts: to Lucy Simler, Associate Director of the Center for Early Modern History, for her skilled and cheerful management of the conference; to the graduate students who provided a lively and accurate record of our discussions – Steve Alvin, Jim Brown, Tim Coates, Jennifer Downs, Ed Kern, Seong-hak Kim, John Ness, Allyson Poska, Hal Parker, Matt Sobek, and Malcolm Thompson; to Julieann Carson, formerly Associate Dean of the College of Liberal Arts at the University of Minnesota and now Dean of the College of Liberal Arts at Willamette University, for her help in raising the vital matching funds for our National Endowment for the Humanities grant; to Douglass C. North, Luce Professor of Law and Liberty at Washington University, and Michael N. Pearson, Professor of History at the University of New South Wales, for urging us at our planning meetings to be more ambitious; and to Edward L. Farmer and Russell R. Menard, my colleagues in history at Minnesota, and Geoffrey Parker, Nowell Professor of History at the University of Illinois, for their sage counsel in preparing and organizing papers for inclusion in this volume. If readers of these essays have half the pleasure and learn half as much as I have from association with all of those responsible for them, the project may be accounted a success.

Map 1. The world from an Atlantic perspective

Map 2. The world from a Pacific perspective

Map 3. Western Europe in 1650

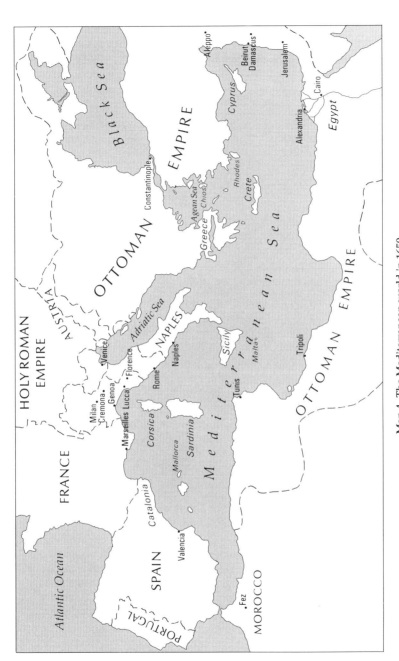

Map 4. The Mediterranean world in 1650

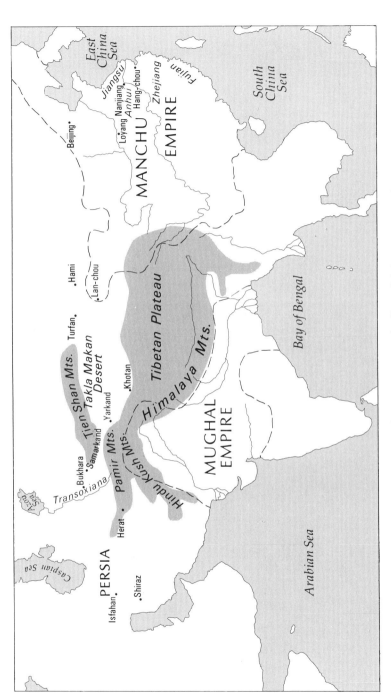

Map 5. Asia in 1650, showing towns on the Central Asian caravan route

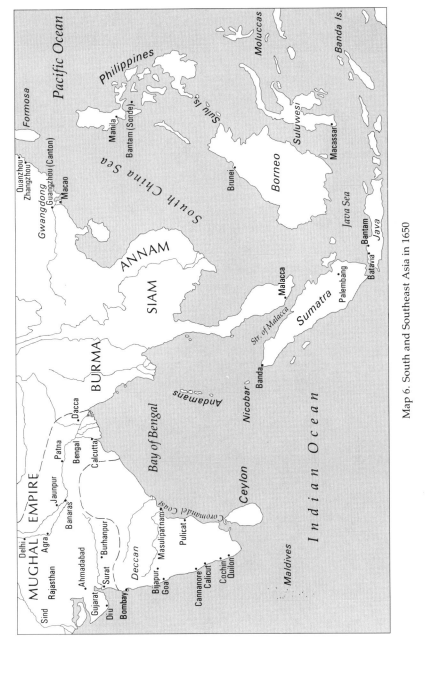

Map 6. South and Southeast Asia in 1650

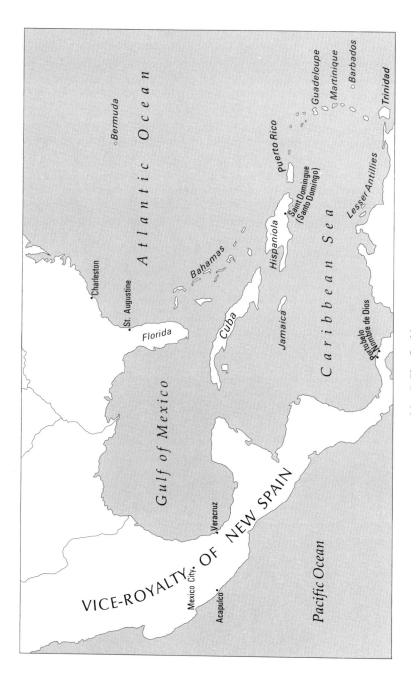

Map 7. The Caribbean in 1650

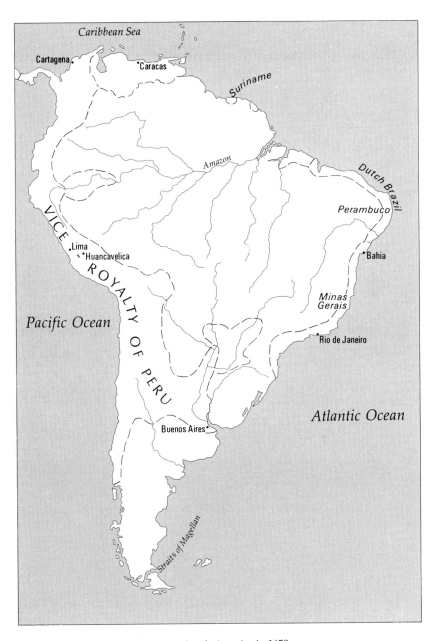

Caribbean Sea

Cartagena

Caracas

Suriname

Amazon

Dutch Brazil

Perambuco

VICE

Lima
Huancavelica

Bahia

ROYALTY

Minas
Gerais

Pacific Ocean

OF

Rio de Janeiro

PERU

Atlantic Ocean

Buenos Aires

Straits of Magellan

Map 8. South America in 1650

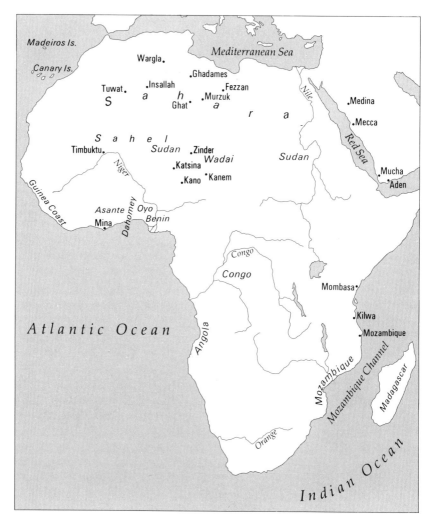

Map 9. Africa in 1650

Introduction

JAMES D. TRACY

IN the wake of European expansion, global trade branched out into countless new and exotic forms of exchange. In some cases the novelty consisted merely in transporting by sea goods that hitherto had reached their final destination overland. Thus when the Portuguese began carrying pepper and fine spices round the Cape, they threatened to undercut the caravans that brought these precious goods to entrepôts in the eastern Mediterranean.[1] Cowry shells from the Maldive Islands had long been used as currency in West Africa, but after about 1600 they came by ship from Europe, as part of the slave trade, instead of by caravan across the Sahara.[2] More dazzling to the imagination are the many instances in which goods never before heard of in certain parts of the world became, sometimes quite suddenly, objects of an intense demand. For example, Mexican silver shipped to Manila paid for Chinese silks, which were bought up on arrival in Acapulco by the same merchant firms (usually run by peninsular Spaniards) who controlled the trade with Spain by way of Veracruz.[3] Armenian merchants, who had developed close ties with the English through the trades in English broadcloth and Persian silk, used their own ships to send the brightly colored cloths of the Coromandel Coast from the English outpost at Madras to the Philippines, again in return for Mexican silver.[4] In Gujarat, on India's northwest coast, Muslim shippers of Surat prospered by exporting cottons to the Red Sea port of Mocha, favored for this trade because the silver that paid for the cloth was brought by Egyptian traders visiting the coffee markets of Yemen; ultimately, the precious metal in question came, by way of

[1] See Chapter 1.
[2] See Chapters 9 and 10.
[3] D. A. Brading, *Miners and Merchants in Bourbon Mexico, 1767–1810* (Cambridge, 1971), 97.
[4] Sinappah Arasaratnam, *Merchants, Companies, and Commerce on the Coromandel Coast, 1650–1740* (Oxford, 1986), 158; Bruce Masters, *The Origins of Western Economic Dominance in the Middle East: Mercantilism and the Islamic Economy in Aleppo, 1600–1780* (New York, 1988), 24–25.

1

Spain and Venice, from the mines of Mexico and Bolivia. In this way, Spanish silver reals became the principal coin of trade in the Indian Ocean, if not in the mainland Mughal Empire.[5]

When Europeans intruded themselves into the Red Sea cloth trade, as they managed to do for many if not all of the flourishing trades of the Indian Ocean, they bought coffee for re-export to Europe, so that by the end of the seventeenth century, the aroma of this exotic beverage mingled with that of American tobacco in the coffeehouses of London, Madrid, Paris, and Amsterdam. In the eighteenth century, the English East India Company (EIC) gradually prevailed over its Dutch rival, the Vereenigde Oost-Indische Compagnie (VOC), in the race to satisfy Europe's extraordinary appetites for the silk and the cottons of Bengal and for the tea of China.[6] Meanwhile, the consumption of tea helped fuel a new explosion of sugar production on Caribbean plantations, worked by black slaves bought in West Africa and paid for by such diverse imports as Brazilian sugar, Coromandel and Bengali cottons, and cowry shells.[7] What is most striking about these linkages is the way they affected, for good and ill, the lives of ordinary people in many different parts of the globe. Precious goods from far-off Asia certainly reached Europe in the Middle Ages, but they were enjoyed only by the few, and the minuscule quantities involved cannot have had any effect on Asian producers. In the early modern centuries, however, unknown thousands of cotton weavers and silk winders and cloth washers in India's inland villages were set to work meeting the demands of new export markets in Europe and Asia;[8] millions of Africans were wrenched into brutal servitude in alien lands; and humble folk of the Atlantic nations had a few hard-won amenities, like the Irish railway man who, according to the song, worked all day for sugar in his tay.

It is thus beyond any dispute that the early modern era (roughly 1500–1750) witnessed a great increase in the integration of trade on a global scale, just as the succeeding industrial age has seen still greater strides toward the formation of a global economy. What remains in many respects in doubt is the contemporary impact or significance of these new configurations of long-distance trade. Adam Smith be-

---

[5] As in Das Gupta, *Indian Merchants and the Decline of Surat, 1700–1750* (Wiesbaden, 1979), 4–5, 135–9; K. N. Chaudhuri, *The Trading World of Asia and the English East India Company, 1660–1760* (Cambridge, 1978), 183.

[6] On the coffee trade, see Chapter 3; Om Prakash, *The Dutch East India Company and the Economy of Bengal, 1630–1720* (Princeton, 1983).

[7] On the eighteenth-century sugar trade, see Chapters 3 and 4.

[8] Chaudhuri, *Trading World of Asia*, chap. 11; Prakash, *Dutch East India Company and the Economy of Bengal*, 160–2, 98–117.

lieved that the nearly simultaneous discoveries of America and of a passage to India were the two greatest and most important events in recorded history, and so it might have seemed to one who could see the benefits of England's newfound place at the center of a world market.[9] But it is far less clear what meaning the new connections had for those who lived in the sixteenth or even the seventeenth century. One might expect the discovery of hitherto-unknown regions to have a dramatic impact on European thought, but J. H. Elliott has argued that it took about 150 years for the European imagination to grasp the real novelty of the "new world."[10] In like manner, Europe's new access to the riches of the East might not have seemed as impressive as one would think, especially because even modern scholars have not been able to agree on how to calculate profit and loss for organizations as complex as the EIC or the VOC.[11] Moreover, although there can be no question of the enormous changes wrought by Europeans in the Americas, not least through the importation of African slaves, it is far less evident what difference a few European trading posts made for the vast realms of Asia, or even for Asia's well-established networks of seafaring commerce.[12] By way of introduction, then, it will be appropriate to say a word here about the separate but related questions of quantity and competition: What effects did the new linkages have on the volume and composition of trade in various regions (section I), and how did Europeans fare in competition with the trading nations of Asia, whose general levels of culture and business acumen were at least equal to their own (section II)?

I

In very broad terms, one may say that the American and Asian branches of the new European trade networks were joined together by a stream of silver; as Chaudhuri has put it, the influx of American bullion increased European purchasing power and made possible the acquisition of Asian goods.[13] But the mechanisms of this many-sided exchange are only selectively documented. Generally speaking, even the trades that do not involve Europeans have to be studied through the lens of documents produced by Europeans. The great Asian empires had customs houses in major ports, but their records have not

---

[9] Adam Smith is quoted in Chaudhuri, *Trading World of Asia*, 1.
[10] *The Old World and the New, 1492–1650* (New York, 1971).
[11] See Chapter 6.
[12] For a view that minimizes European impact on Asia, see Rhoads Murphey, *The Outsiders* (Ann Arbor, 1977).
[13] Chaudhuri, *Trading World of Asia*, 455.

survived, and court chroniclers usually have no more than a passing interest in trade or in the odd foreigners known in India as "hat men."[14] One may doubt how well the European interlopers understood their hosts, but at least they recorded in copious detail their impressions of strange lands and stranger customs.[15] In Europe itself, the archives of the major port cities are richly stocked with records of duty on incoming goods or treasure and of merchandise loaded on ships sent overseas. In recent decades the prodigious labor of many scholars has made it possible to consult printed summaries of such important data series as port statistics for Seville and Lisbon and shipping lists for all outbound voyages of the VOC.[16] Yet these invaluable records give an impression only of European trade, which in some parts of the globe (notably in the Indian Ocean) was only a fraction of the whole. More-over, any series of figures generated by a government's fiscal needs represents a compromise of some unknown proportion between the zeal of officials and the self-interest of merchants and importers; at times, official statistics may conflict sharply with information from private sources, as in the case of Spanish silver imports in the early seventeenth century.[17]

There is also room for debate about how trade is affected by cyclical movements in the larger economies of various regions. For example, the stance that one takes on the apparent "crisis of the seventeenth century" in Europe has considerable bearing on how one interprets the data for overseas trade.[18] Also, trade statistics may point toward a rise or fall in volume, but they do not in themselves offer an expla-nation for these trends. For example, from about 1685 to about 1715, import figures indicate a definite slackening of European trade with Asia. This trough between two periods of expansion may reflect dif-ficulties attendant on the last and bloodiest of the wars of Louis XIV. Alternatively, it may reflect a reported drop in imports of Brazilian gold and Spanish silver during the same period – except that other

---

[14] Bernard Lewis, *The Muslim Discovery of Europe* (New York, 1982).

[15] In addition to works that have been published there are those buried in company archives, like Simon Deodati's account of a journey from Agra to Surat, cited by Das Gupta, *Indian Merchants and the Decline of Surat*, 139–45.

[16] On Seville see Pierre Chaunu and Huguette Chaunu, *Séville et l'Atlantique*, 12 vols. (Paris, 1953–60); cf. Pierre Chaunu, *Les Philippines et le Pacifique des Ibériques* (Paris, 1960). For the connection between these two works, seen in retrospect, see "Vingt ans après," in Pierre Chaunu, *Seville et l'Amerique* (Paris, 1977), 9–15. For Lisbon, Frédéric Mauro, *Portugal et l'Atlantique* (Paris, 1960). For shipping lists of the VOC, J. R. Bruijn, F. S. Gaastra, and I. Schöffer, *Dutch Asiatic Shipping in the Seventeenth and Eighteenth Centuries*, 3 vols. (The Hague, 1979–87).

[17] See Chapter 7.

[18] See Chapters 2 and 7.

evidence suggests an increase in the flow of bullion from Europe to Asia in the same period.[19] Finally, the regional economies of the globe were not so well integrated that one may presume that cycles of expansion or contraction necessarily operated on a global scale. Chapters 2, 3, and 4 will show that the eighteenth century witnessed an extraordinary expansion in European trade with both Asia and the Americas. But for historians of India, the issue is whether or not there was a decline of trade during the same period, although it has recently been suggested that evidence for the decline may amount to nothing more than a relative absence of European records.[20]

If long-distance trade is necessarily a function of the economies that it links together, one may also envision circumstances in which economic development is a function of trade. In practice, discussion of this point is often linked to a debate about the terms of trade that pits the latter-day disciples of Adam Smith against the intellectual descendants of Karl Marx. Smith believed that the benefits of trade between regions with differing levels of economic development (like town and country) ought to be "mutual and reciprocal." If exchange between the Old World and the New did not fit this pattern, it was because "the savage injustice of the Europeans rendered an event, which ought to have been beneficial to all, ruinous and destructive to several of those unfortunate countries." Nonetheless, according to Smith, nothing was more likely to restore the proper balance "than that mutual communication of knowledge and of all sorts of improvements which an extensive commerce from all countries to all countries naturally, or rather necessarily, carries along with it." At a far more abstract level, but still consistent with the tenor of Smith's argument, modern economists have been concerned to establish the conditions under which free trade will result in "factor price equalization," or a comparable competitive position for all trading nations. On the other hand, those who believe that trade can be equal do not necessarily believe that it is long-distance trade that spurs economic development.[21] By contrast, Marx, in his chapter "Historical Remarks on Merchant Capital," does not recognize even the possibility of an equal exchange between nations unequal in power: "A dominant merchant capital presents itself everywhere as a system of plunder, just as its development,

---

[19] Chaudhuri, *Trading World of Asia*, 9, 64, 163–4, 456.

[20] Arasaratnam, *Merchants, Companies, and Commerce on the Coromandel Coast*, chap. 5.

[21] Smith, *The Wealth of Nations* (New York, 1982), 416, 479–80, 573, 590; John S. Chipman, "A Survey of the Theory of International Trade, Part III: The Modern Theory," *Econometrica* 34 (1966): 18–76; Patrick O'Brien, "European Economic Development: The Contribution of the Periphery," *Economic History Review*, 2d ser., 35 (1982): 1–18.

whether under the merchant peoples of ancient or of modern times, is bound up with violent plunder, piracy, enslavement, and colonial subjugation." One of Marx's modern disciples, Eric Wolf, coins the phrase "tributary mode of production" to describe the whole range of societies with whom European traders came into contact. Wolf sees local producers in these societies falling into a state of dependence, either through excessive specialization in the products bought by Europeans ("commodity peonage") or, more directly, through slavery or through the provision by the Europeans of goods on which indigenous peoples become physically dependent, like alcohol. Another version of the same argument insists that it was profits from unequal trade with other parts of the world that permitted Europe to industrialize and thus strengthen its dominant position.[22]

For historians, this underlying debate about the terms of trade takes on very different meanings in different parts of the world. For North America, scholars debate the merits of the "staples thesis," which holds that the economic development of a given subregion is critically dependent on the characteristics of its "staple," or dominant export crop. Thus the products of New England's family farms have "spread effects," which stimulate other sectors of the economy, but the sugar produced on slave plantations in the Caribbean islands does not.[23] For Latin America in the early modern era and Africa in the nineteenth century, historians have to take a position one way or the other on the "development of underdevelopment" argument put forward by André Gunder Frank and others, which holds that the contemporary economic plight of many Third World nations is traceable to exploitative policies of the colonial era.[24] Asia, even more than other regions of the globe, is simply too vast and too variegated to be brought under a single common denominator. In the Middle East, the decline by 1700 of a traditional caravan center like Aleppo clearly is related to the increased importance of maritime trade routes controlled by Europeans.[25] In India, scholars are now suggesting that European demand may have stimulated the productive sectors of the economy of the subcontinent, even if Indian long-distance shipping was not able

[22] Marx, *Das Kapital*, vol. 3 (Mainz and Leipzig, 1966), chap. 8, esp. p. 343; Eric Wolf, *Europe and the People without History* (Berkeley, 1982), 83–8; André Gunder Frank, *World Accumulation, 1492–1789* (New York, 1978).

[23] John S. McCusker and Russell R. Menard, *The Economy of British America* (Chapel Hill, 1985), pts. 1 and 2.

[24] Frank, "The Development of Underdevelopment," *Monthly Review* 18 (1966): 17–31; idem, *World Accumulation, 1492–1789*; for Africa, see the comments of Ralph Austen, *African Economic History* (New York, 1987), 1–5.

[25] Masters, *Origins of Western Economic Dominance in the Middle East*.

to survive into the nineteenth century.[26] By contrast, Rhoads Murphey contends that prior to 1800 no more than 5 percent of China's total domestic product was involved in trade with the "southern barbarians."[27] This complexity makes it worthwhile to take a closer look at changing relations between European and Asian merchants.

II

W. H. Moreland, perhaps the leading historian of India during the last generation of British rule, believed that the arrival of the Portuguese ushered in a new age for the Indian Ocean. Although recognizing that Muslim shipping remained active in some areas, Moreland thought that the Portuguese effectively controlled the principal channels of trade. This view was still influential in 1959, when K. M. Panikkar dated the "age of European dominance" in India from the coming of Vasco da Gama.[28] Since then, however, a new and flourishing school of historians of trade in the Indian Ocean has emphasized the continuing vitality of Asian maritime commerce after 1500 and even after 1600. J. C. van Leur, a Dutch scholar whose essays were published in English translation in 1955, was the first to discredit some of Moreland's views. To be sure, his characterization of post-1500 long-distance commerce in Asia as a "pedlar" trade has been criticized as just another form of the Eurocentric bias that van Leur deplored in Moreland. On the other hand, no one has yet contended that the religious or caste groups into which indigenous merchants of the great Asian entrepôts were organized ever achieved the institutional solidarity of a European trading company or a European municipal corporation like the one Portuguese traders formed at Macao.[29] In this sense, even so powerful a figure as Mullā ʿAbduʾl Gafūr, who was able in the 1690s to rally the merchants of Surat to a successful defiance of the Dutch and English fleets, might be considered vulnerable as an individual, and indeed was vulnerable once his enemies were able to isolate him.[30] But the common European perception that wealthy Indian merchants of this type lived in constant dread of having their

[26] Prakash, *Dutch East India Company and the Economy of Bengal,* 223–36; Arasaratnam, *Merchants, Companies, and Commerce on the Coromandel Coast,* 350–1.
[27] Murphey, *The Outsiders,* 9.
[28] W. H. Moreland, *India at the Death of Akbar* (London, 1920); K. M. Panikkar, *Asia and Western Dominance* (New York, 1959).
[29] Van Leur, *Indonesian Trade and Society* (The Hague, 1955); Das Gupta, *Indian Merchants and the Decline of Surat,* 13–14; George Bryan Souza, *The Survival of Empire: Portuguese Trade and Society in China and the South China Sea* (Cambridge, 1986), 226–99. See also Chapter 8.
[30] Das Gupta, *Indian Merchants and the Decline of Surat,* 94–134.

goods confiscated by despotic rulers has been called into question.[31] Moreover, van Leur was plainly wrong to think that the Asian "peddlars" involved in the overseas trade dealt only in luxury goods. For example, Surat's prosperity in the age of Mullā ʿAbduʾl Gafūr was founded on the export of cheap white cottons that were an article of mass consumption in the Arab lands.[32] The only true peddler in India, as Chaudhuri says, "was the solitary owner of a pack bullock."[33]

Van Leur also contended that the Portuguese never really gained control of the vital trades in pepper and fine spices, and this part of his argument is now accepted on all sides.[34] Because the Portuguese failed to capture Aden, at the entrance to the Red Sea, they could never fully implement Albuquerque's grand strategy of controlling the choke points of maritime commerce. Both the west coast of India and the Strait of Malacca were patrolled by the Portuguese, but Muslim shippers were able to bring fine spices from the Moluccas through the Straits of Sunda to Atjeh in northern Sumatra for transshipment directly to the Red Sea and from there to Alexandria, where Venetian merchants were able after all to carry on their traditional spice trade.[35] Steensgaard confirmed this part of van Leur's argument by showing that there was no dramatic increase in the volume of pepper and spices reaching Europe until the coming of the VOC and the EIC in the early seventeenth century. It might be noted, however, that there has been some tendency to rehabilitate the now-tarnished reputation of Portuguese commerce, especially by calling attention to the private traders who continued to prosper even as the Estado da India lost one outpost after another to the attacks of the VOC.[36]

These marauding Dutchmen and their somewhat more peaceful English counterparts quickly grasped, in the wake of the Portuguese, that participation in the intra-Asian "country trade" would diminish the need for importing bullion from Europe to pay for Asian goods. Their determination to move in on various branches of the country trade posed a far more direct and formidable challenge to long-distance

---

[31] Compare Arasaratnam, *Merchants, Companies, and Commerce on the Coromandel Coast*, 221, with Chaudhuri, *Trading World of Asia*, 256.

[32] M. N. Pearson, "India and the Indian Ocean in the Sixteenth Century," in *India and the Indian Ocean, 1500–1800*, ed. Ashin Das Gupta and M. N. Pearson (Calcutta and Oxford, 1987), 74.

[33] Chaudhuri, *Trading World of Asia*, 137.

[34] Arasaratnam, *Merchants, Companies, and Commerce on the Coromandel Coast*, 113–15.

[35] See Chapter 1.

[36] N. Steensgaard, *The Asian Trade Revolution of the Seventeenth Century* (Chicago, 1974), 95–103, 157–69; see Subrahmanyam and Thomaz in the forthcoming volume *The Political Economy of Merchant Empires*.

shippers in Asia, especially to the various Muslim communities, whom the Europeans lumped together as "Moors." In the southeast corner of the Southeast Asian archipelago, the Dutch fought a long and ultimately successful battle to bar their Asian and European rivals from buying fine spices in the Moluccas, culminating with Dutch occupation of Bantam in 1682.[37] Scholars have detected a major shift even before this date in Indian overseas trade, away from the archipelago, to which access was becoming more difficult, and toward new markets in the Persian Gulf and the Red Sea.[38] Meanwhile, the VOC and the EIC between them cleared the Bay of Bengal of Portuguese and Burmese pirates and gained important privileges for trade along the rivers of Bengal, thus opening this rich and productive region to more intense trade with Asia as well as Europe. In particular, the produce of Bengal made it easier for Europeans to tap directly into the markets of south China, rather than dealing with Chinese intermediaries in Bantam or peninsular Southeast Asia.[39]

Steensgaard shows how the companies were able to pay for the upkeep of war fleets and fortresses from the profits of their country trade, instead of being dependent on subsidies from a cash-starved metropolitan government, as the Estado da India was. In addition, Chaudhuri's monumental study of the EIC makes a powerful case for the superior economic rationality of economic decisions made within the framework of "business constitutionalism," in which fundamental policies were articulated by the company's directors with remarkable consistency over the decades, even if there were problems of implementation.[40] Nonetheless, indigenous merchant communities did not simply wither away as soon as the VOC and the EIC had set up their factories in entrepôts like Surat and Masulipatnam. For example, Arasaratnam finds that in the seventeenth century Coromandel merchants triumphed over the European companies in areas where they could still trade in freedom and security. Europeans were never able to break into the export from Thailand of rubies and elephants (the great beasts died more frequently on European ships than on Indian vessels). Hence Coromandel traders could use the high profit margins on these commodities to sell Indian cloth in Thailand below cost and drive the Europeans from the market. Owing to difficulties

---

[37] The best overview is F. S. Gaastra, *Geschiedenis der VOC* (Haarlem, 1982).

[38] Das Gupta, *Indian Merchants and the Decline of Surat*, 4–6.

[39] Prakash, *Dutch East India Company and the Economy of Bengal*, chap. 2; Holden Furber, *Rival Empires of Trade in the Orient, 1600–1800* (Minneapolis, 1976), 129–38, 175–7.

[40] Steensgaard, *Asian Trading Revolution of the Seventeenth Century*, 111–14, 131–41; Chaudhuri, *Trading World of Asia*, esp. chap. 2.

of this kind, European factories in Thailand were all withdrawn before 1700.[41]

The implication of Arasaratnam's argument is that European companies did best where they were able to use their naval power to good
advantage. Certainly it was by naked force that the Dutch gained control of the highly localized trade in fine spices, and they threatened
to monopolize the pepper trade after their successful raid on the free
port of Macassar on Sulawesi (1663) and their capture of Cochin on
the Malabar Coast (1665).[42] But a policy of force also had its limitations. For one thing, fear of a Dutch monopoly in the pepper trade
seems to have been one of the reasons why the English concentrated
on the export of Indian textiles, which proved to have a far more
elastic market in Europe.[43] Also, the Europeans were not masters of
every sea, as the Omanis proved when they took Muscat and Mom-
basa from the Portuguese and made the former the leading entrepôt
on the Persian Gulf.[44] More importantly, force employed in zones
where control of trade was not possible tended to be counterproductive. Thus when the Dutch tried to compel Malabar pepper growers
to bring their produce to Cochin, they ended by giving new life to the
free of Calicut, Cochin's historic rival. On the Coromandel Coast,
where the VOC was unusually strict about controlling trade from its
ports, local traders and investors freely collaborated with the French
and the English, whose settlements flourished in the latter half of the
seventeenth century, but not with the Dutch, whose settlements stagnated.[45] More broadly speaking, the fact that Europeans prospered at
least as much through association with Asians as through competition against them has led some scholars to characterize the period
from 1500 to about 1750 as "an age of partnership."[46]

European shipping was dominant throughout Asian waters by the
end of the eighteenth century, but the companies were not the chief
beneficiaries, because the VOC had seen its "country" fleet dwindle

---

[41] Arasaratnam, *Merchants, Companies, and Commerce on the Coromandel Coast*, 142–5.

[42] Kristof Glamann, *Dutch Asiatic Trade, 1620–1740* (Copenhagen and The Hague, 1958), chap. 4.

[43] The shift of emphasis from pepper to textiles in the exports of both companies, with the EIC leading the way, is amply documented in the tables in Glamann, *Dutch Asiatic Trade*, and Chaudhuri, *Trading World of Asia*.

[44] Das Gupta, *Indian Merchants and the Decline of Surat*, 71–2.

[45] Ashin Das Gupta, *Malabar in Asian Trade, 1740–1800* (Cambridge, 1967), 11–32; Arasaratnam, *Merchants, Companies, and Commerce on the Coromandel Coast*, 161–3.

[46] M. N. Pearson, "Introduction," in *The Age of Partnership: Europeans in Asia before Dominion*, ed. Blair B. King and M. N. Pearson (Honolulu, 1979), a volume of essays dedicated to Holden Furber, who coined the phrase.

considerably,[47] and the EIC was now preoccupied with the land empire it acquired in Bengal after the battle of Plassey (1757). Instead, long-distance maritime commerce was more and more in the hands of European private traders, especially British shippers based in Calcutta.[48] These private traders were in the happy position of benefiting from the privileges that the companies had extracted from local rulers, without having to bear the cost of maintaining warships and fortresses. Yet it does not appear that Asian shipping was defeated by the profit margins of European competitors, or at least not solely. Das Gupta convincingly traces the decline of Surat to the nearly simultaneous decline of the three Islamic dynasties whose empires were linked commercially through Surat: the Ottomans, the Safavids of Iran, and the Mughals. Similarly, Arasaratnam connects the decline of the Coromandel ports with political turmoil in the hinterland, and Prakash links the decline of Bengali shipping to the withdrawal of investment in trade by the Mughal political elite.[49] If the European companies had an advantage, it may have been a superior ability to withstand political crises. The only thing that is completely clear is the end of the story. As Das Gupta remarks, by about 1800 "the Indian ship had sailed into oblivion."[50]

European dominance of the shipping lanes was of course a prelude to the great age of European imperial power, in the nineteenth and early twentieth centuries. As many scholars have suggested, the age of European ascendancy can be seen in perspective now that it has come to an end. One might even say that it is particularly appropriate in this present age of a new global interdependence to look more closely at that preimperial "age of partnership," or perhaps "age of competition," when westerners and Asians vied on even terms. Certainly this volume is conceived in the belief that the time is ripe to examine early interactions between Europeans and other peoples in ways that are no longer colored either by the arrogance of imperialism or by the passions of newborn and as yet insecure nationalisms.

Herman van der Wee leads off a first group of essays with a description of the fifteenth-century trading empire of the Venetian Re-

---

[47] Ashin Das Gupta, "India and the Indian Ocean in the Eighteenth Century," in *India and the Indian Ocean, 1500–1800*, 151.

[48] P. J. Marshall, "Private British Trade in the Indian Ocean before 1800," in ibid.

[49] Das Gupta, *Indian Merchants and the Decline of Surat*, passim; Arasaratnam, *Merchants, Companies, and Commerce on the Coromandel Coast*, chap. 6; Prakash, *Dutch East India Company and the Economy of Bengal*, 223–36.

[50] "India and the Indian Ocean in the Eighteenth Century," 134.

public, which provided in more ways than one a model for the commercial networks and the armed outposts of the Portuguese, the Dutch, and the English. Carla Rahn Phillips traces the growth and development of the overseas trading empires of Portugal and Spain during the early modern centuries; contrary to mistaken assumptions, the Spanish Empire, like the Portuguese, was based on trade from its beginnings. Niels Steensgaard draws together new calculations for the burgeoning colonial trades of England and the Netherlands, showing that "the introduction of colonial commodities was the largest change and the major cause of growth in north European long-distance trade between the medieval period and the middle of the eighteenth century." Paul Butel presents French trade as outgrowing its historic dependence on Dutch and German intermediaries because of a dramatic surge in the eighteenth-century colonial trades, paralleling the trends found by Professors Phillips and Steensgaard. On more special issues, Jaap R. Bruijn offers evidence for the continuing inventiveness and profitability of Dutch shipping, even after the VOC was clearly seen to be in decline; and Larry Neal shows that share prices of EIC and VOC stock closely followed real fluctuations in the fortunes of the rival companies. Finally, Ward Barrett critically reviews the literature and presents composite estimates for the bullion flows, mainly from the Americas to Europe and from Europe to Asia, that made the formation of global trading networks possible.

Frédéric Mauro introduces a second set of essays by comparing the merchant communities of old Europe with those that European traders found on the scene in the Asian entrepôts. Herbert S. Klein summarizes advances made in recent literature on the slave trade, emphasizing that it was Africans, not Europeans, who set the terms of trade. Ralph A. Austen shows how the caravan trade of West Africa, sheltered behind the rain forest disease barrier, continued to prosper in spite of shipping routes that now brought some of the same goods to the West African coast. Morris Rossabi explains how disruptions in the central Asian caravan trade during the seventeenth century can be traced to political turmoil at several key points along the caravan routes rather than to competition from European shipping. Irfan Habib, focusing on two major mercantile communities in India, describes how institutions like brokerage, deposit banking, bill-money, and insurance were created "out of India's own commercial fabric." Finally, Wang Gungwu describes how the coming of the Europeans at first stimulated the trade of the Hokkien Chinese communities in Luzon and Nagasaki but ended by making these traders into mere instruments of Spanish or Dutch aims because they lacked a protector, given the indifference of the Ming emperors to such matters.

Professor Habib ends his essay by asking whether the final triumph of the Europeans was due to a superiority in weaponry rather than to any superiority in business organization. That is exactly the question of central concern in *The Political Economy of Merchant Empires.* This second volume will include contributions by José Jobson de Andrade Arruda, Thomas Brady, K. N. Chaudhuri, Dennis Flynn, Russell R. Menard, Douglass C. North, Geoffrey Parker, M. N. Pearson, Anne Perotin-Dumon, Jacob Price, Sanjay Subrahmanyam, and Luis Felipe F. R. Thomaz.

CHAPTER 1

Structural changes in European long-distance trade, and particularly in the re-export trade from south to north, 1350–1750

HERMAN VAN DER WEE

INTRODUCTION

THE European long-distance re-export trade has not yet been the object of much quantitative research for the period of the late Middle Ages and early modern period.[1] Of course, some excellent quantitative information on Dutch and English re-exports from the seventeenth century onward is available, thanks to the work of Charles Wilson, Ralph Davis, David Ormrod, K. N. Chaudhuri, and others, but these statistics cover only the very end of the period to be examined here. Moreover, they concern European re-exports from north to south rather than the trade in the other direction, which is the subject of this paper.[2]

In the European re-export trade from south to north, Italy for centuries was the leading power. During the late Middle Ages it became the focal point of a very dynamic urban re-export trade of Near and Far Eastern wares to the rest of Europe, a trade that in its turn stimulated all other sectors of long-distance and local commerce in Eu-

During my research for this paper, Mr. Jan Materné was of great help, and I am very grateful to him.

[1] I define re-export trade as the exporting of previously imported goods without additional processing. For detailed definitions of re-export trade, see D. W. Pearce, *The Macmillan dictionary of Modern Economics* (London, 1981), 369; C. Ammer, *Dictionary of Business and Economics* (New York, 1977), 357; and *Ökonomisches lexikon* (Berlin, 1979), 3:47–8.

[2] A recent survey is given in D. Ormrod, "English Re-exports and the Dutch Staple Market in the Eighteenth Century," in D. C. Coleman and P. Mathias, eds., *Enterprise and History: Essays in Honour of Charles Wilson* (Cambridge, 1984), 89–115.

14

rope. The discovery of alternative sea routes to Asia around 1500 by Portugal and Spain disturbed Italy's dominant position, but it did not lead to an immediate decline of its re-export trade from south to north. On the contrary, Italy reacted vigorously and adapted its economic structure and its re-export trade, the latter regaining strength from the second third of the sixteenth century onward. In the beginning of the seventeenth century, however, Italy had to give in: not to the Portuguese or the Spanish but to the Dutch and the English, keeping for itself a role in the re-export trade from the Levant.

I will focus mainly on Italy's dynamic role in the world's long-distance trade during the late Middle Ages and Early Modern period and particularly on Italy's dominant role in Europe's re-export trade from south to north during the same time span. The role of the Portuguese, Spanish, Dutch, and English in the re-export trade will be examined in more detail in other chapters. Because of the absence of viable statistics, my overview is based mainly on qualitative information and is limited to a *status questionis* of the problem of structural changes in Italy's long-distance trade.

THE RISE TO COMMERCIAL PREEMINENCE
OF THE ITALIAN CITY-STATES
IN THE LATE MIDDLE AGES

During the late Middle Ages the Italian city-states emerged as the leading centers for long-distance trade in the Mediterranean, in the Black Sea, and along the Atlantic coasts of northwestern Europe. This hegemony was the outcome of a long historical process and linked Italy's destiny with developments in Europe north of the Alps, in the Middle East, and in Asia.

The commercial revival of Italy had its roots in the early Middle Ages, but it accelerated quickly in the beginning of the second millennium, when two dynamic movements of long-distance trade over land came in touch with Italy's maritime potential in the Mediterranean area. The first of these movements was the new expansion of the overland traffic from China and India via central Asia and Persia to the Black Sea. For some time, the main link to the Black Sea – the destination of caravans from the Far East and South East – was an overland route along the Volga controlled by the Swedes and Russians. But Byzantium's political and economic resurgence, supported by Italy's revival, soon shifted the center of gravity of east–west trade from the shores of the Black Sea to Byzantium, whose trade in turn came increasingly under the control of the Italian sea-republics. Thanks to their navies, the Italian sea-republics were able to give effective military assistance to Byzantium, when needed, and in return obtained commercial privileges. The Italian sea-republics and their merchants established themselves firmly in the Byzantine market, gradually weakening the position of the Greeks, Syrians, and Jews in this growing center of world trade. At the same time the Italians were allowed to found factories and colonies on the shores of the Black Sea, and by doing so, they gained control of the east–west trade in the whole area. Italian commercial dynamism in the Black Sea reinforced the commercial power of Byzantium and thereby also consolidated the Italian position in Byzantium itself. Swedes and Russians shifted their trade routes to the west and concentrated mainly on the staple market of Byzantium for trade with the South East and Far East and for their increasing trade with the Middle East and the Mediterranean.[3]

The second dynamic movement of long-distance trade over land started from the delta of the Rhine, Meuse, and Scheldt rivers in northwestern Europe. It was based on an active overland trade by Flemish, northern French, Brabant, and Rhineland merchants. They exported woolen cloth on a large scale to Italy, where it was re-exported to Spain, North Africa, and the Middle East. Soon Italy's commercial rise also affected northwestern Europe. The emergence and prosperity of the fairs of Champagne in the twelfth and thirteenth centuries were due mainly to the successful penetration of Italian merchants into the European market north of the Alps: the Italians first took over from the northern merchants the long-distance overland trade from Champagne to the south; then the Italians moved farther north, obtaining control over the whole overland traffic from the northwestern European delta area of the Scheldt, Meuse, and Rhine to the south.[4]

During the fourteenth century the pattern of international long-distance trade just described underwent fundamental changes. Traditional overland traffic was increasingly disrupted. In the course of the thirteenth century the Mongolian and Ottoman campaigns and conquests were already threatening the trade routes from central Asia to Byzantium. They paralyzed these routes in a catastrophic way during the next century. During the fourteenth century the long-distance overland trade through France also came under pressure. The rise of central royal power in France met with increasing resistance at the

---

[3] R. S. Lopez, *The Commercial Revolution of the Middle Ages, 950–1350* (New York, 1976), 92.

[4] F. Braudel, *Civilisation matérielle, économie et capitalisme, XVe–XVIIIe siècle*, vol. 3 of *Le temps du monde* (Paris, 1979), 92.

periphery, generating conflict and violence. The famines and the great epidemics of the fourteenth century aggravated the situation by generating misery and insecurity on a large scale. The Hundred Years' War (1337–1453) was the biggest blow of all: It destabilized French political life for a very long period and disintegrated the economy by inflating transaction costs for long-distance overland trade.[5]

The consequences of the disruption of the traditional overland trade routes were far-reaching. The disruption weakened Byzantium's economic position and for that reason accelerated its decline, which was sealed by the capture of the city in 1453. The disruption also quickened the decline of the fairs of Champagne, which began shortly after the end of the thirteenth century.

There were positive effects too. The crisis, indeed, generated important shifts in the structure of international trade: it encouraged and stimulated, both in Asia and in northwestern Europe, long-distance maritime trade.[6]

In Asia the shift was clear-cut and had great importance for the growth of trade in the ports of the Nile delta and Syria. Transcontinental trade from the Far and South East, via central Asia and Persia to the Black Sea and Byzantium, was increasingly overshadowed by the expansive, long-distance maritime trade in the Indian Ocean, linking India and East Africa directly with the Red Sea and supplying from there the Middle East markets and ports, such as Damascus, Amman, Aleppo, Beirut, Cairo, Tripoli, and, above all, Alexandria.[7] Arab merchants had been in control of this long-distance oceanic trade for centuries. But only now were they able to fully integrate into it the European trade of the Mediterranean. The disruption of the overland traffic in central Asia, Persia, and Anatolia must have been a decisive factor in the attraction of the Italians to the ports of Syria and Egypt. The consolidation of political power during the Mamluk period must also have had beneficial effects on trade in the same area.

In Europe north of the Alps the shift from transcontinental to maritime long-distance trade was not as complete as in Asia and the Middle East, but it was also evident. At the end of the thirteenth century the

---

[5] J. A. Boyle, "The Last Barbarian Invaders: The Impact of the Mongol Conquests upon East and West," in *The Mongol Empire, 1206–1370* (London, 1977), 1–15; and M. T. Caron, *La société en France à la fin du Moyen Age*, Documents histoire, vol. 18 (Paris, 1977), 9.

[6] H. van der Wee, "Un modèle dynamique de croissance interséculaire du commerce mondial, XIe–XVIIIe siècles," *Annales: Economies, Sociétés, Civilisations* 25 (1970): 100–26.

[7] E. Ashtor, "The Venetian Supremacy in Levantine Trade: Monopoly or Pre-Colonialism?" *Journal of European Economic History* 3 (1974): 5–53.

first Italian galleys from Florence, Venice, and Genoa left the Mediterranean for northwestern Europe, going mainly to Bruges, Antwerp, and London. During the fourteenth and fifteenth centuries this direct maritime link between Italy and the North Sea ports became a regular one, replacing to some extent overland trade via France.[8] The expansion of the north-south maritime trade stimulated commercial activity in ports along the new sea route: The ports of Catalonia, Mallorca, and Valencia and of Andalusia, Portugal, and the French Atlantic coast benefited from the galleys moving northward; all of them felt Italian influence and power. Finally, in Bruges and London the Italians encountered the merchants of the Hanseatic League. The solidarity of the league prevented a successful further penetration of Italian commercial power into the north of Europe, but the presence of their galleys in Bruges and London enabled the Italians to fully integrate the maritime growth of northern Europe and the Baltic into their own northward expansion.

VENICE'S MARITIME HEGEMONY
IN THE FIFTEENTH CENTURY

During the fourteenth century, Italian predominance in the long-distance maritime trade of the Mediterranean and northwestern Europe, even apart from the Hansa area, was never complete. Catalonia and Sicily became strong competitors in the Middle East trade. Southern France, the Dalmatian coast, and the islands of Rhodes, Malta, and Cyprus were also able to get small shares of it (Table 1.1).[9]

In fact, the maritime hegemony of Italy was rather complex. Venice and Genoa were major rivals, but they both remained leaders in the old declining trade of Byzantium and the Black Sea, and both acquired at the same time predominance in the expanding Syrian and Egyptian trade. Both cities also played a leading role in the maritime trade with northwestern Europe, but in this area they had to share

---

[8] R. Doehaerd, "Les galères génoises dans la Manche et la Mer du Nord à la fin du XIIIe et au début du XIVe siècle," *Bulletin de l'Institut Historique Belge de Rome* 19 (1938); 32–3; and H. Laurent, "Choix de documents inédits pour servir à l'histoire de l'expansion commericale des Pay-Bas en France au Moyen Age (XIIe–XVe siècles)," *Bulletin de la Commission Royale d'Histoire* 98 (1934): 380.

[9] Ashtor, "Venetian Supremacy," 7; idem, "L'apogée du commerce vénitien au Lavant: Un nouvel assai d'explication," in *Venezia centro di mediazione tra oriente e occidente (secoli XV–XVI): Aspetti e problemi* (Florence, 1977), 1:308–9; and F. Melis, "Note sur le mouvement du port de Beyrouth d'après la documentation florentine aux environs de 1400," in M. Mollat, ed., *Sociétés et compagnies de commerce en Orient et dans l'Océan Indien: Actes du Huitième Colloque International d'Histoire Maritime (Beyrouth 5–10 Septembre 1966)* (Paris, 1970), 372.

Table 1.1

Harbor Traffic in Beirut and Alexandria

according to Port of Origin

	Beirut (1394-1408),%	Alexandria (1404-1405),%
Catalonia	25.8	21.0
Basques	---	5.2
Biscaye	1.6	---
Provence	3.4	2.6
Perpignan	2.6	---
Venice	32.0	5.2
Genoa	30.2	23.6
Gaeta	0.1	---
Ancona	0.5	---
Pisa	---	2.6
Toscana	3.3	---
Sicily	0.1	13.1
Ragusa	---	5.2
Pera	---	2.6
Cyprus	---	2.6
Malta	---	2.6
Rhodes	---	5.2
Other ports	0.4	8.5
Total	100	100

Source: See n. 9.

the lead with Florence, which was particularly interested in the trade in English wool.[10]

[10] R. A. Goldthwaite, *The Building of Renaissance Florence: An Economic and Social History* (Baltimore, 1982), 31.

Venice, Genoa, and Florence were able not only to increase their influence outside Italy but also to extend their political power in Italy beyond the limits of their own walls. They became mighty city-states by annexing surrounding countryside, villages, and towns. They also tried to bring Mediterranean islands under their control. Venice was successful in Crete, Cyprus, and several others; Genoa was successful in Chios and Rhodes, albeit to a lesser degree than Venice.[11]

During the fifteenth century, the concentration of political and maritime power in the hands of Venice, Genoa, and Florence tended to increase. This tendency intensified the struggle for maritime hegemony among the three: Florence and Genoa had to give in, and Venice emerged, from the second quarter of the fifteenth century onward, as the leading commercial and financial center of Europe.[12] Structural shifts in the pattern of world trade help explain the emergence of Venice as the center of European world trade. These shifts were determined by geographical and geological factors, by socioeconomic and political circumstances, and by the changing nature of the export and re-export trade.

Geographical and geological factors in the fifteenth century favored Venice at the expense of Genoa and Florence. The Hundred Years' War undermined the French economy, disrupting Genoa's closest and traditionally richest market. Genoa therefore followed a strategy of increasing its commercial and financial links with Spain. But penetration into the Spanish market proved to be very slow and costly.[13] The strong position of the Catalonian and Valencian ports in the Mediterranean trade was not easy to overcome. The benefits of financing Portuguese and Spanish explorations in the Atlantic Ocean and along the West African coast were not immediate and would become visible only at the turn of the century, after the great event of the opening of new oceanic sea routes to the West and East Indies. Even then, the Genoese had to be patient: Seville's boom and the "siècle des Génois" linked with it would begin only in the middle of the sixteenth century.[14]

Venice, by contrast, was geographically favored by the development of Europe's world trade in the fifteenth century. German colo-

---

[11] G. V. Scammell, *The World Encompassed: The First European Empires, c. 800–1650* (New York, 1981), 106, 119–20, 186.

[12] Ashtor, "Venetian Supremacy," 48.

[13] J. Heers, *Gênes au XVe siècle: Civilisation méditerranéenne, grand capitalisme et capitalisme populaire* (Paris, 1971), 321–2.

[14] F. Braudel, *La Méditerranée et le monde méditerranéen à l'époque de Phillippe II* (Paris, 1966), 2:454ff.

nization in central, eastern, and northern Europe in the thirteenth and fourteenth centuries had been a great success. It had created attractive markets, which Venice had helped to develop and expand, in collaboration with merchants, entrepreneurs, and bankers of south German cities. Venice's geographical position had been crucial in this respect. Its unique harbor facilities and its sheltered location at the end of the long Adriatic Sea were complemented by excellent Alpine routes, such as the Brenner Pass, which provided the easiest overland access from Italy to the vast "hinterland" of central and eastern Europe.[15] The revival of mining in central and southern Europe beginning in the fifteenth century soon reinforced the stimulus emanating from the central and east European economy: Innovations in mining techniques attracted south German and Venetian investment in the silver and copper fields of the Harz Mountains, Bohemia, Tirol, and, later, Bosnia and Serbia.[16] At this moment the south Germany–Venice commercial axis reached its zenith, symbolized in the Fondacco dei Tedesci, the impressive staple house and residence of the south German merchants in Venice.[17]

The flourishing north German Hansa also had contact with the south German–Venetian axis. The Hansa's relations with the west were mainly with the markets of Bruges and London, but Hansa towns also had access to the south German markets and Venice along the great north European rivers, such as the Vistula, Oder, Neisse, and Weser. The most important overland link between the Hansa and the south German–Venetian axis was along the Rhine and was dominated by Cologne, leader of the western Hansa towns (Lübeck was leader of the eastern Hansa towns). Part of the Hansa trade in Bruges and Antwerp did not go southward via the maritime route to the Mediterranean but followed the Rhine route via Cologne to south Germany and Venice. Traffic along the Rhine route grew quickly from the second third of the fifteenth century onward, when the Brabant fairs, the fairs of Frankfurt, and those more inland in Germany were linked by the south German and Venetian alliance. During the fif-

---

[15] F. C. Lane, *Venice, A Maritime Republic* (Baltimore, 1973), 227.

[16] H. Kellenbenz, "Final Remarks: Production and Trade of Gold, Silver, Copper, and Lead from 1450 to 1750," in H. Kellenbenz, ed., *Precious Metals in the Age of Expansion: Papers of the Fourteenth International Congress of the Historical Sciences*, Beiträge zur Wirtschaftsgeschichte, vol. 2 (Stuttgart, 1981), 307–63.

[17] B. Pullan, ed., *Crisis and Change in the Venetian Economy in the Sixteenth and Seventeenth Centuries* (London, 1968), 1–2; and H. Kellenbenz, "Venedig als internationales Zentrum und die Expansion des Handels im 15. und 16. Jahrhundert," in *Venezia centro di mediazione*, 281–2.

teenth century, south German merchants established themselves in increasing numbers in Antwerp.[18]

Social and economic factors also favored Venice at the expense of Genoa and Florence during their struggle for commercial hegemony in Europe. Florence's power was based on industrial development, export-led growth, and international finance. High-quality woolen cloth (manufactured using English wool and Flemish techniques), high-quality silk cloth (manufactured using Levantine silk and Levantine techniques), and sophisticated international banking became the leading sectors of the Florentine economy. This structure accentuated the inequality of wealth and income. It made large segments of the labor force, particularly those with marginal incomes, vulnerable to economic fluctuations, thus generating and aggravating social conflict. In the end it weakened Florence's economic position in the world.[19]

Genoa's social structure also encompassed more inequality than the Venetian one. Investments in the eastern Mediterranean and in Spain were increasingly financed by large family companies, the predecessors of the big Genoese banking houses of the sixteenth and seventeenth centuries. The rich Genoese families were taking political control of the town, and by doing so, they intensified social tension. In the first half of the fifteenth century this tension reached a climax: No fewer than thirteen urban uprisings and revolutions took place in Genoa between 1413 and 1453.[20]

Venice, by contrast, was characterized during the same period by social stability and political efficiency. Several social and institutional factors were responsible. Wealth was more equally distributed among Venetian merchants than it was in the other city-states. Trade was less concentrated, and political institutions worked in such a way that large segments of the world of commerce and finance were involved in the decision-making process of town and state. Industry was not yet oriented toward mass production of standardized high-quality goods, which would make the sector dependent on the erratic fluctuations of export demand. Instead, industry was based on more stable activities such as artisanal luxury products, with an inelastic export demand, and a large-scale, state-owned shipbuilding and ship-repairing industry.[21]

[18] H. van der Wee, *The Growth of the Antwerp Market and the European Economy (Four-teenth–Sixteenth Centuries)*, 3 vols. (Louvain, 1963), 2:130–1.
[19] Goldthwaite, *Renaissance Florence*, 167.
[20] Scammell, *The World Encompassed*, 167.
[21] F. C. Lane, "Venetian Shipping during the Commercial Revolution," in Pullan, *Crisis and Change*, 47–58.

Venice also had some vital assets in the field of commercial policy, which was characterized by a spirit of aggressive state mercantilism "avant la lettre."[22] Venice's large state-owned commercial fleet was a powerful tool in its diplomatic and political strategy for maritime hegemony. Strict navigation laws provided that only Venetian fleets could bring spices to the city of the doge. Efficient organization of maritime traffic made Venetian galley convoys regular, fast, and reliable, giving them a substantial advantage over their competitors.[23] Venice's tight control over its colonies Cyprus and Crete and over other islands gave it strategic military and commercial bases in the eastern Mediterranean (Genoa tried to obtain the same advantages on Chios and Rhodes but never succeeded in gaining complete control; instead, both islands became increasingly independent staple markets). A large network of highly skilled diplomatic representatives (state consuls and official factors) in the Middle East and in Europe supplied commercial information to the state and its merchants and provided the latter with reasonable safety and protection.[24] Finally, Venetian legislation intensified commercial protectionism and discrimination, so reinforcing the foundations of Venice's staple market. Success reached its zenith in the fifteenth century, when Venice became the world center of the re-export trade from the Far and Middle East, and even from the western Mediterranean, to the rest of Europe.[25]

THE RE-EXPORT TRADE FROM SOUTHERN EUROPE IN THE LATE MIDDLE AGES

The commercial rise of Italy in the beginning of the second millennium was based to a large extent on the long-distance re-export trade of luxury goods and fabrics from North Africa and increasingly from the Middle, Far, and South East. This re-export trade was financed mainly by exports of woolen textiles from northwestern Europe (later also from Italy itself) and increasingly by exports of silver and copper or copperware from central Europe.[26]

The structural shifts in the long-distance trade between east and west and in its control, as described previously, did not fundamentally change the types of goods being re-exported. The replacement

---

[22] G. V. Scammell, *The World Encompassed*, passim.
[23] See in this context, however, B. Doumerc, "La crise structurelle de la marine vénitienne du XVe siècle: Le problème du retard des mude," *Annales: Economies, Sociétés, Civilisations* 40 (1985): 605–23.
[24] Lane, *Venice, A Maritime Republic*, 287–8.
[25] Ashtor, "L'apogée du commerce vénitien," 324–6.
[26] Ashtor, "Venetian Supremacy," 13.

of the traditional overland routes, ending in Byzantium, by the maritime routes along the Indian Ocean and the Red Sea, ending in Syria and Egypt, did not fundamentally affect the composition of the goods supplied by the Far, South, and even Middle East, although there were some significant changes in the structure of the east–west trade.

First, the range of luxury goods increased as long-distance trade between east and west expanded under the dynamic influence of Italian and Arab merchants. To this "rich trade" belonged, traditionally, Byzantine, Persian, and Chinese silk fabrics, Persian tapestries, fancy cotton fabrics from India, Chinese porcelain, all kinds of aromatics and perfumes (such as incense and musk), ivory, precious woods, pearls, gems, jewels (such as Indian emeralds, rubies from Burma, sapphires from Ceylon), various dyes, all sorts of spices (pepper, ginger, cinnamon, saffron, cloves, sugar, and many others), and numerous medicines and drugs (such as Chinese galingale and the aloes of Socotra).[27] It can be taken for granted that over the centuries the supply of these luxuries became much more differentiated, not only because the intensification of the maritime trade in the Indian Ocean and the Red Sea opened up new centers of supply but also because European demand increased strongly, particularly during and after the Crusades, when demonstration effects came to the fore, and during the fifteenth century, when a long period of higher living standards began.

A second mechanism of change in Italian re-export trade to the north during the late Middle Ages was import substitution. In the beginning of the second millennium Italy's role was still overwhelmingly commercial. Italy imported luxury goods from North Africa and the Middle East and re-exported a large number of them north of the Alps, in exchange for European goods, which were re-exported to the south and east. During this period Italy was, industrially speaking, still underdeveloped. But its commercial successes during the twelfth and thirteenth centuries would soon change the situation. Whereas the Italian towns during the eleventh and twelfth centuries still imported gold coins from Byzantium, Sardinia, and North Africa and re-exported some of them north of the Alps, from the middle of the thirteenth century onward, Florence, Genoa, and Venice, although remaining big importers of gold powder and gold coins from North Africa and the Middle East, started minting their own coins for export to the north.[28]

[27] K. Glamann, "The Changing Patterns of Trade," in *The Cambridge Economic History of Europe* (Cambridge, 1977), 5:185–289.
[28] Lane, *Venice, A Maritime Republic*, 148.

In textiles the changes were more significant. Lucca, Florence, Venice, and other Italian towns began importing raw silk from the Levant for the production of silk fabrics. The original aim was to substitute Italian fabrics for Levantine ones on the domestic market, but soon the Italian products found their way north of the Alps. In the case of cotton the changes went still further. Milan, Cremona, and other towns began to import cotton from the east in order to produce fustian, a mixture of cotton and wool. Their success was so great that Italian production could not satisfy both home demand and the increasing export demand north of the Alps. Italian merchants then introduced production in south Germany, which soon superseded the Italian industry. Ulm, Augsburg and Nürnberg became leading export centers, selling fustians all over Europe. Italy's role was now to be a center for the re-export of cotton as a raw material from the Levant to south Germany, and Venice was best located to dominate this staple trade.[29]

Import substitution, extending into export-led growth, was also to be found in other branches of industry: The Venetian glass-, mirror-, and crystal-making industries, the Venetian majolica industries, and the Venetian and other Italian jewelry crafts are the best examples, but the Italian and French paper industries should also be mentioned. A similar phenomenon, very famous and successful though in the opposite direction (i.e., north to south), should be noted here: the substitution of high-quality Florentine woolens for Flemish ones and their re-export to North Africa and the Middle East.[30]

Spices were not, in general, suited to import substitution. But there were exceptions: Sugar, for example (still considered during the late Middle Ages as belonging to the category of spices), was a product that received much attention. Originating in Southeast Asia, production of cane sugar had been moving slowly westward, reaching Palestine in the Middle East about the beginning of the second millennium. Venetians started planting it in Cyprus and Crete, and it later reached Sicily and Malta. The Genoese introduced it in southern Spain, from where it moved, in the course of the fifteenth century and with the help of Genoese, Portuguese, and Flemish capital, to the Atlantic islands (first to the Canaries and Madeira and later, in the sixteenth century, to the Azores and São Tomé).[31] Although the introduction

---

[29] M. F. Mazzaoui, *The Italian Cotton Industry in the Later Middle Ages, 1100–1600* (New York, 1981), 28–59.

[30] See in this context H. van der Wee, ed., *The Rise and Decline of Urban Industries in Italy and the Low Countries during the Late Middle Ages and the Early Modern Times* (Louvain, 1988).

[31] C. Verlinden, "From the Mediterranean to the Atlantic: Aspects of an Economic

of cane sugar in the Middle East was originally aimed at import substitution, the rapid extension of production westward soon became
export-oriented. Cane sugar was a success story and, for that reason,
a vital product of the European re-export trade. The city councils of
Genoa and Venice tried hard to maintain control over the trade, but
the Portuguese crown, supported by Genoese, south German, and
Flemish private bankers, was in the end able to dominate it.[32] However, this did not occur until the fifteenth century was already close
to its end.

In the other sectors of the spice trade, the Italian city-states – and
Venice in particular – did much better. Between 1420 and 1496 Venice
was able to maintain a very strong position in re-exporting spices from
the Middle East to Europe and in re-exporting woolen cloth to Syria,
Egypt, and the Levant.[33] During a period of considerable expansion
of spice consumption in Europe, such a predominance in the re-export
trade was a tremendous asset in Venice's struggle for maritime hegemony. A tentative estimate puts Venice's share in the total spice
trade (including sugar) under 45 percent about 1400 and over 60 percent a century later.[34] Pepper remained the leading article of the spice
trade, the volume of its re-export still growing in absolute terms during the fifteenth century. But in the course of that century the relative
position of pepper deteriorated to the advantage of the other spices.
Demand clearly was differentiating in Europe. The increase in European pepper consumption during the fifteenth century was probably
less than 25 percent, whereas the demand for spices other than pepper increased by 155 percent.[35] Prices during the fifteenth century
reflect the growth of the world trade in spices. They not only tend to
fall more rapidly than the general price level, no doubt another factor
in the increase in demand, but their convergence throughout Europe
reflects the development of trade links. Comparisons between the price
movements of spices at the Venetian and Antwerp markets during
the fifteenth century are a case in point.[36]

Three other shifts concerning the re-export trade from and to the
Middle East should be mentioned. First, during the fifteenth-century,

Shift (Twelfth–Eighteenth Century)," *Journal of European Economic History* 1 (1972):
625–46.

[32] J. Baxa and G. Bruhns, *Zucker im Leben der Völker: Eine Kultur- und Wirtschaftsgeschichte* (Berlin, 1967), 15–16.

[33] Ashtor, "Venetian Supremacy," 48.

[34] C. H. H. Wake, "The Changing Pattern of Europe's Pepper and Spice Imports, ca.
1400–1700," *Journal of European Economic History* 8 (1979): 392.

[35] C. H. H. Wake, "The Volume of European Spice Trade at the Beginning and the
End of the Fifteenth Century," ibid. 15 (1986): 635.

[36] van der Wee, *Antwerp Market*, 3:20.

Venetian trade to Egypt, in particular to Alexandria, grew at the expense of its trade to Syria. As Venice was the predominant trading partner with the Middle East, this meant that Alexandria became the leading exporter of spices from the Middle East, and Egypt began to overshadow Syria in trade relations with Europe.[37] Second, import substitution in Europe had a negative effect on industrial activity in Iraq, Syria, and Egypt. The introduction of cane sugar plantations in the Mediterranean islands, southern Spain, and the Atlantic islands virtually terminated the export of sugar from the Middle East. The introduction of paper factories in France and Italy had the same unfavorable effect on the exports of paper from the Middle East. The increasing imports of north European, Italian, and south German textiles by the Middle East had no less disastrous effects on the traditional textile sectors of Syria, Egypt, and Iraq.[38] Third, import substitution in Europe and exports of European textiles to the Middle East had a favorable effect on Europe's balance of payments. The effect, however, was insufficient to restore equilibrium. The sharp increase in European consumption of spices and other luxury goods imported from the Middle East gradually undermined Europe's traditional surplus. The deficit became critical about 1400, but its reduction was not possible until the second third of the fifteenth century, when innovations in mining techniques stimulated the production of silver in central and southern Europe.[39] As mentioned above, Venice, for geographical and commercial reasons, benefited most from the increasing flow of silver from north to south; thus, the south German–Venetian axis was a crucial variable in the emergence of Venice as the leading European center of the re-export trade from south to north and in Venice's rise to maritime and financial hegemony in the Mediterranean and Europe.

THE RISE OF THE PORTUGUESE RE-EXPORT TRADE AND VENICE'S TEMPORARY RECOVERY (FIFTEENTH TO SIXTEENTH CENTURIES)

The increasing predominance of Venice in the Mediterranean and North Sea trade during the fifteenth century was accompanied by a parallel growth of maritime activity from the Iberian Peninsula, especially from Portugal, into the Atlantic Ocean.

During the fourteenth and fifteenth centuries Portuguese shippers

---

[37] Wake, "Spice Imports," 634–5.
[38] Ashtor, "L'apogée du commerce vénitien," 318–20.
[39] Ashtor, "The Volume of Levantine Trade in the Later Middle Ages (1370–1498)," *Journal of European Economic History* 4 (1975): 609.

added to their traditional skills the technical innovations that had been introduced in Italian and Hanseatic shipbuilding and navigation. The Portuguese kings took advantage of these advances in Portuguese shipping and increasingly used their fleets for maritime exploration and military conquest. The islands of Madeira, the Canaries, and the Azores were discovered and annexed beginning in the fourteenth century. During the same period exploration of the western coast of Africa prepared the way for the discovery of the Cape of Good Hope and the route to East Africa and India.[40]

When exploring the western coast of Africa, the Portuguese not only discovered gold but also found spices, which they could sell in northern Europe. The re-export of West African spices from Lisbon to Flanders and Brabant was already an important trade before 1500. It remained significant until the middle of the sixteenth century, when English and French ships began importing spices directly from West Africa.[41] The successful re-export trade of West African spices induced the king of Portugal to send official agents to Bruges and Antwerp to represent his interests. These interests suddenly widened in 1498, when Vasco da Gama reached Calicut and returned to Portugal, his ships loaded with Asian spices. But an expansion of the spice trade required increased imports of copper and silver from the north and greater financial support. The imports could be found most easily at Antwerp, where merchants from the Aachen area and south Germany were selling both metals in increasing quantities. Extra loans could be obtained from Genoese, Flemish, and south German merchants at the money markets in Flanders and Brabant.[42]

Thus was created a Lisbon–Antwerp commercial axis. In 1501 the first ship from Lisbon loaded with Asian spices arrived at the Antwerp harbor. From 1503 the re-exports of Asian spices from Lisbon to Antwerp were large and regular.

Not only did the king of Portugal try to increase his sales of spices at the Antwerp market, but with the help of Italian financiers, he wanted to monopolize the re-export trade in African and Asian spices for the whole of Europe. In 1508 rights to the Portuguese crown monopoly of spices were leased to the Affaitadi and Gualteroti, which probably accounts for the appearance of Asian spices, re-exports from

[40] C. Verlinden, "From the Mediterranean to the Atlantic," 625–46; and V. Magalhães Godinho, "Création et dynamisme économique du monde atlantique (1420–1670)," *Annales: Economies, Sociétés, Civilisations* 5 (1950): 32–6.
[41] V. Magalhães Godinho, *L'économie de l'empire portugais aux XVe et XVIe siècles* (Paris, 1969).
[42] H. van der Wee, "World Production and Trade in Gold, Silver, and Copper in the Low Countries, 1450–1700," in Kellenbenz, *Precious Metals in the Age of Expansion*, 79–86.

Lisbon, at the fairs of Lyons beginning in 1508. Shortly afterward, re-exports form Lisbon were also penetrating into central and eastern Europe, even into Italy.[43]

The success of the re-export trade in spices from Lisbon to the rest of Europe was, without doubt, at the expense of the Italian trade, in particular that from Venice. At the same time, the weakening of the Venetian spice trade was not only due to Portuguese competition. After the death of the Mamluk sultan of Egypt in 1496, the Mediterranean spice trade was hindered by serious internal turmoil. The Turks took advantage of the situation by extending their political ambitions to Syria and Egypt. Tensions led to the outbreak of the Turkish–Venetian War in 1499. The end of the war in 1503 did not lay to rest Turkish expansionism, and Syria and Egypt came definitively under Ottoman control in 1517.[44] During the same period the Portuguese were using military means to prevent the export of Malabar spices along the traditional Muslim sea route to the Mediterranean. In 1505 the Portuguese founded their Indian empire officially. They defeated the Mamluks and Gurjeratis in the Indian Ocean. They set up factories along the Indian coast. They built military fortifications and naval bases. They took control of many of the strategic entries to the ocean, such as the Cape of Good Hope, Socotra at the entrance of the Red Sea, Bahrein and Hormuz in the Persian Gulf, and Malacca at the entrance to the South China Sea. Finally, they subjugated the small Muslim states of East Africa and conquered the islands of Madagascar and Mauritius.[45]

Between 1510 and 1530 the Portuguese predominance in the re-export trade in African and Asian spices to the rest of Europe via Lisbon and the Antwerp staple market reached its peak.[46] Half of the revenue of King John III of Portugal in the 1520s came from this re-export trade. By contrast, the revenue that the Mamluk sultan derived from the transit trade in spices from Syria and Egypt toward Italy, still very high in the early 1490s, fell drastically at the beginning of the sixteenth century. Venice's share in the re-export of spices to Lisbon and Antwerp had decreased so much that in 1527 the Venetian Senate, in despair, offered to purchase the spice monopoly of the Portuguese crown, a proposal that was not accepted.[47]

Portugal was not able to maintain for long its near-monopoly posi-

[43] van der Wee, *Antwerp Market,* 2:127ff.; and V. Vazques De Prada, *Lettres marchandes d'Anvers* (Paris, 1960), 89.

[44] Lane, *Venice, A Martime Republic,* 349.

[45] K. Glamann, "European Trade, 1500–1750," in *The Fontana Economic History of Europe* (Glasgow, 1976), 475–81.

[46] Godinho, *L'empire portugais,* passim.

[47] Glamann, "Changing Patterns of Trade," 284.

tion in the re-export trade in spices. It lost this position shortly after 1530, when the Mediterranean, and Venice in particular, recaptured a good share of the re-exports of Asian spices to Europe north of the Alps.[48]

From the early 1530s spice shipments from the Middle East to Venice increased sharply again. In the 1530s in Lyons the share of spices arriving via the Mediterranean, which during the French–Habsburg war of the 1520s had risen to about half, reached 85 percent. These spices, however, were not imported exclusively from Venice but came in increasing quantities directly via Marseille from Alexandria, Istanbul, and the Anatolian ports.[49]

In the 1530s "Venetian" spices also reappeared in large quantities in central Europe, in the Baltic area, along the Rhine route, and even on the Antwerp market. The strong position of the Antwerp staple market for Asian spices was soon severely eroded. With it came the decline of the Antwerp Feitoria de Flandres, which closed in 1548.[50]

Of course, re-exports of spices from Lisbon to Antwerp and the north did not disappear at once. They still remained important for a while, together with Venetian and other re-exports. During the second half of the century, however, the Portuguese position receded further relative to that of Venice.[51]

The reasons for the decline of the Portuguese re-export trade in spices and for the revival of the Venice–Marseille trade are complex. First, there was a gradual deterioration of Portugal's military and naval strength from the second third of the sixteenth century and particularly during the last third of that century. The weakening of royal power in Portugal led to the annexation of the country by Philip II of Spain and to a relaxation of military control in the Indian Ocean. After the Portuguese conquest of the Malabar Coast, the Muslim merchants, who had in previous centuries dominated the spice trade in the area, moved to Sumatra, trying to set up a trade in Indonesian pepper directly from Sumatra to the Red Sea via the more open, southern belt of the Indian Ocean. By doing so the Muslims were able to rebuild slowly the Asian spice trade to the Red Sea. During the second half of the sixteenth century, profiting from the fact that Aden, at the entrance to the Red Sea, had withstood the Portuguese, Muslim merchants intensified their efforts and succeeded partly in reviving

[48] Braudel, *La Méditerranée*, 2:495ff.
[49] R. Gascon, "Un siècle du commerce des épices à Lyon, fin XV- fin XVI-siècles," *Annales: Economies, Sociétés, Civilisations* 15 (1960):646ff.
[50] van der Wee, *Antwerp Market*, 2:156ff.
[51] Glamann, "European Trade, 1500–1750," 475–82.

the old spice routes to Cairo-Alexandria and in particular to Damascus-Beirut. These routes, however, never recaptured their predominant position of the fifteenth century. The main reason for their relative failure was the rise of an alternative spice route to the Mediterranean, one closely linked with the impressive growth of the Ottoman Empire under Sultan Soliman the Great.[52]

When the Portuguese at the beginning of the sixteenth century were able to block the supply of Malabar spices along the Red Sea to Damascus-Beirut and Cairo-Alexandria, Venice was forced to limit its visits to both markets. But the temporary weakening of the Mediterranean spice trade did not entail a decline in the whole Levant trade. On the contrary, Venetian merchants and other Italian, French, and Catalan traders continued to visit the Levant markets to buy goods such as cotton and raw silk, wheat and salt, cotton and silk luxury fabrics, precious stones, gems, jewels, and so on. This Levant trade increased considerably as the general European expansion gained momentum from the second third of the sixteenth century. The Ottoman Empire, which was also entering a period of impressive internal growth, gave another powerful impetus to the Mediterranean trade.[53]

The Ottoman boom was particularly important because it had a double effect. First, the boom increased the demand for European goods. All European ports of the Mediterranean benefited from this, but most of all Venice. A woolen industry, organized on a large scale and oriented toward the Middle East, developed in the city.[54] Venice also took particular advantage of the intensification of long-distance overland trade from Flanders to Italy along the Rhine route and through south Germany and from central Europe to Italy. Textiles from England and Flanders, copperware from Germany, and many other goods from Europe north of the Alps were re-exported in increasing quantities from Venice to Istanbul and to the other Ottoman markets in the Levant.[55]

The other effect of the Ottoman boom was to increase the home demand for oriental products, that is, luxury goods and spices from the Far East. Because of their growing military power east of Anatolia, the Ottomans started putting pressure on the overland routes in Persia. The Portuguese took advantage of this, turning Hormuz on the Persian Gulf into a huge staple market for oriental goods (in particular

[52] Godinho, *L'empire portugais*, passim.
[53] Braudel, *La Méditerranée*, 2:493ff.
[54] Pullan, *Crisis and Change*, 11ff.
[55] Lane, *Venice, A Maritime Republic*, 297ff.

for Malabar spices) intended for the Ottoman territories. From 1543 onward the customs of Hormuz were fully and directly integrated into the tax system of Portugal, an indication of their growing share in public revenue.[56]

Malabar spices and other oriental goods passing the staple of Hormuz continued their way westward along the Persian Gulf. From Basra they reached Baghdad and Aleppo by caravan. From Aleppo they were re-exported to the Anatolian markets and Istanbul, and increasingly to western Europe. Venice and the other west Mediterranean ports involved in the expanding Levant trade soon came into contact with the new spice route. Because of its growing importance in supplying the Ottoman market, Aleppo became very attractive to west Mediterranean buyers as well. Gradually Aleppo (and its port Tripoli in Syria) rose to prominence, becoming the leading staple market for oriental goods and spices in the Levant, distributing them partly to the Ottoman markets and partly to the Venetians and others, who re-exported them to Europe north of the Alps. Aleppo at the turn of the century surpassed Alexandria and Damascus by far, and it maintained this leading position far into the seventeenth century.[57]

Meanwhile, the pattern of the European re-export trade in Asian, Atlantic, and American products had changed fundamentally once again. From the end of the sixteenth century English and Dutch ships, in growing numbers, penetrated into the Mediterranean.[58] English and Dutch merchants started selling Baltic grain and west European textiles, first to Italian merchants, then directly to Levantine merchants. With their earnings, they started to buy Levantine and other oriental products directly.[59]

When the Thirty Years' War (1618–48) broke out in Germany, the Venetian overland re-export trade in Levantine and Asian products collapsed entirely. Amsterdam in the meantime emerged as the leading European staple market for these products, because the Dutch East India company, founded in 1602, succeeded in replacing the Portuguese merchants in the spice trade via the Cape of Good Hope, and because Dutch shipping to the Levant supplied Asian goods directly from the Mediterranean to Holland.[60] From this moment onward European re-exports from Asia no longer went from south to north but

---

[56] Godinho, *L'empire portugais*, passim.
[57] S. Faroqhi, "The Venetian Presence in the Ottoman Empire (1600–1630)," *Journal of European Economic History* 15 (1986): 373–83.
[58] F. Braudel and R. Romano, *Navires et marchandies à l'entrée du Port de Livourne (1547– 1611)* (Paris, 1951).
[59] Braudel, *La Méditerranée*, 2:517ff.
[60] F. S. Gaastra, *De Geschiedenis van de VOC* (Haarlem, 1982), 35 ff.

went increasingly in the opposite direction. When later in the seventeenth century the London staple market surpassed Amsterdam, the structure of the re-export trade did not fundamentally change. Even the newcomers in the Far East trade of the late seventeenth and early eighteenth centuries, such as Sweden, Denmark, France, and the Austrian Netherlands, did not alter the pattern.[61]

During the decade after 1602 the volume of trade moving through Venice fell dramatically. Venice's share in the revived Mediterranean spice trade shrunk considerably during these years; the exports of Venetian woolen cloth to the Levant dropped sharply.[62] The crisis at the beginning of the Thirty Years' War made things worse: it was the last, fatal turning point in the definitive decline of Venice's re-export trade of Asian goods to the rest of Europe. Genoa, the other great maritime power of Italy, succeeded for a while in maintaining some international trade activity because of its financial links with the Spanish Empire. But when the financial siècle des Génois was over, after the bankruptcy of the Spanish government in 1627, Genoa's trade also decayed quickly. The historic role of Italy as transmitter of Asian and African wares to the rest of Europe had come to an end.

[61] F. S. Gaastra and L. Blusse, eds., *Companies and Trade*, Comparative Studies in Overseas History, vol. 3 (The Hague, 1981), passim.
[62] R. Romomo, "Between the Sixteenth and Seventeenth Centuries: The Economic Crisis of 1619–22," in G. Parker and L. M. Smith, eds., *The General Crisis of the Seventeenth Century* (London, 1978), 176ff., 184ff.; D. Sella, *Commercio e industria a Venezia nel secolo XVII* (Venice and Rome, 1961), passim.

CHAPTER 2

The growth and composition of trade in the Iberian empires, 1450–1750

CARLA RAHN PHILLIPS

IN planning the conference on merchant empires that formed the basis for this collection of papers, the Early Modern Group at Minnesota originally included diverse topics under the general headings of northern and southern Europe. This paper was designed to provide a general background for the long-distance trade of southern Europe between 1350 and 1750, surveying the published literature on Mediterranean and Iberian trade in those crucial centuries. The inquiry was to be limited to long-distance trade outside Europe, omitting discussion of internal European commercial networks. In this way we hoped to clarify the role of merchants and trade in establishing European influence around the globe. In other words, the focus of the conference was not on the growth of world trade in the early modern period but on the role of European merchants and their governments in furthering world trade. Primarily for that reason, we decided not to include lengthy discussion of the Ottoman Empire, although the interaction of Christian Europe with the Islamic world was crucial to the development of global commerce in many ways. In Immanuel Wallerstein's terminology, the Ottoman Empire of the sixteenth century was a separate world-system from Europe, uniting an economic and trading network with political authority and distributive power. The Ottoman system would be absorbed by the expanding capitalist world-economy after 1750, but for the whole of the period considered here, it remained a separate, autonomous system, linked with Europe by a trade in luxury goods.[1]

---

[1] Wallerstein, "The Ottoman Empire and the Capitalist World-Economy: Some Questions for Research," *Fernand Braudel Center for the Study of Economies, Historical Systems, and Civilizations, Review* 2 (Winter 1979): 389–98; Halil Inalcik, "Capital Formation in the Ottoman Empire," *Journal of Economic History* 29 (1969): 97–140. Other

During the conference itself, our focus shifted somewhat, and the division between northern and southern Europe seemed less useful than it had at the planning stage. Moreover, we became less concerned with Mediterranean trade and more concerned with the trade that developed beyond the confines of Europe. The task of this paper shifted to a survey of the literature on the first great merchant empires of Europe – the Portuguese and the Spanish. Separately and together, they spanned the globe and lasted through the early modern period and beyond. Nonetheless, the Iberian empires have not been well studied by scholars writing in English, nor well integrated into the general history of world trade. This is particularly true in the United States, where the tendency has been to leave the Iberian empires to specialists in Latin America, Africa, and Asia, and to concentrate on the later empires established by northern Europeans, which included the future United States. Perhaps an element of nationalistic hostility entered into this neglect as well, particularly with regard to Spain. During the early modern period, Spain reached the peak of its political and economic power, both in Europe and around the globe. Holland and England shaped their national identities and founded their North American colonies in opposition to Spain and in an atmosphere of anti-Spanish sentiment. One may argue that this sentiment has continued to shape United States historiography, even in a seemingly neutral topic such as world trade. The wealth of published material on the Iberian empires, especially in non-English-language scholarship, deserves to be more widely known. The object of this paper is to survey some recent work on the topic, although it cannot pretend to offer a comprehensive summary.

Of primary concern will be the practical and quantitative aspects of trade between the Iberian powers and their empires overseas: How was trade established and maintained? How long did it take to make a round-trip? How many ships were involved, and how did their number change over time? What trade goods were involved, and how did the composition and volume of trade change over time? In the long list of items that figured prominently in international seaborne trade, two present special problems of interpretation – slaves and precious metals. They will be mentioned here because of their central roles in Iberian trade, but they will receive fuller and more specialized

work from different perspectives also finds the Ottoman Empire retaining its economic autonomy during the early modern period. See, e.g., Michel Morineau, "Naissance d'une domination: Marchands européens, marchands et marchés du Levant aux XVIIIe et XIXe siècles," in *Commerce de gros, commerce de détail dans les pays méditerranéens: XVI–XIX siècles* (Nice, 1976), 145–84.

treatment in chapters 7 and 9. Similarly, the arrangements between merchants and states will be touched upon only briefly in this essay, as they form the subject of several other contributions in the second volume of the collection.

The framework used here will be chronological and empirical rather than theoretical. Immanuel Wallerstein's theoretical framework for the evolution of the world economy has provided the stimulus for much fruitful discussion.[2] Wallerstein deals with the relationship between the internal organization of government, society, and labor and the external role of a given nation in the world-economy. Unfortunately, his characterization of the internal economies and labor relations of Portugal, Spain, and their empires suffers greatly from overgeneralization. Moreover, he has very little to say about the composition and volume of trade within the empires. Thus, his categories of analysis are not particularly helpful for the purposes of this paper.

Another possible theoretical approach was formulated by the late Fernand Braudel, who contributed so much to our understanding of the early modern centuries. Braudel chose to organize his analysis of European trade around a succession of key financial centers such as Venice, Antwerp, Amsterdam, and London, all of them combining political, commercial, and financial functions.[3] That is too restrictive an approach for the Iberian empires. In about 1600, when Spain and Portugal shared a king, their empires had one main political center (Madrid), two commercial centers (Seville and Lisbon), and several financial centers (in the hiatus between the decline of Antwerp and the rise of Amsterdam). Braudel's categories make it impossible to understand how the Iberian empires were organized, and they risk ignoring the connection between trade and government. Braudel even suggested that Philip II of Spain should have moved his capital to Lisbon in order to forestall the rise of Amsterdam.[4] This notion ignores the fact that Lisbon lacked a rich agricultural hinterland such as those that supported the other cities he mentioned. More important, Lisbon would not have been able to command the financial support of Castile, a crucial element in Spain's imperial administration.

A broad theoretical approach may some day emerge that can encompass the complexity of the Iberian empires. In the meantime, it

---

[2] Wallerstein, *The Modern World-System*, vol. 1, *Capitalist Agriculture and the Origins of the European World-Economy in the Sixteenth Century* (New York, 1974); and idem, *The Modern World-System*, vol. 2, *Mercantilism and the Consolidation of the European World-Economy, 1600–1750* (New York, 1980).

[3] Braudel, *The Perspective of the World*, vol. 3 of *Civilization and Capitalism, Fifteenth–Eighteenth Century*, trans. Siân Reynolds (New York, 1984), 27–35.

[4] Ibid., 32–3.

seems best to use a more traditional approach and concentrate on an empirically based analysis of changes over time. Of special concern in this paper will be the timing of shifts in the volume of trade. Wallerstein has structured his analysis of world trade around the notion of a "long expansionist phase roughly from 1450 to 1650, followed by a long (overlapping) period of *relative* contraction or stagnation from 1600 to 1750."[5] Published work on trade in the Iberian empires suggests several refinements in that general timetable, as we shall see.

Historians have often dealt with trade as independent from the broader economy or have treated it largely as a stimulus for the sluggish agrarian and manufacturing sectors. It makes better sense to recognize that trade was linked to the broader economy, even if we cannot always understand the nature of the links. The vast majority of Europeans depended on a local agrarian economy for their livelihood through the early modern period and beyond. International trade had supplied very few of their needs during medieval times, mostly high-priced luxuries.[6] During the early modern centuries some areas – primarily coastal trading cities – were regularly supplied with basic foodstuffs by sea, and low-priced bulky goods were becoming an important part of international commerce within Europe.[7] This change occurred along with improved ships and navigational aids and such innovations as maritime insurance and law, business partnerships, and credit instruments, which formed the "commercial revolution" of the late Middle Ages.[8] The Mediterranean was most closely identified with that commercial revolution, which laid the foundations for the trading empires of Portugal and Spain.

The best figures we have for Mediterranean trade are sporadic indications of the total number of ships on a given route (see Table 2.1). Because of the importance of Mediterranean trade, it is surprising to learn how few ships were involved. In the mid–fourteenth century, just after the arrival of the Black Death, Venice sent an average of one ship to the Levant every two years. By the end of the fifteenth century an annual average of five to seven galleys made the trip. In the mid–fifteenth century Venetians also sent a dozen "round ships" a year to Syria. How large the individual ships were and how much merchan-

---

[5] "Ottoman Empire," 392.

[6] Wilhelm Heyd, *Histoire du commerce du Levant au Moyen-age*, trans. F. Reynaud, 2 vols. (Leipzig, 1885–6; reprint, Chicago, 1967), provides detailed descriptions of the products traded and the routes used.

[7] Jacques Heers, *L'Occident aux XIVe et XVe siècles: Aspects économiques et sociaux* (Paris, 1973), 170–1.

[8] Robert S. Lopez, *The Commercial Revolution of the Middle Ages, 950–1350* (New York, 1971).

dise they carried are not known, although we have some information on individual cargoes and merchants.[9] Genoese trading volume is even less well known. An annual average of six ships of all types traded to the Levant in the late 1360s. The city as a whole had a fleet of twenty-four to twenty-six ships during the late 1450s and early 1460s, but unfortunately, we have no information about their size.[10]

Catalonia, whose trade ran far behind that of Venice and Genoa, was sending just over two ships a year to the Levant at the end of the fourteenth century and five to six during the 1420s. Thereafter, Catalan trade slackened briefly, before rising again to about 4.5 ships per year in the 1450s and early 1460s. By the late fifteenth century fewer than two ships per year traveled to all ports from Catalonia, probably due to the Catalonian civil war.[11] Even the small Italian port of Ancona surpassed Catalonia during the late fifteenth century, sending an average of 2.4 trading ships each year to all destinations.[12]

The problems faced by Catalonia in the late fifteenth century did not typify the Mediterranean as a whole, however. Much evidence suggests that the late fifteenth century saw a revival of population, agriculture, manufacturing, and trade in the Mediterranean economy.[13] The late fifteenth century also witnessed the beginning of a shift in the nexus of European trade from the Mediterranean to the Atlantic. Merchants from the Mediterranean had been trading beyond the Strait of Gibraltar for several centuries, with Italians, Catalonians, Castilians, and Basques well established in port cities on the Atlantic coast. As the business climate in the eastern Mediterranean deteriorated during the fifteenth century, due in part to the increasing hostility of the Ottoman Turks, many merchants intensified their efforts in the Atlantic, some of them settling among the growing Italian communities in Iberia.

The Portuguese, with few interests in the Mediterranean, had long viewed the Atlantic as their major trading area, even before they began to expand outward. With the Castilians, they served as intermediaries between the Islamic and Christian worlds of the western Med-

---

[9] Eliyahu Ashtor, *Levant Trade in the Later Middle Ages* (Princeton, N. J., 1983), 79, 194–9, 318, 328–30.

[10] Jacques Heers, *Gênes au XVe siècle: Activité économique et problèmes sociaux* (Paris, 1961), 639–45.

[11] Ashtor, *Levant Trade*, 488; Mario Del Treppo, *Els mercaders catalans i expansió de la corona catalano-aragonesa al segle XV*, trans. Jaume Riera i Sans (Barcelona, 1976), 371.

[12] Ashtor, *Levant Trade*, 508–9.

[13] Frederic C. Lane, *Venice: A Maritime Republic* (Baltimore and London, 1973), 225–39; Harry A. Miskimin, *The Economy of Later Renaissance Europe, 1460–1600* (Cambridge and New York, 1977).

Glossary of Terms Used in the Tables

arroba   Castilian weight equivalent to 25 pounds of 16 ounces
     each, or 11.5 kilograms.

caixa   Portuguese measure used for sugar, literally meaning
     "box." In Brazil, it was equivalent to 30 arrobas.

fanega   Castilian measure of volume used for various
     agricultural products, its weight varying accordingly. A
     fanega of cacao weighed 110 libras, or 4.4 arrobas.

livre/libra A Castilian pound, or 1/25 of an arroba.

rolo   Portuguese measure used for tobacco, literally meaning
     "roll." In the trade between West Africa and Brazil, it
     seems to have been equivalent to 3 arrobas.

tonelada Spanish measure of the carrying capacity of a ship,
     roughly equivalent to the French tonne de mer (sea ton) of
     1.42 cubic meters. Although Chaunu claims that the size of
     the official Spanish tonelada changed during the sixteenth
     century, much evidence suggests that it did not.

iterranean and eastern Atlantic and as conduits for the gold of West
Africa.[14] The gold, fish, and slaves of North Africa, plus African de-
mand for the agricultural products of Iberia, fueled rivalry between
Portuguese and Castilian merchants and attracted Genoese mer-

[14] Antonio Henrique R. de Oliveira Marques, *History of Portugal,* 2 vols. (New York,
  1972), 1:91–4.

Table 2.1

Shipping Volume

Years	Total years with available data	Trader	Ships per year	Average weight of known ships (in toneladas)	Total toneladas per year	Comments	Source
1345-69	25	Venice	0.5				a
1381-90	10	Venice	4.9				a
1391-1400	10	Venice	7.5				a
1401-10	10	Venice	5.8				a
1411-20	10	Venice	7.1				a
1421-30	10	Venice	6.1				a
1422-52	31	Venice	12.0				a
1431-40	10	Venice	6.2				a
1441-50	10	Venice	6.1				a
1390-99	10	Catalonia	5 to 8				a

1390–1404	15	Catalonia	2.1		b
1405–14	10	Catalonia	5.6		b
1414–24	11	Catalonia	5.8		b
1424–34	11	Catalonia	5.1		b
1435–44	10	Catalonia	3.3		b
1445–54	10	Catalonia	3.8		b
1455–64	10	Catalonia	4.5		b
1465–1504	40	Catalonia	0.9		a
1453–98	46	Ancona	2.4		a
1462–1566	105	All	1.4	Alum to northern Europe	c
1566–1650	85	All	2.4	Alum to northern Europe	c
1501–13	13	All	1.0	Alum to Venice	c
1531–39	9	All	0.9	Alum to Venice	c
1540–52	13	All	0.8	Alum to Venice	c
1553–65	13	All	0.6	Alum to Venice	c
1566–78	13	All	0.2	Alum to Venice	c
1571–1614	44	All	7.4	Alum to Rome	c

Table 2.1. (*Cont.*)

Years	Total years with available data	Trader	Ships per year	Average weight of known ships (in toneladas)	Total toneladas per year	Comments	Source
1578–90	13	All	0.5			Alum to Venice	c
1590–1602	13	All	1.3			Alum to Venice	c
1629–1707	79	All	4.7			Alum to Rome	c
1602–25	24	Holland	10.0			Shipments to Asia	d
1602–1780	179	Holland	25.1			"	d
1626–70	45	Holland	22.0			"	d
1671–1750	80	Holland	29.0			"	d
1750–80	31	Holland	26.0			"	d
1721–25	5	All	609.0			Ships entering and	e
1731–35	5	All	945.3			leaving Lisbon	e
1746–50	5	All	919.6			"	e
1751–55	5	All	866.6			"	e
1756–60	5	All	830.8			"	e
1761–65	5	All	912.6			"	e
1766–70	5	All	854.4			"	e

						Ships to and from the Spanish Indies	
1771-75	5	All	763.6			"	e
1776-80	5	All	806.8			"	e
1506-10	5	Spain and others	45.2	99.1	4,480.0		f
1511-15	5	"	55.8	99.3	5,540.0	"	f
1516-20	5	"	88.4	99.5	8,802.0	"	f
1521-25	5	"	96.6	107.7	7,456.0	"	f
1526-30	5	"	96.6	109.8	10,594.0	"	f
1531-35	5	"	103.8	114.2	11,858.0	"	f
1536-40	5	"	115.6	130.8	15,124.0	"	f
1541-45	5	"	127.6	131.1	17,515.6	"	f
1546-50	5	"	174.8	145.7	25,456.0	"	f
1551-55	5	"	131.2	163.6	21,463.2	"	f
1556-60	5	"	109.8	158.7	18,062.0	"	f
1561-65	5	"	132.6	175.1	23,213.0	"	f
1566-70	5	"	132.2	211.8	27,984.8	"	f
1571-75	5	"	133.0	210.1	30,466.0	"	f
1576-80	5	"	102.4	296.9	30,225.8	"	
1581-85	5	"	131.0	266.9	34,959.6	"	f
1586-90	5	"	177.2	216.2	38,317.8	"	f

Table 2.1. (*Cont.*)

Years	Total years with available data	Trader	Ships per year	Average weight of known ships (in toneladas)	Total toneladas per year	Comments	Source
1591-95	5	Spain and others	184.0	197.9	32,465.2	Ships to and from the Spanish Indies	f
1596-1600	5	"	188.6	236.2	39,816.0	"	f
1601-05	5	"	151.6	259.8	39,400.2	"	f
1606-10	5	"	193.0	236.2	45,593.4	"	f
1611-15	5	"	165.2	230.7	38,117.6	"	f
1616-20	5	"	173.4	238.6	41,369.1	"	f
1621-25	5	"	155.0	247.1	38,304.8	"	f
1626-30	5	"	117.6	318.8	36,920.4	"	f
1631-35	5	"	98.8	278.9	27,549.4	"	f
1636-40	5	"	95.4	288.5	27,561.0	"	f
1641-45	5	"	71.2	325.8	22,999.8	"	f
1646-50	5	"	73.2	301.3	22,056.0	"	f
1651-55	5	"	49.2			"	f
1656-60	5	"	34.2			"	f
1661-65	5	"	30.8			"	f

1666-70	5	"	31.0		=	f
1671-75	5	"	43.6		=	f
1676-80	5	"	39.0		=	f
1681-85	5	"	40.2		=	f
1686-90	5	"	33.6		=	f
1691-95	5	"	29.4		=	f
1695-99	5	"	35.0		=	f
1717-20	4	"	30.5	296.5	7,782.7	" g
1721-25	5	"	52.8	300.5	10,216.0	Not all ships were listed g
1726-30	5	"	39.4	320.4	9,483.4	with tonnages g
1731-35	5	"	36.4	362.8	11,973.7	g
1736-40	5	"	31.8	333.3	9,264.5	g
1741-45	5	"	46.2	235.2	9,831.1	g
1746-50	5	"	51.4	322.2	16,369.7	g
1751-55	5	"	62.0	331.0	19,449.9	g
1756-60	5	"	60.4	393.6	22,277.9	g
1761-65	5	"	69.6	407.4	24,038.0	g
1766-70	5	"	97.2	336.4	28,059.9	g

Table 2.1. (Cont.)

Years	Total years with available data	Trader	Ships per year	Average weight of known ships (in toneladas)	Total toneladas per year	Comments	Source
1771–75	5	"	84.0	351.7	24,831.3		g
1776–78	3	"	102.7	414.1	29,401.6		g

a Eliyahu Ashtor, Levant Trade in the Later Middle Ages (Princeton, N.J., 1983), 79, 194–9, 318, 328–30, 343, 488.

b Mario Del Treppo, Els mercaders catalans i expansió de la corona catalano-aragonesa al segle XV, trans. Jaume Riera i Sans (Barcelona, 1976), 371.

c Jean Delumeau, L'alun de Rome (XVe–XIXe siècle) (Paris, 1962), 268, 240, 312.

d Auguste Toussaint, "Atlantique et Océan Indien. La route impériale des Indes," Anuario de Estudios Americanos 26 (1968):635.

e Virgilio Noya Pinto, Ouro brasileiro e o comercio anglo-portugues (São Paulo, 1979), 296.

f Pierre Chaunu, with Huguette Chaunu, Seville et l'Atlantique, 1504–1650, 8 vols. in 12 (Paris, 1955–60), 6(1):168, 337.

g Antonio Garcia-Baquero González, Cadiz y el Atlantico (1717–1778), 2 vols. (Cádiz, 1976), 2:123–37.

chants as well.[15] During the fifteenth century, Castile and Portugal both saw Africa as a rich market and as a field for the extension of their religious struggle with the Islamic world. The Portuguese established colonies and sugar plantations in the Azores and the Madeira islands, and the Castilians did likewise in the Canaries.[16]

Portugal exported salt, wine, fresh and dried fruit, oil, honey, and dried shellfish to northern Europe, as well as cork, hops, and other industrial raw materials. In return, northern Europe sent grain and flour, dried and salted fish, dairy products, metals, wood and other forest products for shipbuilding, and textiles and other manufactured goods.[17] The Mediterranean powers also carried on a regular and lucrative trade with northern Europe by the late fifteenth century, with merchant colonies established in England, France, the Netherlands, and the Germanies in considerable numbers.[18] Wool exports from Castile were an important part of this trade, which also involved bulky items such as salt, alum, and a wide range of agricultural and manufactured goods from the Mediterranean and beyond.[19]

Although the period that is often called the age of discovery was by definition unique, the process of commercial and colonial expansion had extensive roots in the medieval centuries. By the fifteenth century, the peoples of the Iberian Peninsula had a long history of commercial activity in the Mediterranean and the Atlantic, in both luxuries and articles of general consumption. They were well supplied technologically and administratively to pursue commercial opportunities outside the boundaries of Europe, leading the way beyond the familiar and into the unknown.[20]

Compared with trading powers in the Mediterranean, Portugal

---

[15] Heers, *Gênes*, 57–74.

[16] Bailey E. Diffie and George D. Winius, *Foundations of the Portuguese Empire, 1415–1580* (Minneapolis, 1977), 41–51; Marques, *History of Portugal*, 1:145–8, 151–9; Vitorino Magalhães Godinho, *A expanção quatrocentista portuguesa: Problemas das origens e da linha de evolução* (Lisbon, 1944), 138–40; Manuela Marrero Rodríguez, "Desfase entre la piratería y la Mediterránea," *Anuario de Estudios Americanos* 25 (1968): 595–9.

[17] Antonio Henriques de Oliveira Marques, *Hansa e Portugal na idade média* (Lisbon, 1959), 108–37; Virginia Rau, "Les courants du trafic du sel portugais du XIVe au XVIIIe siècle," in *Le rôle du sel dans l'histoire*, ed. Michel Mollat (Paris, 1968), 53–71.

[18] Heers, *Gênes*, 406–410; Jean-Albert Goris, *Etude sur les colonies marchandes méridionales (Portugais, Espagnols, Italiens) à Anvers, 1477–1566* (Louvain, 1925); Wendy R. Childs, *Anglo-Castilian Trade in the Later Middle Ages* (Manchester, England, 1978).

[19] Michel Mollat, *Le rôle du sel dans l'histoire*, 209; Jean Delumeau, *L'alun de Rome (XVe–XIXe siècle)* (Paris, 1962), 18–21; Jean-Claude Hocquet, *Le sel et la fortune de Venise*, 2 vols. (Lille, 1978–9), deals with the salt trade in a much wider context than the title indicates, tracing the story from 1200 to 1650.

[20] Vitorino Magalhães Godinho, *L'économie de l'empire portugais aux XVe et XVIe siècles* (Paris, 1969), 30–41.

seemed ill-endowed to play a major role in European expansion. With a surface area of about 89,000 square kilometers and about a million inhabitants in the early fifteenth century, it was far smaller than its potential rivals.[21] Nonetheless, its location, maritime tradition, and centralized monarchy more than compensated for Portugal's slim resources, and the West African trade began to pay for itself very early on. Despite the rivalry of Castile in the late fifteenth century, Portugal had a near monopoly on the trade in gold, slaves, *malagueta* pepper, and Sudanese ivory from about 1440 until the early sixteenth century. Profits could be as high as fourfold on cloth and much higher on slaves, and those profits underwrote further exploration down the West African coast. By 1487–8 Portuguese explorers had reached the Cape of Good Hope, and by 1498 Vasco da Gama had sailed all the way to India and back, fulfilling the dream of finding a sea route to the rich markets of Asia.

The Portuguese crown moved quickly to secure the safety of the route. Da Gama had encountered strong Muslim opposition, and the Portuguese believed they would have to force their way into the Asian trade routes. In those early years, Portugal also intended to drive the Muslims from the Christian holy places of the Middle East. After establishing a fort at Hormuz on the Persian Gulf, from 1503 until the mid–sixteenth century Portugal tried to block the Red Sea route of the Mamluks and monopolize the spice trade. This adversely affected Venetian trade for several decades, but Portugal's attempted blockade of the Red Sea was never totally effective. By 1560 Venice had recovered much of its trade and expanded it thereafter.[22] The Portuguese allied with the Persians, first against the Mamluks, then against the Ottoman Empire, to gain help in achieving their economic and political ends. Although the Ottoman ouster of the Mamluks changed the power structure in the area, a fruitful partnership between trade and conquest was well established early in Portuguese expansion.[23]

In India, strong local rulers made any thought of Portuguese domination unrealistic. Pedro Álvares Cabral's voyage in 1500 opened

---

[21] In the early sixteenth century, when we first have fairly reliable figures, Portugal's population had risen to 1.4 million, compared with 7 million in Spain, 14 in France, 4 in the British Isles, over 6 in Morocco, and 16 in the Ottoman Empire. Godinho, *L'économie de l'empire portugais,* 18.

[22] Lane, *Venice,* 290; Vitorino de Magalhães Godinho, *Os descobrimentos e a economia mundial,* 4 vols., 2d ed. rev. (Lisbon, 1981–82), 3:81–94.

[23] Godinho, *Os descobrimentos,* 1:193–5, 2:176–81. Michael Naylor Pearson, *Merchants and Rulers in Gujarat: The Response to the Portuguese in the Sixteenth Century* (Berkeley and Los Angeles, 1976), 56, thinks that Portugal could have entered and shared the trade in India peacefully, but much evidence suggests otherwise.

Cochin and Cannanore on the west coast of India to Portuguese trade, and during the first decade of the sixteenth century, other emissaries negotiated trading agreements with local rulers and set up fortresses and trading posts.[24] By the end of the first decade of the sixteenth century, Portugal controlled the routes that would sustain its African and Asian trade, with seven forts in two captaincies, one for the Red Sea and the other for the Malabar Coast of India. The Portuguese had amply demonstrated the superiority of European firepower at sea, following the principle that a successful trading empire must control the routes and ports of call that define it.[25] Military expenses have usually been ignored by economists, but Frederic Lane argued that such violence was part of a sound investment strategy when it secured trading opportunities. When military expenses served only to coerce profits through plunder, however, the strategy was not economically sound, eventually costing more than it was worth.[26]

The round-trip from Lisbon to Goa on the west coast of India could take as long as one and one-half years or as little as six months, depending on the rhythms of the wind and water currents of the eastern Atlantic and the Indian Ocean. Between 1500 and 1635, about seven ships left Lisbon each year for India, and about four began the return trip. Varying greatly in size, the ships used by the Portuguese in the early sixteenth century seem to have averaged about 400 tons. By midcentury, the average size had risen to about 600 tons, and at the end of the century, monstrous carracks of 1,500 and even 2,000 tons were not uncommon in the Portuguese trade.[27]

Although ships were usually instructed not to stop on the way from Lisbon to India, Mozambique Island off the southeastern coast of Africa became a frequent port of call on the outbound voyage. With an active trade to Goa and several other Indian ports, Mozambique served as an exchange point for gold, ivory, and slaves from Africa, and Indian textiles, Chinese porcelain, and other items from the east.[28]

---

[24] Godinho, *L'économie de l'empire portugais*, 563–74.

[25] Carlo M. Cipolla, *Guns, Sails, and Empires: Technological Innovation and the Early Phases of European Expansion, 1400–1700* (New York, 1965), 106–9; K. N. Chaudhuri, *Trade and Civilisation in the Indian Ocean: An Economic History from the Rise of Islam to 1750* (Cambridge and New York, 1985), 67–73.

[26] Niels Steensgaard, "Violence and the Rise of Capitalism: Frederic C. Lane's Theory of Protection and Tribute," *Fernand Braudel Center for the Study of Economics, Historical Systems, and Civilizations, Review* 5 (Fall 1981): 247–74.

[27] C. R. Boxer, "The *Carreira da India*," in *From Lisbon to Goa, 1500–1750: Studies in Portuguese Maritime Enterprise* (London, 1984), I:33–4; Godinho, *L'économie de l'empire portugais*, 665–76.

[28] C. R. Boxer, "The Principal Ports of Call in the 'Carreira da India' (Sixteenth–Eighteenth Centuries)," in *From Lisbon to Goa*, 2:33–8.

A diversity of products and activities characterized all areas of the Portuguese trading empire. To obtain gold in West Africa, Portuguese merchants moved into the production of grain, livestock, sugar, and indigo, invading networks formerly controlled by local Muslims. Likewise in the Atlantic islands, they dealt in grain, raisins, sugar, milling, livestock, dyestuffs, shellfish, sealskins, and wood, as well as a range of other products. Taking slaves in the Canaries and on the Guinea coast proved especially lucrative, even when the Portuguese had to pay for the slaves with items such as horses, which were also useful to exchange for gold.

As spices lured the Portuguese around Africa to the Indian coast and beyond, a similar pattern of multiple exchanges and multiple products continued. Portuguese colonists entered the local agricultural economy, producing for the Asian market that ultimately supplied the spices, drugs, and exotic woods that the Portuguese carried to Europe. Thus, whereas it is accurate in some senses to focus on gold in the West African trade and spices in the Indian Ocean and Far Eastern trades, we should keep in mind that those were not the only items involved. Without agricultural products, it would have been nearly impossible to sustain the trade as a whole.[29] Like salt, grain, and alum in the medieval Mediterranean, ordinary trade goods in Africa and Asia underwrote the more famous products for which the trade was known.

Before the Portuguese reached India, they bought spices on the West African coast. The pepper called "grains of paradise," or malagueta, in medieval trading manuals had been used as a condiment and a medicine in Europe from the thirteenth century on, obtained from trans-Saharan caravans at the markets of Alexandria and Arzila. It was sold in Florence, Genoa, and Barcelona by about 1440 and probably reached Lisbon as well. The Portuguese were bringing it by sea from West Africa between Senegal and the Guinea coast by about 1450 and sending it from Lisbon to Flanders by about 1460. From about 1485 on, they encountered another sort of pepper in Guinea, attached to a stem and called *pimienta de rabo*.

Except for a hiatus in the 1460s, the Portuguese crown claimed a monopoly on all imports of gold, slaves, and pepper. The government set the price for pepper, but it was naturally forced downward as supplies increased in the mid– to late fifteenth century. By the late fifteenth century, increasing demand for exotic spices in general pushed prices upward again and stimulated further Portuguese exploration.[30]

---

[29] Godinho, *L'économie de l'empire portugais*, 832–3.
[30] Godinho, *Os descobrimentos*, 2:148–54.

Guinean pepper competed well with Indian pepper on European markets, because of its lower price. Malagueta pepper had no Asian equivalent and continued to supply part of European demand even after the Portuguese had established themselves in India. The amount of malagueta imported was small – perhaps 1,000 to 1,300 quintals per year – in the second decade of the sixteenth century. Nonetheless, that was more than any other individual spice except the pepper and ginger from India's Malabar Coast.

Vitorino Magalhães Godinho provides much of the quantitative evidence for Portuguese trade in India. The agreements arranged by the Portuguese set the purchase price for pepper. By bringing in copper, which was in great demand, they were able to buy pepper at very favorable terms. On the west coast of India around 1500, copper could be exchanged for from 2.5 to over 4 times its weight in pepper. In 1558, after the Portuguese had been established in India for half a century, the net profit on pepper imported to Lisbon was 89 to 152 percent. By then, most of the pepper was loaded in Cochin and Quilon.

Other spices and drugs obtained in India played a smaller role in the total trade, even though their unit profits could be much higher than that for pepper. Ginger was loaded at Cannanore. Cinnamon, produced on the Malabar Coast but mostly on the island of Ceylon, generated very high profits. Ceylon was only eight days' sailing from Calicut, and although the area was often disturbed by warfare, the voyage was relatively safe, compared with routes in East Asia. Profits could run as high as tenfold for the round-trip from the southwest coast of India to Ceylon in the late sixteenth century – an enormous return for such a short voyage. Another sixfold profit accrued by transporting cinnamon from India to Hormuz on the Persian Gulf or to Diu in northwest India. Other luxury spices, such as cloves, nutmeg, and mace, came from farther east, but they were sold for about the same price as cinnamon and ginger in Cairo.

By the mid–sixteenth century, Goa, which had been the military and administrative center for the Portuguese in India since 1511, was becoming the commercial center as well. Though Cochin was still important for its large pepper market and for a king whose friendship the Portuguese wanted to retain, only one ship a year loaded there by the 1550s. The last Portuguese shipments were sent to Cochin in 1611–2; by then the whole structure of Asian trade had changed.[31]

Overall, spices and drugs dominated Portugal's Asian trade for most of the sixteenth century, rising dramatically in volume and generating

[31] Godinho, *L'économie de l'empire portugais*, 586, 596–616, 631–2, 643, 652–4, 820–8.

an impressive profit for the Portuguese crown and for private merchants. Despite Portuguese efforts to establish a monopoly over Asian spice supplies, the traditional routes to the eastern Mediterranean revived and even prospered in the late sixteenth century.[32] The expansion of trade was ample enough to support the Portuguese and their Asian and Italian rivals as well. Individual Portuguese merchants established themselves all over the Far East, participating in local trading networks, settling down and marrying, and sometimes, though not always, maintaining contacts with Portuguese officials.[33]

Long before the Portuguese arrived in Asia, the great terminals for the Asian trade were Hormuz (on the Persian Gulf) and Aden (on the Red Sea) in the west, and Malacca (on the Malay Peninsula) in the east, supplemented by smaller ports at both ends. The Portuguese reached the great emporium of Malacca in the early years of the sixteenth century, but their primary base remained in western India. From Malacca, trading vessels traveled east to the Spice Islands in January, arriving at Great Banda, the key producer of nutmeg and mace, in February. Banda also served as a redistribution point for cloves and for the exotic aromatic woods whose fame had reached Europe in the Middle Ages.[34] Sumatra was one of the world's largest suppliers of pepper. Although Sumatran pepper was reputedly inferior in quality to the pepper produced on India's Malabar Coast, it was more sought after by the end of the sixteenth century. The monsoon governed trade in the Far East, causing the round-trip from Malacca to Great Banda and the Spice Islands to last nineteen to twenty months. Another supply route was between the emporium at Malacca and Borneo, Ternate, Tidore, and Amboina. Again because of the monsoons, a round-trip from Malacca (mid-August departure) to Borneo and its environs could last twenty-two months.

The total round-trip from India to East Asia took thirty months for the Banda route and twenty-three for the Borneo route – much longer than the round-trip from Portugal to India. Only the extremely high profits from successful voyages could justify their time and expense. Cloves bought in the Spice Islands and sold in India in the mid–sixteenth century yielded a profit of at least 100 percent, after paying royal taxes that approached half the value of the shipment. Indian textiles sold in the Far East could earn another 100 percent, minus

---

[32] Lane, *Venice*, 291–2; Chaudhuri, *Trade and Civilisation*, 74–9.
[33] Godinho, *L'économie de l'empire portugais*, 783–6.
[34] Robert Putnam, *Early Sea Charts* (New York, 1983), 112–13, contains a map of Malacca and the Moluccas (Spice Islands) made in Amsterdam in 1595. It also includes drawings of red, yellow, and white sandalwood and nutmeg with its cortex of mace.

expenses. The price of mace in Calicut was twelve to fifteen times what it cost in Great Banda, and the price of nutmeg was thirty times higher. As an added incentive, neither spice had to pay royal taxes. Even pepper, a relatively bulky, low-profile item in this exotic trade, rose fourfold in value between Malacca and China.[35]

Despite the obvious attraction of the East Asian trade circuits, the Portuguese did not establish bases on those routes until the mid sixteenth century. Initially, they faced no serious European competition in the area, and they were reluctant to develop Far Eastern sources of supply that would undercut the profits of their factories in India. After the Spanish arrived in the Philippines in 1565, the Portuguese moved belatedly to secure their position. An interlude of free trade for spices began in 1570 to encourage more private investment. The Portuguese government also established bases at Amboina and Tidore and instituted annual fleets from western India to Malacca. One ship or small fleet went on from Malacca to make the Banda circuit, and another made the Borneo circuit.[36]

As in West Africa in the early sixteenth century, the Portuguese could not prevent other European powers from encroaching on their trade. The Spanish were clearly in the Far East to stay. If any doubts remained, the acquisition of the Portuguese throne by Philip II of Spain in 1580 laid them to rest. The Spanish arrived in the Far East with their anti-Muslim zeal intact, something the Portuguese had long since abandoned as counterproductive. Spanish raids against local Muslim leaders turned the Muslims against the Portuguese. A general anti-Portuguese revolt in 1570 exposed the weakness of the Portuguese position and began a steady erosion of their hegemony. The Dutch would present an even greater threat. The Portuguese captaincy in the Far East was too far from Goa to be under strict control, and it was to the advantage of local merchants and settlers, including the Portuguese, to trade with Dutch interlopers.

In the last decades of the sixteenth century, Portugal's Far Eastern empire faced attack on all sides. Even the Cape route, relatively secure for most of the sixteenth century, was attacked in 1586 by the English pirate Francis Drake. Similar attacks on Portuguese ships continued intermittently thereafter, leading to losses that have been estimated at 11 percent on outbound voyages and 15 percent on return voyages.[37] These attacks were part of a global struggle between the

---

[35] Godinho, *L'économie de l'empire portugais*, 580–2, 656, 804–11.
[36] Godinho, *Os descobrimentos*, 3:135–44.
[37] See Godinho, *L'économie de l'empire portugais*, 668–73, for an analysis of losses to Dutch and English interlopers.

Iberian powers and their rivals. Having observed the wealth that flowed into Spain and Portugal from their colonies, the English, the Dutch, and the French developed colonial aspirations of their own. Because the most lucrative colonies were already under the control of Spain and Portugal, late arrivals could succeed only at their expense. After the union of Spain and Portugal in 1580, they shared a king, but their empires remained legally separate. Portuguese residents of Macao and Nagasaki traded with the Spanish in Manila as with any other foreign power.[38] Nonetheless, the Dutch, already in rebellion against Spain, became enemies of Portugal as well. One can argue that the Dutch would not have attacked the colonies of an independent Portugal, but that is doubtful as long as the Portuguese tried to maintain a trading monopoly.[39] England also attacked the Portuguese empire, turning against one of its oldest allies in its search for overseas wealth.

If Spain and Portugal were to defend their position, they would need to mobilize their resources at home and abroad. Cooperation and mutual aid might have enabled them to combat incursions from their European rivals, but instead competition and mutual suspicion held Spain and Portugal apart. The Dutch landed at Bantam in 1596, eventually establishing themselves in the area of the Malay Peninsula. Wisely avoiding India, where Portugal was still strong, and the Spanish Philippines, they seized upon the weak links in the Portuguese Empire. Asian merchants often allied with the Dutch against the Portuguese and recaptured their position in the Far Eastern trade. By the first third of the seventeenth century, the Portuguese had been driven out of the Spice Islands. English and Dutch forces acting together during the Thirty Years' War even closed the port of Goa in 1623. Armed conflict over control of the spice trade in the late sixteenth and early seventeenth centuries may have cut production by as much as half, although it is far from certain that armed conflict was the only cause of the fall in production. The trade as a whole experienced a slump in the 1620s and 1630s, according to Anthony Disney.[40]

The Portuguese continued sending ten to twenty ships each year to Goa in the seventeenth and eighteenth centuries, their numbers rising and falling with global rhythms of trade.[41] Nonetheless, when

---

[38] C. R. Boxer, "A Note on the Triangular Trade betwen Macao, Manila, and Nagasaki, 1580–1640," *Terrae Incognitae* 17 (1985):51–60.

[39] See Godinho, *Os descobrimentos*, 3:158–64.

[40] Disney, *Twilight of the Pepper Empire: Portuguese Trade in Southwest India in the Early Seventeenth Century* (Cambridge, Mass., 1978), 50–55; Godinho, *L'économie de l'empire portugais*, 589–90.

[41] Boxer, "Ports of Call," in *From Lisbon to Goa*, 2:64–5.

they found themselves being squeezed out of the Far East, the Portuguese shifted their focus to the other side of their trading world – Brazil. The Treaty of Tordesillas in 1494 had assigned most of the Western Hemisphere to Castile's sphere of influence, but it soon became clear that a sizable chunk of land extended eastward into the Portuguese sphere. Sailing to the southwest to pick up winds and currents to round the tip of southern Africa, ships often came very close to Brazil, and Bahia became a frequent port of call for ships bound from Europe to the Far East.

Although Brazil has often been viewed as an afterthought in Portuguese empire building, it was part of the empire from the beginning.[42] Portugal did little to develop its claims to Brazil during the early sixteenth century, although King João III (1521–57) recognized the vulnerability of an Asian empire held together only by fleets and fortresses. Potentially, Brazil was much more tenable than the commercial empire in the east. The route from Portugal to Brazil was shorter, less dangerous, and less dependent on annual wind patterns. Moreover, the Portuguese found it easier to establish themselves in Brazil than they had in the Far East. The ancient civilizations of Asia, densely populated and firmly governed, did not suffer the incursions of foreigners easily. In Brazil, on the other hand, the Portuguese found a long coastline with access to a rich interior, sparsely inhabited by scattered tribes. Local peoples had few defenses against European technology and diseases and often tried to avoid contact with the newcomers altogether.

Encouraged by a lack of local resistance, the Portuguese reproduced the agro-maritime economy that they knew at home, almost independent of the local population. They also developed an export economy based on the rich forest products of the interior, using coerced Indian labor. As the sixteenth century progressed, the Portuguese began to use increasing numbers of slaves from Africa in an expanding plantation economy.[43]

During the period of Spanish–Portuguese union, Brazil was effectively developed as a colony and linked by trade to Europe and Africa. Whereas the Far Eastern empire had been characterized by a relatively low volume of high-priced goods such as spices, the Brazilian empire was characterized by high-volume, low-priced goods from the beginning. Brazilwood and other aromatic and building woods

---

[42] José Roberto do Amaral Lapa, *A Bahia e a Carreira da India* (São Paulo, 1968), 301–2.
[43] H. B. Johnson, "The Portuguese Settlement of Brazil, 150–1580," in *The Cambridge History of Latin America*, ed. Leslie Bethell (Cambridge and New York, 1984), 1:268–75.

continued to be important exports.[44] Sugar production on large plantations developed during the late sixteenth century, and sugar rapidly became the most valuable of Brazil's exports, even more valuable than gold (see Table 2.2). Sugar continued to hold that position into the nineteenth century.[45]

It is nearly impossible to separate production from export in many of the estimates for Brazilian sugar. In the early years, we can assume that most of the production was exported. From about 180,000 arrobas of sugar per year in the 1560s, the volume rose to about 600,000 arrobas in 1600, and over 700,000 arrobas in about 1610.[46] Although it was still a semiluxury in seventeenth-century Europe, sugar became an important speculative commodity, which generated new plantations and eventually lowered the unit cost. Even before sugar became an article of mass consumption in the eighteenth century, it was subject to a buyer's market like other consumer goods. Sugar production was a profitable venture in the long run, although its annual returns were far from secure. Calculations of the profits and losses for one famous sugar mill from 1622 to 1634 show that it often ran at a loss.[47] Yet, in a world economy that was generally depressed in the middle third of the seventeenth century, Brazil and its sugar held up well.[48]

Unfortunately, the figures we have for the seventeenth century are incomplete. The Dutch captured and held important sugar-producing areas in northeastern Brazil from about 1624 to about 1654, and we lack continuous figures for Portuguese production and exports in the same period. Dutch exports rose abruptly from about 48,000 arrobas per year in 1631–5 to about 298,000 arrobas in 1641–5, and then fell equally abruptly to about 32,000 arrobas in 1646–50.[49] It is not clear what happened to Portuguese production and export in the 1630s, but the period 1640–60 likely registered a decline from earlier levels.

---

[44] Frédéric Mauro, *Le Portugal, le Brésil et l'Atlantique au XVIIe siècle (1570–1670)* (Paris, 1983), 132–141. This is a revised and expanded version of the author's *Le Portugal et l'Atlantique au XVIIe siècle (1570–1670)* (Paris, 1960).

[45] Stuart B. Schwartz, *Sugar Plantations in the Formation of Brazilian Society: Bahia, 1550–1835* (Cambridge and New York, 1985), 422–3.

[46] Ward J. Barrett and Stuart B. Schwartz, "Comparación entre dos economias azucareras coloniales: Morelos, México y Bahia, Brasil," in *Haciendas, latifundios y plantaciones en América Latina*, ed. Enrique Florescano (Mexico, 1975), 540–2. The Castilian arroba was equivalent to 25 Castilian pounds of 16 ounces, or 11.5 kilograms.

[47] Frédéric Mauro, "Comptabilité théorique et comptabilité pratique en Amérique portugaise au XVIIe siècle," in *Etudes économiques sur l'expansion portugaise (1500–1900)* (Paris, 1970), 140–5. See also Mauro, *Portugal, Brésil et l'Atlantique*, 239–53.

[48] Mauro, *Portugal, Brésil et l'Atlantique*, 275–82.

[49] Ibid., 291–2. The total for 1632 should read 23,111-$\frac{3}{4}$. Similar figures are reported in Eleazar Cordova-Bello, *Compañías holandesas de navegación, agentes de la colonización neerlandesa* (Seville, 1964), 84–5, for the peak of Dutch exports.

Total production seems to have recovered by the 1670s, but the data are too sparse to be sure.[50] Sugar production had a multiplier effect on the economy as a whole because it required capital investment for mills and slave labor.[51] Portugal held the contract *(asiento)* for supplying slaves to the Spanish Empire on and off from 1573 to 1676, which was generally lucrative for the contractors.[52]

The cultivation of tobacco in Brazil followed many of the same patterns as sugar, although it began later. Seventeenth-century Europe had a seemingly insatiable demand for tobacco, which Columbus and his men first encountered in Cuba. In the seventeenth century, it held a high value in the West African slave trade, then dominated by the Dutch.[53]

Overall, imperial trade seems to have stimulated the home economy in Portugal. Traditional exports such as salt, fish, wine, and oils increased production to keep up with rising demand. Wheat and meat production, on the other hand, remained insufficient for Portugal's needs and continued to be supplemented with supplies from northern Europe and from the Portuguese Empire.[54] Within Europe, France was the most important trading partner of Portugal for most of the seventeenth century, especially in the 1670s. Although Portugal and France exported many of the same products, for a while their trade prospered. France sent grain and hides south in exchange for salt and exotic re-exports from Brazil and the Far East. Once France established tropical colonies of its own in the Caribbean, it had no further need for Portugal's colonial production. Portugal then turned to other countries, especially England, for the cloth, hides, and agricultural products formerly supplied by France.[55]

As long as the Dutch remained in northeast Brazil, they took full advantage of their position, producing sugar for the European market, preying on Portuguese and Spanish shipping in the Caribbean,

---

[50] Frédéric Mauro, "Portugal and Brazil: Political and Economic Structures of Empire, 1580–1750," in *Cambridge History of Latin America,* 1:457–8.

[51] Frédéric Mauro, "L'économie européenne et l'Atlantic Sud aux XVIIe et XVIIIe siècles (Brésil et Portugal)," in *Etudes économiques sur l'expansion portugaise,* 122–5. Ordinarily, labor is considered an expense, not a capital investment. In the case of a slave economy, however, the labor force is owned like other capital goods.

[52] Frédéric Mauro, "L'Atlantique portugaise et les esclaves (1570–1670)," *Revista da Facultade de Letras, Universidade de Lisboa* 22(2) (1956):5–52; Enrique Otte and Conchita Ruiz-Burruecos, "Los Portuguese en la trata de esclavos negros de las postrimerías del siglo XVI," *Moneda y Crédito* 85 (1963): 3–40; Enriqueta Vila Vilar, "La sublevación de Portugal y la trata de negros," *Iberoamerikanisches Archiv* 2(3) (1976): 171–92.

[53] Piere Verger, *Bahia and the West African Trade, 1549–1851* (Ibadan, 1970), 5–6.

[54] Mauro, *Portugal, Brésil et l'Atlantique,* 315–21, 327–30, 387–405, 421–3.

[55] Mauro, "Empire portugais et le commerce franco-portugaise au milion du XVIIIe siècle," in *Etudes économiques sur l'expansion portugaise,* 90–5.

Table 2.2

Sugar Exported from America

Years	Total years with available sources	Total weight	Weight unit	Weight per year in arrobas	Source
From Spanish Colonies:					
1566–1570	3	169,350.0	arroba	56,450.0	b
1581–1585	4	127,670.0	arroba	31,917.5	b
1586–1590	3	31,020.0	arroba	10,340.0	b
1593–1596	3	16,807.0	arroba	5,602.3	b
1607–1609	3	17,099.0	arroba	5,699.7	b
1613–1615	2	8,692.0	arroba	4,346.0	b
1616–1620	4	47,027.0	arroba	11,756.0	b
1651–1655	5	27,553.0	arroba	5,510.6	c
1656–1660	3	5,040.0	arroba	1,680.0	c

1661–1665	2	970.0	arroba	485.0	c
1666–1670	2	467.0	arroba	233.5	c
1671–1675	3	9,373.0	arroba	3,124.3	c
1681–1685	3	4,442.0	arroba	1,480.7	c
1686–1690	4	3,154.0	arroba	788.5	c
1691–1695	4	366.0	arroba	91.5	c
1696–1699	2	70.0	arroba	35.0	c
1717–1720	4	10,761.0	arroba	2,690.3	d
1721–1725	5	48,081.5	arroba	9,616.3	d
1726–1730	5	23,436.0	arroba	4,687.2	d
1731–1735	5	61,150.0	arroba	12,230.0	d
1736–1738	3	50,960.0	arroba	16,986.7	d
1747–1750	4	211,089.0	arroba	52,772.3	d
1751–1755	5	429,925.0	arroba	85,985.0	d
1756–1760	5	1,226,525.0	arroba	245,305.0	d
1761–1765	5	1,143,299.0	arroba	228,659.8	d
1766–1770	5	1,230,725.0	arroba	246,145.0	d
1771–1775	5	520,006.5	arroba	104,001.3	d
1776–1778	3	104,779.0	arroba	34,926.3	d

Table 2.2. (*Cont.*)

Years	Total years with available sources	Total weight	Weight unit	Weight per year in arrobas	Source
From Portuguese Colonies					
1581–1586	6	33,216.7	arroba*	5,536.1	a
1560–1570	11			180,000.0	a
1580	1	350,000.0	arroba	350,000.0	a
1582	1	350,000.0	arroba	350,000.0	a
1600	1	600,000.0	arroba	600,000.0	f
1610	1	735,000.0	arroba	735,000.0	a
1617	1	1,000,000.0	arroba	1,000,000.0	a
1618	1	500,000.0	arroba	500,000.0	a
1620	1	25,552.0	arroba	25,552.0	a
1627	1	900,000.0	arroba	900,000.0	a
1630	1			1.3–1.5 million	a
1631	1	6,440.0	caixa	193,200.0	a
1638–1642	5	1,800,000.0	arroba	360,000.0	a

Year					
1641	1	20,000.0	caixa	600,000.0	a
1643	1			1-1.2 million	a
1645	1	40,000.0	caixa	1,200,000.0	a
1647	1	8,000.0	caixa	240,000.0	a
1650	1	2,100,000.0	arroba	2,100,000.0	a
1652	1	3,500.0	caixa	105,000.0	a
1656	1	53,221.0	caixa	1,596,630.0	a
1657	1	42,000.0	caixa	1,260,000.0	a
1666	1	15,000.0	caixa	450,000.0	a
1670	1	2,000,000.0	arroba	2,000,000.0	a
1712-1715	4	85,850.0	caixa	643,875.0	e
1716-1720	5	47,720.0	caixa	286,320.0	e
1721-1725	3	28,591.0	caixa	285,910.0	e
1726-1730	4	32,800.0	caixa	246,000.0	e
1731-1735	5	38,780.0	caixa	232,680.0	e
1736-1740	5	27,012.0	caixa	162,072.0	e
1741-1745	5	60,522.0	caixa	363,132.0	e
1746-1750	5	76,833.0	caixa	460,998.0	e
1751-1755	5	61,106.0	caixa	366,636.0	e

Table 2.2. (Cont.)

Years	Total years with available sources	Total weight	Weight unit	Weight per year in arrobas	Source
1756–1760	2	11,757.0	caixa	176,355.0	e
1761–1765	5	86,704.0	caixa	520,224.0	e
From The Dutch in Brazil					
1631–1635	4	190,726.3	arroba	47,681.6	a
1636–1640	5	945,158.3	arroba	189,031.7	a
1641–1645	5	1,488,604.0	arroba	297,720.8	a
1646–1650	5	161,715.0	arroba	32,343.0	a

* from Madeira Islands

a Mauro, Portugal, Brésil, et l'Atlantique, 209 for Madeira, 277–81 for Portuguese

Brazil, 291–2 for Dutch in Brazil.

b Pierre Chaunu, with Huguette Chaunu, Séville et l'Atlantique 1504-1650, 8 vols. in 12 (Paris, 1955-60), 6(2):1004-5.

c Lutgardo García Fuentes, Comercio español con América (1650-1700) (Seville, 1980), 517-18.

d Antonio García-Baquero González, Cádiz y el Atlantico (1712-1778), 2 vols. (Cadiz, 1976), 2:222-47.

e Virgilio Noya Pinto, Ouro brasileiro e o comercio anglo-português (São Paulo, 1979), 196-9.

f Ward J. Barrett and Stuart B. Schwartz, "Comparación entre dos economías azucareras coloniales: Morelos, México y Bahia, Brasil," in Haciendas, latifundios y plantaciones en América Latina, ed. Enrique Florescano (Mexico, 1975), 540-42.

and importing slaves from their bases in West Africa. The effort seems to have been repaid by handsome profits.[56] When they were ousted from Brazil after 1654, they carried their sugar and tobacco cultivation to the Lesser Antilles. At the same time the French and English were developing agriculture on islands that they had claimed. Eventually, island exports competed with those from Brazil in European markets. Moreover, the mercantilist policies of France in the late seventeenth century effectively closed many European markets to Portuguese products.

By about 1670 such changes had a sharp downward effect on prices in Lisbon. Sugar fell from 3,800 reis per arroba in 1650 to 1,300–1,400 reis in 1688. Tobacco fell from 260 reis per arratel (459 grams) in 1650 to 70 reis in 1688. Although prices in Europe for many goods were falling at the same time, the declines for sugar and tobacco were much sharper. Portugal's trade also suffered because of the general downturn in trade from the Spanish Empire. With less silver entering Seville, less went on to Lisbon, and Dutch vessels made fewer stops in Lisbon and Setúbal than before. The Portuguese government tried unsuccessfully to keep foreign goods out of Lisbon. Their efforts to stimulate manufactures were more effective, and a devaluation of the currency made Portuguese goods cheaper for foreign buyers. The Portuguese also founded a company in 1685 for the purchase of slaves, one of the few still-profitable aspects of their transatlantic trade.[57] What ultimately restored prosperity was another shift in the dominant product of the empire – this time a move back to gold.

In the early years of European expansion, the Portuguese had often traded slaves obtained in the Congo for gold elsewhere in Africa. Around 1695, gold was found in several locations in Brazil, most notably in Bahia and what would become Minas Gerais. The Minas district also yielded diamonds, as if all the riches of the world were concentrated in one place. The boom that resulted had immediate and far-reaching consequences for Brazilian society.[58] One immediate ef-

---

[56] C. R. Boxer, *The Dutch in Brazil, 1624–1654* (Oxford, 1957), 277–90.

[57] Vitorino Magalhães Godinho, "Le Portugal, les flottes du sucre et les flottes de l'or (1670–1770)," *Annales: Economies, Sociétés, Civilisations* 5(1950):184–8.

[58] Summaries of the literature can be found in James Lockhart and Stuart B. Schwartz, *Early Latin America: A History of Colonial Spanish America and Brazil* (Cambridge and New York, 1983), 369–88; A. J. R. Russell-Wood, "Colonial Brazil: The Gold Cycle, c. 1690–1750," in *The Cambridge History of Latin America*, ed. by Leslie Bethell (Cambridge and New York, 1984), 2:547–600. See also Michel Morineau, "Or brésilien et gazettes hollandaises (1699–1806)," *Revue d'Histoire Moderne et Contemporaine* 25 (1978): 3–60; reprinted in *Incroyables gazettes et fabuleux métaux: Les retours de trésors américains d'après les gazettes hollandaises (XVIe–XVIIIe siècles)* (Cambridge and New York, 1985), 120–217.

fect of these discoveries was to increase the demand for African slaves to work the mines. Reversing the pattern of the fifteenth century, in the late seventeenth and eighteenth centuries, Brazilian gold was used to purchase slaves. The gold boom, like the earlier expansion of sugar production, also affected other branches of trade. Portugal was by no means in sole control of its trade, however. English merchants and ships ultimately acquired two-thirds of the gold that arrived in Portugal, in exchange for cloth and other trade goods. Brazilian gold also flowed to Amsterdam and Seville to finance trade, not incidentally altering the relative value of gold and silver in Europe.[59]

Michel Morineau has questioned the notion that Brazilian gold was the predominant spur to the eighteenth-century European economy, but there is no question that the amount of gold flowing into Europe was enormous.[60] In 1703 alone it surpassed all the gold that the Portuguese had ever obtained from Mina and Guinea in Africa, or that Spain had obtained annually from its American colonies in the sixteenth century. By the second decade of the eighteenth century, Brazilian gold far surpassed all of those sources together, plus exports from Sofala in East Africa and Sumatra in the Indian Ocean. Ten to fifteen years of Brazilian gold exports equaled all that had been sent to Seville from Spanish America in the century and a half before 1660.[61] During the peak years of 1741–60, Brazil sent an average of 14,600 kilograms of gold to Europe each year.[62] Morineau estimates the total gold sent from Brazil to Europe in the eighteenth century as from 800 to 850 tons, with a margin of error of 10 percent.[63] The Brazilian gold boom would last from 1695 to about 1770, when it entered a half-century of depression.

Other trade from Portuguese Brazil confirms the idea of a boom in the eighteenth century. Between 1697 and 1719, approximately 276 ships left Brazil for the Mina Coast, more than 2.5 times as many as had sailed in the previous two decades. Most of their cargo consisted of tobacco from Bahia, largely third-quality small and broken leaves, twisted into ropes or rolls *(rolos)* and brushed thickly with molasses

[59] Mauro, "Economie européenne," 128–9; Godinho, "Portugal, les flottes du sucre et les flottes de l'or," 196–7.

[60] *Incroyables gazettes*, 122–45.

[61] Godinho, "Portugal, les flottes du sucre et les flottes de l'or," 192–3; Morineau, *Incroyables gazettes*, 190–7.

[62] Virgilio Noya Pinto, *Ouro brasileiro e o comercio anglo-portugues: Uma contribução aos estudos da economia atlantica no seculo XVIII* (São Paulo, 1979), 114, 248–52; Frédéric Mauro, "De l'or du Minas au café do Paraíba: Remarques d'histoire comparée," in *Etudes économiques sur l'expansion portugaise*, 236.

[63] Morineau, *Incroyables gazettes*, 139–145, discusses the various estimates of gold sent from Brazil to Europe.

Table 2.3

Tobacco Exported From America

Years	Total years with available data	From:	To:	Ships per year	Total amount	Weight unit	Amount per year (in arrobas)	Source
1609-13	5	Indies	Spain		39,748.8	arroba	7,949.8	a
1651-55	4	Indies	Spain		4,607.0	arroba	1,151.8	b
1656-60	4	Indies	Spain		6,096.0	arroba	1,524.0	b
1661-65	4	Indies	Spain		2,377.0	arroba	594.3	b
1666-70	3	Indies	Spain		555.0	arroba	185.0	b
1671-75	4	Indies	Spain		564.0	arroba	141.0	b
1676-80	4	Indies	Spain		1,469.0	arroba	367.3	b
1681-85	4	Indies	Spain		5,156.0	arroba	1,289.0	b
1686-90	4	Indies	Spain		13,258.0	arroba	3,314.5	b
1691-95	5	Indies	Spain		14,217.0	arroba	2,843.4	b
1696-99	4	Indies	Spain		7,189.0	arroba	1,797.3	b
1681-85	5	Brazil	Mina	2.2				c
1686-90	5	Brazil	Mina	6.4				c

1691–96	6	Brazil	Mina	8.2			c
1697–1700	4	Brazil	Mina	15.0			c
1701–05	5	Brazil	Mina	20.4			c
1706–10	5	Brazil	Mina	22.8			
1711–15	4	Brazil			65,600.0	rolo	16,400.0	d
1716–20	5	Brazil			34,128.0	rolo	20,476.8	d
1721–25	3	Brazil			47,197.0	rolo	47,196.9	d
1729–30	2	Brazil			21,000.0	rolo	31,500.0	d
1734–35	2	Brazil			16,335.0	rolo	24,502.5	d
1736–40	3	Brazil			18,350.0	rolo	18,350.1	d
1741–45	5	Brazil			37,444.0	rolo	22,466.4	d
1746–50	4	Brazil			28,226.0	rolo	21,169.5	d
1751–55	4	Brazil			30,811.0	rolo	23,108.4	d
1762–63	2	Brazil			30,000.0	rolo	45,000.0	d

a Pierre Chaunu, with Huguette Chaunu, Séville et l'Atlantique, 1504–1650, 8 vols. in 12 (Paris, 1955–60), 6(2):1033.

b Lutgardo García Fuentes, Comercio español con América (1650–1700) (Seville, 1980), 527–28.

c Pierre Verger, Bahia and the West Africa Trade, 1549–1851 (Ibadan, 1970), 11.

d Virgilio Noya Pinto, Ouro brasileiro e o comercio anglo-portugues (São Paulo, 1979), 202.

to hold them together (see Table 2.3). As the trade developed, the aroma and flavor of this distinctive product made it a key item for the slave trade. Though the government and merchants in Lisbon disapproved of direct trade between Brazil and Africa, they could not prevent it.[64] Tobacco exports from Brazil between 1711 and 1730 averaged about 12,000 rolls a year, declining in subsequent decades to about 7,000 rolls.[65]

During the seventeenth century, about seventy to ninety vessels a year arrived in Lisbon from various ports in Brazil. During the eighteenth century, Lisbon hosted an enormous volume of shipping traffic, serving as an emporium for all of Europe (see Table 2.1). In the early 1720s, an average of 609 ships a year visited Lisbon. The peak came in 1731–5, when an average of 945 ships sailed in and out of the port each year. Usually at least half of the ships were English.[66] Although we lack precise information about the fleets and their contents, we do know that some Brazilian ports specialized in cotton, responding to the growing needs of the early Industrial Revolution.[67] In the nineteenth century, the fleets from Brazil would become quite specialized: Ships from Rio de Janeiro carried mostly gold but also some silver pesos and hides from Buenos Aires; ships from Bahia carried sugar, tobacco, and brazilwood; ships from Pernambuco carried wood and sugar; and ships from northern ports carried cacao. It is logical to assume that some of this regional specialization had developed in the course of the eighteenth century.

The export of hides from Brazil rose sharply from the late 1720s on, reaching a peak of about 263,000 hides per year in 1761–5 (see Table 2.4).[68] Sugar exports during the eighteenth century showed a good deal of fluctuation within a generally upward trend. Various estimates put Brazilian sugar production at 1.5–2.5 million arrobas in the 1750s and 1760s, perhaps falling to 1.4 million by around 1776, and alternately rising and falling thereafter for the rest of the century (see Table 2.2). If these figures can be trusted, Brazilian sugar production in the late eighteenth century was double its level in 1600, even though it had fallen to about 10 percent of total sugar production in the Amer-

---

[64] Verger, *Bahia and the West African Trade*, 5–11; Russell-Wood, "Colonial Brazil: The Gold Cycle," in *Cambridge History of Latin America*, 2:591–3.

[65] Noya Pinto, *Ouro brasileiro*, 202.

[66] Ibid., 296. See Mauro, "Portugal and Brazil," in *Cambridge History of Latin America*, 1:461–3, for Portugal's trade with England.

[67] Godinho, "Portugal, les flottes du sucre et les flottes de l'or," 191–2.

[68] Noya Pinto, *Ouro brasileiro*, 208–11.

icas.[69] With allowances made for the incompleteness of the data, the estimates for Brazilian sugar production confirm the creation of a mass market for what had been a high-priced luxury in the medieval world.

For the first half of the eighteenth century, Portuguese Brazil experienced a spectacular cyclical boom in an imperial trade that had begun over three centuries before. By then, however, the limits of the empire were plain to see. To maintain, govern, and defend an empire required an enormous investment, not only in money but also in personnel and technical support such as shipping. Portugal faced a chronic shortage of all three, plus a poor agrarian economy that limited population growth. Given its resources, Portugal had been well matched with an Asian empire of fortresses and trading posts, linked together by sea. The high per-unit profits on that trade had more than repaid the risk and expense involved, until other, better-endowed European powers determined to break Portugal's attempted monopoly. After Spanish, Dutch, and English merchants entered the direct trade with Asia, Portugal abandoned its pretense at monopoly, but individual Portuguese merchants stayed on in Asia and continued to make a profit from local and international trade.[70]

Most of the official Portuguese presence shifted to Brazil, however, which changed the structure of risks for the government in Lisbon. Although a land-based empire in Brazil was technically more defensible and easier to exploit than the Asian string of fortresses and trading posts, it required a vast investment for sugar mills, mines, and slave-based plantations, as well as for government and defense. High investment costs and dependence on a volatile world market made the Brazilian empire as financially tenuous for the Portuguese as their Asian empire had been militarily tenuous. Nonetheless, it survived. Unlike the cost of trying to monopolize the Asian spice trade, the expenses for Brazil were investments in the productive capacity of the country. By the late eighteenth century, more of the gold produced in Brazil remained there, to fund government and business. Over the course of three centuries, the Portuguese Empire had evolved from its early days of violent incursions into distant markets to a mature colonial empire, governing and fostering growth in the colony as well as exploiting it.

---

[69] Schwartz, *Sugar Plantations*, 164, 422–3. Noya Pinto, *Ouro brasileiro*, 196–9, cites far lower figures, based on official government statistics.

[70] Sanjay Subrahmanyam, "Staying On: The Portuguese of Southern Coromandel in the Late Seventeenth Century," *Indian Economic and Social History Review* 22 (Oct.– Dec. 1985): 445–63.

Table 2.4

Hides Exported From America

Years	Total years with available data	Number of hides	Number of hides per year	Source
From Spanish America				
1561-65	4	109,016.0	27,254.0	a
1568-70	3	313,326.0	104,442.0	b
1568-70	3	358,448.0	119,482.7	a
1571-75	5	414,075.0	82,815.0	a
1576-80	5	429,964.0	85,992.8	a
1581-85	5	672,465.0	134,493.0	a
1586-90	5		128,900.0	a
1593-95	3	245,965.0	81,988.3	a
1606-08	3	257,236.0	85,745.3	c
1606-10	5	418,773.0	83,754.6	b
1610-12	3	161,000.0	53,666.7	c
1611-15	4	338,292.0	84,573.0	b

1616–20	4	347,405.0	86,851.3	b
1617–20	4	312,087.0	78,021.8	c
1651–55	5	197,180.0	39,436.0	d
1656–60	5	125,745.0	25,149.0	d
1661–65	5	87,509.0	17,501.8	d
1665–70	6	46,790.0	7,798.3	d
1671–75	5	58,186.0	11,637.2	d
1676–80	5	51,963.0	10,392.6	d
1681–85	5	33,194.0	6,638.8	d
1686–90	3	31,206.0	10,402.0	d
1691–95	5	44,909.0	8,981.8	d
1696–99	3	28,138.0	9,379.3	d
1717–20	4	14,930.0	3,732.5	e
1721–25	5	54,030.0	10,806.0	e
1726–30	5	59,529.0	11,905.8	e
1731–35	5	43,740.0	8,748.0	e
1736–38	3	44,636.0	14,878.7	e
1747–50	4	184,706.0	46,176.5	e
1751–55	5	184,706.0	36,941.2	e

Table 2.4. (Cont.)

Years	Total years with available data	Number of hides	Number of hides per year	Source
1756-60	5	263,696.0	52,739.2	e
1761-65	5	336,762.0	67,352.4	e
1766-70	5	538,429.0	107,685.8	e
1771-75	5	934,954.0	186,990.8	e
1776-78	3	293,593.0	97,864.3	e
From Portuguese Brazil				
1711-15	4	125,600.0	31,400.0	f
1716-20	5	220,157.0	44,031.4	f
1721-25	4	178,756.0	44,689.0	f
1726-30	4	384,000.0	96,000.0	f
1731-35	4	405,570.0	101,392.5	f
1736-40	3	455,339.0	151,779.7	f
1741-45	5	614,942.0	122,988.4	f
1746-50	5	600,487.0	120,097.4	f
1751-55	5	1,040,418.0	208,083.6	f

1756–60	4	565,810.0	141,452.5	f
1761–65	5	1,314,334.0	262,866.8	f
1766–70	5	833,936.0	166,787.2	f

a Eufemio Lorenzo Sanz, Comercio de España con América en la época de Felipe II, 2 vols. (Valladolid, 1980), 1:546, 620–1, 2:425.

b Pierre Chaunu, with Hugette Chaunu, Séville et l'Atlantique, 1504–1650, 8 vols. in 12 (Paris, 1955–60), 6(2):1012–13.

c Michel Morineau, "Gazettes hollandaises et trésors américains," Anuario de Historia Económica y Social 2 (1969):336.

d Lutgardo García Fuentes, Comercio español con América (1650–1700) (Seville, 1980), 517–18.

e Antonio García-Baquero González, Cadiz y el Atlántico, (1717–1778), 2 vols. (Cadiz, 1976), 2:222–47.

f Virgilio Noya Pinto, Ouro brasileiro e o comercio anglo-portugues (Sao Paulo, 1979), 208–11.

The empire of Spain followed a similar trajectory, with roughly similar timetables of expansion and contraction of trade during the early modern period. Spain shared the Iberian Peninsula with Portugal, and their two empires dominated European overseas enterprise until the late sixteenth century. They even shared a royal dynasty for sixty years, from 1580 to 1640. Nonetheless, the Spanish and Portuguese empires were more different than they were alike. The Portuguese set out to establish regular trade with Asia, developing a land-based colonial empire in Brazil only later. The Spanish likewise set out to establish regular trade with Asia, but geography and circumstances changed their plans. Instead of a string of trading posts, they founded a land-based colonial empire whose characteristics and extent were far different from the factory and fortress empire of the Portuguese.

The dramatic story of Christopher Columbus's 1492 voyage toward Asia will undoubtedly attract considerable scholarly attention in the next several years, as we approach its five-hundredth anniversary.[71] Born in Genoa to a family involved in manufacturing and commerce, Columbus acquired his early seafaring experience in trade to the eastern Mediterranean and formulated his notion of sailing west toward Asia, the source of spices and other luxury goods, during a nine-year sojourn in Portugal. When the Portuguese king declined to back him, Columbus tried his luck in Spain, gaining the support of Queen Isabella of Castile. Instead of finding a westward route to Asia, Columbus unwittingly reached the two continents that would come to be called North and South America. Even before he died in 1506, dozens of other explorers had begun to map out the true dimensions of the vast New World that he had claimed for Castile.[72] Although peoples in the New World had gold and systems of exchange, their commercial arrangements had little in common with the sophisticated trading networks of Asia, Europe, or Africa. To trade profitably with the New World, Castilians would have to organize, govern, and develop it for themselves. Columbus had the possibilities of trade uppermost in his mind in his early letters about the islands where he landed, and a list of prices survives for dozens of goods in the market on Hispaniola in

---

[71] The best full biographies of Columbus are Samuel Eliot Morison, *Admiral of the Ocean Sea: A Life of Christopher Columbus,* 2 vols. (Boston, 1942); Jacques Heers, *Christophe Colomb* (Paris, 1981); Juan Manzano Manzano, *Cristóbal Colón: Siete años decisivos de su vida, 1485–1492* (Madrid, 1964); and Paolo Emilio Taviani, *Christopher Columbus: The Grand Design,* trans. from the 1980–2 Italian edition by William Weaver (London, 1985).

[72] Juan Gil, "Marinos y mercaderes en Indias (1499–1504)," *Anuario de Estudios Americanos* 42 (1985): 297–499.

1503.[73] Mercantile concerns were central to the Iberian empire from its beginnings, although they were often overshadowed by further exploration and conquest in the early decades.

Many of the men who sailed with Columbus had little education and less self-discipline. Freed from the normal constraints of law and supervision, they ran amok in the Caribbean islands, provoking the natives to warfare and plundering the available wealth at will. The crown began sending royal bureaucrats to the new settlements almost immediately, but it took decades to bring order out of the chaos. For nearly all of the four centuries that the empire lasted, trade and colonization were legally a monopoly of Castile and its inhabitants, despite numerous exceptions to the law in practice. Nonetheless, this paper will follow conventional usage and refer to the "Spanish" empire in the survey that follows. The early years of conquest, together with European diseases, nearly annihilated the native population of the Caribbean islands.[74] Those years also produced enough wealth to finance further exploration. As early as 1506, fortunes made in Cuba were being used to finance voyages elsewhere. Financial backing primarily from Spain lasted only through the first fifteen years of the empire.[75] Spanish colonists introduced sugar cultivation in the Caribbean, raiding the mainland coast for Indian labor. When those Indians succumbed to disease and overwork as rapidly as the islanders had, African slaves began to be imported to labor in the plantations.[76]

From 1519, when Hernán Cortés set out from Cuba to the continent, the center of activity for the empire shifted to the west. Founding a town at Veracruz, the members of the expedition authorized Cortés to continue into the interior, toward the seat of a powerful empire that local peoples had described. By 1521 Cortés and his men

[73] Letter from Juan de Ayala to Ferdinand and Isabella of Spain, 1503, James Ford Bell Library, University of Minnesota.

[74] Carl Ortwin Sauer, *The Early Spanish Main* (Berkeley and Los Angeles, 1969). Fernando Iwasaki Cauti, "Conquistadores o grupos marginales: Dinámica social del proceso de conquista," *Anuario de Estudios Americanos* 42 (1985): 217–42, points out that the Spanish conquest was essentially a popular enterprise, brought under royal control after the fact.

[75] Ralph Davis, *The Rise of the Atlantic Economies* (Ithaca, N.Y., 1973), 39–41. Chapters 3, 8, and 10 of the same book deal well with the economy of Spanish America. A brief general summary of Spanish conquest and colonization is J. H. Elliott, "The Spanish Conquest and Settlement of America," 1:149–206, and "Spain and America in the Sixteenth and Seventeenth Centuries," 1:287–340, in *Cambridge History of Latin America*.

[76] Stuart B. Schwartz, "Indian Labor and New World Plantations: European Demands and Indian Responses in Northeastern Brazil," *American Historical Review* 83 (June 1978): 43–79; William D. Phillips, Jr., *Slavery from Roman Times to the Early Transatlantic Trade* (Minneapolis, 1985), 195–217.

had overthrown the Aztec Empire in the Valley of Mexico. Replacing the Aztecs as overlords of that vast region, the Spanish consolidated their hold on the mainland. Cortés fully recognized that the excesses of the Caribbean years must be avoided, for economic as well as ethical reasons. Consequently, the generation of conquistadores was weaned from conquest by grants of land and labor services. A decade after Cortés and his Indian allies defeated the Aztecs, Francisco Pizarro conquered the Inca Empire of Perú. There, armed struggles among the conquistadores and a native uprising postponed the restoration of order and the installation of a viable colonial regime, but eventually bureaucracy overcame anarchy. Even before the situation stabilized, however, an active commerce developed.[77] Although debate over the morality of the conquest would continue in Spain for decades, there could be no turning back. The empire was an established fact.

Within the first fifty years after the first voyage of Columbus, the Spanish crown licensed expeditions all over South America and as far north as the southern quarter of North America.[78] Local and regional governments were staffed by bureaucrats from the peninsula and integrated with the central government in Madrid. A system of taxes and tribute payments was established on the model of the Aztec and Inca systems. In addition to sustaining the local economies, production in the Indies supplied large quantities of gold, silver, precious gems, and industrial raw materials for Europe. Following the common mercantilist approach, the Spanish government sought to ensure that its colonies would support the home economy rather than compete with it. The colonies were organized to supply what Spain did not produce and to purchase manufactured goods and some agricultural products from Spain. Foreigners were legally excluded from direct trade with what the Spanish called the Indies; instead they had to deal through the port of Seville in the sixteenth and seventeenth centuries and through the port of Cádiz for much of the eighteenth century. Although monopoly trades rarely find favor with modern analysts, contemporary observers more often complained about being excluded than about the notion of monopoly itself.[79]

The system regulating trade to the Spanish Empire was set up in

---

[77] Teodoro Hampe Martínez, "Actividad mercantil del puerto de Lima en la primera mitad del siglo XVI," *Anuario de Estudios Americanos* 42 (1985): 549–71.

[78] See the map from Francisco Morales Padrón, *Historia general de América*, 2d ed. (Madrid, 1975), 336–7.

[79] Boxer, *Dutch in Brazil*, 3, cites the early seventeenth-century Antwerper Willem Usselincx, who urged the Dutch government to follow the Spanish example.

1503, under the so-called House of Trade (Casa de Contratación). From Seville, it supervised and regulated private trade and the vessels that carried it, and saw that tribute and the taxes on trade were collected and turned over to the crown. The merchants themselves had primary jurisdiction over commercial disputes, working through their Consulado in Seville.[80] Although merchants generally preferred to arrange their own transport, it soon became clear that an organized system of convoys was the best way to protect shipping across the Atlantic. By the 1540s one fleet each year sailed for the Indies, dividing into two parts in the Caribbean. One part sailed on to New Spain (Mexico) and the other to Tierra Firme (northern South America) and then to Panamá. Later, two separate fleets served the two destinations.

In the late sixteenth and early seventeenth centuries, the New Spain fleet tended to leave Cádiz about July 1, arriving at the outer Caribbean islands sometime in August and at Veracruz sometime in September, escaping the worst of the pestilential summers on the Mexican coast. Wintering over and doing business in Veracruz, it left for Havana in May or early June, continuing home to Spain by the end of summer.[81]

The Tierra Firme fleet typically left Spain from March to May, reaching Cartagena de Indias by about June and moving on to the Isthmus of Panamá about two months later. Treasure and merchandise from South America would meet the fleet at Nombre de Dios for a brief but intense commercial fair. In the late sixteenth century, the fair was moved to Portobelo, but both towns were small and unhealthful, blossoming into international marketplaces during the sojourn of the fleet and then settling back into their habitual torpor.[82] Returning to Cartagena, the Tierra Firme fleet usually wintered over before returning to Spain the following summer. On the homebound voyage, both fleets aimed to pass through the Bahama Channel before August to avoid the hurricane season.[83]

For the early years of imperial trade, figures on volume are very hard to come by. In their monumental study of the Indies trade, Pierre

---

[80] Eduardo Trueba Gómez, "La jurisdicción marítima en la carrera de Indias durante el siglo XVI," *Anuario de Estudios Americanos* 39 (1982): 93–131.

[81] Pierre Chaunu, with Huguette Chaunu, *Séville et l'Amérique aux XVIe et XVIIe siècles* (Paris, 1977), 232–3.

[82] Enriqueta Vila Vilar, "Las ferias de Portobelo: Apariencia y realidad del comercio con Indias," *Anuario de Estudios Americanos* 39 (1982): 275–340.

[83] Cesáreo Fernández Duro, ed., *Disquisiciones náuticas*, 6 vols. (Madrid, Sucesores de Rivadeneyra, 1876–81), 2:167–8; Eufemio Lorenzo Sanz, *Comercio de España con América en la época de Felipe II*, 2 vols. (Valladolid 1980), 2:276–8.

Chaunu and Huguette Chaunu relied on the number of ships and their recorded or calculated tonnage (see Table 2.1).[84] By the 1520s nearly a hundred ships each year carried merchandise across the Atlantic between Spain and its American colonies. Together, the ships represented about 9,000 *toneladas* of carrying capacity, each tonelada being equivalent to about 1.42 cubic meters. By the late sixteenth century, a yearly average of 150–200 ships was involved in the Indies trade each year, with a total tonnage of about 30,000–40,000 toneladas (an average of 200 toneladas per ship).[85] The number of ships had doubled since the 1520s, and their average size had also doubled, leading to a fourfold increase in carrying capacity. For comparison, Fernand Braudel has estimated that there were about 350,000 tons of shipping capacity in the Mediterranean in the late sixteenth century and 600,000–700,000 tons in the Atlantic for all maritime activities, including fishing.[86]

In the late sixteenth and early seventeenth centuries, a regular guard squadron of six to eight galleons usually accompanied the Tierra Firme fleet; the New Spain fleet had a smaller escort of two galleons. The Tierra Firme squadron collected the year's treasure at Portobelo and returned to Spain as the escort of the previous year's merchant fleet.[87] Although the convoy system was not as all-inclusive as its planners intended, it still accounted for about 85 percent of the trade. Even when convoys were abolished in the late eighteenth century, 85–90 percent of the trade still used the same timing and routes, which had proved ideal for sailing conditions in the Atlantic.[88]

The system of imperial trade was fed by production in the Indies, reorganized from traditional patterns to suit the needs of interna-

[84] Chaunu assumed that the definition of the Spanish *tonelada* changed over time and adjusted the given tonnages to weighted figures *(unités ponderées)*, in terms of the modern international ton of 2.83 cubic meters (Pierre Chaunu, with Huguette Chaunu, *Séville et l'Atlantique, 1504–1650*, 8 vols. in 12 [Paris, 1955–60], 6[1]:29–30). Fortunately, Chaunu printed the given tonnages as well as his *unités ponderées*, because scholars have generally rejected his weighted figures. Michel Morineau has argued persuasively that the Spanish tonelada was equal to the contemporary French sea ton *(tonneau de mer)* of 1.42 cubic meters (*Jauges et méthodes de jauge anciennes et modernes* [Paris, 1966], 31–4, 64, 115–16).

[85] Chaunu, *Séville et l'Atlantique*, 6(1):168, 337.

[86] *The Mediterranean and the Mediterranean World in the Age of Philip II*, trans. Siân Reynolds, 2 vols. (New York, 1972), 1:445–8.

[87] Most standard histories make no distinction between timetables for merchants fleets and guard squadrons, often assuming an annual round-trip for all. See, e.g., Clarence Henry Haring, *Trade and Navigation between Spain and the Indies in the Time of the Hapsburgs* (Cambridge, Mass., 1918), 207–8. For a discussion of the divergent timetables, see Carla Rahn Phillips, *Six Galleons for the King of Spain: Imperial Defense in the Early Seventeenth Century* (Baltimore, 1986), 11–14.

[88] Chaunu, *Séville et l'Amérique*, 22–3.

tional commerce. Livestock introduced from Europe multiplied easily in the New World, which had few domestic animals and no cattle, horses, or pigs before Spaniards brought them across the Atlantic. Soon hides and tallow became major exports for the transatlantic trade. Other important exports were sugar, indigo (a blue vegetable dye), cochineal (or *grana*, a red dye derived from small insects), exotic woods for construction and dye making, and a wide range of aromatic and medicinal plants, either native to the Americas or introduced there for export production.[89] A Dutch writer in the early seventeenth century noted that combined plant and animal products from the Indies exceeded the more famous gold and silver in value.[90]

Figures for the exchange of individual products become available from about 1550 on. By the early 1560s, about 27,000 hides a year were exported from the Caribbean islands and New Spain (see Table 2.4). By the early 1570s, the number had risen to about 83,000, and by the early 1580s to over 134,000.[91] One recent study estimates the value of hides shipped in the late sixteenth century at an average of 78,000,000 *maravedís* a year. Exports of sugar from Spanish America were estimated at just over half that, about 40,000,000 maravedís per year. The yearly export of sugar could fluctuate widely (see Table 2.2). Fairly reliable figures show a yearly average of about 32,000 arrobas in 1581–5 and only about 10,000 in 1586–90, at a time when the Spanish colonies were under attack from pirates. Indigo, estimated to have been worth about 30,000,000 maravedís a year in the late sixteenth century, also experienced wide yearly fluctuations. Figures for indigo do not become available until the late 1570s, averaging between 1,000 and 2,000 arrobas each year from then until the end of the century. One of the most valuable single items was cochineal, estimated at about 125,000,000 maravedís a year in the late sixteenth century, or nearly 42 percent of all products from the Indies (see Table 2.5). Its price showed considerable fluctuation from year to year, but its quantity rose fairly steadily, from about 1,800 arrobas in the late 1550s, to about 8,000 in the late 1580s.[92]

[89] Chaunu, *Séville et l'Atlantique*, 6(2):1039, contains a list of forty-eight products typically exported to Spain. See also Alfred W. Crosby, *Ecological Imperialism: The Biological Expansion of Europe, 900–1900* (Cambridge and New York, 1986).
[90] Willem Usselincx, cited in Boxer, *Dutch in Brazil*, 2–3.
[91] Chaunu, *Séville et l'Atlantique*, 6(2):1012–13; Lorenzo Sanz, *Comercio de España con América*, 1:620; Michel Morineau, "Gazettes hollandaises et trésors américains," *Anuario de Historia Económica y Social* 2 (1969): 336 (this article and several others were collected in *Incroyables gazettes*, cited in n. 58).
[92] Lorenzo Sanz, *Comercio de España con América*, 1:546, 580, 591, 1004–5; Chaunu, *Séville et l'Atlantique*, 6(2):980–1, 988–9; Morineau, "Gazettes," 336.

Table 2.5

Cochineal Exported from the Indies to Spain

Years	Total years with available data	Total weight	Weight unit	Weight per year	Reduced to arrobas	Unit price in ducats	Source
1556-60	4	7,169.5	arroba	1,792.4	1,792.4		a
1561-65	5	14,155.0	arroba	2,831.0	2,831.0		a
1566-70	5	30,025.0	arroba	6,005.0	6,005.0		a
1571-75	5	34,318.0	arroba	6,863.6	6,863.6		a
1576-80	5	42,520.0	arroba	8,504.0	8,504.0		a
1581-85	5	40,838.0	arroba	8,167.6	8,167.6	58.4	a
1586-90	5	36,000.0	arroba	7,200.0	7,200.0	51.9	a
1591-95	5	31,494.0	arroba	6,298.8	6,298.8	74.7	a
1596-1600	3			7,500.0	7,500.0	95.3	a
1603-04	2	207,280.0	livre	103,640.0	4,145.6		b
1606-10	5	22,189.0	arroba	4,437.8	4,437.8		c
1606-10	5	568,500.0	livre	113,700.0	4,548.0		b
1611-15	5	10,716.0	arroba	2,143.2	2,143.2		c
1611-15	3	163,250.0	livre	54,416.7	2,176.7		b

1616-20	5	27,595.0	arroba	5,519.0	5,519.0	c
1616-20	5	942,921.0	livre	188,584.2	7,543.4	b
1717-20	4	37,466.0	arroba	9,366.5	9,366.5	d
1721-25	5	37,225.0	arroba	7,445.0	7,445.0	d
1726-30	5	41,639.5	arroba	8,327.9	8,327.9	d
1731-35	5	58,407.0	arroba	11,681.4	11,681.4	d
1736-38	3	12,394.0	arroba	4,131.3	4,131.3	d
1747-50	4	71,707.0	arroba	17,926.8	17,926.8	d
1756-60	5	70,122.0	arroba	14,024.4	14,024.4	d
1761-65	5	89,679.5	arroba	17,935.9	17,935.9	d
1766-70	5	93,845.0	arroba	18,769.0	18,769.0	d
1771-75	5	161,306.5	arroba	32,261.3	32,261.3	d
1776-78	3	66,154.8	arroba	22,051.6	22,051.6	d

a Eufemio Lorenzo Sanz, Comercio de españa con América en la época de Felipe II, 2 vols. (Valladolid, 1980), 1:579-80.

b Michel Morineau, "Gazettes hollandaises et trésors américains," Anuario de Historia Económica y Social 2 (1969):336.

c Pierre Chaunu, with Hugette Chaunu, Séville et l'Atlantique, 1504-1650, 8 vols. in 12 (Paris, 1955-60), 6(2):980-1.

d Antonio Garcia-Baquero González, Cadiz y el Atlántico (1717-1778), 2 vols. (Cadiz, 1976), 2:222-4.

Judging from shipping capacity and the products for which we have quantitative data, the Indies trade represented an enormous change of scale from the late medieval Mediterranean trade and from the Portuguese Asian trade. In many ways, it was a logical extension of the trend toward bulky, low-priced goods that marked the commercial revolution of the late Middle Ages. What changed were the precise items traded, but not their character. The dyestuffs, hides, and woods of the Indies trade were industrial raw materials, as the alum and dyestuffs of the Mediterranean trade had been. The grain and salt trades of the Mediterranean were matched by the trade of the Indies in wine, oil, sugar, and (later) tobacco. Textiles (for which, unfortunately, we lack precise data) were a mainstay of all long-distance trade, for the Indies trade no less than for other routes. Seville became the great collecting point for every possible item of international commerce and was the distribution point for treasure and trade goods from the Indies.

The total value of trade with the Indies is very difficult to quantify. Chaunu estimated that the trade to and from the Indies was two or three times the value of the largest European commerce although it was probably smaller in volume. The volume of trade to the Indies experienced wide fluctuations due to the difficulties of adjusting supply and demand in a trade that could take one to three years for a round-trip.[93] It is difficult to test Chaunu's estimate, although the few figures available tend to support it. For example, reliable figures exist for the export of silver from Venice to the Levant in 1610–14. Its total value was about 5.7 percent of the total value of silver arriving in Seville in the same period.[94] Judging from this figure, the trade of Venice with the Levant, which had regained much of its prosperity in the late sixteenth century, was still far smaller than the Indies trade.

Chaunu relies heavily upon taxes on trade to the Indies to provide a gross estimate of its volume and value. The *avería* tax, which helped to finance armed escorts for the fleets, and the *almojarifazgo* tax on exports from Seville form the basis for his calculations.[95] The almojarifazgo tax collected on goods going from Spain to the Indies suggests a total value for trade of nearly 450 million maravedís a year in the early 1560s, rising to about 850 million in the early 1590s. The avería

---

[93] *Séville et l'Amérique*, 361–2.

[94] Frank C. Spooner, "Venice and the Levant: An Aspect of Monetary History (1610–1614)," in *Studi in onore di A. Fanfani*, 6 vols. (Milan, 1962), 5:652–3.

[95] Chaunu, *Séville et l'Atlantique*, 6(1):468–474, contains five-year averages for these taxes; the tables are discussed on pp. 45–63 of the volume. Lorenzo Sanz, who distrusts figures for shipping volume, also relies heavily on the almojarifazgo tax (*Comercio de España con América*, 2:366–7, 417–20).

tax confirms that same order of magnitude for the outbound shipments. Judging solely from the avería taxes, which were levied on merchandise alone, the outbound cargoes to the Indies were worth about three times as much as the homebound cargoes.[96]

Overall, however, the figures were quite different. The most valuable, as well as the most famous, exports of the Indies were not trade goods but the gold, silver, pearls, and precious stones that constituted the "treasure" of the Spanish Empire. Originally plundered from natives of the Caribbean islands and the Aztec Empire, and later mined, gold dominated treasure exports during the "gold cycle" of the early sixteenth century. Chaunu estimated that 23,000–27,000 kilograms of gold had been shipped to Spain before about 1525.[97] Following the conquest of the Aztec Empire, the exports of gold increased, reaching a peak in the 1550s, with registered exports of over 4,200 kilograms per year.[98] Total gold production has been estimated at close to 23,000 kilograms per year for the early 1530s and about 10,500 for the early 1540s, falling rapidly thereafter to less than 1,000 kilograms per year by the end of the century.[99] Altogether, it has been estimated that 164,000 kilograms of gold were exported from the Indies to Spain in the century and a half before 1660.[100] Its effect on the Spanish and international economies is still the subject of much debate, but it undoubtedly contributed to the European price rise during the sixteenth century.[101]

Several important goldfields were discovered in northern South America in the 1530s and 1540s, along with several silver mines. Enormous deposits of silver were found in 1545 at Potosí in the Viceroyalty of Perú (modern Bolivia), ushering in what could be called the "silver cycle" of the Spanish Empire, far exceeding gold in both volume and value. The Potosí mines proved to be among the richest the world has ever known, although their location above twelve thousand feet in the Andean highlands made mining extremely difficult and expensive. The initial flush of the Potosí discovery produced nearly

[96] Chaunu, *Séville et l'Atlantique*, 6(1):46–51, 466–74.

[97] Ibid., 8(1):511.

[98] Earl J. Hamilton, *American Treasure and the Price Revolution in Spain, 1501–1650* (Cambridge, Mass., 1934; reprint, New York, 1964), 42.

[99] Peter Bakewell, "Mining in Colonial Spanish America," in *Cambridge History of Latin America*, 2:141.

[100] Hamilton, *American Treasure and the Price Revolution in Spain*, 42–5.

[101] J. H. Elliott, *The Old World and the New, 1492–1650* (Cambridge and New York, 1970), 55–68, provides a helpful summary of the debate over bullion and inflation in the sixteenth century. Earl J. Hamilton is the scholar most often associated with the notion that bullion exercised the most important pressure on European prices; see Hamilton, *American Treasure and the Price Revolution in Spain*, 283–306.

84   *Carla Rahn Phillips*

85,000 kilograms of silver each year during the late 1540s. Thereafter, production dropped back to 50,000–60,000 kilograms a year until the late 1570s, when it suddenly jumped to 153,000 kilograms, and from there to a peak of nearly 280,000 kilograms in the late 1580s.[102] Silver exports began modestly in the 1520s, rising to nearly 18,000 kilograms per year in the 1540s, before the great boom. Thereafter they surged to 94,000 kilograms in the 1560s, 112,000 in the 1570s, and 271,000 in the 1590s.[103]

About 20–30 percent of the registered bullion that crossed the Atlantic belonged to the Spanish crown. It came primarily from a tax called the "royal fifth" on both gold and silver, collected from 1504 on, plus fees for assay and coinage. About 8 percent of the royal share came from ecclesiastical taxes that had been given to the crown by the Roman Catholic church. Penalties and condemnations for smuggling, the sale of offices, and various minor taxes also added to the royal share. The single most valuable source of royal income in the late sixteenth century was the royal fifth from Tierra Firme, which made up about 60 percent of the royal share between 1555 and 1600.[104] The rest of the bullion crossing the Atlantic belonged to merchants and other private individuals.

Based largely on treasure receipts and almojarifazgo taxes, Lorenzo Sanz defined a period of expansion in the Indies trade between 1561 and 1579 that was dominated by the returns from New Spain. Despite periodic slumps in the trade and in treasure receipts, the period as a whole produced an annual average of 1,150 million maravedís in treasure receipts. From 1580 to 1600 Peruvian treasure receipts surpassed those from New Spain, averaging 2,400 million maravedís a year. According to Lorenzo Sanz's figures, the highest treasure receipts of the century occurred in 1581–5, and the highest almojarifazgo figures in 1580–5. Thereafter the volume fell briefly, due to pirate raids in the Caribbean. Although treasure receipts would continue to be high for a while longer, the sixteenth century boom was nearing an end.[105]

In all, the total value of royal treasure from the Indies from 1555 to 1600 was about 24,000 million maravedís. Merchants and other private individuals sent about 55,000 million maravedís, for a total of about 79,000 million maravedís. Pearls, emeralds, and other precious

[102] Bakewell, "Mining in Colonial Spanish America," 141.
[103] Hamilton, *American Treasure and the Price Revolution in Spain*, 42.
[104] Lorenzo Sanz, *Comercio de España con América*, 2:166–72.
[105] Ibid., 421–8. The author tends to judge the policies of the Spanish government very harshly, without considering alternatives to the actions taken. He places himself in the awkward position of listing a multitude of supposedly ruinous policies that coexisted with the greatest flow of treasure and goods that the world had yet seen.

stones also formed part of the mineral wealth of the Spanish Indies. Although the figures available for them are difficult to interpret, they added considerably to the total value of the treasure.[106] By modern standards, the gems might equal or surpass the precious metals in value.

Unregistered remittances of treasure undoubtedly accounted for most of the fraud noted in trade to the Spanish Indies. Private individuals were anxious to avoid taxes, but even more, they wanted to avoid the possibility of confiscation of their trading profits. From time to time in the mid–sixteenth century and thereafter, the king of Spain would confiscate incoming treasure to pay pressing bills, particularly in wartime. The rightful owners of the treasure would be compensated with interest-paying government bonds, but that hardly made good the loss of their capital. Although this drastic action happened infrequently, the threat was enough to make some private individuals risk dire penalties to avoid registration. Recently, a careful scholarly investigation of fraud in the late sixteenth century estimated that about 10 percent of the treasure that arrived in Europe never appeared in the registers.[107] Other estimates, especially those for unregistered production, have often ranged far higher, but such estimates have been sharply questioned by many scholars.[108] It should also be emphasized that much of the treasure mined in America stayed in America for both public and private needs, fueling the economic growth of the Spanish colonies. With these points in mind, the estimate of a 10 percent underregistration for treasure remittances in the late sixteenth century seems plausible. Any attempt to give a single global figure for smuggled treasure over time is bound to distort reality, however. It is clear that the level of smuggling varied over time, as we shall see.

Sometime before the end of the sixteenth century the first long expansionary cycle of the Spanish Empire came to an end. Many historians have sought the explanation for this in bullion flows and price differentials. The long European inflation of the sixteenth century,

[106] Summary tables apear in ibid., 207, 240, 253–4. The figures are anayzed on pp. 207–72.

[107] Ibid., 142–46. Hamilton, *American Treasure and the Price Revolution in Spain*, 37–38, noted that "smuggled treasure has been estimated at from 10 to 50 percent of the registered, but there is reason to believe that it was rather nearer the former than the latter figure."

[108] See, e.g., Alexander von Humboldt, *Political Essay on the Kingdom of New Spain*, trans. John Black, 4 vols. (London, 1811; facsimile ed., New York, 1966); D. A. Brading and Harry E. Cross, "Colonial Silver Mining: Mexico and Peru," *Hispanic American Historical Review* 52 (1972): 545–79; and the discussion in Chapter 7 of this volume.

fueled in part by massive bullion flows from the New World, meant that the relative value of silver as a commodity declined. Eventually, demand for silver fell in Europe, making it less profitable to operate New World mines. The result was a decline in silver production. Chaunu and others have broadened that argument to focus on trade as the crucial variable, seeing prices largely as reflections of changes in trade. The physical expansion of Europeans around the globe encouraged long-distance trade to take advantage of global price differences. Once regular trade was established, price differences tended to even out. That created a circumstance in which the diminished value of silver in Europe discouraged transatlantic exchanges.[109] Explanations based primarily on prices and bullion flows can be misleading, however, and Morineau has argued that a bullionist approach distorts our understanding of the global economy.[110]

Another possible explanation for the end of the sixteenth-century expansion focuses on the effects of population decline in the Americas, which supposedly led to a decline in bullion production that strangled trade.[111] Despite the plausibility of such an explanation, it does not take into account that the slump in American bullion production occurred concurrently with or later than a slump in the European economy. The European difficulties may well have begun in the agrarian sector, in a growing imbalance between population size and available resources. Signs of agricultural distress appeared as early as the 1550s in some areas, and nearly everywhere by the 1570s.[112] Ris-

---

[109] Davis, *Rise of the Atlantic Economies*, 99–102; Chaunu, *Séville et l'Amerique*, 355.

[110] Michel Morineau, "D'Amsterdam a Séville: De quelle réalité l'histoire des prix est-elle le miroir?" *Annales: Economies, Sociétés, Civilisations* 23 (1968): 178–205, found that the periodization defined by Nicolas W. Posthumus, based on price history, misrepresented the experience of the Dutch economy as a whole (Posthumus, *Nederlandsche prijsgeschiedenis*, 2 vols. [Leiden, 1943, 1964]). According to Morineau, Dutch economic trends were much closer to general European trends than Posthumus and other historians had thought. Similarly, the influential work of François Simiand, *Recherches anciennes et nouvelles sur le mouvement général des prix du XVIe au XIXe siècle* (Paris, 1932), needs to be revised substantially in the light of a growing body of evidence based on production (Morineau, "Gazettes," 289–91). This anti-bullionist sentiment is a recurrent theme of Morineau's collected articles in *Incroyables gazettes.*

[111] Fernand Braudel, *Wheels of Commerce*, vol. 2 of *Civilization and Capitalism, Fifteenth–Eighteenth Century*, trans. Siân Reynolds (New York, 1979), 173–5; Murdo J. Macleod, "Spain and America: The Atlantic Trade, 1492–1720," in *Cambridge History of Latin America*, 1:371–2; Chaunu, *Séville et l'Amérique*, 353–5.

[112] Wilhelm Abel, *Agricultural Fluctuations in Europe from the Thirteenth to the Twentieth Centuries*, trans. from the 1966 German ed. by Olive Ordish (New York, 1980); Emmanuel Le Roy Ladurie and Joseph Goy, eds., *Tithe and Agrarian History from the Fourteenth to the Nineteenth Century*, trans. Susan Burke (Cambridge and New York, 1982); Maurice Aymard, "The Transition from Feudalism to Capitalism in Italy: The Case That Doesn't Fit," *Fernand Braudel Center for the Study of Economies, Historical*

ing population and prices for agricultural products in the sixteenth century eventually squeezed out demand for manufactured goods. Likely to suffer even more were the goods supplied by international trade, which Chaunu estimated as worth no more than 2 percent of the value of European agricultural production.[113] Europe demanded fewer manufactured goods and imports and could supply fewer exports. Rising prices were therefore symptoms of a crisis in the economy as a whole. Credit and banking crises in 1586, 1596, and 1606–7 suggest that the crisis was spreading outward from the agrarian economy, although it is nearly impossible to separate purely economic events from the political upheavals of the times.[114] By around 1620, ample evidence attests to a widespread European slump in manufacturing, trade, and credit; generally weak economic indicators continued for several decades thereafter.[115]

There is no question that some areas of the international economy could profit during the slump. Mediterranean trade had prospered during the late fourteenth and early fifteenth centuries, another depressed period. In the economic slump that can be defined between about 1620 and 1680, the Dutch enjoyed their golden age in commerce, buoyed in part by the warfare and political disarray of their larger neighbors. Trade across the Pacific to the Philippines also experienced a pronounced contraction after about 1615. It would seem not so much that European trends affected the rest of the world or vice versa as that each area had become part of a larger whole, responding similarly but independently to the same stimuli.[116] Those stimuli are not yet properly understood, but their nature should be sought in the interaction of all parts of economic life.

Once the decline in trade to the Indies set in, fleets sailed irregularly. The famous fairs at Portobelo, having come to life during the

---

Systems, and Civilizations, Review 6 (Fall 1982): 131–208; Carla Rahn Phillips, "Time and Duration: A Model for the Economy of Early Modern Spain," *American Historical Review* 92 (June 1987): 531–62.

[113] *Séville et l'Amérique*, 362.

[114] See José Gentil da Silva, *Stratégie des affaires à Lisbonne entre 1595 et 1607: Lettres marchandes des Rodrigues d'Evora et Veiga* (Paris, 1956), 113–16.

[115] Ruggiero Romano, "Tra XVIe e XVII secolo, Una crisi economica: 1619–1622," *Rivista Storica Italiana* 74 (1962); José Gentil da Silva, *Banque et crédit en Italie au XVIIe siècle*, 2 vols. (Paris, 1969), 1:151–63; idem, *Stratégie des affaires à Lisbonne entre 1595 et 1607*, 113–16; Lane, *Venice*, 400–2; B. E. Supple, *Commercial Crisis and Change in England, 1600–1642: A Study in the Instability of a Mercantile Economy* (Cambridge, 1959).

[116] Pierre Chaunu, *Les Philippines et le Pacifique des Ibériques (XVIe, XVIIe, XVIIIe siècles)*, 2 vols. (Paris, 1960), 1:242–52; idem, *Séville et l'Amérique*, 354–5; Carmen Yuste López, *El comercio de la Nueva España con Filipinas, 1590–1785* (Mexico City, 1984), 31–4.

final spurt of sixteenth-century growth, persisted into the seventeenth century, but at a much reduced level.[117] The convoy system that had served the empire so well in the sixteenth century almost ceased. In the late 1620s, there were still nearly 120 ships per year in the Indies trade, with a cargo capacity of about 37,000 toneladas (see Table 2.1). By the late 1640s, an annual average of fewer than 75 ships carried the trade, and from the late 1650s to the late 1660s, between 30 and 35 ships.[118] The contract for supplying slaves to America was allowed to lapse. MacLeod, assuming that the slave trade was always profitable, has seen evidence of administrative incompetence in the lapsed contract,[119] but it is more likely that the Spanish crown simply found no willing contractors as long as the slump lasted.

The number of hides exported from the Indies declined steadily from the last decade of the sixteenth century, falling to fewer than 8,000 per year in the late 1660s from a peak of over 134,000 in the early 1580s (see Table 2.4).[120] Indigo exports continued to rise until about 1620 and then fell back during the next several decades, although the trend line shows considerable fluctuation.[121] Cochineal experienced a sharp drop between 1600 and 1615 before rising again in 1616–20 (see Table 2.5). Unfortunately, data are lacking after 1620.[122] Sugar exports also seemed to recover in 1616–20 from a several-decade slump, but thereafter they entered a steady decline (see Table 2.2).[123]

The estimated total value of trade to the Indies, based on the almojarifazgo tax, fell from the 1620s to the early 1640s to one-thirtieth of what it had been at the turn of the century. The avería tax presents a more ambiguous picture, although there is no question that it reflects a decline from the 1620s on compared with levels at the turn of the century.[124]

Gold production in the Indies, already below its midcentury levels by the 1580s, fell sharply in the 1590s. Gold exports, however, did not

---

[117] Vila Vilar, "Ferias de Portobelo," 335–7.
[118] Chaunu, *Séville et l'Atlantique*, 6(1):168, 337; Lutgardo García Fuentes, *Comercio español con América (1650–1700)* (Seville, 1980), 417–22.
[119] "Spain and America," 382.
[120] Lorenzo Sanz, *Comercio de España con América*, 1:621; Chaunu, *Séville et l'Atlantique*, 6(2):1012–13; Morineau, "Gazettes," 336; García Fuentes, *Comercio español con América (1650–1700)*, 517–18.
[121] Chaunu, *Séville et l'Atlantique*, 6(2):988–9; García Fuentes, *Comercio español con América (1650–1700)*, 509–10; Morineau, "Gazettes," 336.
[122] Chaunu, *Séville et l'Atlantique*, 6(2):980–1.
[123] Lorenzo Sanz, *Comercio de España con América*, 1:615; Chaunu, *Séville et l'Atlantique*, 6(2):1004–5; García Fuentes, *Comercio español con América (1650–1700)*, 517–18.
[124] Chaunu, *Séville et l'Atlantique*, 6(1)468–70; Vila Vilar, "Ferias de Portobelo," 289. See also John C. Lynch, *Spain under the Habsburgs*, 2d ed., 2 vols. (New York, 1982), 2:200–11, for the slump in the Indies trade and foreign incursions therein.

decline until the 1610s. Silver production held strong until 1600 at least, and exports remained high until the 1640s.[125] Official treasure receipts did not fall definitively until the 1630s, reaching their nadir in the early 1660s.[126] Although the notion of a seventeenth-century crisis in America came under attack for several decades, recent work on fiscal returns has confirmed the decline in treasure receipts for Perú. The situation in Mexico is less clear, but much evidence supports the notion of an economic decline in the middle third of the century.[127] Morineau has been anxious to show that treasure remittances to Europe in the seventeenth century as a whole were higher than those in the sixteenth century, to discredit the notion that bullion flows determined the general shape of the European economy. Morineau rightly questions the accuracy of many official reports, but his own sources suggest lower remittances for several decades in the seventeenth century.[128] One contemporary observer, writing in 1637, thought that the fabled mines of America had been used up.[129]

The Spanish government responded to diminished trade and treasure receipts by attempting to tighten enforcement of the official monopoly. A related development was what has been called the golden age of piracy in the Caribbean, from about 1620 to about 1680. In addition to officially sponsored attacks on the Spanish Empire by the Dutch after 1621, freelance pirates, particularly French and English, preyed on Spanish settlements and commerce in and around the Caribbean, tacitly encouraged by their home governments.[130] These pirates represented a response to the seventeenth-century decline in trade and to the Spanish government's tightened control. With in-

---

[125] Bakewell, "Mining in Colonial Spanish America," 141; Hamilton, *American Treasure and the Price Revolution in Spain,* 42.

[126] Hamilton, *American Treasure and the Price Revolution in Spain,* 34; Antonio Domínguez Ortiz, "Las remesas de metales preciosos de Indias en 1621–1665," *Anuario de Historia Económica y Social* 2 (1969): 568–81; Morineau, "Gazettes," 337; García Fuentes, *Comercio español con América (1650–1700),* 534–41.

[127] Herbert Klein, "La economía de la Nueva España, 1680–1809: Un análisis a partir de las Cajas Reales," *Historia Mexicana* 34 (Apr.–June 1985): 563–5; Herbert Klein and Jacques Barbier, "Recent Trends in the Study of Spanish American Colonial Public Finance," *Latin American Research Review* 23, no. 1 (1988): 47–9.

[128] Morineau, *Incroyables gazettes,* pp. 105–19, 571. He found a stagnation in deposits in the Bank of Amsterdam between about 1650 and 1686 ("Quelques remarques sur l'abondance monétaire aux Provinces-Unies," *Annales: Economies, Sociétés, Civilisations* 29 [1974]: 767–76).

[129] Diego de Colmenares, *Historia de la insigne ciudad de Segovia, y compendio de las historias de Castilla,* 4 vols. (Segovia, 1637; reprinted in 2 vols., Segovia, 1969), 1:316, labeled chap. XVIII, para. XIV.

[130] Hugh F. Rankin, *The Golden Age of Piracy* (New York, 1969); Clarence Henry Haring, *The Buccaneers in the West Indies in the Seventeenth Century* (c. 1910; reprint, Hamden, Conn., 1966).

creased competition for a smaller total trade and a reduced use of Spanish shipping lanes in the Atlantic and the Caribbean by the Indies fleets, the situation was ripe for illegal and often violent incursions into the empire. Apart from the pirates, some interlopers who entered the empire illegally came more or less peaceably and came to stay, some of them later gaining official permission to settle.[131]

During the slump of the seventeenth century, the New World economies turned inward, producing some of the goods they had formerly imported. There is some evidence that per capita agricultural output and consumption both rose, as the reduced population concentrated on better lands.[132] The Spanish crown tried to discourage interregional trade in the Americas, but such trade was too important to the local economies to be discouraged by royal prohibitions. Local and interregional trade increased to fill the gap left by declines in transatlantic trade. Buenos Aires became an important outlet for illegal shipments from across the Andes, relying on a network of roads that was largely in place by 1630.[133]

The end of the seventeenth century saw a recovery in the local and international economy that affected the Indies trade, although precise figures are difficult to find. The best sources for trade in the late seventeenth century are the same shipping registers in Seville that provided information for earlier periods. The merchant Consulado of Seville dominated trade from 1650 to 1700, leaving the government's House of Trade as a mediator between merchants and the state. The official fleets for the Indies were shifted from Seville to Cádiz in 1680, with the acquiescence of the merchants of Seville. Cádiz was much more conveniently located and in many ways more an extension of Seville than its rival. Seville tended to concentrate on the export of agricultural and metal exports, whereas Cádiz concentrated on the re-

[131] María Encarnación Rodríguez Vicente, "Los extranjeros en los reinos del Perú a fines del siglo XVI," in *Homenaje a Vicens Vives*, 2 vols. (Barcelona, 1967), 2:625–6, lists sixty-nine non-Spaniards in Perú in the early seventeenth century who were allowed to remain in exchange for paying a tax. Twenty-four of them were Portuguese, and the rest came from various places in the Mediterranean.
[132] Sherburne F. Cook and Woodrow Borah, "Indian Food Production and Consumption in Central Mexico before and after the Conquest (1500–1650)," in *Mexico and California*, vol. 3 of *Essays in Population History* (Berkeley, Los Angeles, and London, 1971–9), 172–3.
[133] A. P. Canabrava, *O comércio portugués no Rio da Prata (1580–1640)* (São Paolo, 1944), 163–5. Demetrio Ramos Pérez, *Trigo chileno: Navieros del Callao y hacendados limeños entre la crisis agrícola del siglo XVII y la comercial de la primera mitad del XVIII* (Madrid, 1967), 11–12, 31–3, 49–52, shows how Chile became a major producer and exporter of wheat by the late seventeenth century.

export of textiles, wax, and manufactured goods to the Indies. The merchant Consulado of Seville, which included members from both cities, cooperated with foreign merchant enclaves to preserve the monopoly they shared over the Indies trade.

After 1660 the total volume of merchandise shipped across the Atlantic began to show renewed growth, which lasted until the end of the century. Spanish ships and shipping tonnage in the trade stayed quite low, however. The rising volume of trade was handled increasingly by foreign ships. Part of the growth came in traditional products, but new products entered the trade as well. In America, cacao began to be exported in notable quantities from the mid–seventeenth century on, although the heyday of the chocolate craze would come later (see Table 2.6). Tobacco exports from the Spanish Indies increased sharply in the 1680s and 1690s, having been quite small before (see Table 2.3). In Spain the distilled spirit called aguardiente quickly rose to prominence among exports of the late seventeenth century, at the start of an extended rise.[134]

The figures for four other trade items suggest some of the changes occurring on both sides of the Atlantic. Hides, one of the key exports from America in the mid–sixteenth century, continued at a low level, contrary to the rising trend that we find elsewhere in the trade figures. Iron and iron items exported from Spain to the Indies, on the other hand, rose sharply from the late 1660s on, with plowshares and hoes particularly notable. This pattern suggests that population and agriculture in the Indies were reviving and putting pressure on herding in the late seventeenth century, a pattern borne out by other evidence.[135] Paper and wax also began to be sent to the Indies in increasing quantities from the 1660s on, which suggests an increasing tempo of activity, official and private, lay and ecclesiastical.[136]

In the Indies, silver production began to recover after 1660. It had surpassed its late sixteenth-century peak by 1690, presumably responding to an improved trading climate with Europe. The discovery of gold in Brazil about 1695 further stimulated silver production, as its value rose in relation to gold. New Spain, experiencing impressive growth, began to gain a larger share in total exports, whereas Tierra

---

[134] García Fuentes, *Comercio español con América (1650–1700)*, 410–26, 527–8; Antonio García-Baquero González, *Cádiz y el Atlántico (1717–1778)*, 2 vols. (Cadiz, 1976), 2:222–47.

[135] Nicolás Sánchez-Albornoz, "The Population of Colonial Latin America," in *Cambridge History of Latin America*, 2:26–9.

[136] García Fuentes, *Comercio español con América (1650–1700)*, 456–7, 483–4.

Table 2.6

Cacao Exported from Spanish America

Years	Total years with available data	Total weight	Weight unit	Weight per year	Reduced to arrobas	Source
1651-55	5	8,680.7	arroba	1,736.1	1,736.1	a
1656-60	5	10,055.1	arroba	2,011.0	2,011.0	a
1661-65	5	23,251.6	arroba	4,650.3	4,650.3	a
1666-70	4	58,999.4	arroba	14,749.9	14,749.9	a
1671-75	4	31,997.2	arroba	7,999.3	7,999.3	a
1676-80	3	59,047.5	arroba	19,682.5	19,682.5	a
1681-85	2	44,032.5	arroba	22,016.2	22,016.2	a
1686-90	4	16,672.6	arroba	4,168.1	4,168.1	a
1691-95	5	54,105.5	arroba	10,821.1	10,821.1	a
1696-99	3	10,687.4	arroba	3,562.5	3,562.5	a

1717-20	4	402.0	fanega	100.5	442.2	b
1721-25	5	8,425.3	fanega	1,685.0	7,414.2	b
1726-30	5	16,118.0	fanega	3,223.6	14,183.8	b
1731-35	5	92,930.0	fanega	18,586.0	81,778.4	b
1736-38	3	72,184.0	fanega	24,061.3	105,869.9	b
1747-50	4	58,683.0	fanega	14,670.8	64,551.3	b
1751-55	5	139,637.0	fanega	27,927.4	122,880.6	b
1756-60	5	137,052.5	fanega	27,410.5	120,606.2	b
1761-65	5	180,383.5	fanega	36,076.7	158,737.5	b
1766-70	5	216,247.3	fanega	43,249.4	190,297.6	b
1771-75	5	248,861.3	fanega	49,772.3	218,997.9	b
1776-78	3	81,088.3	fanega	27,029.4	118,929.4	b

[a] Lutgardo García Fuentes, Comercio español con América (1650-1700) (Seville, 1980), 517-18.

[b] Antonio García-Baquero González, Cádiz y el Atlántico (1717-1778), 2 vols. (Cádiz, 1976), 2:222-47.

Firme declined. In the long run, the seventeenth-century slump marked a temporary setback for New Spain, but a more lasting one for Tierra Firme.[137]

Estimates for the total flow of treasure from the Indies to Spain differ widely, but they all indicate that the revival in trade and industry was not reflected in official returns to Spain.[138] Widespread smuggling probably explains this discrepancy. From the early 1670s, royal receipts of treasure accounted for over half the total returns, and in the late 1680s and 1690s, they rose to around 90 percent.[139] In contrast, through the sixteenth century, the royal share had rarely surpassed 30 percent.[140] This suggests that private persons had responded to the seventeenth-century slump in trade by avoiding official registration of their treasure. By the time trade began to increase again, smuggling had become ingrained in their behavior. Concerted government efforts to enforce registration reduced the royal share of treasure to 30 percent by the late 1710s.[141] By then total receipts were far higher than the official figures for the late seventeenth century, but smuggling had declined. Despite the increased flow of bullion across the Atlantic in the late seventeenth century, European prices stayed fairly low until about 1730, which belies any direct or simple correlation between bullion and prices.[142]

In the late seventeenth century the labor shortage in the Indies was ameliorated not only by a rise in the local population but also by a

---

[137] John TePaske and Herbert S. Klein, "The Seventeenth-Century Crisis in New Spain: Myth or Reality?" *Past and Present* 90 (1981): 116–35; García Fuentes, *Comercio español con América (1650–1700)*, 413–14. Growth in eighteenth-century mining output in Mexico is documented in Richard L. Garner, "Silver Production and Entrepreneurial Structure in Eighteenth-Century Mexico," *Jahrbuch für Geschichte von Staat, Wirtschaft, und Gesellschaft Lateinamerikas* 17 (1980): 157–85. Ann Zulawski, "Wages, Ore Sharing, and Peasant Agriculture: Labor in Oruro's Silver Mines, 1607–1720," *Hispanic American Historical Review* 67 (August 1987): 405–30, found a later cycle of decline and growth for mines in central Perú, with lower production after 1650 and recovery after 1700. Carlos Daniel Malamud Rikles, *Cádiz y Saint Malo en el comercio colonial peruano (1698–1725)* (Jerez de la Frontera, 1986), found a slump in trade with Perú at the end of the seventeenth and early eighteenth centuries.

[138] García Fuentes, *Comercio español con América* (1650–1700), 534–41; Morineau, "D'Amsterdam à Séville," 196–7, found that money was much more abundant in the United Provinces after about 1686 than in the previous three decades. Because much of the silver in circulation in Europe came from the Spanish Indies, a recovery of trade is the most likely explanation for the increase in silver. At the same time, official returns to Spain remained low.

[139] García Fuentes, *Comercio español con América (1650–1700)*, 534–41; Domínguez Ortiz, "Remesas," 579–81.

[140] Hamilton, *American Treasure and the Price Revolution in Spain*, 34; Lorenzo Sanz, *Comercio de España con América*, 2:254.

[141] García-Baquero, *Cádiz y el Atlántico*, 2:259–65.

[142] Morineau, "D'Amsterdam à Séville," 196–7.

greatly expanded importation of black slaves from Africa. The importation of slaves can be seen not only as a cause of the subsequent increase in plantation production but also as an effect of the improved international market for that production. Dutch merchants held the contract to supply slaves to the Spanish Empire several times during the late seventeenth century. The French held it during the War of the Spanish Succession, and the English acquired it in 1713 by the treaty ending that war, retaining it until 1750. Both the Dutch and the English used their contracts to smuggle trade goods in along with the slaves.

With the revival in trade, piracy became a nuisance even to those powers that had previously given the pirates tacit support. As a result, the golden age of piracy ended once trade revived. English and French bases on Caribbean islands changed almost imperceptibly from pirate enclaves to solid settlements and plantations as their inhabitants saw more to be gained by peaceful trade with the Spanish Empire than by continued piracy against it.[143] Despite the legal monopoly of trade to the Indies by Castile, foreign merchants and foreign goods permeated the Indies trade in the late seventeenth century and through the first quarter of the eighteenth century, some of them licensed by the Spanish government. Foreigners were particularly prominent in the trade to Tierra Firme; New Spain was better controlled and better supplied by the official fleet system.[144]

The Dutch predominated among the foreigners in the Indies trade until the 1690s, when they began to be edged out by the English.[145] One Spanish observer complained in 1687 that three-fourths of the total trade – presumably, trade goods – belonged to "foreigners" of one sort or another. Recent studies suggest, however, that merchants in Seville and Cádiz never lost their dominance of the trade, even in the seventeenth century.[146] According to a French report, before the War of the Spanish Succession, Spain shipped about 40 million livres tournois worth of goods every five years to the Indies and brought

---

[143] Macleod, "Spain and America," 382–3.

[144] Carlos D. Malamud, "El comercio directo de Europa con América en el siglo XVIII," *Quinto Centenario* 1 (1981): 25–52, deals well with the complex issues involved in assessing the volume and impact of direct (contraband) trade.

[145] Richard Conquest, "The State and Commercial Expansion: England in the Years 1642–1688," *Journal of European Economic History* 14 (Jan.–Apr. 1985): 155–72; Joaquim Nadal Farreras, *Comercio exterior y subdesarrollo: España y Gran Bretaña de 1772 a 1914: Política económica y relaciones comerciales* (Madrid, 1978), 205–8.

[146] The Spanish observer is cited in Antonio Domínguez Ortiz, "Los caminos de la plata americana," *Boletín de la Academia Nacional de la Historia* (Caracas) 62, no. 248 (1979): 816. Klein and Barbier, "Recent Trends," 51–3, present the brief for continued Spanish dominance.

back 150 million worth in treasure and merchandise.[147] Overall, it would appear that Spain continued to control its empire, despite serious incursions from foreign goods and merchants.

The War of the Spanish Succession (1701–13) affected the recovery of American trade very little at first, but a slump in the 1710s and 1720s temporarily slowed growth. During the war, many foreigners were allowed to trade legally in the Indies, in recognition that they and their goods were indispensable. Regular Spanish fleets also sailed every two to three years between Cádiz and Veracruz from 1706 on, each supplying an important, though small, fraction of the total needs of the colonies.[148]

After the war, the new Bourbon government in Spain began a concerted effort to tighten control over the Indies trade. Ordinances in 1720 reestablished the fleet system for New Spain, to the benefit of the merchants in Cádiz.[149] About 85 percent of the ships sailing to and from the Indies touched at Cádiz between 1717 and 1765. The only legal ports to rival Cádiz for outbound voyages were generally in the north, a much less favored coastline for the westward currents and winds. Return voyages stopped more frequently in the north, both legally and illegally. Nonetheless, merchants based in the Indies and smaller merchants in Spain resented the advantages accruing to Cádiz, and it was becoming clear that the fleet system had outlived its usefulness. Erratic sailings in the 1720s and early 1730s often found no market for their goods. Increasingly, ships to New Spain traveled individually, outside the fleets, and piracy revived as well.

To some historians, the reasserted government control over the Indies trade in the early eighteenth century marked the first full-blown mercantilism in the Spanish Empire.[150] It involved not only the revived fleets but an effort to drive out unnaturalized foreigners established in the Indies. Although Spain and France were both ruled by the Bourbon dynasty, French merchants were eventually excluded from the Indies. So were the Dutch, to a large extent. The English resisted Spanish pressure for a time and were willing to fight a war to remain. During the hostilities, which lasted from 1739 to 1748, foreign ships were allowed to trade legally with the Indies, which may explain why so few official figures exist for trade in that period.

---

[147] Braudel, *Wheels of Commerce*, 176.

[148] Valentín Vázquez de Prada, "Las rutas comerciales entre España y América en el siglo XVIII," *Anuario de Estudios Americanos* 25 (1968): 203.

[149] García-Baquero, *Cádiz y el Atlántico*, 1:151–62, discusses this and later reforms of the fleet system.

[150] Ibid., 67–74.

Thereafter, in a new commercial treaty in 1750, the English South Seas Company gave up the contract for supplying slaves and the right to send one vessel each year to the Spanish Indies, rights that had given them the excuse to trade openly despite the official monopoly.[151] The fleet system was effectively abandoned from 1749 on for the Caribbean and South America, although Cádiz and the estuary of the Guadalquivir retained their monopoly over trade with New Spain for three more decades.[152]

During the eighteenth century, Spain also chartered several privileged companies for the Indies trade, something that had been discussed since the early seventeenth century but never implemented. The Royal Guipuzcoan Company of Caracas was established in 1728 for trade between the Basque province of Guipúzcoa and Venezuela. With a de facto monopoly that lasted until 1780, the company prospered, benefiting from the boom in cacao in the middle decades of the eighteenth century and effectively taking back the trade with Venezuela from the Dutch.[153] Following thereafter were the Royal Company of Havana in 1740, designed to develop agriculture and trade in Cuba; the Royal Company of San Fernando of Seville in 1747 for parts of the South American trade not covered by other companies; and the Royal Company of Barcelona in 1756 for the islands of Santo Domingo, Puerto Rico, and Margarita.[154]

The Barcelona company marked the culmination of several decades of Catalan penetration into the Indies trade. Agricultural production, shipbuilding, distilling, and manufacturing in Catalonia all expanded strongly during the eighteenth century, as in the rest of Spain, supplying the Indies markets and in turn being supplied by them.[155] By about 1750, "after four decades, Spain had regained unrestricted exercise of its commercial monopoly over the American empire."[156]

The trade across the Pacific between New Spain and the Philippines followed a pattern very similar to that for the Atlantic trade. Recovery from the seventeenth-century depression began about 1680

---

[151] Eleazar Córdova-Bello, *Compañías holandesas de navegación neerlandesa* (Sevile, 1964), 57; Geoffrey J. Walker, *Spanish Politics and Imperial Trade (1707–1789)* (London, 1979), 205–16.

[152] Vázquez de Prada, "Rutas," 206–8; Walker, *Spanish Politics and Imperial Trade,* 219–25.

[153] Vázquez de Prada, "Rutas," 210–11; Roland Dennis Hussey, *The Caracas Company, 1728–1874* (Cambridge, Mass., 1934); Brading, "Bourbon Spain and Its American Empire," 411–12; García-Baquero, *Cádiz y el Atlántico,* 1:135–6.

[154] García-Baquero, *Cádiz y el Atlántico,* 1:135–6.

[155] García-Baquero, *Cádiz y el Atlántico,* 1:563–9; Carlos Martínez Shaw, *Cataluña en la carrera de Indias, 1680–1756* (Barcelona, 1981), 72–94.

[156] Brading, "Bourbon Spain and Its American Empire," 412.

and then experienced a setback in the early eighteenth century before rising sharply again. Tax figures document the importance of the China trade to Manila. They also document the high cost to Spain of maintaining its distant outposts in Asia. Between 1591 and 1780, the Philippines are estimated to have cost about 10–15 percent of the total income from the Indies. By maintaining a presence in the Far East, Spain gained a strategic outpost of great importance and a way to control the flow of silver to Asia. The merchants of New Spain were the primary beneficiaries of the Asian trade, profiting from it without having to underwrite its defense. On their own account, they sent several times as much silver to the Far East as the crown did. It has been estimated that 4,000–5,000 tons of silver crossed the Pacific to Asia from 1570 to 1780.[157]

Debate in the mid–eighteenth century centered on whether to keep the system of fleets, fairs, and privilege. The Spanish government made concessions to various ports left out of the official companies, which progressively weakened the remaining monopoly privileges. During the Seven Years' War (1756–63) the government opened trade with the Caribbean islands to nine Spanish ports and in 1778 allowed some foreign shipping into the Indies trade as well. Although this was not quite the "free trade" promised by the official decree, free trade soon followed. The Caracas company lost its monopoly in 1780, and the last few restrictions on free trade were raised in 1789.[158] The establishment of free trade marked a final triumph and a coming of age for the merchants and the economy of the Spanish Indies.

Regarding the volume of trade during the eighteenth century, the best sources are the same records for shipping and taxes that Chaunu used for the period before 1650. The only two complete series for the eighteenth century are the number of ships per year and their total tonnages (see Table 2.1). The figures show a rise from about thirty ships per year in the late 1710s to about one hundred ships per year in the late 1770s. Tonnages followed the same trend, with a rise from nearly 7,800 toneladas per year in the late 1710s to an average of about 26,000 toneladas in the 1760s and 1770s. The eighteenth-century peak was therefore about two-thirds as high as the peak of the late sixteenth century.[159] At the same time the European economy and its shipping capacity were expanding even more. One estimate places the total capacity of all of Europe's fleets at 3.5 million French tons by

[157] Chaunu, *Philippines et le Pacifique*, 1:253–69.
[158] Vázquez de Prada, "Rutas," 214–21.
[159] García-Baquero, *Cádiz y el Atlántico*, 1:539–44, 2:137–9.

the end of the eighteenth century, up from just 2 million a century earlier.[160]

Incomplete series for taxes indicate a general rise in trade to the Indies during the eighteenth century. By volume, Spain produced about 45 percent of the cargoes for the Indies, mostly in agricultural products and raw materials such as wine, oil, aguardiente, and iron. By value, however, Spanish products probably made up less than 20 percent of most fleets.[161]

Return cargoes from the Indies continued to be mainly in traditional items, with the steepest increase in volume from the late 1740s on. Sugar exports rose over a hundredfold between 1717–20 and 1766–70, reflecting intensified production in Cuba (see Table 2.2). Cacao exports from the Indies rose spectacularly from the 1730s on, increasing seventeenfold between 1726–30 and 1771–75 (see Table 2.6). The number of hides exported rose over eighteenfold, and cochineal exports nearly quadrupled (see Tables 2.4 and 2.5). Cochineal would continue to be an important American export in the period 1778–1821, but other agricultural products would decline greatly. The production and export of indigo showed sharp rises between about 1695 and 1725, declines in the 1730s and 1740s, and increases thereafter. In value, bullion made up 77.6 percent of the total cargoes to Cádiz between 1747 and 1778.[162]

On the whole, the eighteenth century saw the consolidation of a strong and economically viable American empire, less dependent upon Spain after three centuries of investment and development but still benefiting from imports of people and capital from the peninsula.[163] American exports were part of a balanced economy, no longer organized primarily to supply the European market. By contrast, in 1789 the slave plantations on the French island of Saint Domingue (the former Santo Domingo) yielded nearly as much in exports as all of Spanish America combined. One recent author noted that "if the ex-

---

[160] Ruggiero Romano, "Per una valutazione della flotta mercantile europea alla fine del secola XVIII," *Studi in onore di Amintore Fanfani*, 6 vols., 5:578–80.

[161] Brading, "Bourbon Spain and Its American Empire," 415–16, mentions just 16 percent for the 1757 fleet. García-Baquero, *Cádiz y el Atlántico*, 1:552–5; on p. 555 García-Baquero implies that agricultural production in Andalusia followed the rhythm of trade and was thus stimulated by demand. The reality could have been just the opposite, with increased agricultural production in Andalusia stimulating trade in Spanish agricultural products.

[162] García-Baquero, *Cádiz y el Atlántico*, 2:222–47, 349; Javier de la Tabla Ducasse, *Comercio exterior de Veracruz, 1778–1821: Crisis de dependencia* (Seville, 1978), 239–40.

[163] Garner, "Silver Production," documents the importance of Spanish contributions to the Mexican mining boom of the eighteenth century.

port earnings of the $14\frac{1}{2}$ million inhabitants of Spanish America barely exceeded the output value of a single island in the Caribbean, it was because the bulk of its population found occupation and sustenance in the domestic economy."[164]

There is no question that the volume of long-distance trade from southern Europe increased enormously during the early modern period, most of the increase coming from the overseas trading empires first developed by the Portuguese and the Spanish. During the same period trade within Europe, by land and sea, seems to have increased as well, along with population and agricultural and industrial output. Because much of the increase in trade within Europe was related to overseas colonies and markets, it is difficult to separate long-distance and intra-European trade. Nonetheless, it seems likely that the total volume of trade was substantially higher in 1750 than it had been in 1350.

The relationships between trade flows and other parts of the economy are infinitely complex. Although the discovery of silver in Spanish America (ca. 1545) and the discovery of gold in Brazil (ca. 1695) undoubtedly influenced the expansive phases of trade that followed them, it would be unwise to neglect other factors, such as changes in population size and in agricultural and industrial production, to explain that expansion. In other words, trade was not necessarily the driving force in the early modern economy, although it was often more visible and measurable than other activities. The role of trade can be fully understood only in relation to the economy as a whole. Trade to and from the Iberian empires served as a conduit for European agricultural and manufactured goods and American treasure, both inside and outside official channels. As precious metals from the Spanish and Portuguese empires flowed around the world, they supported the growth in global trade that characterized the early modern period.

The long-term expansion in trade carried within it several shorter-term fluctuations. Between about 1350 and 1450, the volume of trade in the Mediterranean seems to have declined, although some merchants in Italy and the Levant were able to profit despite the depression. Their success has often tended to mask the general contraction that followed the Black Death. From about 1450 to about 1610 or 1620, the global volume of trade expanded greatly, most visibly in the Asian trade of the Portuguese and the transatlantic trade of the Spanish.

---

[164] Brading, "Bourbon Spain and Its American Empire," 426.

Then, from about 1620 to about 1680, a major slump occurred in the volume of trade across the Atlantic, across the Pacific, and within Europe, if the available figures can be trusted. By about 1680, most of the available figures had turned upward again. The eighteenth century experienced a generally upward trend, although with at least one setback. This pattern for long-distance trade is strikingly similar to the timetable now established for the European population and economy as a whole. It seems clear that a global system had emerged during the early modern centuries, linked by trade but not determined by it.

CHAPTER 3

The growth and composition of the long-distance trade of England and the Dutch Republic before 1750

NIELS STEENSGAARD

INTRODUCTION

INTERCONTINENTAL trade in the period known variously as the age of commercial capitalism and the age of European expansion is a well studied but still-elusive field of historical research. Numerous detailed studies on particular branches of trade, areas of production, commercial routes, or points of distribution, often based on sources that make quantification possible, offer a mass of information on various aspects of the history of trade. At the same time the totality remains elusive; the information is not easily compared or summed up, not even when it happens to be complete and reliable. Any attempt to sum up our knowledge of the volume and composition of early modern long-distance trade must remain preliminary and open to revision.

More than twenty-five years ago F. Mauro appealed to his colleagues to cooperate internationally in order to reconstruct the commodity flows between continents in this period.[1] Since then more details and better statistical information have been uncovered, but his plea for cooperation among scholars was not heard, and today we are not much closer to a comprehensive understanding of the economic interrelations between the continents in the early modern period than we were twenty-five years ago. It is to be hoped that this volume will be a step in the right direction, especially because of the growing interest, not only among historians, in the history of intercontinental

[1] F. Mauro, "Towards an 'Intercontinental Model': European Overseas Expansion between 1500 and 1800," *The Economic History Review*, 2d ser., 14 (1961): 11.

trade in the early modern period. The books of Frank, Wallerstein, and Wolf have drawn attention to the significance of these centuries for our understanding of the distribution of wealth and power in the contemporary world. Their views and basic assumptions are contradictory and remain controversial, but the problems they have raised as social scientists are a challenge to the historical profession.[2] It is not my task, however, to unravel these problems, but only to offer a modest contribution by trying to determine some quantitative aspects of the trade between northern Europe and the overseas world.

The north European countries entered into regular relations with the world overseas only after 1600. Therefore – and keeping the general theme of the volume in mind – attention will be focused on the period after 1600. This approach has its obvious shortcomings from an institutional point of view, because the groundwork for the successful competition of the Dutch and the English with the pioneer colonial powers, the Spanish and the Portuguese, was laid in the preceding centuries. On the other hand, the composition of long-distance trade shows a remarkable continuity from the medieval period to the seventeenth century. Medieval trade in northern Europe was primarily a trade in bulky necessities of life: grain, butter, cheese, fish, wine, timber, wool, woolen and linen textiles, woad, potash, salt, iron, copper, lead, and tin.[3]

By the middle of the sixteenth century the Netherlands had emerged as the most highly developed market economy in Europe, but the commodities handled in foreign trade were much the same: woolen, linen, and silk textiles, wine, grain, woad, copper, salt, wool, oil, and alum. These are all recognized from medieval trade; the only significant change is the introduction of sugar and spices to the Netherlands market through Lisbon. Though not entirely unknown in medieval trade, these commodities were obviously of growing importance in the sixteenth century.[4]

If we move onward to the seventeenth century, this trend becomes more distinct. For the purpose of weighting the indices for his *Nederlandsche prijsgeschiedenis*, Posthumus selected forty-four commodities representative of the selling and buying on the Amsterdam exchange.

[2] André Gunder Frank, *World Accumulation, 1492–1789* (New York, 1978); Immanuel Wallerstein, *The Modern World System*, vol. 1, *Capitalist Agriculture and the Origins of the European World-Economy in the Sixteenth Century*, and vol. 2, *Mercantilism and the Consolidation of the European World-Economy, 1600–1750* (New York, 1974 and 1980); Eric R. Wolf, *Europe and the People without History* (Berkeley, 1982).

[3] M. M. Postan, *Medieval Trade and Finance* (Cambridge, 1973), 92–102.

[4] Wilfrid Brulez, "The Balance of Trade of the Netherlands in the Middle of the Sixteenth Century," *Acta Historiae Neerlandicae* 4 (1970): 20–48.

Most of the commodities are familiar from medieval commerce: Grain, fish, wine, wool, textiles, potash, salt, iron, copper, lead, tin, flax, honey, hemp, and wax accounted for a little more than half. New, or rather of greater importance, are Mediterranean commodities and, most significantly, tobacco, sugar, and spices, which by the seventeenth century accounted for nearly 20 percent of the turnover on the Amsterdam exchange.[5]

The information on English foreign trade confirms these indications. In the 1660s wine, timber, wool, linen textiles, flax, and hemp accounted for 29 percent of the London imports; silk and silk textiles, thread, fruit, dyes, and oil accounted for 32 percent. None of these commodities were new compared with medieval trade, but the proportions reflect a more intensive exchange of commodities between the north and the south of Europe. The most interesting development, however, is the growing importance of Asian and American commodities, already accounting for more than 24 percent of London's imports in the 1660s. This trend strengthens over the next century. The calculations of Ralph Davis of English imports from 1752 to 1754 show a nearly unchanged proportion for the old commodities of the trade of northern Europe, with wine, timber, woolen and linen textiles, iron, flax, and hemp accounting for 31 percent of imports. But because the share of silk, silk textiles, fruit, dyes, and oil had declined to 17 percent, the imports from Asia and America now constituted 46 percent of English imports.[6]

The registers of the Sound Toll, in principle a register of all the commodities entering or leaving the Baltic, offer additional evidence on the slow change in the composition of north European long-distance trade. The dominance of the traditional commodities continues through the seventeenth century and most of the eighteenth century, grain, ashes, flax, hemp, iron, and timber traveling to the west, and salt, fish, woolen textiles, and wine to the east. Historians in general agree that the early decades of the seventeenth century marked a high point in the history of Baltic trade. Then, for over a hundred years, the traditional commodities show decline, stagnation, or very slow growth. The only significant exception is the mixed category "colonial commodities," which increased by about 500 percent from the middle of the seventeenth to the middle of the eighteenth century (Table 3.1).

---

[5] N. W. Posthumus, *Nederlandsche prijsgeschiedenis,* vol. 1 (Leiden, 1943), XCVII.

[6] Ralph Davis, "English Foreign Trade, 1660–1700," in W. E. Minchinton, ed., *The Growth of English Overseas Trade* (London, 1969), 96 f.; idem, "English Foreign Trade, 1700–1774," in ibid., 119. See also Table 3.22.

Table 3.1

Annual Average Transport of Selected Commodities

through The Sound

	Colonial commodities (1,000 pd*)	Salt (lasts)	Fish (lasts)
1631–40	1,440	25,002	10,965
1641–50	2,001	31,728	12,187
1651–60	1,495	26,583	6,106
1661–70	1,826	18,917	3,515
1671–80	2,796	25,799	3,927
1681–90	3,615	24,936	4,609
1691–1700	3,665	21,237	3,468
1701–10	3,052	18,632	1,499
1711–20	4,337	22,981	3,127
1721–30	7,553	26,176	3,680
1731–40	8,556	26,635	4,125
1741–50	10,296	35,290	4,793
1751–60	12,644	33,886	7,378

* The Dutch pound (pd) is 494.09 grams. The English pound (lb) is 453.55 grams.

Note: Based on Nina Bang and Knud Korst, ed., Tabeller over Skibs- og Varetransport gennem Oresund, part 1 (1497-1660), vol. 2 and part 2 (1661-1783), vol. 2:1-2 (Copenhagen 1922-45). The data are not complete, 2, 2 and 6 years are unrecorded in the three decades between 1631 and 1660. From 1661 to 1720 Swedish ships were not entered in the Sound Toll registers.

Only in the years 1635, 1646 and 1655 is it possible to analyze the category "colonial commodities", which also included

Table 3.1. (*Cont.*)

commodities from the south of Europe, but there can be no doubt that throughout the seventeenth and eighteenth centuries growth was most pronounced in the trade in overseas commodities, especially sugar, tobacco and dyes; cf. Hans C. Johansen, "How to pay for Baltic Products," in Wolfram Fischer, R. Marvin McInnis and Jürgen Scheider, eds., The Emergence of a World Economy (Wiesbaden, 1986). In the relatively peaceful years 1784-1792 the annual averages for the six most important colonial commodities were (in units of 1,000 pounds)

Sugar	19,101	Tobacco	3,581
Coffee	7,065	Logwood	3,312
Rice	4,585	Pepper	212

These indicators of the composition of north European trade from the Netherlands, England, and the Baltic have been presented to illuminate one important point. There was a remarkable continuity in the composition of north European trade from the medieval period to the middle of the eighteenth century. There were few innovations in production or revolutionary changes in consumer taste to stimulate the opening of new markets or new lines of production of major importance. Although the trade in commodities from southern Europe was increasing, the most conspicuous change was the introduction of the colonial commodities.

THE COLONIAL TRADES OF ENGLAND AND THE DUTCH REPUBLIC

The direct participation of the north European countries in the trade outside Europe before 1600 was insignificant. Silver from America and the Portuguese imports of sugar and spices reached the north through the Netherlands, particularly Antwerp, which by the middle of the sixteenth century had become the central market for colonial commodities in northern Europe.[7]

The revolt in the Netherlands and the fall of Antwerp disrupted the normal channels of trade but did not stop the exchange of commodi-

---

[7] Brulez, "The Balance of Trade of the Netherlands"; Herman van der Wee, *The Growth of the Antwerp Market and the European Economy (Fourteenth–Sixteenth Centuries)* (Louvain, 1963), 3 vols., 1:127–30, 15–6.

ties. In spite of the war, colonial commodities continued to be carried to northern Europe by Dutch ships in the last decades of the sixteenth century, while English privateers in their own efficient manner contributed to the north European supply of colonial commodities, particularly sugar.[8] Antwerp also imported considerable amounts of sugar through Portuguese merchants until the 1620s.[9]

Within a few decades after 1600, however, the Dutch and the English broke the Iberian monopolies and entered directly into trade relations with Asia and into trade and colonization in America. This was not a mere substitution of one set of entrepreneurs for another but was also a shift in business methods that lowered the economic costs and extended the market for exotic goods in Europe.

In what follows, the quantitative aspects of the north European trade with Asia and America will be reviewed. The quantitative evidence is limited and offers difficult problems of interpretation, especially as far as the early period is concerned. The overall task is facilitated, however, by the fact that only a few commodities composed the bulk of the colonial imports; pepper, spices, textiles, tea, and coffee dominated the Asian trade, and sugar and tobacco, the American.

To facilitate comparisons, weights and values in this paper have in several instances been converted into kilograms and pesos. The weights are no great problem; standard conversions of 454 grams for the English pound (lb) and 494 grams for the Dutch pound (pd) have been used. Currency conversions are more complicated. I have used as a standard the Spanish pre-1728 peso (piece of eight rials, piaster) of 25.56 grams of fine silver, which nearly equals the rix-dollar of 25.98 grams.[10] Conversions from pounds (£) have been made on the assumption that the rate of exchange was stable at the ratio of 4.3:1. Conversions from Dutch guilders (fl.) have been made on the basis of the silver equivalents recorded by Posthumus.[11]

In the study of short-term trends such conversions are obviously worse than useless, because of the fluctuations of the rates of exchange. For the present purpose, however, where long periods of

[8] J. R. Bruijn, "De vaart in Europa," in *Maritime geschiednis der Nederlanden,* vol. 2 (Bussum, 1977), 232–5; K. R. Andrews, *Trade, Plunder, and Settlement* (Cambridge, 1984), 250.

[9] Hans Pohl, "Die Zuckereinfuhr nach Antwerpen durch portugesische Kaufleute während des 80 jährigen Krieges," *Jahrbuch für Geschichte von Staat Wirtschaft und Gesellschaft Lateinamerikas* 4 (1967): 356–7.

[10] Artur Attman, *American Bullion in the European World Trade, 1600–1800* (Göteborg, 1986), 101.

[11] Posthumus, *Nederlandsche prijsgeschiedenis,* CXIII: 1601–10, 11.02 grams; 1611–20, 10.73; 1621–60, 10.28; 1661–80, 9.74; 1681–1760, 9.61.

time and long distances are concerned, the advantage of being able to compare weights and values immediately outweighs, in my opinion, the distortions caused by the conversions.

Trade with Asia

Historians have one good reason to defend the monopolies in the early modern trade between Europe and Asia – the companies left wonderful archives. We have also good reason to be grateful to the colleagues who have made the statistical evidence preserved in the vast archives accessible. With very few exceptions the companies covered the total interchange of commodities between northern Europe and Asia before the middle of the eighteenth entury; as a rule, therefore, we are much better informed about Asian trade than about trade across the Atlantic, where most of the evidence must be drawn from customs records and official trade statistics.

Invoice values. The series of invoice values is one of the most complete series, preserved from the Dutch East India Company (VOC) from the 1620s and from the English East India Company (EIC) from 1664. In general the invoice values reflect a f.o.b. price, though practice might vary regarding packing and transport to the port. This is only of minor importance, but other peculiarities have a more distorting influence on the series of invoice values as indicators of economic activity.

First, commodities obtained under monopolistic conditions, typically the fine spices (cloves, nutmeg, mace, and cinnamon), were invoiced at an artificially low buying price that did not include the costs of obtaining and defending the monopoly. Such costs were entered as part of the general costs of the factory or the general costs of the establishment in the Indies.[12]

Second, the VOC used different rates of exchange in the East and in the Netherlands, the Spanish peso being accounted as 60 st. (3 fl.) in Batavia ("light" money) but as 48 st. (2.4 fl.) in the Netherlands,

---

[12] In the accounts of the VOC the factories in Batavia, Ternate, Amboina, Banda, and, later, Macassar and Ceylon always showed an annual loss. See G. C. Klerk de Reus, *Geschichtlicher Überblick der Niederländisch-Ostindischen Compagnie*, Verhandelingen van het Bataviaasch Genootschap van Kunsten en Wetenschappen, vol. 47 (1894), Appendix X. The costs of monopoly included not only military expenses but also in some cases the destruction of surplus stocks – for instance, 4.5 million pounds of cloves and 1.5 million pounds of nutmeg in 1718–19 (Kristof Glamann, *Dutch Asiatic Trade, 1620–1740* [Copenhagen, 1958], 109).

beginning in the 1650s.[13] This irregularity, which reflected the assumed profit from bringing silver coin to Asia, influenced the bookkeeping of the company, but not in a simple manner. It is to be assumed that accounts in the East were kept partly in light money, partly in Dutch money, but it is hardly possible to determine the exact proportions.[14] Here the figures have been reproduced without any regard to the differing rates of exchange. In all probability, therefore, the invoice figures after the middle of the seventeenth century are to an increasing degree on the high side. This tendency is to some extent counterbalanced by the artificial invoice value of the spices.

These reservations hardly change the impression of the general development of the company trade to Asia that can be gained from Table 3.2. We have no complete figures for the early part of the seventeenth century, but we know that the English trade to the Indies was on a much smaller scale than that of the Dutch before 1660, particularly in the decades 1620–50. The number of outward bound ships to Asia from England and the Netherlands indicates the relative strength of the two nations:[15]

	Dutch	*English*
1601–10	59	20
1611–20	117	65
1621–30	148	53
1631–40	151	52
1641–50	162	64
1651–60	226	97

In the 1630s the north European trade with Asia lost its impetus, but beginning in the middle of the century growth was considerable, the invoice figures reaching a peak in the 1680s that was not attained again until 1711–20. Probably this decline is a result of the wars, as indicated by comparing the annual invoice values from 1681 to 1717 according to years of war and years of peace (Table 3.3).

Growth was resumed in the long period of peace in the first half of the eighteenth century, and only the decade 1731–40 saw a decline in Dutch trade and near stagnation in the English trade. Probably this

[13] Glamann, *Dutch Asiatic Trade*, 54ff.; J. P. de Korte, *De jaarlijkse financiële verantwoording in de VOC* (Leiden, 1984), 32–3, 39.

[14] J. J. Steur, *Herstel of Ondergang: De voorstellen tot redres van de VOC* (Utrecht, 1984), 302, n. 24, assumes that the Indian accounts before 1664 were kept in Dutch money, and from 1664 to 1773, half in Dutch money and half in light money.

[15] N. Steensgaard, "European Shipping to Asia, 1497–1700," *Scandinavian Economic History Review* 18 (1970): 9, table 3. See also K. N. Chaudhuri, *The English East India Company: The Study of an Early Joint Stock Company, 1600–1640* (London, 1965).

Table 3.2

Annual Average Imports from Asia

(Invoice Values in Thousands of Pesos)

	VOC	EIC	Both companies
1621-30	402.8		
1631-40	870.5		
1641-50	954.5		
1651-60	1,017.2		
1661-70	980.8	437.2	1,418.0
1671-80	1,299.2	1,215.8	2,515.0
1681-90	1,669.8	1,634.7	3,304.5
1691-1700	1,592.9	744.2	2,337.2
1701-10	2,015.8	1,161.4	3,197.1
1710-20	2,370.0	2,056.7	4,426.7
1721-30	3,176.8	2,723.2	5,900.0
1731-40	2,506.6	2,820.3	5,326.9
1741-50	2,418.7	3,345.0	5,763.7
1751-60	3,163.9	3,348.2	6,512.1

Sources: For the VOC see F. S. Gaastra, "De verenigde Oost-Indische Compagnie in de zeventiende en achttiende eeuw: De groei van een bedrijf," Bijdragen en medelingen betreffende de geschiedenis der Nederlanden 91 (1976): table III, 254. For the EIC see K. N. Chaudhuri, The Trading World of Asia and the English East India Company, 1660-1760 (Cambridge, 1978), table C.2, 508-10 (covering 1664-1760). Annual values for the VOC are in G. C. Klerk de Reus, Geschichtlicher Überblick der Niederländisch-Ostindischen Compagnie (1894), appendix V.

decade was characterized not so much by a general European recession in the colonial trade as by the growing competition from new entrepreneurs, particularly the French. After this recession, growth was resumed, and by the middle of the eighteenth century the in-

Table 3.3

Annual Average Invoice Values

according to Conditions of War and Peace

(in Millions of Pesos)

	EIC	VOC	Both companies
1681–87	2.1	1.9	4.0
1688–97	0.4	1.4	1.8
1698–1703	1.7	2.2	3.9
1704–09	0.8	1.9	2.7
1710–17	1.7	2.3	4.0

Sources: Kristof Glamann, <u>Dutch Asiatic Trade, 1620–1740</u> (Copenhagen, 1958); J. P. de Korte, <u>De Jaarlijkse financiële verantwoording in de VOC</u> (Leiden, 1984).

voice values for the imports of the two companies were at least four times what they had been a century before.

Sales values. Invoice values, in principle covering only the direct purchase of commodities in Asia, represent only a minor part of total company turnover. Sales values – that is, the receipts from company sales in Europe – are a more comprehensive measure of company activities. Unfortunately the English series is known only for the period 1711–45, whereas the corresponding Dutch series is known in its full extent from 1641 onward. For the period before 1711 the English series can, however, be reconstructed with some confidence on the basis of the series of sales values for the most important commodities published by Chaudhuri (Table 3.4).

In 1661–70, the first decade for which a reconstruction of the sales values may be attempted, the total European sales of the two companies amounted to nearly 5 million pesos; in the next decade sales were more than 6 million. The recession of the war years appears less

Table 3.4

Annual Average Imports from Asia

(Sales Values in Thousands of Pesos)

	VOC	EIC	Both Companies
1641-50	3,184.0		
1651-60	3,387.2		
1661-70	3,515.1	1,184.9	4,700.0
1671-80	3,476.8	2,913.4	6,490.2
1681-90	3,926.1	3,395.0	7,381.1
1691-1700	4,786.7	2,610.9	7,397.6
1701-10	5,242.7	3,173.9	8,416.6
1711-20	6,152.3	5,661.1	11,813.4
1721-30	6,973.6	7,090.8	14,064.4
1731-40	6,277.7	5,526.5	11,804.2
1741-50	6,003.1	7,555.1	13,558.2
1751-60	7,064.1		

Sources: For the VOC see de Korte, *De jaarlijkse Financiële Verantwoording*, 45, table 12. For the EIC see, for the period 1711-45, Chaudhuri, *Trading World of Asia*, 438, table A.24, "sales receipts." For the period 1661-1710 total sales of the eight most important commodities have been calculated on the basis of Chaudhuri's tables C.8-C.10, C.14, C.15, C.18, C.19 and C.24. They have been weighted as in invoice values, and the total has been inflated in accordance with this weight to account for "other commodities." Records are incomplete for the decades 1661-70 and 1701-10.

pronounced in this series; apparently the companies could compensate for a fall in imports by raising prices in Europe and perhaps also by reducing their stocks of Asian commodities. The decade 1731–40, on the other hand, shows a decline in sales values as well as in invoice values, confirming the assumption that this was a period of marked competition in the European–Asian trade. During the three decades 1721–50 the total receipts of the two companies appear to have stagnated at 13.5–14 million pesos. The overall increase in sales values since the middle of the seventeenth century is less impressive than the one observed for the invoice values. Over the long term, gross profits in the Asia trade declined.

If the relative positions of the two companies are compared, we find that the VOC had great difficulty in defending its leading position after the reconstruction of the EIC in 1657. During the long period 1640–90, growth in the VOC was modest, in sales values from 3.2 to 3.9 million pesos, while the EIC went from practically nil to 3.4 million. In the following decades the trade of the VOC increased at a faster rate, but the VOC did not maintain its lead in every decade before 1750.

When Tables 3.2 and 3.4 are compared, an impression of the gross profits in the Asia trade is obtained. A precise picture is not possible, as the annual sales never exactly corresponded to the annual imports. Imports might be held back or accumulated stocks might be sold out in response to the demand conditions. Nevertheless, some conclusions may be drawn from the comparison of the crude figures. There are obvious parallels between the gross profits of the two companies. Profits declined in the period of fast growth up until the 1680s. They rose during the decades of war but fell off again beginning in the 1720s. The companies were under attack as national monopolies, but they had to compete in an international market. The gross profits of 100–250 percent should not be interpreted as evidence of unusual profitability and the monopoly status of the companies. Over the long term, profits were reduced and it was vital for the companies to adjust to competition and innovations. The EIC successfully cut its costs and selected the most profitable branches of trade after its reconstruction, while the VOC slowly eroded its own reserves in the East, though still paying out dividends, which preserved its image as a profitable company far into the eighteenth century.[16]

Composition of the imports from Asia. Over the long term, gross profits declined, although a difference of 100 percent between the buying and the selling price was a minimum or even below a minimum indicating when a commodity profitably might be brought from Asia to Europe. Only a few items of trade with a mass demand in Europe

---

[16] F. S. Gaastra, "The Shifting Balance of Trade of the Dutch East India Company," in Leonard Blussé and Femme Gaastra, eds., *Companies and Trade* (Leiden, 1981), 62–4; de Korte, *De jaarlijkse financiële verantwoording*, 71–8.

Table 3.5

Distribution of Main Imports from Asia

(Invoice Values in Percentage)

VOC

	1619-21	1648-50	1668-70	1698-1700	1738-40
Spices	17.55	17.85	12.05	11.70	6.1
Pepper	56.45	50.34	30.53	11.23	8.1
Sugar	–	6.39	4.24	0.24	3.7
Tea and Coffee	–	–	–	4.24	32.2
Drugs and Dyes	9.84	8.52	5.84	8.29	2.8
Saltpeter	–	2.07	5.08	3.92	2.6
Metals	0.10	0.50	5.74	5.26	1.1
Textiles and silk	16.06	14.16	36.46	54.73	41.1
Others	–	0.17	0.06	0.39	2.3
Total	100.00	100.00	100.00	100.00	100.0

EIC

	1664-70	1696-1705	1731-40
Pepper	20.01	6.14	4.30
Tea	0.02	1.55	9.26
Coffee	0.63	1.24	5.35
Indigo	3.98	1.87	–
Saltpeter	5.07	2.24	2.43
Textiles	62.59	64.53	65.35
Silk	0.48	13.56	11.06
Others	7.22	8.87	2.25
Total	100.00	100.00	100.00

Sources: For the VOC 1619-1700 see Glamann, Dutch Asiatic Trade, 13, table II; For 1738-40 J. R. Bruijn, F. S. Gaastra and I. Schöffer, eds., Dutch-Asiatic Shipping in the 17th and 18th centuries, vol. 1 (The Hague, 1987), 192, table 41. The figures for the EIC are calculated on the basis of Chaudhuri, Trading World of Asia, tables C.8 – C.10, C.14, C.15, C.18, C.19, and C.25.

Table 3.6

Distribution of Main Imports from Asia,

(Sales Values in Percentages)

	VOC					
	1648-50	1668-70	1698-1700	1738-40	1745-50
Spices	26.36	28.43	24.78	23.63	23.18
Pepper	32.89	28.99	13.31	11.43	10.18
Sugar	8.80	2.02	0.20	3.00	0.25
Tea and coffee	-	0.03	4.10	24.92	28.32
Drugs and dyes	7.35	5.86	6.57	2.70	1.34
Saltpeter	4.30	7.63	4.00	3.54	4.58
Metals	0.70	2.99	2.94	0.58	0.21
Textiles and silk	17.54	23.77	43.45	28.27	29.04
Others	2.06	0.28	0.65	1.93	2.90
Total	100.00	100.00	100.00	100.00	100.00

	EIC	
	1664–70	1691–1700
Pepper	19.46	10.48
Tea and coffee	0.63	3.22
Drugs and dyes	4.40	1.95
Saltpeter	9.23	4.61
Textiles and silk	57.84	74.89
Others	(8.44)	(4.85)
Total	100.00	100.00

Source: For the VOC see Glamann, Dutch Asiatic Trade, 14, table II; J. J. Steur, Herstel of Ondergang, (Utrecht, 1984), appendix VIIIa (1745–50). The figures for the EIC are calculated on the basis of Chaudhuri, Trading World of Asia, tables C.8– C.10, C.14, C.15, C.18, C.19, and C.2

could support such high costs. Typically these were commodities that could only be produced economically under tropical conditions. A number, however, were soon transferred to the Western Hemisphere: indigo, sugar, ginger, and later coffee. Pepper and fine spices remained an Asian specialty throughout our period, and so did the most interesting item, the cotton textiles from India, the economic production of which became possible in Europe only after a major technological revolution.

A large number of different commodities were imported from Asia to Europe, but the trade was dominated by a few items. Pepper, spices, textiles, and silk were never less than three-fourths of total imports before 1740. Toward the very end of our period tea and coffee must be included among the most prominent imports (Tables 3.5 and 3.6). There were, however, changes in the relative importance of the dominant imports over time. Such changes cannot be explained by innovations in production; they must be understood against the background of the preferences of the European consumers and the ability of the companies to discover such preferences and use them to their advantage. Most importantly, the market for some commodities approached a point of saturation, while at the same time other commodities found a market with an apparently indefinite capacity to expand.

Pepper. Before the discovery of the sea route to Asia, pepper was by far the most important single item in the European–Asian trade. In the sixteenth century pepper still took up the larger part of the cargo space in the returning Portuguese carracks – in the known examples, 65–89 percent.[17] Toward the end of the sixteenth century pepper still reached Europe, not only on the Portuguese ships but also along the caravan routes through the Levant and Venice. With the establishment of the two north European East India companies, pepper became cheaper in Europe, and the route overland could no longer compete economically. At the same time pepper consumption in Europe presumably rose, particularly in the north. Shortly after 1600 European pepper consumption may be estimated at 2,250,000 kg, at a wholesale value of 1,450,000 pesos.[18]

During the first half of the seventeenth century, pepper remained the most important single import to Europe from Asia. The long-term

---

[17] N. Steensgaard, "The Return Cargoes of the Carreira in the Sixteenth and Early Seventeenth Century," in Teotonio R. de Souza, ed., *Indo-Portuguese History: Old Issues, New Questions* (New Delhi, 1985), 22, table 2.3.

[18] N. Steensgaard, *The Asian Trade Revolution of the Seventeenth Century* (Chicago, 1974), 151–4; 168, Table 12.

price trend of pepper, however, was declining. It may be followed in a fairly continuous series from the Amsterdam exchange. From an index of 145.5 (basis period 1721–45) early in the seventeenth century, prices fell to an index of 57.3 in 1680–4. After this low point, prices were stabilized at a higher level (c. 65–87) until 1730–4, when a new rise in pepper prices began.[19]

Behind this long-term development we find a bitter struggle between the companies, which at times led to an oversupply of the European market. In the period 1620–38 the average Dutch import of pepper can be estimated at 2,500,000 pd a year. In the same period the average English import was a little more than 1,100,000 lb a year.[20] The average annual imports of both companies would be 1,750,000 kg – a figure that accords well with the estimate of total European consumption referred to earlier, the margin being filled by Portuguese imports.

Throughout the 1640s and 1650s the English company imports were irregular and of less importance than in former decades, whereas the average annual Dutch import in the period 1641–56 was 4,600,000 pd, or about 2,250,000 kg. In 1664 the Dutch import reached 6,200,000 pd (more than 3,000,000 kg), and in 1670 9,200,000 pd (more than 4,500,000 kg).[21] By this time, however, the English were back as serious rivals in the pepper trade, the company importing 1,500,000 lb annually in the late 1660s and 4,000,000 lb annually in the 1670s.[22] The repercussions of this fight were felt from Amsterdam and Bengal, where prices in the years around 1680 reached the lowest level of the century,[23] to Java, where Bantam, the chief supplier of pepper to the competitors of the Dutch, became a possession of the VOC in 1682.

The English were worried. In 1687 the board of the EIC wrote that "if ever they [the Dutch] come to be Masters of that Commodity [pepper] as they are already of nutmegs, mace, cloves and cinnamon, the sole Profit of that one Commodity, Pepper being of generall use, will be more to them than all the rest and in all probability sufficient to defray the constant charge of a great Navy in Europe."[24] But their worry was unfounded, partly because it proved impossible to mo-

---

[19] Posthumus, *Nederlandsche prijsgeschiedenis*, 174–6.
[20] Glamann, *Dutch Asiatic Trade*, 78; Chaudhuri, *English East India Company*, 148, table V.
[21] Glamann, *Dutch Asiatic Trade*, 80, 82–3.
[22] K. N. Chaudhuri, *The Trading World of Asia and the English East India Company, 1660–1760* (Cambridge, 1978), 529–30, table C. 14.
[23] Posthumus, *Nederlandsche prijsgeschiedenis*, 174–6; Om Prakash, *The Dutch East India Company and the Economy of Bengal, 1630–1720* (Princeton, N.J., 1985), 160.
[24] Chaudhuri, *Trading World of Asia*, 317.

nopolize pepper, because the English soon found alternative supplies, and partly, and more importantly, because the market was becoming saturated with pepper. The dumping prices of the 1670s and
1680s did not lead to a much larger demand.

In 1688 the board of the VOC, the Heren XVII, estimated the annual Dutch and English company requirements for pepper at 7,200,000
pd (about 3,550,000 kg).[25] For the period 1715–32 the total import of
the two companies is known (annual averages):[26]

EIC	1,510,000 lb	680,000 kg
VOC	5,510,000 pd	2,720,000 kg
		3,400,000 kg

In the period 1740–5 the total import of the two companies was still
at nearly the same level. The average annual English import was
1,628,000 kg.[27] We know the value but not the volume of Dutch pepper imports in the same years. Assuming the same prices in England
and Amsterdam, the volume of the Dutch import would be about
1,900,000 kg, making the total annual import of the two companies
about 3,500,000 kg.[28]

Without knowledge of the volume of pepper reaching Europe
through other channels, the calculation must remain incomplete.
Nevertheless, it is striking that the company import of what used to
be the bulk of the import from Asia to Europe hardly doubled over
more than a century. Pepper remained an important and profitable
commodity, but it could not support an expansion of the Asia trade;
the market had reached a point of saturation already in the seventeenth century.

The fine spices. Taken together, the fine spices cloves, nutmeg, and
mace constituted the second most important European import from
Asia in the sixteenth century; the demand for cinnamon was still rather
slight. The Portuguese had gained a foothold in the spice-producing
islands in the East, but not a monopoly. The Dutch strategy in the
Moluccas and later in cinnamon-producing Ceylon soon changed from
ousting the Portuguese to establishing a complete world monopoly.
The English attempts to acquire a share in the monopoly came to an
end shortly after 1620, less because of the so-called massacre of Am-

[25] Glamann, *Dutch Asiatic Trade*, 74.
[26] Chaudhuri, *Trading World of Asia*, 529–30, table C.14; Glamann, *Dutch Asiatic Trade*, 297, table XIV.
[27] Chaudhuri, *Trading World of Asia*, table C.14.
[28] Steur, *Herstel of Ondergang*, appendix VIIIb.

boina than as a result of the strained liquidity of the EIC. The English company could not afford the outlays required to achieve and defend its share of the monopoly.

The area where cloves, nutmeg, and mace were produced was well defined but not easily controlled. The Dutch could prevent the large ships of their European competitors from visiting the Spice Islands, even though the Spaniards from the Philippines retained a foothold in the Moluccas until 1663, but they found it more difficult to control the traffic of the numerous small Southeast Asian ships, which used to trade with textiles and rice to the specialized markets of the Spice Islands. The people of the Spice Islands were among the first victims of specialization for the world market. The raids against rival traders and the extirpation of unauthorized spice trees by the VOC not only made life dangerous for their rivals but also made life miserable for the local population. When the Spaniards finally left their stronghold in the Moluccas in 1663 and Macassar acknowledged Dutch suzerainty in 1669, the Dutch company had acquired one of the most effective monopolies in history.

The price paid by the local population was evident, but there was also a price to be paid by the VOC. Throughout the period 1648/50 to 1778/80 the sales revenue from spices constituted 24–28 percent of the total sales revenue of the company in Europe, but the spice factories consistently showed a loss in the balance sheets of Batavia.[29]

It has been a matter of debate whether the monopoly was worth the price. The spices remained an important part of the business of the VOC, perhaps most importantly in the trade within Asia, but in the trade to Europe it was a trade with small potential for growth. The estimates of the European demand for spices in the early seventeenth century and the actual imports in the middle of the seventeenth and middle of the eighteenth centuries indicate a decline rather than a growth in European spice consumption (Table 3.7).

The difference between the estimate of total European consumption and actual sales in the middle of the seventeenth century may be explained by the fact that the monopoly was not yet perfect – some spices still reached Europe through other channels. In the following decades the monopoly was perfected, and the company in periods deliberately kept the European market undersupplied in order to raise prices. When the European price on cloves was stabilized in 1677 at 3.75 fl. a pound, demand had declined; the average annual sales in the period 1677–1700 were 264,000 pd. Nutmeg went through a longer

---

[29] See n. 12.

Table 3.7

Estimates of Demand and Actual Sales of Fine Spices in Europe--
VOC ca. 1620, 1655 and 1740-50.

<u>ca. 1620</u>

	Estimate					
Cloves	450-500,000 pd.					
Nutmeg	400,000 pd..					
Mace	80,000 pd.					
Total	930-980,000 pd.					

<u>ca. 1655</u>

	Estimate			Sales		
Cloves	400-425,000 pd.	360,000 pd.		ca.1,260,000 fl.		
Nutmeg	340-350,000 pd.	270,000 pd.		ca. 729,000 fl.		
Mace	120,000 pd.	100,000 pd.		ca. 600,000 fl.		
Total	860-895,000 pd	730,000 pd.		2,589,000 fl.		

<u>1740-50</u>

			Sales		
Cloves	ca. 300,000 pd.		1,189,000 fl.		
Nutmeg	ca. 866,000 pd.		866,000 fl.		
Mace	ca. 523,000 pd.		523,000 fl.		
Cinnamon	ca. 450,000 pd.		1,270,000 fl.		
Total	ca.2,139,000 pd.		3,848,000 fl.		

Source: For the 1620 and the 1655 estimates and sales see
Glamann, <u>Dutch-Asiatic Trade</u>, 93, 97-98; for 1740-50 see Steur,
<u>Herstel of Ondergang</u>, appendix VIIIb. The value of sales ca. 1655
and the volume of sales 1740-50 are calculated on the basis of
price data from N. W. Posthumus, <u>Nederlandsche Prijsgeschiedenis</u>
(Leiden, 1943).

period of receding prices and rationing of supplies to Europe before
the price was stabilized in 1703 at the same level as the price of cloves:
3.75 fl. a pound.[30]

The sales value of the three fine spices remained nearly the same

[30] Glamann, *Dutch Asiatic Trade,* 101–3.

from the middle of the seventeenth to the middle of the eighteenth century, although the quantities had become smaller. The increase in the total revenue from fine spices was gained only by the growing popularity of a fourth, cinnamon from Ceylon, which by 1740–50 had become the most prominent of the fine spices imported by the company, cinnamon alone accounting for 8 percent of the total sales revenue in Europe.

Possibly the monopoly policy of the VOC was self-defeating in that the very high profits – 300–460 percent – may have prevented an increase in European spice consumption. On the other hand, the saturation of the European pepper market in the period of low prices seems to indicate that the elasticity of demand for this kind of commodity was low. Although the high prices on fine spices undoubtedly had a negative effect on European spice consumption, it is by no means sure that a low price policy would have increased the turnover in terms of value.

Although this is a speculative argument, there can hardly be any doubt that the spice monopoly diminished the ability of the VOC to maneuver in a changing world. Large investments were sunk into the eastern archipelago, and the whole structure of the company trade in Asia as well as in Europe was tied to a constant flow of spices. It was a safe source of income but had little potential for development, whereas the European rivals, first the EIC, promoted a trade in new commodities with a much larger potential market: textiles, tea, and coffee.

Textiles. A wide variety of textiles came to be imported from Asia by the East India companies, but by far the most important of these were the many kinds of Indian cotton goods. The Indian cotton fabrics were important in Asian trade already before the arrival of the Portuguese. They were perhaps the most important manufactured commodity in world trade at the time of the discoveries. Their penetration of the European market came late, however. Indian textiles were of practically no account in the European trade with the Levant, and only small quantities were brought to Europe on the Portuguese carracks in the sixteenth century.[31] When in 1623 the board of the EIC had decided to venture into this new line of business, they were well aware of its novelty: "calicoes are a commodity whereof the use is not generally known, the vent must be forced and trial made into all ports."[32]

From the moment the companies took up trade in Asia, the impor-

---

[31] Steensgaard, "Return Cargoes," 22, table 2.3.
[32] Chaudhuri, *Trading World of Asia*, 195.

tance of Indian textiles was forced upon their attention. Silver was the main European export to Asia; it might be invested in spices in Southeast Asia, but obviously it was far more advantageous to invest the silver in Indian textiles and barter for pepper or spices or sell the textiles for cash in the islands of Southeast Asia. For the VOC this became the determinant for its trade in Indian textiles, while the EIC, because of its weaker position in Southeast Asia and its need for "quick returns," made the first bold attempts to market the Indian calicoes in Europe.

In 1619–21 textiles, silk, and cotton accounted for 16.06 percent of the invoice value of the commodities imported into Europe by the VOC, but calicoes were only a minor item, hardly more than 12,000 pieces a year. In 1642 the company order for the European market was at a higher level, about 60,000 pieces a year at an invoice value of about 150,000 fl. Probably this order was more than the actual import in 1648–50, when silk and textiles accounted for only about 10 percent of the total invoice value.[33] This, however, did not mean that the VOC was unfamiliar with the trade in Indian cottons. In the six seasons between 1631 and 1658 from which figures have been preserved, the Dutch export of calicoes from Surat averaged 277,000 pieces at a value of 489,000 fl., but this export was primarily directed toward Asian destinations.[34] Similarly, on the Coromandel Coast only a third of the Dutch exports in 1652, including indigo, were bought for the Dutch market; two-thirds were destined for Southeast Asia.[35]

Meanwhile the EIC had made the first serious attempt to introduce the Indian textiles into Europe with imports reaching a maximum of 221,500 pieces in 1625.[36] The experiment seems to have been moderately successful, but the internal problems of the company and particularly the hunger years in Gujarat after 1630 stopped further development. The only known figure from the following years (the import of 66,000 pieces in 1639) indicates that the trade was continued but at a lower level.[37]

---

[33] Glamann, *Dutch Asiatic Trade*, 13, 134, 136, 137.

[34] H. W. van Santen, "De verenigde Oost-Indische Compagnie in Gujarat en Hindustan, 1620–1660" (diss., University of Leiden, 1982), table I, 32–3.

[35] Tapan Raychaudhuri, *Jan Company in Coromandel, 1605–1690* (The Hague, 1962), 134, n. 251.

[36] Chaudhuri, *English East India Company*, 193.

[37] Ibid. In 1638 the board of directors wrote to the factors in Surat that "calicoes in general . . . were in times past a main support of that Indian trade, and were here in good use and well requested and been sold to some profit while their making was answerable to their first cost; but since they have declined in goodness from their former manufacture and increased so much in their prices, they are now become here at a stand in their use, and other country's clothing being better made and

Unfortunately the information concerning this early experiment in Indian textiles on the European market is scant. In all probability the imports mainly consisted of cheap, plain goods, which had to compete with linen on the English market, but there was also some re-export; in 1627 33,500 pieces were re-exported, mostly to the Mediterranean.[38]

The lack of information also makes it impossible to follow the development of the English trade in cottons during the "dark decades" of 1640–60. From the VOC, however, we can follow the sales of the Amsterdam chamber in a series that extends from 1650 to 1734 (Table 3.8). Assuming that the sales of Amsterdam made up the conventional 50 percent of the total company sales, total sales were rather stable at 85,000–90,000 pieces a year at a sales value of 400,000–500,000 pesos until 1670.

So it was the reconstructed EIC that in the 1660s made the real breakthrough for the Indian textiles on the European market, importing on an average 199,000 pieces a year during the last seven years of the decade, 578,000 pieces annually during the 1670s, and 707,000 during the 1680s. The 1680s were the culmination and end of the first boom in Indian textiles. Only in the 1720s did the English imports and the combined imports of the two companies reach the same levels as far as quantities are concerned, whereas the income from sales was increasing by the first decade of the century, reaching a total value of more than 6 million pesos in the 1720s.

The spectacular success of the introduction of Indian cotton textiles on the European market in the last decades of the seventeenth century is one of the most remarkable examples of innovation in preindustrial long-distance trade. Although it has caught the attention of historians as well as contemporaries, the mechanisms behind this unusual achievement are still imperfectly understood. On the supply side, the rising European demand caused some strain, but apparently not more than the Indian structures of production could easily absorb. The Indian weavers were able to deliver without any fundamental changes in technique or organization. On the demand side, the cotton textiles in all their variety had a number of qualities that appealed to the European customers and that could not be imitated in Europe before the introduction of a completely new technology in textile manufacturing in the last decades of the eighteenth century.

cheaper succeeded in calicoes' room." Quoted in K. N. Chaudhuri, "Some Reflections of the World Trade of the Seventeenth and Eighteenth Century: A Reply," *Journal of European Economic History* 7 (1978): 225–6.
[38] Steensgaard, *Asian Trade Revolution*, 174, table 14.

Niels Steensgaard

Table 3.8

Estimated EIC and VOC Average Textile Imports

(in Pieces and Thousands of Pesos)

	VOC		EIC		Both companies	
	Pieces	Sales	Pieces	Sales	Pieces	Sales
1651–60	89,800	465.7				
1661–70	87,800	417.1	199,000	686.9	286,800	1104.0
1671–80	137,200	500.1	578,000	1993.3	715,200	2493.4
1681–90	347,600	995.7	707,000	2617.5	1,054,600	3613.2
1691–1700	277,600	1027.0	296,000	1845.2	573,600	2872.2
1701–10	349,800	1445.7	277,000	2674.8	626,800	4120.5
1711–20	409,600	1668.7	552,000	3493.0	961,600	5161.7
1721–30	489,800	1732.7	783,000	4466.4	1,272,800	6199.1
1731–40	250,000	650.9	765,000	4237.2	1,015,000	4888.1
1741–50			772,000	5005.2		
1751–60			527,000	4251.1		

Sources: For the VOC see Glamann, Dutch Asiatic Trade, 143, table 26, recording sales of cotton at Kamer Amsterdam. To arrive at the total sales, the sales of Amsterdam have been doubled. The figures for the EIC include Chinese silk piece goods, which, however, constituted more than 2 percent of total imports only in twelve of the years. For 1664–1704 see Chaudhuri, Trading World of Asia, table C.24. The data for the decades 1661–70 and 1701–10 are incomplete. The figures for the decades 1711–60 are calculated on the basis of Chaudhuri, Trading World of Asia, 302, tables A.13 and C.24.

Cottons were relatively cheap and were washable and comfortable and therefore not only served as substitutes for linen and woolen textiles but also catered to new tastes. Another asset was that various qualities of fabric were available. The most expensive printed or patterned fabrics appealed to a fashionable and lavish public in the European capitals, and the cheapest qualities were in demand for the slaves in the West Indian plantations.[39]

Of course the protectionists in Europe were worried: "As ill weeds grow apace, so these manufactured goods from India met with such a kind reception that *from the greatest gallants to the meanest Cook Maids,* nothing was thought so fit to adorn their persons as the Fabrick from India," wrote an English pamphleteer.[40] In England the use of "all calicoes painted, dyed, printed or stained in the East Indies" was prohibited in 1700.[41] In France the import, production, and use of painted calicoes were banned in 1686, a prohibition that reputedly cost the lives of 16,000 persons before it was retracted in 1759.[42] As similar restrictions were introduced in several European countries, one may indeed wonder how the trade could continue and even to expand, if at a slower rate, in the eighteenth century, but the explanation is probably to be found in the wide range of qualities available in India and to the simple fact that premodern governments always found it difficult to ensure that laws were complied with.

In the Netherlands the textile producers protested against the competition from the manufactured goods as they seem to have done all over Europe, but the Republic did not interfere. This should have given the VOC an advantage, at least in the Dutch market, but it does not seem to have been the case, because the EIC remained by far the largest importer of cotton textiles, the VOC following far behind (Table 3.8). A partial explanation can be found in the fact that the EIC enjoyed a favored position in Bengal even before Plassey, but probably the most important difference was in the commercial structure of the two companies. The decision-making process in the EIC was more decentralized, and it was easier for the English to maneuver in the complicated and volatile textile market. The ability of the English to compete in an open market is documented by the high figures for re-export, particularly to northwestern Europe (Table 3.9).

The fact that the value of the re-exports regularly exceeded the value of the imports is not as surprising as it may appear; it reflects the principles on which the official English trade statistics were based. "Prices on importation were supposed to represent 'first cost' in the country of origin. Freight, insurance, warehousing in this country, the costs of handling and the services rendered by merchants justify

---

[39] Chaudhuri, *Trading World of Asia,* 277–82.
[40] Pollexfen in 1681, quoted in Prakash, *Dutch East India Company,* 201.
[41] Chaudhuri, *Trading World of Asia,* 294.
[42] Eli F. Heckscher, *Mercantilism,* rev. (2d) ed. (New York, 1955), 1:173.

Table 3.9

English Imports and Re-exports of Calicoes,

Annual Averages, Official Valuation

(Thousands of Pounds)

	Imports	Re-exports	Re-exports, to northwestern Europe
1699-1701	363	340	239 (70%)
1722-24	437	484	419 (87%)
1752-54	401	499	434 (87%)

Sources: Ralph Davis, "English Foreign Trade, 1700-1774," in W. E. Minchinton, ed., The Growth of English Overseas Trade (London, 1969), 119.

a higher valuation when re-exported."[43] These principles, however, would have a distorting effect of some consequence for the interpretation of the official trade statistics. Logically, there would be a tendency to underestimate the value of overseas commodities with high freight and transaction costs as compared to imports from origins closer to England, as will appear from a comparison between invoice value, sales value, and official valuation (Table 3.10). The same distortion can be detected in the valuation of tobacco and sugar imports (Tables 3.16 and 3.21).

Coffee. "Next to the introduction of Indian textiles to the European market, the import of coffee and tea was the most important contribution of goods from the East in modern times."[44] It was, however, a contribution that came late in our period. During the seventeenth century imports of both coffee and tea were insignificant; they were exotic drugs, not the everyday substitutes of wine and beer that they were to become during the following century.

Coffee was probably the first of the two to gain wide popularity,

[43] T. S. Ashton in his introduction to Elizabeth Boody Schumpeter, *English Overseas Trade Statistics, 1697–1808* (Oxford, 1960), 8.
[44] Glamann, *Dutch Asiatic Trade,* 184.

Table 3.10

Values of Calico and Silk Imports to England

(in Thousands of £)

	Invoice value	Sales value	Official valuation
1722-24	429	1,030	437
1752-54	582	1,029	401

Sources: Invoice values are from Chaudhuri, Trading World of Asia, table C.24; sales values are calculated on the basis of Chaudhuri's tables A.13 and C.24. Official valuation is from Davis, "English Foreign Trade, 1700-1774."

and from the 1690s coffee was considered a commodity with a regular and profitable market by both companies. The next decades saw a dramatic development in the coffee trade, first a wild scramble for supplies from Yemen and then the rapid rise to prominence of new areas of production.

This dramatic development is well illustrated by the English participation in the coffee trade. English imports from Mocha rose rapidly to an apex of 23,852 cwt in 1724 (about 1,213,000 kg); in that year coffee constituted 21 percent of the total invoice value of the company imports from Asia. But this peak was followed by an immediate decline, both in absolute and relative terms. After 1730 the annual import averaged 9,000 cwt (about 548,000 kg) and accounted for only 4–6 percent of the imports.[45]

The development in the Dutch purchases in Mocha paralleled that of the English. By 1715 Dutch purchases might exceed 1 million pd a year. In the years 1717–22 Dutch purchases averaged 1,640,000 pd annually (about 815,000 kg). But in the following five years Dutch purchases in Mocha slumped to 646,000 pd (about 321,000 kg) a year.[46]

Behind the decline and stabilization of the Mocha trade of the com-

---

[45] Chaudhuri, *Trading World of Asia*, table C.9.
[46] Glamann, *Dutch Asiatic Trade*, 195–6, 201, table 37.

panies lay the emergence of new centers of production. The first was Java. In 1711 984 pd of coffee had been shipped from Batavia to Europe, the first result of a deliberate transfer of the cultivation of coffee from Yemen, which before had enjoyed a world monopoly in the production of coffee, to Dutch-controlled Java. Thirteen years later more than 2,000,000 pd of coffee entered the company warehouses in Batavia in one year.[47] "While 90 percent of the quantities of coffee imported in the season of 1721 came from Mocha and only 10 percent were Java coffee, the ratio five years later was the exact opposite."[48]

As early as the 1730s Asian coffee met with competition from West Indian coffee in the European market. In 1737 the VOC raised its order for coffee from Asia to 6,000,000 pd; it is doubtful, however, if this order was met over a sustained period of time.[49] The average annual import of coffee by the VOC during the 1740s was sold for 1,700,000 fl., corresponding to approximately 1,500,000 pd of coffee. Both the Dutch and the English continued to buy coffee in Yemen, but the early transfer of the coffee cultivation had given the Dutch a lead in this line of business. By the middle of the eighteenth century coffee accounted for about 10 percent of the Dutch imports but only for 5 percent of the English.

Tea. Tea became popular in Europe in much the same period as coffee, perhaps slightly later. The largest quantity of tea imported by the EIC in one year before 1700 was 38,000 lb in 1690. A steady increase in annual imports did not begin until 1713.[50]

Unfortunately we have few quantitative data on the Dutch tea trade in the early period, when the easy contact with the Chinese through the junk trade to Batavia may have given them an advantage. In 1710, for example, it was reported that tea had been brought into England from Holland.[51] During the next few years English shipping to Canton became regular, but the VOC hesitated until 1728 before taking up regular sailings for fear of jeopardizing the valuable junk trade to Batavia. The Dutch lost ground in the rapidly expanding tea trade during the 1720s because of this delay; in the decade 1720–30 the

---

[47] Ibid., 208, table 39.
[48] Ibid., 206.
[49] Ibid., 210.
[50] Chaudhuri, *Trading World of Asia*, table C.19.
[51] Ibid., 388. If the imports according to the official trade statistics (Schumpeter, *English Overseas Trade Statistics*, table XVI) are compared with the registered company imports (Chaudhuri, *Trading World of Asia*, table C.19), it would appear that tea reached England legally through other agents than the EIC in the first two decades of the eighteenth century.

Table 3.11

Annual Average English Tea Imports

(in Thousands of Kilograms)

	Quantity	Growth rate
1721-30	401.4	
		31
1731-40	527.2	
		73
1741-50	913.7	
		85
1751-60	1688.2	

Source: Chaudhuri, Trading World of Asia, 388, table A.17.

average annual Dutch tea import was 234,776 pd, whereas the corresponding English figure was 793,491 lb.[52]

The amazing rate of growth in the English tea trade in the first half of the eighteenth century has been documented by Chaudhuri (Table 3.11), but the total import of tea to northern Europe may have been growing even faster in these decades, when Canton became the preferred investment for all the smaller companies (Table 3.12). By the 1740s tea accounted for about 13 percent of the sales revenue of the VOC, by the 1750s it was probably close to 20 percent of the sales of the EIC, and the trade in tea had started in earnest only a few decades before. The companies had found a totally unexpected, popular market for this new commodity.

Trade with America

Monopoly companies were not successful in the Atlantic trade, so generally the statistics available to determine the growth and composition of the trade with the Americas are less satisfactory than is the case with European–Asian trade. The task is made easier, however, by the fact that two commodities, sugar and tobacco, overshadowed everything else in the imports to Europe from America. Sugar and tobacco alone accounted for three-fourths of the English imports from America before the middle of the eighteenth century, the rest being made up of a large number of miscellaneous commodities, and

[52] Glamann, *Dutch Asiatic Trade*, 225, table 43.

Table 3.12

Annual Average Tea Exports from Canton

for All Nations (in Thousands of Kilograms)

	EIC		VOC		OTHERS		TOTAL	
	Quantity	Growth Rate	Quantity	Growth Rate	Quantity	Growth Rate	Quantity	Growth Rate
1719-25	417		-		354		771	
		19		-		30		48
1726-33	498		181		460		1139	
		26		118		125		80
1734-40	629		392		1034		2055	
		43		134		85		82
1741-48	899		916		1918		3733	
		55		39		39		43
1749-55	1,390		1,275		2661		5326	

Source: Louis Dermigny, La Chine et l'occident: Le commerce à Canton au XVIIIe siècle (Paris, 1964), 539.

we have no reason to believe that the composition of the Dutch imports was much different. Only in the very last decades of our period did a few new commodities, such as rice and coffee, begin to be of importance (Table 3.13).

Sugar. Sugar, originally from Asia, could be and was cultivated and produced in Southern Europe, but in the sixteenth century the Portuguese revolutionized the sugar trade by bringing production to the Atlantic islands and, more importantly, to Brazil and organizing the mills and plantations as specialized units, working for the distant European market. In the late sixteenth century Brazilian sugar production is estimated at 600,000 arrobas (about 8,500,000 kg), and in 1625, on the eve of the Dutch invasion, at 960,000 arrobas (about 14,000,000 kg.)[53]

The Low Countries participated in the Portuguese sugar trade not only as distributors in northern Europe but also trading to Brazil. The direct north European involvement in American sugar production and

[53] Stuart B. Schwartz, *Sugar Plantations in the Formation of Brazilian Society* (Cambridge, 1985), 165.

Table 3.13

Relative Amounts of American Imports Entering

England--Official Valuations (in Percentages)

	1663-9	1699-17	1722-4	1752-4
Tobacco	16.4	22.5	15.7	20.9
Sugar	60.8	56.9	55.3	48.5
Rice	-	-	3.0	6.2
Miscellaneous	22.8	20.6	26.0	24.4
	100.0	100.0	100.0	100.0

Source: Davis, "English Foreign Trade, 1600-1700," in

Minchinton, Growth of English Overseas Trade, idem, "English

Foreign Trade, 1700-1774," in ibid., 119.

large-scale participation in the sugar trade, however, occurred in the same decisive decades after 1600 when the direct trade between northern Europe and Asia also began.

This new development was closely related to the struggle between the Dutch Republic and the Spanish Empire. From 1629 to 1654 the Dutch West India Company controlled large parts of the sugar-producing areas in Brazil and disrupted trade and production in the areas not under their control. In the years 1637–44, when their dominion over Brazil was at its peak, the average annual import of sugar to the Netherlands from Brazil was a little more than 8,000,000 pd, at an average value of 1,500,000 pesos. In the same years the VOC import of sugar was also considerable, 1,950,000 pd a year from 1637 to 1642, bringing the total of Dutch annual sugar imports around 1640 close to 5,000,000 kg.[54]

Probably this brought the Dutch sugar market close to saturation – in 1642 the board of directors of the VOC reduced their orders for

[54] J. J. Reesse, *De suikerhandel van Amsterdam, van het begin der 17de Eeuw tot 1813* (Haarlem, 1908), CXX, CXIII.

Table 3.14

Annual Average VOC Sugar Imports from Asia

Years	Lbs.
1621–30	17,549
1631–40	814,698
1641–50	1,100,215
1651–60	1,226,359
1661–70	542,881
1671–80	415,484
1681–90	2,536
1691–1700	48,304
1701–10	1,503,558
1711–20	2,702,580
1721–30	3,950,909
1731–40	3,489,350
1741–50	366,094
1751–60	741,890

Source: J. J. Reesse, De suikerhandel van Amsterdam, van het begin der 17de Eeuw tot 1813 (Haarlem, 1908), CXIII–CXV.

sugar from Asia because of declining prices – but the high level of imports seems to have been maintained throughout the 1650s.[55] The decade 1650–60 is characterized as the first flourishing period of the Dutch sugar-refining industry, with fifty to sixty refineries in operation in 1660.[56] In the same decade the average annual import of Asian sugar was over 1,200,000 pd (Table 3.14).

The boom period came to an end during the 1660s. In 1669 the owners of refineries in Amsterdam declared that their business was declining because of English laws, the high customs rates on sugar in

[55] Glamann, *Dutch Asiatic Trade*, 153.
[56] Reesse, *De suikerhandel van Amsterdam*, 30f.

France, Sweden, and Denmark, and the rise of a refining industry in Hamburg. They claimed that one-third of the refineries had closed for these reasons.[57] According to the earliest known customs register from Amsterdam, imports in 1667/8 were only a little more than 7,000,000 pd.[58]

When the information on imports of sugar by the VOC is compared with the data on prices, a stagnation or, rather, a slow growth in the Dutch sugar imports in the last decades of the seventeenth century seems indicated. In the same period the import of sugar from Surinam must have been of growing importance, having reached a level of nearly 10,000,000 pd a year around 1700 (Table 3.15). From the apex of the 1650s the VOC imports fell off to nearly nothing in the decade 1681–90. Significant increases began only after 1700, reaching nearly 4,000,000 pd a year in the decade 1721–30. Prices had been high before the Dutch definitely gave up their dominion over Brazil in 1654, but from 1655 prices showed a downward trend. In England prices for muscovado (raw sugar) fell from about £4 a hundredweight in the 1650s to £2 in the years around 1660 and to a low point of 16s. a hundredweight in 1686–7.[59] The same trend is repeated in Amsterdam, where prices on muscovado fell from about 0.5 fl. per pound in the early 1650s to a low point of 0.16 fl. per pound in 1688.[60]

The first half of the eighteenth century was a new age of prosperity for the Amsterdam sugar industry. From 1700 to 1748 the number of refineries in Amsterdam rose from twenty to ninety-five.[61] During the same period the sugar production of Surinam grew from around 10,000,000 pd a year to around 20,000,000 pd a year (Table 3.15), and by the middle of the eighteenth century raw sugar from France was arriving in Amsterdam in nearly the same quantity.[62]

The rise of the English sugar-producing colonies in the West Indies was closely intertwined with the Dutch attempt to conquer the Portuguese sugar empire in Brazil. Barbados, the first of the Caribbean islands to take up production of sugar in earnest, was founded as a tobacco colony, but with the steep decline in tobacco prices that ter-

[57] Ibid., 37–8.
[58] H. Brugmans, "Statistiek van den in- en uitvoer van Amsterdam, 1. october 1667–30. september 1668," *Bijdragen en Mededelingen van het Historisch Genootschap* 19 (1898): 175.
[59] Richard S. Dunn, *Sugar and Slaves* (Chapel Hill: University of North Carolina Press, 1972), 205, n. 26.
[60] Posthumus, *Nederlandsche prijsgeschiedenis*, 119.
[61] Reesse, *De suikerhandel van Amsterdam*, 47.
[62] J. P. van de Voort, "De Westindische plantages van 1720 tot 1795" (diss., University of Nijmegen, 1973).

Table 3.15

Annual Average Sugar Exports

from Surinam

	Quantity (lb)	Price (fl./lb)	Sales value (1,000 pesos)
1701-10	9,835,080	0.19	702.3
1711-20	14,543,660	0.15	802.0
1721-30	20,408,880	0.14	1,073.9
1731-40	17,928,440	0.11	741.2
1741-50	18,590,480	0.18	1,257.7
1751-60	16,230,300	0.17	1,037.0

Sources: Quantities are from J. P. van de Voort, "De Westindische plantages van 1720 tot 1795" (diss., University of Nijmegen, 1973). Prices are from Posthumus, Nederlandsche prijsgeschiedenis.

minated the first tobacco boom in 1629 and another decline in 1635–40, the settlers shifted to alternative lines of production, at first ginger, cotton, and indigo. The rise in sugar prices during the Dutch enterprise in Brazil was a strong inducement to take up sugar production, even if the technique was complicated and demanded a high outlay of capital. Already by 1643 the first shipment of sugar from Barbados to England gave evidence of the ability and willingness of the settlers to follow the market. The shift to the new crop was facilitated in 1645, when the Dutch West India Company began offering slaves (which had become difficult to dispose of in the intended market because of the disruptions in Brazil) at cheap prices and with an extended period of credit. During the 1640s and 1650s the economy of Barbados became totally geared to the production of sugar; by 1655 the export to England is estimated at 17,500,000 lb (about 8,000,000 kg).[63]

[63] Robert Carlyle Batie, "Why Sugar? Economic Cycles and the Changing of Staples on

Table 3.16

Annual Average English Sugar Imports

	Quantity	Official valuation	Estimated sales value
	(1,000 kg)	(1,000 pesos)	(1,000 pesos)
1663 and 69	8,555		
1690	13,010		
1698–1700	23,849		
1701–10	19,693	2,253	3,212
1711–20	29,615	3,479	4,161
1721–30	38,929	4,592	4,039
1731–40	41,410	4,884	3,732
1741–50	42,422	5,100	5,985
1751–60	58,015	6,121	9,173

Sources: Quantities before 1701 are from Richard B. Sheridan, Sugar and Slavery (Baltimore, 1974), 22, table 2.1; after 1701, E. B. Schumpeter, English Overseas Trade Statistics, 1697–1808 (Oxford, 1960), table XVI. Official valuations are from Schumpeter, table XV, and sales prices are from Sheridan, appendix 5, 496–7.

The scattered evidence on the volume of English sugar imports in the seventeenth century indicates a long-term rise in production and consumption (Table 3.16). The average import in the two years 1663 and 1669 was 169,250 cwt (approximately 8,500,000 kg). The official evaluation of this quantity was £256,000; to this should be added English imports from southern Europe, presumably Portugal, valued at

the English and French Antilles, 1624–54," *Journal of Carribean History* (November 1986): 18, 21, 1.

£36,000.[64] In 1683 English sugar imports can be estimated at a little more than 18,000,000 kg.[65] In the very first years of the official English trade statistics, 1698–1700, English sugar imports averaged 47,000 cwt, or nearly 24,000,000 kg, so from the last decades of the seventeenth century the English imports were probably on a considerably higher level than those of the Dutch.[66]

Growth continued in the eighteenth century, and by the middle of the century annual imports were more than 50,000,000 kg. According to the official valuation, the value of the sugar imports increased during the first half of the eighteenth century from more than 2 to more than 5 million pesos, but the actual market value was presumably higher.

An interesting feature in the English sugar trade is the very large share of imports that came to be retained for domestic consumption. From 1698 to 1750, 40 percent of English imports were re-exported, but this percentage declined throughout the first half of the eighteenth century to a level of 8–13 percent in the middle decades. Over the whole period 1698–1750 only 19 percent of the English sugar imports from the West Indies were re-exported.[67] In spite of the protected market and relatively high prices, the English per capita sugar consumption must have been considerably higher than the general European level already quite early in the eighteenth century.

Another remarkable feature in the development of the sugar trade is its competitive character and the need for innovative ingenuity in the business. The global increase in sugar production in the second half of the seventeenth century took place under conditions of a long-term fall in prices. The Brazilians apparently never recovered their dominant status in the world market or even the prewar level of production, being hampered not only by a high level of taxation but also by more traditional and less efficient methods of marketing than those employed by their new rivals. In the West Indies only the planters who were able to consolidate their estates and who followed a cost-conscious policy in production and marketing were able to survive and continue the profitable expansion.[68]

---

[64] Ralph Davis, "English Foreign Trade, 1660–1700," in W. E. Minchinton, ed., *The Growth of English Overseas Trade* (London, 1969), 96.

[65] According to Dunn, 360,000 cwt (*Sugar and Slaves,* 203, n. 77); according to Richard B. Sheridan, 372,000 cwt (*Sugar and Slavery: An Economic History of the British West Indies, 1623–1775* [Baltimore, 1974], 398).

[66] Sheridan, *Sugar and Slavery,* 22, table 2.1.

[67] Ibid.

[68] Carl Bridenbaugh and Roberta Bridenbaugh, *No Peace beyond the Line: The English in*

Table 3.17

Annual Average English Sugar Imports

in Periods of Peace and War

1698-1703	24,477 English tons
1704-09	17,161 English tons
1710-17	27,114 English tons

Sources: Sheridan, <u>Sugar and Slavery</u>; Schumpeter, <u>English Overseas Trade Statistics</u>.

The sugar trade was sensitive to the conditions of war and peace in Europe; an outbreak of war made prices rise in Europe and fall in the West Indies, the larger margin of profit reflecting the increased risk.[69] A breakdown of the volume of English sugar imports after 1698 distributed according to years of war and years of peace shows the same pattern that was found in the East India trade, though less pronounced (Table 3.17).[70]

The most important new development in the last decades of the seventeenth century and into the eighteenth century, which can only be briefly referred to here, was the rapid rise to prominence of the French sugar-producing colonies. Estimates of the total Dutch, French, and English production in the 1680s and the 1750s are shown in Table 3.18.

Tobacco. Like the other colonial trades of the north the trade in tobacco began in the early decades of the seventeenth century, when the Dutch and the English simultaneously challenged the Iberian monopolies. The tobacco trade, however, got its own impetus from the surprising spread of the epidemic (as some would think) of tobacco smoking over Europe and the rest of the world.

In spite of lacunae, particularly for the dramatic period 1640–69, we

the *Carribean, 1624–1690* (New York, 1972), 280–305; Sheridan, *Sugar and Slavery,* chaps. 11–13 and passim.

[69] Sheridan, *Sugar and Slavery,* 404.

[70] Noel Deerr, *The History of Sugar,* 2 vols. (London, 1949), 1:193–9.

Table 3.18

Estimates of Sugar Production,

(in Thousands of Kilograms)

	1680s
French colonies (1683)	9,315
Dutch colonies (1688)	2,516
English colonies (1682-3)	18,832
	30,663

	1750s
French colonies (excluding Santo Domingo)	47,400
Santo Domingo	(38,500)
Dutch colonies	8,000
English colonies	47,000
	(140,900)

Sources: Figures from the 1680's are from Sheridan, Sugar and Slavery, 397. Figures for the 1750's are from Noel Deerr, The History of Sugar, 2 vols. (London, 1949), 1:212, 233; Sheridan, Sugar and Slavery, 22.

are reasonably well informed of the development of tobacco production in the English colonies from its first beginnings (1,250 lb in 1616) (about 50,000,000 lb a year) to the middle of the eighteenth century (Table 3.19).

It is far more difficult to determine the volume of direct Dutch import from America. The Dutch plantations did not grow much tobacco of their own, but in all probability tobacco was imported from the colonies of other nations, especially in the decades in the middle of the seventeenth century, when English control over their colonies was weakest. Smuggling undoubtedly continued even later, but the volume and direction of English re-exports indicate that by far the largest part of the production of the main suppliers, the Chesapeake

Table 3.19

Annual Average English Tobacco Imports

(in Thousands of Kilograms)

1616–20	10
1621–30	73
1631–40 (6 years)	478
–	–
1669	6,798
1671–80 (6 years)	9,028
1681–90 (7 years)	11,630
1691–1700 (9 years)	13,189
1701–10	12,565
1711–20	14,057
1721–30	17,673
1731–40	19,846
1741–50	27,794
1751–60	30,646

Sources: Russell R. Menard, "The Tobacco Industry in the Chesapeake Colonies, 1617-1730: An Interpretation," Research in Economic History V (1980): appendix, 187ff.; U.S. Bureau of the Census, Historical Statistics of the United States: Colonial Times to 1970 (1975); Jacob M. Price, France and the Chesapeake: A History of the French Tobacco Monopoly, 1674-1791, and of its Relationship to the British and American Tobacco Trades, 2 vols. (Ann Arbor, 1973), 2:843-4, table 1.

colonies Virginia and Maryland, was carried to Europe by way of England. The most dangerous rivals of the American planters and the English merchants were not interlopers but European peasants, who discovered the market value of the tobacco crop in a period of agricultural hardship.

It is well known how an unexpected international tobacco boom carried the Chesapeake colonies and the island colonies in the West Indies through their first difficult years. Already in the 1620s the high prices of the first years could not be maintained in spite of the expanding market. The West Indian planters gave up tobacco growing, but the Chesapeake colonies compensated for lower prices by expanding production, and before the Civil War the annual export to England had passed 1,000,000 lb (Table 3.19). According to Russell Menard the growth ratio was leveling off by the 1630s, though growth continued in a fluctuating market until the middle of the 1680s. The next thirty years was a prolonged period of near stagnation, but after 1715 and until the end of the colonial period, growth was resumed at a considerable rate.[71]

Between 1640 and 1669 English tobacco imports from the Chesapeake increased from 1,400,000 to 15,000,000 lb. Unfortunately quantitative data from this long period are lacking, but Menard's analysis of the economic fluctuations in the Chesapeake colonies indicates that a recovery from the first depression took place between the middle of the 1640s and the middle of the 1650s, probably supported by an increase in Dutch interest in the tobacco trade.[72] The early 1660s are characterized by many complaints of bad markets, but the English import of 15,000,000 lb in 1669 was part of a new prosperity.

For the present purpose, the most important point to emerge from Menard's analysis of the economic fluctuations in the Chesapeake region is the observation that the long period of growth and receding prices, which continued until the 1680s, was closely related to higher efficiency and falling costs of production, transport, and handling of the tobacco. Tobacco became cheaper and found new outlets as a commodity of mass consumption, not only in England but also on the Continent, as evidenced by the high figures for re-export.[73] By the middle of the 1680s, however, the possibilities for further reductions in the costs of production were exhausted, and growth could not resume until demand had reached a level where higher prices became

---

[71] Russell R. Menard, "The Tobacco Industry in the Chesapeake Colonies, 1617–1730: An Interpretation," *Research in Economic History* 5 (1980): 113–14.

[72] Ibid., 132, 152.

[73] Jacob M. Price, *The Tobacco Adventure to Russia* (Philadelphia, 1961), 5 and passim.

Table 3.20

Annual Average English Tobacco Imports

in Periods of Peace and War

1681-87 (3 years)	23,700,000 lb
1688-97 (9 years)	27,800,000 lb
1698-1703	31,500,000 lb
1704-09	27,500,000 lb
1710-17	28,100,000 lb

Source: See sources for Table 3.19.

realistic. When a new period of growth began after 1715, it coincided with rising costs of production and higher prices, indicating an increase in demand, particularly in the English re-export markets.

In this chronology tobacco deviates from the pattern, closely related to the war years, that we found both in the East India trade and in the sugar trade. The wartime fluctuations may be traced in the tobacco trade as well, but on a background of long-term stagnation (Table 3.20).[74]

Seen from the English point of view, a major difference between the sugar trade and the tobacco trade was the much larger importance of the re-export – and therefore dependence on the Continental market – of tobacco. For 1671 the English re-export of tobacco is estimated at $33\frac{1}{3}$–37 percent of the imports; scattered figures from London indicate that the share of the re-export was rising during the following decades, and in 1696–9 the average re-export from England was 63 percent of imports. During the period 1711–54 the average proportion of re-exports rose from 64 to 84 percent.[75]

The earliest statistical evidence on the Dutch tobacco trade comes from the preserved Amsterdam customs register for 1667/68. Tobacco was registered by value, not by volume: import, 271,467 fl.; export,

[74] Menard, "Tobacco Industry"; U.S. Bureau of the Census, *Historical Statistics of the United States: Colonial Times to 1970* (1975); Jacob M. Price, *France and the Chesapeake: A History of the French Tobacco Monopoly, 1674–1791, and of Its Relationships to the British and American Tobacco Trades*, 2 vols. (Ann Arbor, 1973).

[75] Price, *Tobacco Adventure to Russia*, 5; idem, *France and the Chesapeake*, 2:849, table 2c.

526,736 fl.[76] These figures are so modest that one has good reason to doubt their reliability. Even considering the energetic development of domestic production and assuming, as is probable, that the direct importation of tobacco from America to the Netherlands was inconsiderable after the introduction of the Navigation Acts, imports from England alone must have been on a larger scale. The Netherlands was the "normal" market for English re-exports of tobacco in the seventeenth century. Frequently English shipmasters were instructed to unload their tobacco in a conveniently located English port in order to comply with English laws and then to take the tobacco back on board and continue to the Netherlands. Of 1,306,000 lb of tobacco imported into Plymouth in 1668, 1,057,000 lb were re-exported in the same year, most to the Netherlands.[77] Assuming an Amsterdam price a little below 0.30 fl. per pound, shipments from Plymouth alone would be worth more than the total registered imports into Amsterdam in 1667/68.

The unreliability of the Dutch statistics may, however, be of minor importance for our present purpose. England was the channel through which by far the largest part of tobacco imports from America passed into northern Europe. The competition met by the English-imported Virginia leaves in the Dutch market came not from overseas tobacco but from *inlandsche tabaksblader*, leaves grown and cured in the Netherlands. By 1675 Dutch tobacco production may be estimated at 5–6 million pounds a year. The decades around the turn of the century, when Chesapeake production stagnated, were the peak years for Dutch tobacco production. The apex was reached around 1710, when Dutch production approached Chesapeake production at 15–18 million pounds a year. According to Roessingh, in the following decades lower transportation costs and therefore cheaper American tobacco reduced demand for Dutch-produced tobacco leaves.[78]

We have no continuous series for wholesale tobacco prices in England, but considering the importance of the Amsterdam market as an outlet for English re-exports, the Amsterdam prices may, with some reservations, be used as a substitute. It must be assumed that the Amsterdam price, considering the privileged position of the English traders in the Chesapeake, was higher than the English price, but

---

[76] Brugmans, "Statistiek van den in- en uitvoer," 176, n. 80.
[77] Price, *Tobacco Adventure to Russia*, 6, n. 6.
[78] H. K. Roessingh, "Tobacco Growing in Holland in the Seventeenth and Eighteenth Centuries: A Case Study of the Innovative Spirit of Dutch Peasants," *Acta Historiae Neerlandicae* 11 (1978): 42ff., table 1; cf. idem, *Inlandse tabak: Expansie en contractie van een handelsgewas in de 17e en 18e eeuw in Nederland* (Zutphen, 1976), 238.

even with this reservation it appears probable that the value of to-bacco, as of other overseas commodities, was underestimated in the official English statistics (Table 3.21).

COLONIAL TRADE BY THE MIDDLE OF THE EIGHTEENTH CENTURY

In the introduction to this paper I suggested that the introduction of colonial commodities was the largest change and major cause of growth in north European long-distance trade between the medieval period and the middle of the eighteenth century. To prove this point, ideally one should have complete series for all ports and commodities, which we shall never have. Indeed it is rarely possible to obtain exact measures of the share of colonial commodities in total turnover. By the middle of the eighteenth century, however, we can get an idea of the order of magnitude for at least the two largest trading nations. The years 1752–4 have been selected as the "ideal" period, mainly because this triennium has been analyzed in detail by Ralph Davis as far as the English trade is concerned, and because 1753 is a bench-mark in the history of Dutch trade, thanks to the customs records preserved from that year.

The importance of the colonial trade in overall English foreign trade is obvious (Table 3.22). According to the official valuation, 46 percent of the commodities imported into England came from America or the East Indies, and 45 percent of English exports were either sent to overseas destinations (26 percent) or were re-exports of colonial commodities to other destinations (19 percent). When one considers that (1) bullion, which was the most important English export to the East Indies, was not registered, and (2) the principles of official valuation automatically implied an underregistration of commodities brought from very distant places, there can hardly be any doubt that more than half of English foreign trade by the middle of the eighteenth century directly or indirectly depended on the intercontinental trade.

It is more difficult to determine the volume of overseas trade in Dutch foreign trade. When estimating the turnover of forty-four commodities at the Amsterdam exchange on the basis of the customs register preserved from 1753, Posthumus allowed 30.4 percent for the six colonial commodities included in his list: nutmeg, pepper, mace, to-bacco, sugar, and indigo. Brugmans, on the other hand, has warned against the tendency to exaggerate the importance of the exotic Asian trade in the economy of the Republic; he estimated the share of the East India commodities in the foreign trade of the Netherlands at 12

Table 3.21

English Tobacco Imports

	Quantity	Official Valuation	Amsterdam price	Amsterdam value
	(1,000 lb)	(1,000 pesos)	(fl./pd)	(1,000 pesos)
1701–10	28,902	912	0.31	3,081
1711–20	28,528	989	0.32	3,139
1721–30	33,606	1,355	0.23	2,658
1731–40	37,561	1,513	0.22	2,841
1741–50	48,015	1,937	0.20	3,302
1751–60	48,048	1,870	0.20	3,305

Source: Quantities and official valuations are from Schumpeter, English Overseas Trade Statistics, tables XVI and XV. Prices at Amsterdam are from Price, France and the Chesapeake, 2:852, table 4.

Table 3.22

The Colonial Share in English Exports and Imports

1752-4, Official Valuations

	Exports		Imports	
	£1,000	%	£1,000	%
America	2,334	20	2,684	33
Asia	784	6	1,086	13
Total colonial	3,118	26	3,770	46
Colonial re-exports	2,222	19		
Combined colonial exports and re-exports	5,304	45		

Source: Davis, "English Foreign Trade, 1700-1774," 119.

percent by the middle of the eighteenth century (without allowing for re-export, however).[79]

The evidence uncovered more recently seems largely to confirm Brugmans's conclusions. On the basis of the 1753 customs registers Johannes de Vries had estimated the total foreign trade of the Republic by the middle of the eighteenth century at 124–35 million guilders. This estimate does not include the trade with Asia and America and the re-export of Asian commodities. We are now able to add a figure for imports from Asia; for imports from America we have no better estimate than the one made by B. van der Oudermeulen in the late eighteenth century, but it appears to be confirmed by other evidence (Table 3.23).[80] We have no data on the value of exports to America

[79] Posthumus, *Nederlandsche prijsgeschiedenis*, XCVII; I. J. Brugmans, "De Oost-Indische Compagnie en de welvaart in de Republiek," *Tijdschrift voor Geschiedenis* 61 (1948): 226–7.

[80] Johannes de Vries, *De economische Achteruitgang der Republiek in de achttiende eeuw*, 2d ed. (Leiden, 1968), 27; Steur, *Herstel of Ondergang*, appendix VIIIb; Brugmans, "Statistiek van den in- en uitvoer," 227, n. 1.

Table 3.23

Estimated Annual Quantities and Sales Values of Colonial Imports, 1752-4

(in Pieces, Thousands of Kilograms, and Thousands of Pesos)

	England		The Netherlands		Total	
	Quantity	Sales Value	Quantity	Sales Value	Quantity	Sales Value
Asia:						
Calicoes and						
silk	604,000[a]	4,853[b]	?	1,893[c]	?	6,746
Pepper	1,061[a]	404[d]	1,679[d]	677[c]	2,740	1,081
Tea	1,544[a]	1,627[e]	1,215[f]	1,176[f]	2,759	2,803
Coffee	502[a]	344[d]	1,393[d]	615[c]	1,913	959
Silk	156	?	?	264[c]	?	?
Cloves	0	0	93[d]	479[c]	93	479
Nutmeg	0	0	120[d]	342[c]	120	342
Mace	0	0	44[d]	208[c]	44	208
Cinnamon	0	0	230[d]	823[c]	230	823
Miscellaneous	?	(1,475)[g]		965[h]	?	?
Total		(8,743)		7,442		(16,185)

America:

Sugar	46,939[i]	7,135[j]	9,300[k]	920	59,239	8,055
Tobacco	26,940[i]	3,689[d]	0	0	26,940	3,689
Coffee	?	?	1,427[l]	499[d]	?	?
Miscellaneous	?	(3,608)[m]	?	?	?	?
Total		(14,432)		(1,419)		(15,851)
Colonial total		(23,175)		(8,861)		(32,036)

[a] Chaudhuri, Trading World of Asia, tables C.9, C.14, C.18, C.19 and C.24.

[b] Calculated from ibid, tables A.13 and C.24.

[c] Steur, Herstel of Ondergang, bijlage VIIIb.

[d] Computed using the average prices on the Amsterdam exchange, according to Posthumus, Nederlandsche prijsgeschiedenis. The method is fairly reliable as far as the VOC imports of spices and pepper are concerned, but it is suspect when it is used to estimate the English imports of pepper, coffee and tobacco. The ratios between the estimated sales values and the known invoice values (see n. g), however, accord nicely with the usual gross profits of the EIC.

[e] Computed using the average sales prices for all qualities sold by the VOC from 1750 to 1755; Steur, Herstel of Ondergang, 274, n. 76.

[f] Includes 479,000 kg imported and sold on private account, ibid, 274, n.76.

Notes to Table 3.23. (Cont.)

g Sales values have been estimated for four items, textiles, pepper, tea and coffee, (nn. b, d and e). Invoice values for each separate item and for total EIC imports are from Chaudhuri, Trading World of Asia, tables C.2, C.9, C.14, C.19, and C.24.

	Invoice Value	Estimated sales value	Ratios
Calicoes and silks	£460,445	£1,129,000	1:2.45
Pepper	£34,516	£94,000	1:2.72
Tea	£158,288	£378,000	1:2.39
Coffee	£35,644	£80,000	1:2.24

These four items account for 83.12 percent of English imports according to invoice value. When the average markup is applied to the remaining 16.88 percent, the sales value of the miscellaneous category can be estimated at £343,000, and the total sales value, at £2,033,205.

h Steur, Herstel of Ondergang, VIIb; with the addition of 534,000 pesos for tea, imported and sold on private account.

i Schumpeter, English Overseas Trade Statistics, table XVI.

j Computed using the average wholesale price as recorded by Sheridan, Sugar and Slavery, 497. Because most of the English sugar imports were retained for the home market, Amsterdam prices are not a good indicator.

k The average import from Surinam during 1752-4 was 8,824,000 kg (Reesse, De suikerhandel van Amsterdam, CXXIV); a little more than 1,000,000 kg has been added to account for imports from other Dutch colonies (cf. van de Voort, "De Westindische plantages," bijlage XVI).

l Van de Voort, "De Westindische plantages," bijlage XVII.

m Miscellaneous, including coffee, has been estimated to be 25 percent of the total imports from America (table 3.13).

from the Netherlands, but presumably they were at a lower level than imports. On this basis we may attempt the following reconstruction:

Trade with Europe	125–35	million guilders
Imports from Asia	18.4	
Imports from America	2.25	
Exports to Asia and America	2	
	147.29–157.29	million guilders

According to this estimate the imports from Asia accounted for 13.6–14.7 percent of the total foreign trade of the Netherlands, while the corresponding figures for America were only 1.7–1.8 percent. When colonial exports are added, the figure may be 14–15 percent. Posthumus estimated that about half the imports from Asia were re-exported, a reasonable guess but not much more. If it is accepted for colonial commodities as a whole, 20–25 percent of Dutch foreign trade by the middle of the eighteenth century depended on Dutch trade overseas. It should be added, however, that this is seen from a strictly Dutch point of view. From a European point of view the proportion would be higher, because the Netherlands had taken over a large part of the distribution of French colonial imports in northern Europe.

Finally, a quantification of the English and Dutch colonial trade by the middle of the eighteenth century has been attempted in Table 3.23. Anyone familiar with the sources or with the economic history of the early modern period will know how many errors this table may contain. The figures cannot possibly be accurate. They cannot be completely wrong either. Seen from a modern point of view, the figures are piteously small. Seen within the context of the eighteenth century, they were huge. The trade in colonial commodities had become an important part of north European economic activity by the middle of the eighteenth century, and it was beginning to leave an impression not only on habits of consumption, but also on habits of investment and spending.

CONCLUDING REMARKS

A number of facts have emerged from this rapid survey of the Dutch and English colonial trade that may be of wider interest for the theme of this volume. First, two minor observations can be made concerning long- and middle-term fluctuations. Over the long term the colonial trade commands special interest because it showed vigorous and sustained growth during a period when growth in traditional sectors of the economy was sluggish and innovations in production and changes in consumer habits elsewhere were few. The middle-term fluctuations appear to be closely related to the conditions of war and peace in Europe.

These long- and middle-term fluctuations were not uniform and unilinear, however. The composition of the colonial trade was not static; the introduction and dispersal of colonial commodities followed patterns that seem to be repeated again and again. I shall try to formulate these patterns provocatively in four (historical) laws.

1. *The law of unpredictability of success.* Sugar may perhaps not be so much of a surprise, but who could have imagined the success of tobacco, coffee, tea, or even calicoes on the European market?

2. *The law of cost-reducing innovations.* When the first profits from the introduction of a new overseas commodity on the European market had been made, competition was always fierce, and entrepreneurs in colonial production and trade could not count on profits. The producers and merchants had to be conscious of the fluctuations of the market, the initiatives of their rivals, and possible cost reductions, particularly reductions of transaction costs, if they wanted to survive and flourish. The Portuguese bilateral trade with Asia was taken over by the more sophisticated organization of the companies. The Brazil sugar planters were beaten by the West Indians when the slave plantation was perfected as an economic machine. Planters had to pack their tobacco tighter and devise efficient marketing techniques for sugar. The list of examples can easily be lengthened.

3. *The law of saturation.* Some commodities (but not all) were affected by the law of saturation. When consumption of pepper and spices had reached a certain level, there was no point in lowering the prices to stimulate an increased demand.

4. *The law of geographical transfer.* (In fact, this is only a variant of the law of cost-reducing innovations.) When a commodity had become popular, its production was transferred to other areas that had abundant factors of production or that were closer to the market. Sugar, indigo, and ginger are early examples. The eastward transfer of tobacco cultivation is interesting because it meant competition between a cheaper, low-quality product, produced by European peasants, and a more expensive, high-quality product, produced by slave labor. But the two most interesting examples are the two largest of the colonial commodities by the middle of the eighteenth century: calicoes and sugar. Each had to await a technological revolution before it could follow the law of geographical transfer and be produced close to the main consuming centers. But eventually these revolutions occurred.

CHAPTER 4

France, the Antilles, and Europe in the seventeenth and eighteenth centuries: renewals of foreign trade

PAUL BUTEL

THANKS to the dynamism of merchant communities along the Atlantic coast and to the exploitation of a young colonial empire, French foreign trade expanded during the eighteenth century. This expansion was based upon the growth in the Antilles trade, which was in turn based upon the mastery of European markets in the re-export of colonial products. The tempo of this growth is estimated to have been greater than that of its rivals – in particular, English commerce. F. Crouzet notes that despite the setback dealt by the collapse of Law's system, French commerce at first grew at a tempo nearing that of English commerce. However, beginning about 1735 it exhibited a more rapid and precocious acceleration that doubled its value in less than seventeen years: from 221 million livres in 1735 to more than 500 million in 1752–4. In Crouzet's words, the years 1735–55 were the golden age of French commerce.[1] Indeed, during the next twenty years, until the American War of Independence, this commerce continued to grow (notwithstanding a clear tapering off caused by the Seven Years' War), although at a slower rate; trade values reached a peak in 1777. On the eve of the American War of Independence, trade remained less than 750 million livres. Not until after the war did an unmistakable recovery occur, which carried trade to its record level on the eve of the French Revolution.[2] Figure 4.1 shows this growth clearly.

Translated by Frederick Suppe, Ball State University.

[1] "Angleterre et France au XVIIIe siècle: Essai d'analyse comparée de deux croissances économiques," *Annales: Economies, Sociétés, Civilisations* 21 (1966): 264.

[2] In current prices, the average annual value for 1784–8 reached 1,062 million livres, nearly five times what it was in 1716–20. Exports led this growth, exceeding 500 million livres in 1787.

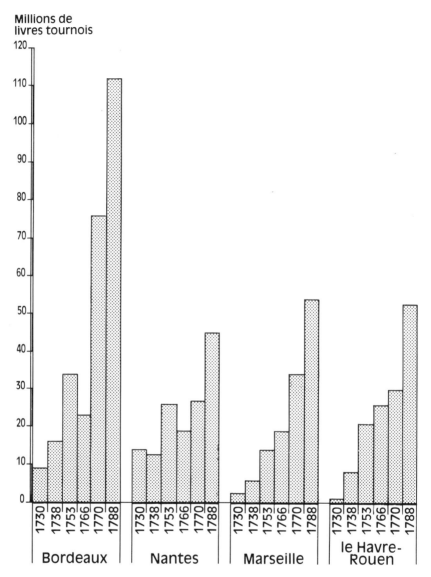

Figure 4.1. Colonial trade in the eighteenth century (*Sources:* J. Meyer, *Histoire du Havre* [Toulouse, 1975], 84; C. Carrière, *Négociantes marseillais au XVIIIe siècle* [Marseille, 1973], 45–65; P. Butel, *Les négociants bordelais, l'Europe et les îles au XVIIIe siècle* [Paris, 1974], 393)

To better understand the factors underlying this growth, one must analyze the heritage of the preceding century. One must not neglect the results of Colbert's policies regarding maritime and colonial trade. Also, the Antilles, colonized since the time of Richelieu, gave French merchants a new position in international commerce. The important naval wars at the end of Louis XIV's reign, between France, Holland, and England, expressed the vigor of international competition created by the early momentum of the Antilles trade in France. Meanwhile, the traditional dynamism of Mediterranean merchants continued, and the first effects of the East Indian trade were also being felt.

This age of the foundation of the French commercial empire cannot be explained unless one tries to discover the situation at the end of the sixteenth century, after the troubles of the Wars of Religion. The financial means for colonial development during the reigns of Louis XIV and Louis XV came from very diverse transactions: those of the Middle Ages, carrying products of the soil (wines, brandies, fruits, and salt), which linked southern France with Nordic Europe; cloth from the north and west of France sold to the Iberian countries; and finally the extension of Atlantic trade, in particular the fisheries of Newfoundland.

THE LEGACIES OF THE FIFTEENTH AND EARLY SEVENTEENTH CENTURIES

The expansion of the "good" sixteenth century (a period of increasing wealth) allowed merchants to restore traditional trade developed during the preceding centuries. Factors essential for this renewal appeared at the end of the fifteenth century. The long stagnation that had prolonged the crises of the fourteenth century finally came to an end. As M. Mollat notes, an economy stimulated by new commercial possibilities and the acceleration of monetary circulation succeeded a contracted, regional economy. There was an increase in trade, with new products appearing, such as spices from Lisbon and, more regionally, wood from Languedoc, which, together with wine, composed the cargoes loaded at Bordeaux and Bayonne in Montaigne's day. The French isthmus between the Nordic seas and the Mediterranean assumed its full economic potential.[3]

Growing Mediterranean activity corresponded with the opening of northwestern European markets. The markets of Bruges and then of Antwerp were favored hereafter with the trade of Rouen, Nantes, and even Bordeaux.[4] At the same time England, Spain, and Portugal

[3] M. Mollat, *Histoire de Rouen* (Toulouse, 1982), 102.
[4] Ibid.

constituted the markets for the linens from Brittany, Anjou, and Poi-
tou, which departed from Nantes. This port also shipped Breton grain
to the Iberian peninsula; grain remained a major element in the north–
south trade between France and the Mediterranean.

At the end of the sixteenth century the impact and stimulus of the
early American treasure should not be overestimated. Well before
Columbus's discovery, busy centers of production developed in France,
working for themselves and for export to England, to the Low Countries, and within France.[5] There was, it has been argued, a fragmentation of the French economy. I. Wallerstein has distinguished continental, northwestern and western, and southern regions. The first,
including Paris and the northeast, remained linked with Antwerp;
the second was connected to the New World economy, to Baltic and
Atlantic commerce; and the third remained an exporter of agricultural
products.[6] In fact, trade between north and south still predominated
in the greater part of the country and was a source of great unity in
the French economy.

But did not the Wars of Religion, together with the long period of
troubles linked with them, call into question the results of the good
sixteenth century for more than a generation – from the 1560s to the
1590s? Seemingly, the losses had been great, but in reality the financial means already in place and the maturation of trade would lay the
foundation at least half a century in advance for the successes of Colbert's age.

The economic difficulties of this period have been illuminated by
work done on Nantes, such as the researches of H. Lapeyre, who
analyzed the business of merchants connected with Spain, the Ruiz.
Lapeyre has shown that their activities suffered many setbacks in the
shipment of linens from Maine and Anjou to Spain from 1568–70 onward.[7] All French textiles were apparently affected; the index of exports of Roman alum, which reflects this activity, shows a decrease
during 1566–90 to nearly half of the 1541–66 levels.[8] Normandy was
invaded by English cloth produced at low cost, ending the textile-
based prosperity of Amiens.[9]

Nonetheless, not all commodities were uniformly affected. J. Tan-

[5] M. Morineau, "L'Europe du Nord-Ouest de 1559 à 1642," *Bulletin de la Société d'Histoire Moderne*, 16th ser., 33 (1987).
[6] Immanuel Wallerstein, *The Modern World System*, vol. 1, *Capitalist Agriculture and the Origins of the European World-Economy in the Sixteenth Century* (New York, 1974), pp. 263–4.
[7] *Une famille de marchands nantais, les Ruiz* (Paris, 1955).
[8] J. Delumeau, *L'alun de Rome* (Paris, 1952), 251.
[9] P. Deyon, "Variations de la production textile aux XVIe et XVIIe siècles," *Annales: Economies, Sociétés, Civilisations* 18 (1963): 939–55.

guy has stressed that for Nantes there was an upsurge after the Treaty of Cateau-Cambrésis (1559) until St. Bartholomew's Day (1572). Trade in wine and salt fed prosperity, as it had earlier.[10] When this trade fell off sharply, certain exports resisted the decline. Such was the case with linens from Brittany, which reached a peak in 1608, attaining nine times the volume exported in 1586. It was not until later that English and Dutch demand replaced that of Iberia as the major outlet for these textiles.[11] One of the essential foundations of France's commercial empire – the, at least partial, mastery of the markets of Spain and Spanish America – was established at the end of the sixteenth century. It was to remain nearly stable until the French Revolution. In the mid–seventeenth century Brittany exported more than 8 million livres worth of linen; if one compares this amount with the total value of exports in 1646, nearly 46 million livres, Breton linens represented nearly 17 percent of French exports that year.

Close to Nantes and at certain times its opponent, the Protestant republic of La Rochelle flaunted an insolent prosperity at the close of the sixteenth century. Political factors alone are not the only explanation for this. The traditional trade in wine, brandy, and salt, which was the enduring base of La Rochelle's commerce, was more and more controlled by Dutch businessmen. One may note that French salt remained a constant element in the Baltic trade until the mid–eighteenth century. The French share of salt shipped to the Baltic did not fall below 20 percent during the worst years of the seventeenth century.[12]

In the long term, what is most interesting at La Rochelle is the penetration of foreigners into the re-export trade. The French merchant empire would always be beholden for a great part of its prosperity to the presence of commission agents from Germany and the Low Countries. Dutch merchants, who ascended the Charente as far as Cognac to buy the brandies and wines of the hinterlands, brought industry to this region; they converted windmills in the Charente and Périgord regions into paper factories to produce the "paper of Holland." At La Rochelle the Netherlanders founded sugar refineries. Their close commercial associations with the Protestant merchants proved to be very fruitful in creating the relationships supporting new

---

[10] J. Tanguy, *Le commerce du port de Nantes au milieu de XVIᵉ siècle* (Paris, 1956).

[11] J. Tanguy, *La production et le commerce des toiles bretonnes* (Paris, 1978), provides the following statistics for exports: 1585, 440,348 pieces; 1594, 1,585,474; 1608, 3,949,492; 1621, 380,253.

[12] J. Delumeau, "Le commerce extérieur de la France au XVIIᵉ siècle," *XVIIᵉ Siècle* 70–71 (1966): 81–105.

expansion based on the re-export of colonial products to northern Europe in the eighteenth century.

A similar continuity in the structure of trade is found at Bordeaux, where the traditional ambit of trade with England and the Netherlands expanded at the end of the sixteenth century and even more at the time of Richelieu, thanks to the new growth of the Newfoundland fisheries. For Bordeaux, Newfoundland created the Antilles, by which I mean that it was the fisheries that provided the means of financing trade. Capital for trade came from the Bordeaux region and from a much larger area, including the Paris district, where bankers made sea-venture loans to Bordeaux shipowners during the 1630s. Here, too, as at La Rochelle, the commercial agents of the United Provinces depended upon a network of Protestant merchants that was as dense in the hinterland – in the valleys of the Garonne, the Lot, and the Dordogne – as it was in the Charente. The Netherlanders thereby indirectly stimulated activity in the southwest, developing trade there in brandy and tobacco. Their dominant position was the envy of local merchants.[13]

At Marseille the growth of the silk trade to satisfy the orders of manufacturers in Lyons is clear from the reign of Henry IV to that of Louis XIII, the volume of raw imported silk having doubled between 1613 and 1642. As along the Atlantic coast, what appears to have been a rather modest trade was a preparation for later growth – in this case, trade with the Levant.[14]

The role of the Dutch in stimulating trade is clearly understood in the only comprehensive qualitative source from the mid–seventeenth century, the *Commerce honorable*, written by Jean Eon of Nantes. M. Morineau has studied the mid–seventeenth century Dutch position in France by comparing it with the situation during the following century.[15] In Eon's day Dutch sales rose to 21.4 million livres while purchases increased to 18 million. In the highest rank of sales were the

[13] P. Voss, "Contribution à l'histoire de l'économie et de la société marchande à Bordeaux au XVIIᵉ siècle: L'exemple de Jean de Ridder" (Master's diss., University of Bordeaux III, 1986), 152. A certain hostility against immigrant Dutch merchants sometimes developed. This was the case in 1683 after letters of citizenship were granted to Jean de Ridder, when there were complaints against "foreigners who, under the cover of the bourgeoisie, intrude upon all affairs of the country, depriving the king of one part of his rights and hindering the native-born countrymen in their dealings."

[14] M. Morineau, "Flottes de commerce et trafics français en Méditerranée au XVIIᵉ siècle (jusqu'en 1669)," *XVIIᵉ Siècle* 86–87 (1970): 135–71.

[15] "La balance du commerce frano-néerlandais et le resserrement économique des Provinces-Unies au XVIIIᵉ siècle," *Economische-Historisch Jaarboek* 30 (1963–4): 170–233.

textiles – woolens and serges – with more than 32 percent of the total; spices came next with 15 percent, and Brazilian sugar sold by the Dutch middlemen accounted for 9 percent of the total. The share of goods from the north, which included flax, hemp, lumber, and masts but not grain, was rather small, at 8 percent. A bit later, during the 1660s, Colbert reckoned the value of northern European goods sold by the Dutch, including grain, at 15 million livres. One must remember that the Dutch seemed masters of French commerce; their total sales greatly exceeded those of the English, estimated at 16 million livres. They controlled the supply to France of spices, commodities from the Antilles, and goods from Nordic Europe. A century later the situation had changed because of the growth of the French Antilles trade and because of the direct relationships between French ports and northern Europe, which led to the decline of Dutch intermediaries.

In 1750 the Dutch no longer furnished sugar to France, contenting themselves with the exotic imported commodities of tea, cocoa, and tobacco. Despite the growth of French shipping, which required more naval stores, Nordic products represented a somewhat reduced share – less than 1.6 million livres, or about 7 percent of Dutch sales. The restoration of textile prosperity at Amiens, Lille, Beauvais, and Rouen at the end of the seventeenth century reduced textile imports; the Dutch sold no more than 2.3 million livres' worth, though a century earlier they had imported some 7 million livres' worth. The merchants of Amsterdam preserved a sector of the French market for themselves only in spices, because the Vereenigde Oost-Indische Compagnie (VOC) was able to provide much larger quantities than could be supplied by France's Company of the East Indies.

A spectacular reversal in trade had taken place: France was freed from Dutch domination for the supply of sugar and other commodities from the American islands. Moreover, France had become the greatest re-exporter of colonial goods in Europe; this was the basis for its new commercial empire. In the long run Colbert's struggle was successful. France was ultimately the victor of the sugar wars in Martinique and Guadeloupe during the 1650s and then in Santo Domingo around 1700. An Americanization of French commerce then revealed itself, sustained by the growth of shipping to the Antilles under Colbert. The old commercial networks established by foreigners had ensured the indispensable relationships for re-export to all of northern Europe; the Netherlands figured here as a powerful intermediary while competing with Hanseatic merchants. In the mid–eighteenth century, colonial commodities alone represented more than half of French sales to the United Provinces; their value reached 12.4 million livres, approximately three times that of traditional goods (wines and brandies). This compensated for the decline in Dutch purchases of salt, fruits, and other products of the soil. Sales of salt declined as a result of Portuguese shipments from Setúbal, whose salt replaced that of Brouage and Bourgneuf.[16]

THE EXPANSION OF COMMERCE FROM THE 1660s TO THE 1750s DUE TO COLONIAL TRADE

The rise of the Antilles and the re-export of colonial commodities

French colonial trade commenced at the beginning of Louis XIV's personal rule. In 1664 the merchant fleet was still of modest size. Statistics on ships of more than 100 tons, prepared for Colbert, yield the following comparison of ports.

Le Havre	75	Toulon	9
Saint-Malo	48	Calais	5
Rouen	26	Sables-d'Olonne	5
Marseille	21	Rhuis (Morbihan)	5
Bayonne	19	Dunkirk	4
La Rochelle	18	Granville	4
Honfleur	14	Abbeville	3
Nantes	12	Caudebec	2
Bordeaux	11	Hennebont	2

Ships of less than 100 tons were not counted, and one must emphasize the imperfection of these statistics, since many ships of 50 to 80 tons were used in long-distance trade to the Atlantic archipelagoes and Newfoundland. But the overall impression is one of a mediocre fleet; colonial traffic was quite modest, and the European coastal trade was mainly sustained by foreign ships.[17] Twenty-two years later ships over 100 tons now numbered:

Saint-Malo	117	Nantes	84
Le Havre	114	Bayonne	61
Dieppe	96	Dunkirk	59
La Rochelle	93	Marseille	47

There is a total increase of 75 percent. It is necessary to examine more precisely the Atlantic traffic at Bordeaux, Nantes, and La Rochelle.

[16] M. Delafosse and C. Laveau, *La Commerce du sel de Brouage aux xviie et xviiie siècles* (Paris, 1960), 96–7.

[17] Ships of more than 40 tons: Le Havre, 142; Marseille, 91; Bordeaux, 77; Saint-Malo, 77. There were relatively few ships of medium tonnage suited to the European coastal trade.

Table 4.1

Ship Departures from Bordeaux

	Ships	Tonnage 1651	Ships	Tonnage 1672	Ships	Tonnage 1682
Bordeaux flagged ships	83	(4,972)	107	(5,284)	223	(7,209)
Foreign flagged ships	423	(72,630)	339	(25,613)	935	(94,149)
French flagged ships	1,007	(21,541)	1,699	(45,151)	2,120	(49,164)
Total	1,513	(99,143)	2,145	(76,048)	3,278	(150,522)

Source: Archives de la Gironde, Fonds de l'Amirauté.

Between 1670 and 1679, 273 ships departed from La Rochelle for the Antilles, Africa, or Canada, while 411 departed between 1680 and 1689. From Nantes 64 ships left for the Antilles between 1674 and 1675, 95 had the same destination in 1684–5, and from 1687 to 1688 the traffic grew to 128 ships. At Bordeaux trade in all commodities flourished during the second half of the seventeenth century (Table 4.1).

In 1674 French ships bound for the Antilles departed from the following ports.[18]

[18] Cf. Jonathan Howes Webster, "The Merchants of Bordeaux in Trade to the French West Indies, 1664–1717" (Ph.D. diss., University of Minnesota, 1972).

La Rochelle	35	Marseille	4
Nantes	25	Toulon	2
Dieppe	10	Le Havre	7
Honfleur	10	Rouen	1
Saint-Malo	6	Dunkirk	1

Despite the losses of the Dutch war, a turnaround in transatlantic commerce occurred during the decade 1670–80. As at Bordeaux, growth henceforth depended upon the vigor of French transatlantic commerce (exclusively controlled by local capital in the port) and a major European north–south coastal commerce (with the exception of Iberian commerce, still a Dutch and Hanseatic quasi monopoly) to handle re-exports. Nantes, studied by J. Meyer, is a good example of this growth. The medieval threesome of wheat, wine, and salt was patently incapable, even when combined with cod, of ensuring anything more than slow growth in the best of cases, with small successive advances coupled with prolonged slumps. On the other hand, the opening of colonies accelerated trade; in less than a half century, from 1664 to 1704, the high seas fleet (ships of more than 100 tons) increased more than tenfold, from 12 to 151 ships.[19]

This acceleration was a result of Colbert's policies and can be measured in the eighteenth century, when the rate of expansion for all French commerce was superior to that for English commerce, this growth being essentially due to colonial trade.[20] The average annual value of foreign trade increased from 215 million livres in 1716–20 to 1,062 million in 1784–8, nearly quintupling (these figures in current prices). With a rise in prices of about 60 percent between 1730 and 1780 (less for agricultural products), one must deflate the figures from the end of the century to reduce them to constant values, but this still leaves a very clear progression. In 1716–20 the value of foreign trade barely exceeded half that of English commerce, but on the eve of the revolution it had reached a level close to the latter.

Where did French commerce control local markets?

France was the chief supplier of manufactured goods for Spain and, via Cadiz, for its American empire, whereas the British monopolized the smaller markets of Portugal and Brazil. In 1686 the French consul at Cadiz valued the French linens imported by Spain at 12 million livres; to these should be added the lace, gold, and silver of Tours and Lyons; the hats of Paris; and cloth from Picardy. In return, there were colonial products and especially piasters (12 million livres in

---

[19] J. Meyer, *Histoire de Nantes* (Toulouse, 1977), 135.
[20] Crouzet, "Angleterre et France au XVIIIe siècle," 261.

Table 4.2

The Growth of French Trade

(in Millions of Livres)

	1730 – 1740		1740 – 1754		1765 – 1776	
Colonial trade	32.0	70.2	70.2	120.4	108.0	191.0
Increase	119.0%		71.7%		76.7%	
Northern trade	10.8	24.4	24.4	51.9	53.5	79.9
Increase	107.6%		109.4%		55.4%	
Dutch trade	31.1	44.1	44.1	51.1	52.1	51.01
Increase	29.3%		15.9%		-16.15%	
Spanish trade	44.7	64.1	64.1	73.7	76.4	71.7
Increase	43.1%		14.4%		-6.1%	
Levant trade	12.3	41.0	41.0	53.2	56.2	65.9
Increase	331.0%		29.7%		17.3%	

Source: Bilan du Commerce de la France, Archives Nationales, Paris.

1673).[21] The French also dominated the markets of Italy and the Levant.

Of greatest importance was the spectacular development after 1700 of sugarcane cultivation on new soil on the French portion of Santo Domingo; the French price was very competitive with that of the sugar from the English Antilles, whose exports continued to decrease, in constant livres, from the beginning of colonialization until the middle of the eighteenth century. This growth corresponded to the expansion of European markets, especially those of northern Europe. British exports to the Continent advanced only slowly in absolute terms.[22] The driving force was provided by colonial re-exports, which multiplied eightfold while exports of French products only tripled. For all of France, the greatest acceleration occurred in the 1730s and 1740s, with the value of foreign trade doubling in less than eight years, be-

[21] J. Delumeau, "Le commerce extérieur de la France au XVIIIe siècle." One may contrast the 1669 exports of silk and linen products to England, which had a value of 800,000 livres.
[22] Crouzet, "Angleterre et France au XVIIIe siècle," 263.

tween 1736–9 and 1749–55. For re-exports the tempo of growth was higher still for the whole century, at Bordeaux exceeding 6 percent per year.

Sector by sector, Table 4.2 illustrates the tempo of growth. One is struck by the independent pattern of growth for French trade with the Levant; after having been the most vigorous of all the areas of trade, more than tripling in a decade, its tempo slackened very notably. It is clear nonetheless that this sector participated in the colonial connection, since one stream of re-exportation was directed toward the Levant. The trade with Spain remained one of the most important during this whole period, but its tempo not merely slackened but indeed declined, with a negative balance from 1765 to 1772. The Dutch trade also tended to regress, to the advantage of the trade with the north, the strength of which faithfully echoed that of the colonial trade but which grew even more rapidly during the middle of the century and remained the most vigorous of the European trades after the Seven Years' War.[23]

To be sure, this analysis lacks the final period, that which followed the American War of Independence. If one looks at colonial trade port by port, one finds the volume of trade climbing steeply during the 1780s: compared with midcentury, Bordeaux had tripled its colonial trade by 1787 (110 million livres compared with 34 million), and Le Havre had more than doubled its trade (53 million compared with 21 million). Of all the Atlantic ports, it was Nantes that had the slowest growth (relatively speaking – 45 million livres compared with 26 million). One is also struck by the relative lag in commerce between the Seven Years' War and the American war. The two phases of liveliest expansion were therefore 1730–50 and the few years preceding the French Revolution.

This growth rested upon the redistribution of colonial goods, which were themselves linked to the Dutch–Hanseatic "connection" and by it to the importation into France of grains, textile fibers, and wood from the north. To understand this process we must consider the role of these northern markets in French prosperity.

France, storehouse for northern Europe, and the special position of the Nordic markets

One of the better specialists, P. Jeannin, has shown that one should not be satisfied with measuring the importance of northern markets

---

[23] The value of trade with the north increased sixfold from 1730 to 1772, whereas trade with Holland did not even double.

only in terms of volume of trade. The role of intermediary between France and the countries of northern Europe, filled at first by Amsterdam and then more and more by Hamburg, did not consist solely of importing goods into France for re-export to the north and vice versa. It also included service functions, notably as regards credit, which was so often indispensable to firms since towns in France did not have direct commercial relationships with places beyond the Elbe.[24]

During the 1760s France imported around 10 percent of the raw materials originating from the Baltic. The country held first rank as a supplier of Hamburg and Bremen, delivering to Hamburg almost half of all it received by sea. As the dynamic colonial economy made its effects felt in the Nordic area, it caused the whole curve of French trade to rise, as well as stimulating further growth in the colonial sphere. One must, however, carefully define the specific characteristics of the flow of colonial goods to the Baltic. For France this commerce drained off its "excess," the goods of its colonies; the productive forces of the kingdom, except for viticulture and the manufacturing sector specializing in luxury and fashion goods, made only a small contribution. In return, the imports from the north were sought more as objects of demand for British commerce than as indispensable raw materials.

In the statistical records meant to show the French balance of trade, the term "north" does not refer to the distant north, the Baltic zone, but rather to the Hanseatic cities and "other countries."[25] Denmark and Sweden were removed from this category in 1734, and Russia was removed in 1744. The area that was left included Prussia and the ports of Germany and Poland, but the Hanseatic cities represented the most important part by far. From 1751 to 1780, the "north" in this narrow sense supplied more than 57 percent of French imports from the northern sector in the broad sense (pre-1734) and received more than 77 percent of the exports to the same sector. The "north's" share of the total European trade (not including the Levant) was 7.4 percent of imports and 8.2 percent of exports in 1721–40 and increased to 11.8 and 21.3 percent, respectively, in 1761–80.

The consular reports of Hamburg stress that manufactured articles – items of fashion and silks from Paris and Lyons, all light and valuable – came by road via Strassburg and Frankfurt and did not pass through the ports. The balance-of-trade statistics for France consider only maritime traffic for the north and are therefore incomplete. Ac-

[24] "Les marchés du Nord dans le commerce français au XVIIIe siècle," *Actes du Colloque des Historiens Economistes Français* (Paris, 1973), 71.
[25] Ibid., 69.

cording to these figures, colonial goods – sugar, coffee, and indigo – greatly predominated, representing 79 percent of imports coming from France during the 1760s, compared with less than 14 percent for wines. But colonial goods had attained this rank well before the middle of the century. If one takes account of merchandise arriving by land, worth nearly 5 million livres in 1750, colonial goods represented 60 percent of French exports to the north and wines 10 percent.

Aside from the years when France had a very great shortage of cereals (in 1752 grains represented 20 percent of the exports from Hamburg to France), this trade showed a great deficit for the north.[26] Whereas nearly 100 loaded ships left the Baltic bound for France, 139 loaded ships came from France to the Baltic. The cargoes coming from the west had a greater average value than those from the east. Between 1731 and 1740 nearly 235 ships left French ports for the Baltic, and to these should be added ships bound for Hamburg and Amsterdam, the transfer points where products for the north were re-shipped. Between 1749 and 1755 more than 310 ships coming from France passed through The Sound, and Hamburg and Bremen received between 220 and 240 French ships. These two ports allowed access to the German market and were more oriented toward central Europe than northern Europe. One may note the rather traditional role played by Königsberg and neighboring ports in receiving wine and salt, while Stettin, the port of Frederick II, shipped much wood and received many colonial goods, having overtaken Danzig in this role after 1750.

Of all the French ports, Bordeaux took the greatest share of the northern markets. In 1776–80 Bordeaux shipped more than 78 percent of its exports to the north.[27] As early as the middle of the century, in 1748–52, this port sold six times as many goods as in 1733–7, whereas exports did not even triple during the same period. Immediately after the American war, in 1783, Hamburg became the principal market for coffee and indigo shipped from Bordeaux – 46 percent and 25 percent, respectively, with tonnages of 6,400 and 100 tons – having largely supplanted Amsterdam for these commodities. By the middle of the century Bordeaux had become the greatest French port for the Baltic, assuming, with the help of Dutch and Hanseatic intermediaries, the supply of the wine, brandy, sugar, and coffee markets and a major part in French purchases of merchandise from the north.

This role is explained by the insertion into the Bordeaux merchant

[26] Ibid., 62.
[27] P. Butel, *Les Négociants Bordelais, L'Europe et les îles au xviiie siècle* (Paris, 1974), 47.

milieu of dynamic businessmen, agents from Amsterdam and, particularly during the eighteenth century, from Hamburg, Lübeck, Danzig, and Stettin. Thanks to their arrival in successive stages from the end of Louis XIV's reign to the American war, the agents "doing business with Germany and the Baltic countries" had strengthened their number: the Almanac of 1779 lists sixty-three agents of this type, and one may estimate the number of commercial firms of Germanic origin at some seventy to eighty, representing the largest foreign group in Bordeaux, even more numerous than the important Anglo-Irish colony.[28] New estimates made by W. Henninger put the number of Germans present in Bordeaux during the 1780s higher still, over 130 in 1782–4. This figure represents a very perceptible increase compared with the numbers of Germans present in 1711, 1744, and 1764–5, which the same author sets at 21, 39, and 75, respectively.[29] The inquest by the intendant Aubert de Tourny in 1743 enumerates eighteen traders who were "subjects of the Hanseatic Cities" and gives details of their business.[30] Thus the agent from Hamburg, Jean Christophe Harmensen, carried on northern trade "by the commissions which he has from Hamburg, Danzig, Rotterdam, and Sweden to send wine, sugar, and indigo and to receive in return planks, *merrain,* and *bourdillon*" (these last two products are woods for cooperage).

The recent study by P. Jeannin of the northern trade was based upon the example of one firm in Bordeaux, Schröder and Schyler. This study reveals a clear distribution of Bordeaux's northern clientele into three major levels. One rather large group of merchants regularly imported products from Bordeaux for local or regional distribution. The second level was composed of agents for centers like Danzig who required wine above all and did not indulge in speculation on colonial goods. At the highest level, one finds the traders of Hamburg, some of whom imported considerable quantities of colonial goods and arranged letters of credit for other ports. These Hamburg merchants were, however, far from enjoying a monopoly in this latter sector of credit, since they left an important role to firms from Amsterdam.[31]

---

[28] P. Butel, "Les Négociants allemands de Bordeaux dans la deuxième moitié du XVIIIᵉ siècle," *Wirtschaftskräfte und Wirtschaftswege,* vol. 2, *Wirtschaftskräfte in der europäischen Expansion* (Klett-Cotta, 1978), 597.

[29] *Studien zur Wirtschafts und Sozialgeschichte von Bordeaux im 18. Jahrhundert unter besonderer Berücksichtigung des deutschen Kaufleute,* vol. 1 (Cologne, 1986), 70–1.

[30] Archives de la Gironde, C 4439.

[31] "La clientèle étrangere de las maison Schröder et Schyler de la guerre de Sept Ans à la guerre d'Independance Americaine," *Bulletin du Centre d'Histoire des Espaces Atlantiques* 3 (1986): 21–85. Jeannin calls attention to the dependence of clients in Bremen for their payments, which were always transferred, either through Amsterdam or through Paris (p. 27). Of more than ninety firms in Amsterdam doing business with

The dynamism of these commercial networks stands out in Jeannin's analysis of private commercial papers and confirms the conclusions derived from statistical studies of the balance of trade concerning the overriding importance of northern markets for Bordeaux beginning in the mid-eighteenth century.

This leaves an ambivalent picture regarding the strength of France's commercial empire. It was founded, to be sure, on the growth of the shipping firms backed by very diverse investors, in particular, the financiers of Paris and many of its banking houses. But this strength would not have amounted to much without the constant intervention of foreign firms, based in the Atlantic ports (or Marseille) as well as in northern Europe. Thus, French overseas trade was vulnerable in that it was dependent on others, indeed doubly so. First, the trans-shipping trade that animated France's commercial empire depended on the Antilles trade, and any blows suffered by the latter struck heavily at metropolitan trade. One sees this in dramatic fashion during the "French Wars," the revolution and the Empire, when the colonies were cut off from metropolitan France. Second, French trade could not maintain its growth except by re-exporting to northern Europe. If this trade fell off, as happened during the "French Wars" at the close of the century, the whole trading empire was shaken. It was not until much later, after 1815, that a new equilibrium appeared in French maritime commerce, but by this time the transshipping ports that had been so important in the eighteenth century were banished into the shadow of markets protected by the system of colonial privilege.[32]

Exploitation of Indian Ocean routes and Asian commerce

The most recent research indicates that Colbert's efforts to open Asiatic routes to French trade were crowned with success in the long term. P. Haudrères has analyzed the flood of pamphlets written toward the close of Louis XIV's reign that argued for suppression of the French Company of the East Indies and shows that the company's operations around the middle of the eighteenth century were incontestably a success. Using a comparative approach in presenting the traffic in Asian goods received by Europe by the various companies acting as intermediaries, Haudrères shows that from 1720 onward the sales of the French Company of the East Indies saw a more significant growth

Schröder and Schyler in 1763–75, seventy-five appear to have had only the right to accept payments for the accounts of clients in other cities, especially Bremen and Danzig (p. 24).

[32] P. Butel, "Traditions and Changes in French Atlantic Trade between 1780 and 1830," *Renaissance and Modern Studies* 30 (1986): 142–3.

than the sales of the rival companies. In 1725 the VOC was well ahead in the surge of sales, the English East India Company was in second position, and the French company was in third place. After 1731 a strong growth in French sales stands out, and in 1735 these sales overtook English sales. There was severe competition between the French and English companies during the twenty years before 1759, the year when the English crushed their rivals. After 1760 the English company obtained the best results, overtaking and surpassing even the Dutch sales by the end of the 1760s.[33]

Some numerical indices may give an idea of the progress of French trade. Sales deriving from Asian trade increased rapidly after 1730, increasing from 7 million livres to 17 million in 1733, approaching 20 million per year in the early 1740s, and reaching more than 25 million annually on the eve of the Seven Years' War (1756–63). But the war was not as disruptive as one might have expected, considering that sales were still at 12.5 million in 1757–58. After the war, there was a perceptible recovery, with sales climbing to a bit less than 24 million livres in 1768. From 1725 until 1769, when the company was suppressed, India provided 72 percent of the sales, some 7 to 15 million livres per year. China came next with 21 percent, and 2 to 5 million livres per year, followed by the Mascarene Islands (east of Madagascar) with 7 percent, some 1 million. The position of India tended to diminish while that of China improved. It is fair to say that the variations in sales were more pronounced than for the other companies because of the effects of the wars.

Converting the value of trade into thousands of pesos, as N. Steansgaard has done (Table 3.23), the ten-year averages of sales of the French company can be calculated:

1731–40	1741–50	1751–60
2.823	2.290	2.777

These annual averages are lower than those for the other companies.

Division of sales by products shows that textiles made the strongest advance. White cottons and muslins constituted more than three-quarters of the textile cargoes coming from India, with the remainder composed of dyed linens and silk-stuffs. Sales of these textiles tripled from the 1720s to 1730–45. Orders for the famous "Company of the Indies" porcelains from China, already common during the first half of the century, were increased after the Seven Years' War. Among the bulkier articles, cargoes of cowries (small shells serving as money

---

[33] "La Compagnie Française des Indes (1719–1795)" (thesis, University of Paris IV, 1987), 2:438–40, for the analysis of these sales.

along the coast of Guinea and therefore indispensable for the slave trade) were always present but were of much lesser value. Of the other commodities, it was tea that had the highest value; cargoes of tea increased rapidly in number, and most of it was destined for Great Britain, as contraband. For most of these articles there was a tendency for prices to sink, which did not prevent the levels of profits from remaining high as volume grew. This Asian commerce was definitely linked with the Antilles trade by way of the slave trade. J. Meyer has shown the importance for Nantes of re-exportation of Indian cotton cloth to Africa,[34] and the importance of cowrie shells for the slave trade was just noted. In all these examples one sees the unity of the French commercial empire in its Asian, African, and American networks. The links between these networks explain why at Lorient, the center of sales for the Company of the East Indies, purchases by Nantes firms mainly concentrated upon Indian textiles and cowries; Paris bought spices, silks, and porcelains; Saint-Malo took a great part of the tea (being near England); and Bordeaux was very interested in porcelain. Atlantic coastal France dominated the company's sales just as its businessmen secured the largest part of French maritime commerce.

It is interesting to compare the profits obtained by the French company and by England's East India Company (Table 4.3). The French company's position improved in the middle of the century, before and after the War of the Austrian Succession. This fact is all the more interesting because profits on products from India declined after 1735, and those on Chinese commerce declined after 1745. The increased volume of sales compensated for this tendency.

If one compares the respective positions of the trade with Asia and with America, one sees a difference in scale (sales in millions of livres tournois):

	1750	*1772*
America	92	157
Asia	20	20.4

It was always America that guided French commercial growth, from midcentury to the eve of the American Revolution. But Asian com-

---

[34] *L'armement nantais dans la deuxième moité du xviiie siècle* (Paris, 1969), 161–4, 361. The author stresses very strongly the difference in the value of cargoes bound for the trade with Africa and the value of cargoes bound directly for the American islands. The higher value of the former derived from the place taken in these cargoes by linens from England and Holland before the middle of the century, and then later increasingly from India. Note the importance of these linens in the inventories of shipowners.

Table 4.3

Comparisons in Profits

(in Millions of Livres Tournois, Annual Averages)

	French company	East India Company
1725/6-29/30	4.4	19.7
1735/6-39/40	7.2	19.4
1740/1-44/5	8.3	12.1
1745/6-49/50	2.8	10.8
1751/1-54/5	11.5	7.5
1765/6-69/70	7.8	11.8

Source: Haudrère, Compagnie Fr. des Indes, II, 443.

merce secured profits that were far from negligible. The Mascarene trade had the closest connections to products traded in the Antilles commerce, and it provided the best profits, especially on coffee. We must add that the disparity between the trade with America and that with Asia grew between 1750 and 1772. By 1772, following the cancellation of the company's privileges in 1769, trade with Asia was free, and businessmen from the Atlantic ports and Marseille could undertake voyages to India and China. This does not seem to have increased trade, however. At midcentury, trade with America was almost five times that with Asia, but by 1772 it was more than seven times the value of the Asian trade.

Merchants who had been critical of the commercial privileges of the company met certain difficulties in launching themselves into trade with India and China. Conditions in this trade were much different from those in the American trade: The cycle for turnover of capital was much longer because voyages were longer and wear and tear on ships was heavier. On the route to the American islands a ship could make at least one round-trip voyage per year, sometimes two. A voyage to Asia might last more than twenty months in the 1720s. From 1735 to 1740 the duration of voyages was reduced to nearly eighteen months, but this was still at least twice that of Antilles voyages. In duration the voyages to Asia recall those of the slave trade, but in the latter the shipowners integrated the voyages into the Antilles trade. The Asian voyages remained separate. Their higher costs (the heavier tonnages of ships used for Asia also increased costs) demanded more substantial capital. One notes that the shipowners who devoted themselves to this trade after 1769 had recourse to the procedures of financing, like loans for major ventures, which had disappeared from the Atlantic routes and were relatively costly. Often foreign places had to be called upon to finance these voyages. Thus, at Bordeaux the ship *Maréchal de Mouchy*, equipped in 1783 for India by the firm of Feger and Gramont, combined capital provided by firms from Paris, Basel, Bilbao, and Santo Domingo.[35] Even more than for the Antilles trade, the shipowners had to combine their investments: firms from Bordeaux, Le Havre, and Saint-Malo collaborated during the 1780s for these ventures.

These voyages to Asia via the Ile de France (Mauritius) also represented a far from negligible effort at diversifying trade beyond the too exclusive and dangerous routes to the American islands and the re-export of their products. The spectacular growth of the "Pearl of the Antilles," Santo Domingo, whose progress had eclipsed the trade of its colonial rivals since the beginning of the eighteenth century, had been strongly favored by the nature of the French commercial empire, which was based upon exploitation of privilege, of colonial exclusivity, and of the re-export trade with northern Europe. During the 1770s and 1780s, however, new relationships began to form between these European markets and the Antilles. Merchants from English North America and then from the United States invaded the Antilles markets. England regained a place among European markets for the re-export of Antilles sugar. The situation became less favorable for French business.

The expansion of the Antilles trade, which had advanced French European commerce thanks to the sustained demand of northern European markets for "excess" colonial products, was the main innovation in French commerce since Colbert. It was able to overshadow traditional trade in wines, brandies, grains, and manufactured goods with both northern and Mediterranean Europe. However, it must be strongly stressed that it was this latter trade that provided the capital necessary to launch trade with the American islands and also to create the market demand. The Dutch–Hanseatic connection and the French commercial networks linked to it had prepared for the later growth. From this trade a commercial empire was born, doubtless favored by the mercantilist framework desired by Colbert. But changes in trade happening under cover of the wars of the French Revolution

---

[35] P. Butel, *Les négociants bordelais*, 41.

and of the Empire and the new importance of Hamburg and especially of London at the beginning of the nineteenth century brought
an end to the re-export trade on which the French Atlantic ports had
depended for their prosperity during the seventeenth and eighteenth
centuries.

CHAPTER 5

Productivity, profitability, and costs of private and corporate Dutch ship owning in the seventeenth and eighteenth centuries

JAAP R. BRUIJN

INTRODUCTION

By about 1450 the oceangoing ship had been developed. Out of a mixture of northern European and Mediterranean/Arabian practice in design and rig, called "a marriage" by J. H. Parry, the three-master came into being and was first used for ocean shipping by the Portuguese and Spaniards.[1] In principle this ship did not change until the nineteenth century, when iron and steam made completely different seagoing structures possible. Until then, the use of timber limited the size of ships. But within these restrictions a variety of types of vessels were designed after 1450. These types all were built with two or three masts and topmasts and equipped with square, lateen, and staysails. Improvement in sailing ability was made but did not have a great impact. For the operating costs of ships, changes in cargo-carrying capacity and in the number of crew on board were more important.

In this field, the Dutch made a major contribution at the end of the sixteenth century. The so-called *fluyt*, or flyboat, was then developed. This well-known story is connected with the city of Hoorn and Pieter Janszoon Liorno, regent and merchant as well as shipbuilder. The new feature of the oceangoing fluyt was its full concentration on cargo-carrying capacity. Until this time, ships had always been designed to carry armament; gun platforms, portholes, and reinforced construction were standard. Lacking such features, the fluyt could be lightly

[1] *The Age of Reconnaissance*, 2d ed. (London, 1966), 63.

built; it became much longer compared with its width than other types (1:4–6), and it was soon known for the simplicity of its rig. Fewer crew were needed than before. In a word, the fluyt was cheap and particularly suitable for the transport of bulk commodities. It was soon popular among Dutch and Baltic shipowners.

The fluyt could not defend itself, however, as the other types of vessels could. This was a basic innovation. Either it had to operate in waters where danger of attack was low, or it had to rely upon the assistance of men-of-war. Fluyts were mainly used in comparatively safe (i.e., northern European) waters, and the Dutch admiralities created a system of convoys. This was another Dutch innovation. The fact that the merchant shipping world paid incoming and outgoing duties to the admiralties entitled it to protection at fixed times. Various versions of the fluyt came into being. The *hekboot, bootschip,* and *katschip* were fairly large merchantmen. There were also smaller types, such as the *galjoten, boeiers,* and *hoekers,* which operated in nearby and Baltic waters. The safety of these unarmed or barely armed vessels was not guaranteed in time of war. Foreign privateers captured many, but the gaps in the merchant fleet were always filled quickly. All of this was instrumental in making cheapness and a continuous supply of cargo space the main characteristics of Dutch merchant shipping in Europe during the early modern period.

The vessels used for shipping outside European waters were very different. More defensible ships sailed to Asia, the West Indies, and also into the Mediterranean. These ships were more heavily constructed and were recognizable by rows of gunports on their sides and a square stern. Building and operating costs were much higher than for European shipping. Many more hands on board were needed. This division between the use of unarmed and armed vessels was in practice not as sharp as formulated here. In the long run changes took place. Lightly or barely armed merchantmen also sailed to the West Indies. But cost-saving in comparison with foreign competitors was never an overriding concern of Dutch shipping in distant seas. It had no special advantages. In transport to and from Asia free competition did not exist. Private shipowners were excluded from this activity; all shipping was the Dutch East India Company's own corporate concern.

Much has been written about Dutch merchant shipping and its main characteristics.[2] The pattern of routes has been described as well as the working of the staple market system. But questions about changes

---

[2] See *Maritieme geschiedenis der Nederlanden,* vol. 2 (Bussum, 1977), chapters on types of ships, ship owning, and shipping in Europe and shipping outside Europe.

in the productivity, profitability, and costs of Dutch merchant shipping have seldom been asked in the past, let alone answered; yet these are obvious questions with regard to a merchant empire like that of the Dutch in Europe and overseas. Students have been aware, however, of the research difficulties for early modern Dutch merchant shipping. Portbooks are seldom available, and the same applied to muster-rolls. Registers of names of ships or shipowners were never kept. Only the shipping movements of the East India Company can be followed in some detail.[3] Indirect sources such as incidental charter-parties, ship protests, or assessment rolls have to be exploited for information about types and tonnages of ships or names and numbers of crews used in European and Atlantic waters. Very few private shipowners' accounts have survived. This lack of serial and also qualitative sources and the difference between European and non-European shipping have seriously obstructed the formulation of general assessments about productivity, profitability, and costs. It is only over the past few years that some critical research has been done in this field. Some of the few relevant sources have been exploited. This essay explores new evidence on changes in productivity in Dutch European shipping during the seventeenth and eighteenth centuries, tackles the issue of whether Dutch ship owning was a profitable business or not, and analyzes the costs of shipping for a company in a monopoly position, that is, the East India Company.

PRODUCTIVITY OF DUTCH EUROPEAN SHIPPING

One of the great assets of the fluyt was the small number of seafarers required for handling the ship. Since Violet Barbour in 1930 published her classic article, her comparison of a 1620 Dutch and a 1620 English ship – both of the same burden of 200 tons, but the first with nine to ten crew members and the second with nearly thirty – has always been quoted as proof of Dutch superiority in seafaring efficiency.[4] Whether this is a good and representative example cannot be confirmed by figures taken from a wide sample of seventeenth-century fluyts. The Dutch merchant fleet, however, was not solely composed of fluyts but also of various other types of ships, from frigates to boeiers.

---

[3] J. R. Bruijn, F. S. Gaastra, and I. Schöffer, *Dutch-Asiatic Shipping in the 17th and 18th Centuries*, vol. 2, *Outward-Bound Voyages from the Netherlands to Asia and the Cape (1595–1794)*, and vol. 3, *Homeward-Bound Voyages from Asia and the Cape to the Netherlands (1597–1795)* (The Hague, 1979).

[4] "Dutch and English Merchant Shipping in the Seventeenth Century," *Economic History Review* 2 (1930): 261–90, reprinted in E. M. Carus-Wilson, *Essays in Economic History* (London, 1954), 1:227–53, esp. 246.

One generally assumes that the use of the fluyt was preponderant, although not on all European trade routes. A contemporary figure from 1636 about the size of the fleet permits calculation of the ton-to-man ratio. On an average, fourteen tons were served by one seaman.[5] Available information permits the conclusion that productivity in Dutch European shipping during the first half of the seventeenth century was higher than in other countries. The English merchant fleet in that period still lacked large bulk carriers and consisted mainly of small vessels and the so-called defensible ships.

For the end of the seventeenth century the British historian Ralph Davis has noticed an increased productivity in English shipping. Step by step, Dutch fluyts had been incorporated into the English merchant fleet, especially as a consequence of the capture of hundreds of Dutch merchantmen during the three Anglo-Dutch wars between 1652 and 1674. In the last part of the century English shipwrights had begun to produce ships that could compete with the Dutch fluyt.[6] But had Dutch productivity remained the same as earlier in the century?

Paul C. van Royen has studied the composition of the European merchant fleet of the Netherlands and its manpower around 1700. He has extracted the marrow from the indirect sources already referred to, such as the charter-parties and ship protests. He demonstrates that Dutch shipboard productivity grew immensely after 1636. The total cargo-carrying capacity of this fleet was greater than it had been sixty-five years earlier, although the number of ships and seafarers had stayed the same. The implication is clear. The ton-to-man ratio had changed to 22:1. Van Royen convincingly argues that Dutch masters were in command of bigger ships than their predecessors, but that they had to handle their ships with the same number of seamen. He also proves that these seamen were still of good professional quality.[7]

The role of the fluyt was dominant. More than half, perhaps almost two-thirds, of the European fleet (the smallest vessels used in the trade with northern Germany excluded) consisted of fluyts and related types. The second main type was that of the two- and three-masted galjoten, ships with an average tonnage of about one-third

---

[5] J. Lucassen, "Zeevarenden," in *Maritieme geschiedenis der Nederlanden*, 2:132, and calculations by P. C. von Royen, *Zeevarenden op de koopvaardijvloot omstreeks 1700* (Amsterdam, 1987), 169–79.

[6] R. Davis, *The Rise of the English Shipping Industry in the Seventeenth and Eighteenth Century*, 2d ed. (Newton Abbot, 1972), 47–54, 369–72; G. M. Walton, "Obstacles to Technical Diffusion in Ocean Shipping, 1675–1775," *Explorations in Economic History* 8 (1970): 123–40, esp. 126–8.

[7] *Zeevarenden op de koopvaardijvloot omstreeks 1700*, 169–79.

that of the fluyts. By and large, ships were employed efficiently and rationally: the longer the route, the bigger the ship and the higher the ton-to-man ratio. In the Norwegian timber trade, for example, only fluyts larger than 400 tons were used. Frigates formed a small part of the fleet and operated on the longest stretches, to the eastern Mediterranean and northern Russia. Their ton-to-man ratio was, as can be expected, much lower: 6:1.[8]

What were the causes for the apparent increase in productivity during the seventeenth century? There is no indication of new labor-saving techniques in the handling of ships. Perhaps provisions for armament were even less needed than before, which would have saved hands. Apart from the seas infested by Barbary corsairs, European waters were safer than at the beginning of the century – at least in peacetime. In wartime, masters of merchant ships had learned that resistance against hostile privateers was in most cases of no avail. But the main cause for growth in productivity was the demand for larger means of transport. All types of ships around 1700 were bigger, and probably more fluyts and related types were built than before. This increase in scale was not followed by an increase in manning requirements. A seaman's work on a 300-ton fluyt was not 50 percent greater than on a 200-ton fluyt.

But one important aspect of this growth in scale and higher productivity needs to be considered. Was all of this the result of a gradual development or only the outcome of the temporary boom in Dutch shipping during the last two decades of the seventeenth century? In other words, could these n w standards be maintained long after 1700? Van Royen's study does not raise this question, nor does it touch upon the consequences of the higher productivity for freight rates and competitiveness with the English;[9] it focuses mainly on the seamen and their recruitment. Further data on freight rates and competitiveness for the eighteenth century are not available. For this century, however, a bit more can be said about the profitability of the merchant fleet.

PROFITABILITY OF DUTCH EUROPEAN SHIPPING

Did Dutch shipowners make a profit from their business? Given their long-standing involvement in shipping, a positive answer has usually

---

[8] Ibid.

[9] See G. M. Walton, "Sources of Productivity Change in American Colonial Shipping, 1675–1775," *Economic History Review*, 2d ser., 20 (1967): 67–78; and Douglass C. North, "Sources of Productivity Change in Ocean Shipping, 1600–1800," *Journal of Political Economy* 76 (1968): 953–70.

been taken for granted. In 1979, however, the Belgian historian Wilfrid Brulez argued that shipping itself was not a profitable business. In the Netherlands and elsewhere shipping during the early modern period was only a nominal source of profit or capital accumulation. At first sight, one is surprised by this conclusion. Why then have people for centuries continued to invest their money in ship owning? But Brulez has some good arguments. His main point is the distinction between shipping and trade. The first could offer favorable returns of any significance only in combination with the latter (or with privateering or hire for war purposes). The high level of shareholding in ships and its widespread appeal to all sorts of groups within the population do not necessarily prove that profitability was the only consideration in the choice of investment.[10]

Ralph Davis proposed the same sort of question in 1962 when asking "whether the lure which brought the ever-expanding flow of fresh capital into shipowning [i.e., English], whether the expectation of adequate gains . . . was in fact an expectation that profits would be earned on capital invested at an average rate as good as or better than that encountered in other occupations open to investors." He answers his own question by remarking that one cannot say with precision what "profitable" meant to the merchant/investor of the seventeenth or eighteenth century. He claims that lack of evidence of either solid gains or losses is less important than the fact that investment in the shipping industry continued without abatement and in England even increased. According to Davis, a ship was an investment that offered a fluctuating return, dependent on the duration of voyages and the level of freight rates and repair costs. The element of chance in the returns on the investment was always substantial, though it declined from the seventeenth into the eighteenth century. Chance was also smaller from the point of view of the entire life of the ship than of one single year or voyage.[11]

It is too early for such a well-balanced interpretation of the profitability of Dutch merchant shipping as Davis had made of the English. Much of the basic information is not available. But Brulez's stimulating article has provoked reactions. W. G. 't Hart and Van Royen have argued that the separation between shipping and trade is artificial. There were no shipowners as such. These people were merchants as

---

[10] "De scheepvaartwinst in de nieuwe tijden," *Tijdschrift voor Geschiedenis* 92 (1979): 1–19, also published in English as "Shipping Profits in the Early Modern Period," in *The Low Countries Yearbook* 1981, *Acta Historiae Neerlandicae* 14 (1981): 65–84. See especially pp. 71, 76, and 83 of the English version.

[11] *Rise of the English Shipping Industry*, chap. 17, esp. pp. 383–6.

well. For transport one used one's own tonnage or hired space in another ship. Both authors have provided us with detailed research on an eighteenth-century ship's account book.[12] Their example was soon followed by Mrs. Hendrikje Renkema-Homs and R. S. Wegener Sleeswijk.[13] Their results deserve attention. This sort of research helps to remedy the lack of concrete evidence (at least for the eighteenth century) deplored by Davis and Brulez.

Davis, who himself studied the financial fortunes of four English ships, developed a system according to which running costs can be best subdivided. He used four categories: (1) wages and victuals of the crew, (2) repairs and stores, (3) port charges, lighthouse dues, pilotage, and so on, and (4) normal miscellaneous expenses.[14] Income from freight has to be set against the running costs in order to get an idea about the earning capacity of the ship, and the problems of depreciation and interest cannot be ignored. Another difficulty arises when part of the cargo went on the account of the ship itself.

Using Davis's system as much as possible, Renkema analyzed the financial administration of a fluyt that was continuously freighted by third parties only. The *Juffrouw Christina* was a rather big fluyt of about 450 tons; it was built at Amsterdam in 1717. A group of eight wealthy Amsterdam merchants bought the ship secondhand in 1724. The price was *f*10,160, and an extra *f*3,600 was needed to make the *Juffrouw Christina* (the name of the one woman amongst the owners) ready for sea. The master and his crew of about fourteen were in paid service. In the period 1724–34 no less than twenty-one voyages were made to the Baltic, almost all to Narva (in Russia), outward-bound in ballast, homeward-bound always with timber as the sole cargo. The timber was destined for the vessel's charterers in Amsterdam; all were timber merchants or timber brokers. Insurance was never taken out by the shipowners. At the end of 1734 the owners (except for one, all Baptists and relatives or very close friends of each other) decided to sell the *Juffrouw Christina*. It yielded a higher price than it had cost: *f*11,025. The ship had been properly maintained; it had received new planking in 1727. The owners, most of whom regularly invested in

---

[12] W. G. 't Hart and P. C. van Royen, "Het smakschip De Neufville van der Hoop: Een onderzoek naar de rentabiliteit van de Nederlandse vrachtvaart in de achttiende eeuw," *Economisch- en Sociaal-Historisch Jaarboek* 48 (1985): 150–68, esp. 151.

[13] H. Renkema-Homs, "Het fluitschip 'De Juffrouw Christina,' 1724–1735: Rendementsberekening en prosopografie van de partenhouders" (M.A. thesis, University of Amsterdam, 1987); R. S. Wegener Sleeswijk, "Rendement van 36 Friese partenrederijen (1740–1830)," *Jaarboek Fries Scheepvaart Museum en Oudheidkamer*, 1986, 66–89.

[14] *Rise of the English Shipping Industry*, 365.

English funds or in other ships, had no reason to deplore their decision to buy the *Juffrouw Christina* at a public auction. After their initial investment of ƒ1,720 each, they never had to supply more money. On the contrary, six times they enjoyed the payment of dividends amounting to ƒ18,000. After the liquidation, another ƒ16,240 was divided, or in other words, the investment of ƒ13,760 in the exploitation of the fluyt during 128 months produced a profit of ƒ20,480. According to the internal rate of interest, the return on their capital had been 13.3 percent year year! Dutch public loans around 1730 returned 3 percent, but offered less risks.

't Hart and Van Royen's case study deals with a smak-ship, a small ship that could operate in shallow coastal waters. This one had a cargo-carrying capacity of 100 tons and was manned by four or five men. An Amsterdam textile merchant was the single owner of the *De Neufville van der Hoop*; he had bought it in 1751 secondhand for ƒ4,900. It is not known when this smak-ship had been built. It operated between the Baltic and the French Atlantic coast, sailing east in ballast on one of about every three voyages and the rest of the time carrying a great variety of bulk and miscellaneous goods. In 1764 it was sold for ƒ2,080. Then owner and master together bought another, new ship. *De Neufville van der Hoop* profited from slightly higher freight rates during the Seven Years' War, but it also suffered from wartime risks. Although neutral it was captured by a British privateer and for seven months was detained in Portsmouth. On some of the voyages salt was bought, carried, and sold by the master; the money involved formed an integral part of the ship's accounts. The financial results of these transactions were not exceptional: per ton salt profits were seldom higher than income from transport for charterers. Again, ship-owning was profitable to the owner, Jan Isaac de Neufville. Only a few times during the war did he consider it necessary to take out insurance on his ship. A number of voyages had a negative financial outcome, but the majority showed a profit. The return on his investment over a period of 157 months was 12.2 percent per year.

The third and last case, studied by Wegener Sleeswijk, deals with the financial history of thirty-six ships owned between 1740 and 1830 by a group of Frisian shipowners living far away from the metropolis of Amsterdam. These small and sometimes midsized vessels operated mainly between the Baltic and the French Atlantic coast. There was no writing off of the original sums paid in, and insurance was not taken out. Many times goods were bought and transported on the account of the managing owners. War mostly meant higher profits. One-third of the thirty-six ships did not return the invested capital; the other twenty-four amply did. The overall return on the capital of the whole fleet was about 10 percent per year.

These three examples refute Brulez's verdict of the lack of profitability of Dutch European shipping, at least as far as the eighteenth century is concerned. Brulez's evidence, however, is mainly based on the late sixteenth and seventeenth centuries, a period when there was probably less regularity and safety in trading and shipping. But the case studies also illustrate how difficult it is to make a distinction between shipping and trade. The salt traded on the account of the *De Neufville van der Hoop* is one example of this difficulty, and the discovery of an error in the accounts of the *Juffrouw Christina* is another. In 1727 both its ship's husband, David Leeuw, and its bookkeeper made an error of ƒ1,000. This sum was unjustly distributed amongst the shareholders. Mrs. Renkema was the first one who noticed the error. David Leeuw did not miss the money. The cash in hand of the ship was not kept apart from his other finances. Leeuw also had shares in other ships.

Another point to consider is how representative these cases are for Dutch eighteenth-century shipping. Perhaps it is best to accept that they are representative, as long as the contrary has not been proved. The ships made regular runs, which was normal on those routes. They operated in waters in which most of the Dutch fleet was active. Besides, there is no reason to assume that the managing owners of these ships were better qualified to run a shipping company than their colleagues. Both Leeuw and De Neufville lived on their estates and in their houses on the most prestigious canals of Amsterdam. Bookkeepers handled the accounts. The ships' masters were salaried employees but had different powers. De Neufville's second and much more active master was entitled to look for remunerative cargoes in foreign ports without waiting for instructions from the owner or his foreign agent. The Frisian managing owners were merchants and tradesmen in small cities such as Makkum and Workum.

In this context reference may also be made to an article by Sarah Palmer. She studied the activities of a Woolwich coal merchant and dealer in bricks and stone, John Long. This tradesman also invested in ships and had shares in ten vessels in the period 1815–28. At least half of these vessels were regularly employed in trades other than coal. Palmer examined the accounts of sixteen voyages made by three ships. Despite some missing costs, she argues that the general impression of profitability is irrefutable. She warns against the mistake of assuming that the nonspecialist shipowner, the person for whom shipping investment was a sideline, was less committed to the business than the person for whom shipping was more important. Long's active professional concern for his shipping enterprises supports this.[15] The two Amsterdam shipowners also kept up a regular correspondence with their masters and bookkeepers.

A few concluding observations with regard to our three case studies and to Brulez's argument. The smak-ship *De Neufville van der Hoop* spent less time in port than the fluyt *Juffrouw Christina*. It was in operation three-quarters of the year, whereas the timber trade required only seven months of the year. The running costs of the *Juffrouw Christina* can be divided thus: 32 percent for wages, 18 percent for victualing, 26 percent for repairs and stores, and 24 percent for port charges and related costs. The category of miscellaneous expenditures was negligible. The accounts of the smak-ship do not allow such a division of running costs to be made. Wages required 25 percent of the total. Per ton the average contribution to the earnings from freight was *f*210 for the fluyt (over 128 months) and *f*710 for the smak-ship (over 157 months). The accounts of the *Juffrouw Christina* made possible the calculation of even more detailed figures. During each of the two annual voyages to the Baltic, *f*7.96 per ton was spent on running costs, and *f*10.01 per ton was earned on freight. Details of the same kind are not mentioned in the Frisian study.

The *Juffrouw Christina* and the *De Neufville van der Hoop* both evidently enjoyed a long second life and even started a third life. The fluyt was seventeen years old when sold again; the smak-ship was at least fourteen. These ages are much higher than the seven years that Brulez considers an average.[16] The mean length of time the thirty-six Frisian vessels (new and secondhand) were owned was about ten years. One vessel even sailed thirty-one years for the same owners! But no less than 14 were lost at sea, a high figure in comparison with the 9 vessels lost out of a seagoing fleet of 126 that made almost 6,000 voyages in the years 1746–75 from their home port of Zierikzee in the province of Zeeland.[17]

Recent research has thus provided us with consistent data showing returns of 10 percent and more on the exploitation of merchant ships

---

[15] "John Long, A London Shipowner," *Mariner's Mirror* 72 (1986): 43–62.

[16] Brulez, "Shipping Profits," 67–70. Two of the references quoted by Brulez, Hart and Davis, do not support his argument. Hart gives seven years as the average age of 142 ships mentioned in wills and partitions of property of some Amsterdam merchants in 1644; i.e., seven years was not the average age at the end of the careers of these ships. Davis writes that wooden ships could have a very long life!

[17] E. van der Doe, "Het welvaren van Zierikzee: Omvang, ontwikkeling en functioneren van de koopvaardij in Zierikzee, 1746–1775" (M.A. thesis, University of Leiden, 1986), 79 and 119.

in the old traditional trades of western and northeastern Europe. More general observations on profitability and productivity, let alone on costs of Dutch European shipping in the early modern period, will have to wait for more case studies. Nevertheless, one need not be surprised by our examples of increased productivity and solid profits in that sector of world merchant shipping where free enterprise and competition dominated. That was certainly not the case in shipping to Asia, to which the discussion will now turn.

COSTS OF DUTCH SHIPPING TO ASIA

A shipping company was a single-ship affair. Every ship had a different list of shareholding owners. But shares of different ships could be in the hand of one owner. One ship's husband could have the management of different ships, each with its own accounts. These were common features of seventeenth- and eighteenth-century shipping. And although shipping and trade cannot be separated, a merchant-shipowner would not regularly freight his own means of transport. There were, however, exceptions. The most important exception was the Dutch East India Company. This joint-stock company, founded in 1602 and officially dissolved in 1796, did not use any of these methods. Right from the beginning, three activities were subsumed under one authority: shipowning, freighting, and shipbuilding.

There were reasons for such a management structure. The East India Company had been given the exclusive right of trading and shipping east of the Cape of Good Hope and west of the Strait of Magellan. These privileges had been granted in 1602 by the States General of the Dutch Republic by means of a charter, which was always renewed on expiry. No private Dutch citizen was entitled to any sort of activity within the territory of the company. At that time a chartered company was not an uncommon structure for large-scale activities of a risky nature or involving distant places. For the East India Company, the large capital sum of ƒ6,424,588 had been raised on a long-term basis. This sort of structure had also been applied to the first Dutch whaling enterprises, when in 1614 the Northern Company was granted a monopoly. This monopoly, however, was not prolonged beyond its expiry in 1642, when the motives for it were no longer valid.

Decisions about the size of the company's shipping activities were made by a board of directors, the so-called Heren XVII, which met twice per year. Decisions were executed by six so-called chambers (situated in six cities), who were charged with the construction, equipment, and freighting of the company's ships. Each chamber handled a carefully defined fraction of these activities: The chamber of Amsterdam was responsible for one-half, that of Middleburg (Zeeland) for one-fourth, and the four others for one-sixteenth each. Each chamber owned a building site with ships and storehouses for ship supplies and commodities.

One who studies the company as a shipping organization is struck by the high degree of continuity. The same picture unfolds over two centuries. Wars hardly disturbed it. Only the number of ships annually built, equipped, and freighted varied, indicating either periods of expansion and decline or changes in the intra-Asiatic trade. Approximately 1,600 ships were launched from the company's yards. The six chambers organized 4,789 voyages to the Cape and Asia, two-thirds of which took place in the eighteenth century.[18]

The scale on which the Dutch company operated was quite exceptional, but the way in which its shipping was organized was not. All other European Asiatic companies more or less followed the same practice. They were the owners, though not always the builders, of their own means of transport. It was considered the best manner in which trade with and in Asia could be practiced. The East Indiaman was the favorite type of ship for each company: strong and big, in shape and gunnery like a man-of-war, durable, but much more expensive than the average merchantman in building and maintenance.

In 1639 the directors of the English East India Company stopped building their own ships and sold their two yards along the river Thames. Pressed by financial problems, they switched over to the system of charter contracts with private shipowners. For each round-trip a standard charter-party was signed by the directors of the company and the owners, stipulating among other things freight rates for the diverse kinds of import goods. It became customary for these ships (East Indiamen) to make a number of consecutive voyages, usually four. Later in the eighteenth century the owners and their captains had the tacit right to make another ship available. The term *hereditary bottoms* was then used overtly. Thus, the English company was the exception to the rule that made other Asiatic companies shipowner and shipper all in one, while some were also shipbuilders.[19]

The Heren XVII of the Dutch East India Company did once consider changing their shipping policy, around 1685. They looked at their English competitors, who were convinced that the English sys-

---

[18] Bruijn, Gaastra, and Schöffer, *Dutch Asiatic Shipping in the 17th and 18th Centuries*, chap. 1–3.
[19] Ibid., chap. 6.

tem, which paid only the cost of hiring ships, was more economical.[20] But the Heren XVII remained loyal to their system, right until the end of the eighteenth century. But what were the costs of this system and the financial and organizational benefits? How did it really compare with the English system?

Not much research has been done on the transport costs of the Dutch East India Company. This company bequeathed a huge archive – kept in the State Archive at The Hague – but the documents provide no straightforward insight into the costs of shipping activities. Separate records for each ship were not kept. The company's accounts are still there, though a general analysis of the expenses is possible only from the beginning of the eighteenth century. The term *equipagiën* in the accounts covered all expenses made by the six chambers with regard to shipbuilding, shipping, freighting, and outward-bound cargoes. Among these expenses, there were no entries for construction or repair per ship. The equipagiën costs were divided into a number of elements, grouped around items such as cargo, bullion and bills of exchange, ship's materials and victualing, wages, and costs of embarkation and unloading.

In 1958 the Danish historian Kristof Glamann studied these sources for the first time. For the period 1714–28 he grouped the different elements in such a way that a separation of expenses connected with the dispatch of the ships became possible. He also tried to define an average cost per ton, but he could not discover the correct total tonnage in use during this period.[21] In 1984 J. P. de Korte published an extensive survey of the company's accounts, providing the reader with thousands of figures for further research. He has followed Glamann's system in grouping the different elements of equipagiën costs, but now for the whole eighteenth century.[22] Recently, the annual tonnage dispatched to Asia has also become available.[23] On the basis of Glamann's classification and the new information, calculation of the price per ton in the company's shipping structure may now be possible. This method of calculation is highly speculative and unsophisticated. It takes into account expenses for shipbuilding, shipowning, and outfitting but not items such as depreciation and interest. Comparable seventeenth-century data are lacking.

Among the equipagiën costs, three categories of outlays are rele-

---

[20] I am grateful for my colleague F. S. Gaastra's advice regarding this problem.
[21] *Dutch-Asiatic Trade, 1620–1740*, 2d ed. (Copenhagen and The Hague, 1981), 42–7.
[22] *De jaarlijkse financiële verantwoording in de Verenigde Oostindische Compagnie* (Leiden, 1984), 53–56, and appendices 12A and 12B.
[23] Bruijn, Gaastra, and Schöffer, *Dutch Asiatic Shipping*, 1:42–4 and 174.

vant: (1) ship's materials, (2) victualing, and (3) wages. The materials were used for the construction as well as for the repair and maintenance of ships. Although some part of the victualing was sometimes forwarded to Asia, most of the supplies were consumed on board outward- and homeward-bound vessels. The wages were paid to laborers in the yards and to seamen and soldiers at the moment of enlistment and upon return. In Table 5.1 figures for these expenses have been compiled by decade. The tonnage dispatched and the average price per ton are also shown.

These calculations are not completely accurate for several reasons. The authorities in Batavia also spent money on the wages of those on board, ship repairs, and victualing; De Korte refers to these outlays as costs of shipping and wages in Asia. These costs, however, included a variety of other expenditures not related to the company's European ships. At the Cape, outward- and homeward-bound ships were provided with refreshments, which were not accounted for in the equipagiën costs. All these expenses should have been included, but reasonably correct figures cannot be given. But this inadequacy in the calculation is compensated by the fact that soldiers' wages count in the third column of the table. By and large, one out of each three on board was a soldier and occupied a typical noneconomic position in a shipowner's view; soldiers were not on the payroll of most of the other Asiatic companies. The small amount of clerical staff salaries has not been included in the third column, contrary to the practice of Glamann and De Korte. Although for obvious reasons accuracy cannot be guaranteed, it seems reasonable to write off the soldiers against the extra expenditure overseas. If one accepts this approximation, Table 5.1 presents a rather realistic picture of transport costs during the eighteenth century.

Some other observations: the amounts in the table cover virtually all the company's outlays in the Netherlands for building, repairing, maintaining, equipping and staffing the annual fleets. Losses through disasters and breaking up and additions of new vessels have all been accounted for. The company never took out insurance on its own ships and their cargoes. There is no reason to add a fictional sum for insurance; one would then also have to add the fictional compensation collected by the company for lost ships and cargoes.[24] At a price of about ƒ250 to ƒ290 per ton, the company had its commodities and soldiers transported to and from Asia, at least in the period until 1780;

---

[24] J. Steur used insurance costs in his calculations in *Herstel of Ondergang: De voorstellen tot redres van de VOC, 1740–1795* (Utrecht, 1984), 254.

Table 5.1

Cost of the Company's Shipping in the Eighteenth Century

	Materials	Victualing	Wages	Total	Tonnage	Price per ton
	(ƒ1000)	(ƒ1000)	(ƒ1000)	(ƒ1000)		(ƒ)
1700–10	15,444	9,142	29,608	54,194	186,364	291
1710–20	17,629	10,238	31,830	59,697	228,066	262
1720–30	22,438	11,816	37,846	72,100	289,233	249
1730–40	25,325	12,022	39,916	77,263	280,035	276
1740–50	21,349	14,006	36,516	71,871	252,715	284
1750–60	22,841	11,156	42,733	76,730	278,845	275
1760–70	22,525	11,223	44,626	78,374	291,605	269
1770–80	22,934	12,479	44,032	79,445	290,340	274
1780–90	34,353[a]	12,636	39,986	86,975	243,424	357
1790–96	8,089[a]	3,748	18,446	30,283	94,467	321

[a]Expenses for ship hiring, insurance, etc., included.

Sources: Ed Korte, De jaarlijkse financiële verantwoording in de Verenigde Oostindische Compagnie (Leiden, 1984), appendices XIIA and XIIB (the amounts have been doubled); J. R. Bruijn, F. S. Gaastra, and I. Schöffer, Dutch Asiatic Shipping in the 17th and 18th Centuries (The Hague, 1987), 1:174.

then the situation changed. At this price, transport was available for about two years. The company was never bound by time limits, which were mentioned in the charter-parties of its English competitor. It could always freely dispose of its vessels, including in the East. A Dutch contemporary equivalent for the term *demurrage*, so crucial in the English organization, did not even exist.

Has this line of reasoning and calculating resulted in reliable prices? Our results for the period are confirmed by the only available other price, calculated by Glamann for a voyage to China in 1732: *f*275.[25] Even more interesting are the prices presented in a forthcoming article by K. N. Chaudhuri on the shipping of the English East India Company between 1670 and 1760. The freight price per ton, meticulously calculated by the great expert on the history of the English company, could vary a great deal. Its annual average during the eighteenth century was at its lowest level in the years 1716–40. The English company then had to pay between £24 and £30 per ton. In 1700–15 and 1741–60 prices above £35 were quite common.[26]

To compare these figures with the Dutch figures, the rate of exchange between pounds sterling and guilders has to be known. According to N. W. Posthumus the rate changed from about *f*10.20 in the early eighteenth century to c. *f*12.00 in 1794.[27] This means that the English price in 1716–40 was the equivalent of *f*250 to *f*315, and £35 was equivalent to *f*370. Especially in wartime freight rates fluctuated wildly, and a number of prices quoted by J. Sutton suggest a higher level than £30 throughout most of the rest of the century: 1763, £31–£34 (= *f*326–357); 1772, £34–£37 (= *f*347–377); 1780, £47 (= *f*494); 1785, £20–£24 (= *f*226–266); and 1794, £ (= *f*420).[28]

Two tentative conclusions in this hitherto-unexplored field can be drawn. First, the costs of the Dutch company's own transport system until about 1780 were stable, which compared favorably with the steady rise in the English system of chartering ships. Second, Dutch and English costs were more or less equal between 1700 and 1740. In the period 1740–80 the English system became more expensive. This was the period in which, according to Sutton, "the supply and organization of [English] shipping was . . . taken almost entirely out of the

---

[25] *Dutch-Asiatic Trade*, 47.

[26] To be published in the forthcoming volume, *Companies and Shipping*, ed. J. R. Bruijn and F. S. Gaastra, Leiden Center for the History of European Expansion.

[27] *Nederlandsche prijsgeschiedenis* (Leiden, 1943), 1:595–612. One can also use J. J. McCusker, *Money and Exchange in Europe and America, 1600–1775* (Williamsburg, 1978), 58–60. For fluctuation in the exchange rate between pounds sterling and guilders and the exchange rate's relation to the value of the company's shares, see Chap. 6.

[28] *Lords of the East: The East India Company and Its Ships* (London, 1981), 33–6.

company's control," and an investigation into the high costs became unavoidable.[29] By then the company was almost completely at the mercy of the whims of some Thames-side shipbuilders.

Dutch shipping activities increased enormously in the beginning of the century and from then on remained rather stable. At first, the more voyages were made, the more ships were involved. In the middle of the century, vessels were larger and were used more cost efficiently for transport between the Netherlands and Asia and back. Their role in intra-Asiatic shipping diminished. The average duration of the outward voyage to Batavia had always been about eight months, and the voyage back home, about the same. As a result of some innovations, the duration in both directions was shortened in the period 1750–70.[30] These improvements were, at least to a certain extent, also reflected in the transport costs.

The overall expenditure on shipbuilding and shipping activities seems to have been kept well under control by the Dutch company. The impact of the general rise in costs of building is not noticeable. In 1688 the largest East Indiaman had at the start of its first voyage an estimated value of ƒ98,200. About fifty years later, a sum of ƒ135,000 was needed for such a vessel. And a century later, around 1790, a first-rate East Indiaman was valued at ƒ184,000.[31] Nevertheless, company servants were successful in keeping the expenditure on materials rather stable, between ƒ77 and ƒ84 per ton, with an exception in the 1730s, when expenditures rose to ƒ90. Victualing costs fluctuated between ƒ38 and ƒ49 per ton, except in the 1740s, when victualing cost ƒ55. Both kinds of outlays showed a distinctive downward trend from the 1750s onward. Expenditures on wages show a different picture. These costs fluctuated between ƒ131 and ƒ153, with a maximum of ƒ159 between 1700 and 1710. Wages were by far the biggest outlay in the costs of shipping, increasing since the 1720s. Higher salaries cannot be blamed for this increase. But time and again more seamen and soldiers were enlisted, reaching a peak in the late 1760s with about eight to nine thousand men per year.[32] Whether the labor force in the dockyards also grew is unknown.

Until around 1780 the question of whether owning or chartering ships offered more advantages was seldom discussed by the Heren XVII of the company. This did not mean that the directors had no interest in the costs of transportation. Around 1730 they devoted much

---

[29] Ibid., 32–3.
[30] Bruijn, Gaastra, and Schöffer, *Dutch-Asiatic Shipping,* 1:74, 89, and 174.
[31] Ibid., 27–8.
[32] Ibid., 144, also 163.

attention to the profitability of the new direct trade with China. Expenses and receipts of eleven voyages were brought together in the ledgers under a special heading. Glamann used these figures for a calculation of costs of transport. His result was the price per ton of *f*275, already referred to. He also discovered that the company was familiar with the depreciation of ships and that the term "wear and tear" was known.[33] But these separate accounts and their terminology seem to have been an exception.

During the fourth Anglo-Dutch war (1780–4) and its aftermath, buying and chartering ships were no longer academic questions for the company. British supremacy at sea and a shortage of transport capacity forced the company to sell a number of ships to neutral owners, to buy ships from private shipbuilders, and to hire from private owners. This happened in the years 1782–9 on a rather wide scale. Greater building activities had in the meantime provided for new tonnage. But again, in 1793 and 1794, when war with revolutionary France had broken out, private ships had to be chartered.

Buying and hiring had always been considered temporary measures. One took it for granted that construction and use of one's own means of transport were cheaper. And the experience during and after the war did not change the directors' minds, though freight rates of chartered ships had probably been lower than those of their own ships. After the fourth Anglo-Dutch war, these rates had fluctuated between *f*100 and *f*125 per ton, with an upward tendency to *f*145 and *f*170 in the 1790s. These rates included a skeleton crew; all the other men normally on board East Indiamen were still on the company's payroll. The directors persisted in having a higher opinion of the navigational capabilities of their own personnel. Victualing was in most cases also the company's concern.[34] Hired vessels were smaller than the average East Indiaman, and an extra 10 percent had to be added to the average freight price. More important was the company's decision that cargo on board chartered vessels, unlike cargo on company-owned ships, had to be insured. For return freight a standard of *f*500 per ton was applied. The company could not always use hired cargo capacities to transport extra seamen and soldiers. The fares of ordinary passengers had to be paid to the owners. Time limits were essential features of charter-parties. Short, extra voyages in Asia were

[33] *Dutch-Asiatic Trade*, 45–7 and 260. More detailed figures are in C. J. A. Jörg, *Porcelain and the Dutch China Trade* (The Hague, 1982), 23–5; and De Korte, *De jaarlijkse financiële verantwoording*, 56–8.

[34] E. S. van Eyck van Heslinga, *Van compagnie naar koopvaardij: De scheepvaartverbinding van de Bataafse Republiek met de koloniën in Azië, 1795–1806* (Amsterdam, 1988), 32–3.

seldom possible. Company authorities, in the Netherlands as well as in Batavia, felt themselves hampered by the influence of factors outside their control.

That the Heren XVII were worried in the 1780s and 1790s is not surprising. A look at Table 5.1 shows the much higher expenditure on transport, especially on materials, including ship hiring and insurance costs. One understands their worries even better when one keeps in mind the freight rates then paid by their English competitor, quoted earlier. Ongoing research on the company's shipping policy during this period will soon provide us with detailed information and a better analysis.[35]

Was the increase the result of the old system, the ship hiring, or both? The company never changed its old policy of building, owning, and freighting its own fleet. Nevertheless, the directors eventually realized that the large East Indiaman had become too expensive. Hiring smaller and more simply constructed merchantmen proved the point. One of the company's shipwrights, Willem Udemans, demonstrated convincingly the advantages of a large-sized ordinary merchantman, a pink-ship. He calculated that three pink-ships could carry more cargo than two first-rate East Indiamen. Building costs of this type of vessel, including rigging, amounted to half the price of the East Indiaman. Moreover, it could be managed by a smaller crew. In 1793 the directors finally decided to build pink-ships in their dockyards.[36] The effect of this decision on the transport costs cannot be calculated, because three years later, in 1796, the company was dissolved. The transport system to Asia changed drastically. New directors were absolutely convinced that hiring would be much cheaper. The dockyards were closed. Dutch and foreign merchantmen began to transport the Asian commodities. Armament was no longer a prerequisite. And the continuous stream of European personnel to Asia had come to a standstill. In 1802, a year of peace, Dutch private shipowners agreed upon a price per ton of about *f*190 plus an average of 10 percent.[37]

Were the Heren XVII stubborn and old-fashioned? A definite yes or no cannot be given. The whole structure of the company, with a large overseas empire to be ruled, demanded thousands of personnel: administrators, traders, soldiers, and seamen. That empire had been built by using East Indiamen for conquest in the seventeenth century

---

[35] I. G. Dillo (Leiden) is preparing a Ph.D. thesis on the company's shipping activities after the fourth Anglo-Dutch war.
[36] Bruijn, Gaastra, and Schöffer, *Dutch-Asiatic Shipping*, 1:50–1.
[37] Van Eyck van Heslinga, *Van compagnie naar koopvaardij*, 249.

and for consolidation and defense in the eighteenth century. Prior to 1783 the Dutch navy never sailed even as far as the Cape of Good Hope. From 1602 onward, the company's infrastructure in the Netherlands had been aimed at providing its own means of transport. Soon private shipyards could not offer the same building capacity as the company's yards did, nor did they regularly build the same type of ships. As long as circumstances did not basically change, the company could not afford to switch over to smaller, nondefensible ships with less facilities for transport of personnel. While following the old patterns, the company was successful in keeping its expenditures and the means of transport under control. But because of its method, it failed in the eighteenth century to profit from the general decline in freight rates on other shipping routes. There were no competitors on the route to Asia who could stimulate a rethinking of the old policy. The competitors, too, either used their own East Indiamen or had to pay almost as much to private shipowners, although without the usual administrative burden.

Around 1780 the time was ripe for a reconsideration of the policy. War interrupted the link between the Netherlands and Asia. The company had to resort to private and neutral shipowners. The outlays on transport were more intricate than before. But for the first time the Dutch navy began to participate in and to take over the defense of Asian territories. Company vessels could therefore be unarmed and smaller. From then on, one may call the Heren XVII stubborn and old-fashioned for not noticing the winds of drastic change for Asiatic shipping in general and for the Dutch in particular. Monopolies were no longer taken for granted or considered useful. There was more demand for smaller and cheaper ships, and the Americans began to be serious competitors in the eastern trade. The French revolutionary wars also caused great disruption.

CONCLUDING REMARKS

It is likely that the productivity of Dutch shipping in European waters increased enormously beginning in the seventeenth century. The ton-to-man ratio was improved. Larger ships were used and were more cost efficiently employed. The freight price per ton must have gone down, though evidence is still lacking. Armament did not require extra capital costs or make stowage unproductive. The Baptist owners of the *Juffrouw Christina* used four guns in the hold as ballast! Ship's accounts prove the profitability of eighteenth-century Dutch shipping and also show the involvement of the nonspecialist shipowner. Earning capacity was much greater than assumed by Brulez. The life expectancy of ships should not be underestimated.

The seventeenth-century costs of Dutch transport to and from Asia cannot be calculated. Archival material, recently made available, offers a possibility for developing a method of calculating eighteenth-century prices per ton. If this method is accepted as reliable, one may conclude that the Dutch East India Company kept its transport costs well under control for much of the eighteenth century, when East Indiamen became larger and voyages shorter and more personnel had to be shipped. Its English competitor struggled just then with rising costs despite the supposedly lower level of freight rates on the private shipping market. Around 1780, however, conditions began to turn against the Dutch. The rationale behind the system of building, owning, and freighting one's own ships began to lose its validity.

CHAPTER 6

The Dutch and English East India companies compared: evidence from the stock and foreign exchange markets

LARRY NEAL

THE East India companies of the Dutch and the English represented the most successful examples of merchant organization in the early modern era. Both exploited the possibilities of long-distance trade in highly valued exotic goods from the Orient to western Europe as well as seaborne traffic in the Asian trading world and, eventually, the potential for extracting taxes and tribute within Asia. Both confronted the problems of long voyages, delays in communications, political and commercial competitors in both Europe and Asia, and uncertain control over their agents. It was most likely the combination of the large scale of their operations, the long distances, and the lengthy times that led to the most important institutional innovation made by the two companies. This was the transformation of merchant trading or working capital committed initially to the duration of a particular voyage into fixed or permanent capital committed perpetually to the enterprise. The transformation was effected quickly by the Dutch company, apparently by 1612, whereas the English company had certainly made the transition by 1659.

After this transformation, both companies were joint stock corporations whose shares were actively traded in surprisingly modern stock exchanges in both Amsterdam and London. The daily prices for the English company's shares are available from 1698 on, and the every-other-day prices for the Dutch shares are available for at least the period 1723–94. These are used below to weigh the relative importance of organizational, commercial, and political factors in determining the fortunes of each company over the course of the eighteenth century, when the English company overtook the Dutch. Consistent

195

with Professor Steensgaard's thesis, the conclusion emerges that the two companies shared closely the profits arising from changing commercial possibilities and differed primarily in the way they confronted the problems of internalizing protection costs created by political conflicts. Due to differences in internal organization, the political events of Asia were more important for the Dutch and those of Europe more important for the English.

The financial information used here has been used in its summary form by modern historians as well as contemporary analysts in eighteenth-century Europe. Jean-Pierre Ricard in the early eighteenth century remarked on "the Dutch East India Company's average yearly divided distribution of 22.5 percent on the original subscribed capital," a dazzling figure that, according to the careful research of J. P. de Korte, had been reduced only to 18 percent by the end of the century, when the company had completed its life as a private enterprise.[1] Malachy Postlethwayt's entry on the Dutch East India Company in his 1751 *Universal Dictionary* explained that "one of the reasons why the Dutch East India company flourishes, and is become the richest and most powerful of all others we know of, is its being absolute, and invested with a kind of sovereignty and dominion, . . . [it] makes peace and war at pleasure, and by its own authority; administers justice to all; . . . settles colonies, builds fortifications, levies troops, maintains numerous armies and garrisons, fits out fleets, and coins money." On the English company, he remarked, "[It] is the most flourishing trading company in the kingdom, as likewise one of the greatest in Europe for wealth, power, and immunities; which appears by the ships they constantly employ, the beneficial settlements they have abroad, their large magazines and storehouses for merchandizes, and sales of goods at home, with the particular laws and statutes made in their favour."[2]

Thanks to Professor Steensgaard's path-breaking study, we appreciate better the political significance of these new organizational forms of trade as well as their economic significance. The studies of the Dutch East India Company (VOC hereafter) by Kristof Glamann, J. P. de Korte, and J. R. Bruijn et al. have added immensely to our economic knowledge of that great enterprise over the nearly two centuries of its existence as a private corporation. Likewise, the monumental ef-

---

[1] Jean-Pierre Ricard, *Le Négoce d'Amsterdam: Contenant tout ce que doivent savoir les marchands et banquiers, etc.* (Rouen, 1723), 400; and J. P. de Korte, *De jaarlijkse financiële verantwoording in de VOC* (Leiden, 1984), 93.

[2] *The Universal Dictionary of Trade and Commerce*, 4th ed., 2 vol. (London, 1774; reprint, New York, 1971), s.v. "Dutch East India Company" and "East India Company."

forts of K. N. Chaudhuri have made readily available a wealth of quantitative information on the trade and profits of the English East India Company (EIC hereafter), particularly in the hundred years 1659–1760, during which it displaced the Dutch company as the preeminent trading power between Asia and Europe.[3]

How can we organize the results of these impressive studies into a direct, quantitative comparison of the two companies? This would be useful so we could determine the relative influences of each similarity and contrast upon the progress of the two companies within the context of the northern European economy. Due to differences in internal organization, the bookkeeping practices of the two are sufficiently different that direct comparisons from the detailed records of their trading and financial activities are as difficult now as they were then. The answer, I argue below, is to be found in the quantitative price data left from the operation of highly integrated and reasonably efficient stock markets and foreign exchange markets in London and Amsterdam during the eighteenth century.

PRICES FROM THE STOCK MARKETS

Elsewhere, I have argued that the evaluations of the equity of each joint stock company made by investors trading and speculating in their shares on the stock exchanges of London and Amsterdam represented much the same kind of evaluation that modern stock markets make of corporate enterprises today.[4] Modern finance theory suggests that modern stock markets are efficient in the sense that all information available each day to stock market traders is used fully in the determination of stock prices each day. Although rumor and misinformation, as well as mistakes, will affect short-run price movements, over the not so very long run the best information available on "fundamentals," the usual determinants of a company's profitability, will dominate the movements in share prices. If eighteenth-

---

[3] Niels Steensgaard, *The Asian Trade Revolution of the Seventeenth Century* (Chicago, 1974); Kristof Glamann, *Dutch-Asiatic Trade, 1620–1740* (Copenhagen, 1958); de Korte, *De jaarlijkse financiële verantwoording;* J. R. Bruijn, F. S. Gaastra, and I. Schöffer, *Dutch-Asiatic Shipping in the 17th and 18th Centuries,* 3 vols. (The Hague, 1979–87) (vols. 165–7 in the Grote serie of Rijks Geschiedkundige Publicatiën); K. N. Chaudhuri, *The Trading World of Asia and the English East India Company, 1660–1760* (Cambridge, 1978); and idem, *Trade and Civilisation in the Indian Ocean* (Cambridge, 1985).

[4] "Efficient Markets in the Eighteenth Century? The Amsterdam and London Stock Exchanges," in Jeremy Atack, ed., *Business and Economic History,* vol. 12 (Urbana, Ill., 1983); and idem, "Integration of International Capital Markets: Quantitative Evidence from the Eighteenth to Twentieth Centuries," *Journal of Economic History* 45 (1985): 219–26.

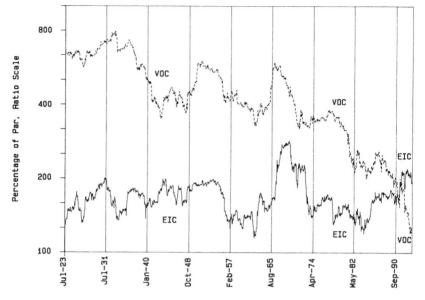

Figure 6.1. English and Dutch East India companies: share prices, 1723–94

century stock markets were efficient in the same way, the information their price movements convey on market fundamentals would be very useful to modern historians.

Figure 6.1 shows the dramatic change in the relative values of shares of the two trading companies as they were traded on the Amsterdam stock exchange and reported irregularly in the *Amsterdamsche Courant.*[5] Although the EIC share prices varied a bit between the London and Amsterdam prices, the movements were very similar and the levels nearly identical.[6] Throughout the period 1723–94, the price of the VOC fell absolutely and relative to the price of the EIC. These are prices of individual shares. We must multiply these by the nominal capital stock in each year to get the total market evaluation of each company. The capital stock of the VOC remained constant at 6,440,220 fl. throughout the period 1650–1790.[7] And the share capital of the

---

[5] J. G. Van Dillen, "Effectenkoersen aan de Amsterdamsche beurs," *Economishe-Historische Jaarboek* 17 (1931): 1–46.

[6] See the analysis of the prices of EIC stock in the two markets in Larry Neal, "The Integration and Efficiency of the Amsterdam and London Stock Markets in the Eighteenth Century," *Journal of Economic History* 47 (1987): 97–115.

[7] De Korte, *De jaarlijkse financiële verantwoording.* appendix 13. Divide the "Dividend bedrag" (total dividends paid) by "Dividend perc." (the dividend yield) to get the nominal capital stock.

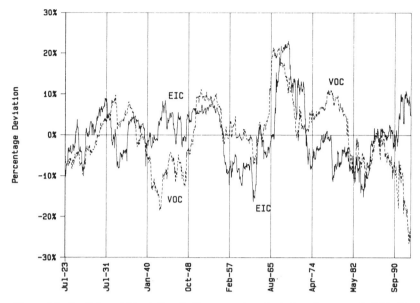

Figure 6.2. English and Dutch East India companies: deviations from trend, 1723–94

English United East India Company remained at £3,194,080 from 1717 through 1785. In 1786, 1789, and again in 1793, its capital stock was raised in stages of £800,000, £1,000,000 and £1,000,000 to a total of £5,994,080. So the decline in share prices for the Dutch company shows precisely the relative decline in total market evaluation. And the fluctuations in share prices for the English company show precisely the rise and fall in the market's evaluation of its total anticipated worth until 1786, when it is understated by increasing amounts.[8]

In addition to this striking difference in trend, the noteworthy feature in the graph is the existence of long-period fluctuations in the prices of each. To analyze the correlations of these between the two companies, Figure 6.2 shows the fluctuations as deviations from a simple linear trend on each series. This indicates that the fluctuations from trend are roughly similar in timing, with the notable exception of the 1730s. It was in this period that not only did the share prices of the VOC drop most dramatically relative to those of the EIC but also

---

[8] In addition to the usual cautionary statements about short-term fluctuations in "the market's" evaluation of a corporation, we should note that the price of VOC stock is really that of stock in the Amsterdam chamber, which represented only half the total enterprise. By the time our coverage begins, however, the variation of share values among the several chambers was likely unimportant.

they moved inversely to, rather than directly with, those of the EIC. Figure 6.2 also shows that the volatility in the price fluctuations of the two stocks was roughly the same.

Can these data be used to make stronger inferences about the historical forces that drove each company's profitability? Critics of modern efficient market theory note that stock prices may reflect not only information about future profit possibilities but also about current battles for control of company decisions that changes in ownership of stock may bring. Much the same arguments have been made about the behavior of stock prices in the eighteenth century.[9]

Josiah Child, for example, in his *Treatise concerning the East-India Trade* in 1681 observed that English investors were wary of buying into the English East India Company:

> Because when we tell Gentlemen, or others, they may buy Stock, and come into the Company when they please: They presently reply, They know that, but then they must pay 280 *l.* for 100 *l.* And when we say the intrinsic Value is worth so much; which is as true as 2 and 2 makes 4, yet it is not so soon Demonstrated to their apprehensions, notwithstanding it is no hard task to make out, that the quick stock of the English East India Company is at this time more than the Dutch quick stock, proportionable to their respective first subscriptions; and yet their Actions now are current at 440 *l.* or 450 *l.* per Cent.[10]

If Child was correct that stock in the EIC at this time was a better buy than stock in the VOC (and there is no reason to suppose he was correct), the difference in values reflected market imperfections. The exclusion of foreigners from purchase of English stock, even though the VOC gave foreigners the right to own stock from the beginning, may be an explanation. By the time the United East India Company merged the Old and New companies in 1709, however, foreigners were clearly given the right to buy and hold stock in the English company. From this time certainly, and probably from the time the New Company was chartered with permission for foreigners to hold its stock, the likelihood was small that such large differences in valuation could be maintained among the informed merchant community.

Although Child in the seventeenth century and all mercantilist writers in the eighteenth century (with the notable exception of Daniel Defoe) regarded the stock markets as reliable arbiters of the rela-

---

[9] For a critique of the efficiency of both eighteenth- and twentieth-century markets, see Philip Mirowski, "What Do Markets Do? The London Stock Market of the Eighteenth Century," *Explorations in Economic History* 24 (1987): 107–29.

[10] *A Treatise concerning the East-India Trade* (London, 1681). By "quick stock" presumably Child means Asian goods in warehouses in Europe.

tive evaluations of the giant joint stock companies of the time, modern scholars have expressed some doubts. The Mississippi and South Sea bubbles are understood by them, as they were by contemporaries, as evidence of unbounded credulity by the investing classes and the ultimate irrationality of the primitive asset markets of the time.[11] Recent historians, however, have tended to upgrade their assessments of these early markets and to emphasize failures of government policy rather than institutional weaknesses in the markets.[12] I have gone so far as to argue that the South Sea Bubble was an original example of a "rational bubble" of the same nature as the rational bubbles occasionally observed in modern financial markets.[13]

For our purposes this debate boiled down to the question of whether the course of stock market evaluations of the joint stock companies represented merely irrational responses by a few large investors to rumors and suspicions, some ad hoc pricing rule adopted in the absence of reliable information, or some rational evaluation of the shares relative to other possible investments. The first position is stated most forcefully by Philip Mirowski, who found no evidence that share prices of the EIC were shaped by profit rates. This contrasted with his evidence that the profits of the London Assurance Company and the Million Bank determined in large part the market evaluation of their shares. It is anomalous that the London stock market could do a good job of evaluating the shares of two companies and not of a third, larger company. Mirowski explained this anomaly by asserting that

both contemporaries and present-day historians identify East India shares as primarily a speculative purchase, due to their dependence upon such imponderables as the state of Indian politics and the relative strength of interlopers in the trade. The effect of the news must have been so extreme upon speculators in the India stock that it spoiled their ability to translate news into prospects of profitability.[14]

Mirowski used the contemporary account books of the three companies to determine their measures of profit rates, arguing this is what the most rational investors would have had available to guide their investment decisions. In equation form:

[11] Burton Malkiel, *A Random Walk Down Wall Street* (New York, 1973); and Charles Kindleberger, *Manias, Panics, and Crashes* (New York, 1978).
[12] Edgar Faure, *Le banqueroute de Law* (Paris, 1977), on the Mississippi Bubble; and P. G. M. Dickson, *The Financial Revolution in England, 1650–1750* (Oxford, 1972), on the South Sea Bubble.
[13] Larry Neal and Eric Schubert, "The First Rational Bubbles: A Re-examination of the Mississippi and South Sea Schemes," unpublished manuscript, 1985.
[14] "The Rise (and Retreat) of a Market: English Joint Stock Shares in the Eighteenth Century," *Journal of Economic History* 41 (1981): 575.

Table 6.1

Regression Results of the Capital Asset Pricing Model

for the Bank of England, the East India Company,

and the Dutch East India Company

Bank of England

Indep. var.	coeff.	std. error	t-value	sig.level
CAP(adj.)	0.999	0.015	67.72	0.0000
R^2(adj.) = 0.99	SE = 5.82	MAE = 4.1	DW = 1.77;	rho = .667

70 observations fitted (1724-94)

English East India Company

Indep. var.	coeff.	std. error	t-value	sig.level
CAP(adj.)	0.925	0.045	20.67	0.0000
R^2(adj.) = 0.86	SE = 17.39	MAE = 12.78	DW = 1.93;	rho = .75

70 observations fitted (1724-94)

Dutch East India Company

Indep. var.	coeff.	std. error	t-value	sig.level
CAP(adj.)	0.913	0.038	24.35	0.0000
R^2(adj.) = 0.92		SE = 45.24	MAE = 32.813	DW = 1.62;	rho = .675

54 observations fitted (1724-78)

English East India Company (Mirowski's Results)

Indep. var.	coeff.	t-value
CONSTANT	164.73	21.36
PR	0.190	0.37
PR-1	0.246	0.48
WAR3	425635.4	0.317

R^2 = 0.001; F = .20

100 observations fitted (1710-1810)

Note: The dependent variable in each regression is the average annual share price. CAP (adj.) is calculated average based on dividend rates, risk-free interest rates, and risk factors as described in the text. SE= standard error of the regression; MAE= mean absolute error; and DW= Durbin-Watson statistic.

Source: Philip Mirowski, "The Rise (and Retreat) of a Market: English Joint Stock Shares in the Eighteenth Century," Journal of Economic History 41 (1981): 575.

$$SP = f(PR_t, PR_{t-1});$$

where SP is the price per share and PR is the rate of profit per share.

Historians of both the Dutch and English companies, however, have been impressed by the extraordinary difficulties faced in calculating true profits, given the problems of goods in transit and of measuring working capital employed in the Asian trading world. If contemporaries were aware of these problems (and of course they were because they were fundamental conditions of long-distance trade in the entire sailing era), they would have been better served by capitalizing actual dividends paid out and taking account of longer-term capital gains.

I have performed my own tests on the performance of the markets by estimating a version of the standard capital asset pricing model (CAPM) used in modern finance. In its simplest form, which is most likely applicable to the eighteenth century, the CAPM argues that the market value of a company's equity is the capitalized value of its annual payouts in the form of dividends. The discount rate used to capitalize the annual payouts can be adjusted to account for the risk factor that investors attach to the financial asset as well as their expectations about future growth of dividends.[15] In equation form, this can be written

$$P_0 = D_1 / (k_1 - g).$$

The variable P_0 is the price per share of the company's equity in time period 0; D_1 is the dividend paid out in the next time period, 1; k_1 is the required rate of return investors demand on the stock in the next time period; and g is the expected rate of growth of dividends over time.

In the regression results presented in Table 6.1, I have calculated the expression on the right-hand side as the single independent variable, which has an expected coefficient of 1.0. In calculating this expression, I have consistently taken g, the expected growth rate of dividends, to be zero, because the period of analysis in each case is well past the initial rapid growth phase of the company in question. The required rate of return investors demand on the stock, k, is a varying discount rate. In modern finance, it is a composite of the short-term return on a risk-free asset actively traded in the capital markets plus a risk factor based on the volatility of the capital markets plus a risk factor for the stock in question that takes into account its volatility relative to that of the entire market. I used the one-year holding re-

---

[15] The model used is adapted from the discussion in the finance textbook by Eugene F. Brigham, *Financial Management*, 4th ed. (New York 1985), chaps. 5 and 6.

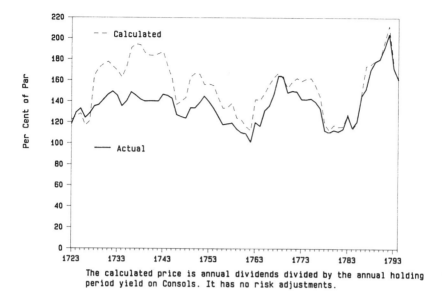

The calculated price is annual dividends divided by the annual holding
period yield on Consols. It has no risk adjustments.

Figure 6.3. Bank of England share prices compared with CAPM-calculated prices

turn on Three Per Cent Consols in the London market as my measure
of the one-period return on a risk-free asset.[16] The data necessary to
calculate the market's volatility as a whole have not yet been en-
coded, so an arbitrary risk factor, the beta coefficient in the opaque
terms of modern finance, was added into the calculation for each
company's stock at certain periods. The graphs in Figures 6.3 through
6.5 plot the annual average share price against the CAPM-calculated
share price without adding risk factors. They show clearly which periods had greater risks for shareholders, because in those periods the
actual share prices are consistently below the calculated share prices,
even though the annual movements are very similar.

For the Bank of England's share prices (Fig. 6.3), the model shows
good tracking ability of the fluctuations throughout the seventy-two-
year period. In the years 1728–45, however, there is clearly an addi-

[16] This required extrapolating the actual Three Per Cent Consol returns back from 1753,
when they began to be quoted in the *Course of the Exchange,* to 1723, when the price
quotes for the VOC began in the *Amsterdamsche Courant.* This was done by using the
return on the Bank of England's Three Per Cent Annuity, the precursor of the famed
Three Per Cent Consol, until 1726, when the Bank issued its first annuity. For the
remaining three years, the return on the South Sea annuities issued in the aftermath
of the bubble was used, because these were the largest single issue of security and
were the most stable in price of any asset in this period.

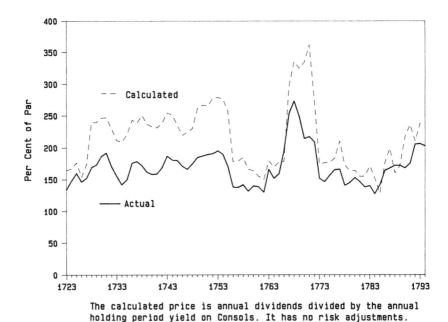

The calculated price is annual dividends divided by the annual
holding period yield on Consols. It has no risk adjustments.

Figure 6.4. East India Company share prices compared with CAPM-calculated prices

tional risk factor attached by investors to the Bank's stock, a risk factor that is considerably reduced over the next period, 1746–76.
Thereafter, Bank stock appears to be as risk-free as the Three Per Cent
Consols. The first period perhaps reflects the uncertainty attached to
the Bank's attempt to take up the functions of the moribund South
Sea Company as financier to the government. Not only had the Bank
engrafted part of the stock of the South Sea Company to its own in
1723, but from 1726 on, it also issued annuities that turned out to be
the precursors of the Three Per Cent Consols. In 1742 its services to
the government were rewarded by a renewal of its charter to 1764
and a strengthening of its monopoly position as the nation's only
joint stock bank. The effect of this was delayed by the panic caused
in 1745 by the advance of the Stuart Pretender to within 127 miles of
London. The Bank's charter was renewed in 1764 and again in 1782.
It benefited in 1774 from the recoinage, which reduced the price of
gold from £4 1s. to £3 17s. 6d.[17] So the deviations of the CAPM from
the actual share prices appear to be consistent with the changed risks

[17] A. Andreades, *History of the Bank of England, 1640–1903*, 4th ed. (reprint, New York,
1967), 143–59.

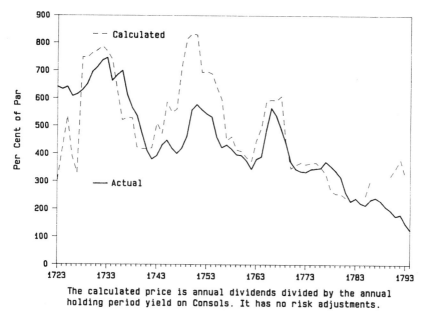

The calculated price is annual dividends divided by the annual
holding period yield on Consols. It has no risk adjustments.

Figure 6.5. Dutch East India Company share prices compared with CAPM-calculated
prices

to shareholders as a result of the periodic changes in the Bank's relation to the government. In the regressions reported in Table 6.1, a
risk adjustment factor of 1.3 was applied during the first period, 1.1
during the third.

In the case of the EIC (Fig. 6.4), a comparable risk factor was evidently in play during the period 1723–56. During the first few years
following the Seven Years' War, the model tracks very closely indeed
and then begins to diverge erratically from 1767 to 1772. Thereafter,
although the levels predicted by the model are close to those actually
realized, the annual movements are erratic. Fairman's account of the
financial history of the company explains convincingly the source of
these deviations of the model.

Early in 1764, the receipt of very unpleasant news from Bengal immediately
caused India stock to fall 14 percent. The general administration of the Company's affairs, both at home and abroad, became afterwards the subject of
much discussion; and, on the 29th August, 1766, the Court of Directors received a notice from the Secretaries of State, that an investigation would take
place in the next Session of Parliament; in consequence of which the price of
their stock fell from 230 . . . to 206, but . . . the dividend being increased to

10 percent., it got up considerably, the average price of the whole year being 254.[18]

The Regulating Act of 1772 followed, which brought the company under the uncertain control of the government. The political uncertainties and financial consequences of this transition of the EIC, from a profit-making holding company operated for the benefit of participating merchants and shipowners to an instrument of the power of the British state in Asia, have been admirably discussed and analyzed by Lucy Sutherland.[19] The vicissitudes of the company's financial dealings with the state, which required annual payments of £400,000 by the company to the Treasury while the Treasury guaranteed the assumption of Indian debts by the company, are detailed in Fairman. These are clearly beyond the capacity of the model to capture. Fortunately, this episode lies outside the time period dealt with in this conference volume. The regression results reported in Table 6.1, however, include the observations for the entire period 1723–94.

The VOC (Fig. 6.5) shows marked divergence from the model at the outset in the mid-1720s and then tracks fairly well until a risk factor appears to be at work from 1743 until 1757. It was in this period that the state was paid yearly an amount equal to 3 percent of the annual dividend as the price for extending the charter of the VOC from 1740 to 1756. Thereafter, it tracks well until 1776. In the period 1755–74 the VOC was able to settle its pledge of 1,200,000 fl. to the government by delivering saltpeter.[20] After this, chaos sets in for the model, but as in the case of the English company just discussed, this reflects the growing financial difficulties of both the company and the government, which led to the formal control of the company by the state in 1785, after several years of skipped dividends. As with the Bank and the EIC, the deviations of the calculated CAPM stock value from the actual prices of the VOC stock appear quite explainable in terms of the changes in the financial constraints placed upon the company by the Dutch government. The first five years and the period after 1782 are omitted in the regression results reported in Table 6.1, and a risk factor of 1.3 is applied during the interval 1745–56.

The regression results are very encouraging to proponents of the idea that participants in the stock markets of the Age of Reason were rational in their economic behavior. The independent variable in each regression is the calculated value of the share prices assuming the

---

[18] William Fairman, *The Stocks Examined and Compared*, 7th ed. (London, 1824), 125.
[19] *The East India Company in Eighteenth-Century Politics* (Oxford, 1952).
[20] Bruijn, Gaastra, and Schöffer, *Dutch-Asiatic Shipping*, 1:7–8.

markets are efficient and our measures of the risk factors are correct. The regression estimates were done using generalized least squares, and the rho-values shown for the first-order autocorrelation were used to correct for serial correlation. The coefficient on the CAP independent variable is statistically significant in each case and is very close to the theoretical value of 1.0, lying within the 95 percent confidence interval, around 1.0 for the Bank of England and just below this interval in the case of the two East India companies. The total variance explained by the simple regressions is quite high even after adjusting for first-order serial correlation in the residuals. The CAPM results on the EIC shares are a marked contrast to the dismal results found by Mirowski for the EIC. They are all the more convincing because the CAPM also does well for the VOC and gives nearly perfect results for the Bank of England.

For our present purpose, relating merchant activity to the course of empire, these results imply that the financial markets of the time give us important, and reliable, information. The stock prices of each company reflected regularly not only the economic calculations of European merchants but their assessments of the political roles played by the management of each company. We have a good retrospective understanding of the profits of each company (even if we are not sure how well the directors of each company understood these at the time) and a good comprehension of the political pressures placed on each company both in Europe and in Asia. The course of stock prices for each company over time tells us how these economic and political events were comprehended by the stockholders of each company. This allows us, in principle, to determine which events were most important in determining the ultimate replacement of the VOC by the EIC as the preeminent trading entity between Asia and Europe.

The summary picture we can draw here is that during the eighteenth century the initial preeminence of the Dutch in the trading nexus between Asia and Europe was being eroded, particularly by the English but doubtlessly also by others. The French company continued to do a large business in Asia until the defeats of the Seven Years' War. The Spanish strengthened their role in the Philippines while the Portuguese continued to play an important entrepôt role in the Asian trading world. Meanwhile, the Austrian, Danish, and Swedish companies made inroads in the Baltic–Asian trade previously monopolized by the Dutch. This may be the inevitable lot of the pioneer profiteer, but the decline took a long time and had an interesting history during its course. When the stock prices of the two companies move

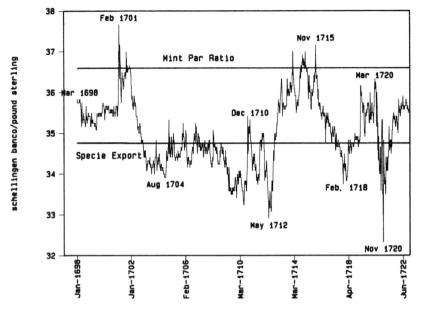

Figure 6.6. London exchange rates on Amsterdam: two-month usance rate, 1698–1722

in similar patterns relative to trend, we may infer that both are experiencing the effects of changed marketing conditions in either Europe or Asia. This is clearly the case in most of the century.

However, there are a number of intervals when the two price series move inversely, indicating one company is gaining on the other, at least relative to trend. For example, the EIC lost relative to the VOC from mid-1731 to 1733, and then from 1736 until 1743 it gained sharply with only a brief setback in 1739. From 1750 through the end of the Seven Years' War in 1763, the VOC gained relative to the EIC, and especially during the war years. After the disturbances at the end of the war, the EIC did marginally better than their Dutch competitors until the Regulating Act of 1772. Thereafter, the VOC again gained relative to the EIC until it began its final collapse, leading to takeover by the Dutch government in 1787. The inverse episodes before the battle of Plassey deserve special attention, especially those in the early and late 1730s and early 1740s, a period of peace in Europe and internal stability in each company's organization.

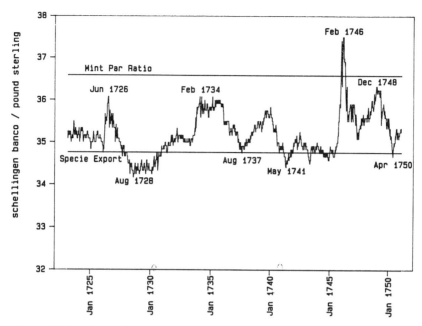

Figure 6.7. London exchange rates on Amsterdam: two-month usance rate, 1723–50

EXCHANGE RATES

Figures 6.6 and 6.7 plot the fluctuations in the exchange rate between London and Amsterdam for the periods 1698–1722 and 1723–50. The rate is the two-month usance rate in London on Amsterdam. In this period exchange rates were always quoted the same way in each city for ease of calculation, so the Amsterdam rates would also be somewhere near 35.5 schellingen banco per pound sterling, which was approximately 1 Flemish shilling below the mint par ratio.[21] Usually the rate would be slightly lower in Amsterdam, say 35s., and slightly higher in London, say 36s. That is to say, the guilder was worth more

---

[21] The mint par ratio between London and Amsterdam for this period was 36.59 Flemish shillings (Fl. s.) (Postlethwayt, *Universal Dictionary*, s.v. "Coin," 4th page of entry). This appears to be in terms of bank money as opposed to current money (the exchange rates given in the exchange currents are for bills of exchange in bank money payable at the Bank of Amsterdam), but even so the rate appears too high for most of our period. But the actual rates observed in Figures 6.3 and 6.4 are seldom below 34.76 Fl. s., which would be approximately the specie export point in peacetime. The rate could obviously fall lower in wartime, as it did during the War of the Spanish Succession.

in Amsterdam than in London, and the pound was worth more in London than in Amsterdam. Sight rates, which begin in Amsterdam on London around 1709 and in London on Amsterdam at the end of 1720, included a premium paid at the city of origin for the right to obtain the foreign currency at the city of destination more promptly. So sight rates in Amsterdam were typically 2 grooten higher than the usance rate, and sight rates in London were a standard 2 grooten lower than the usance rate, save during liquidity crises.

The rates seem to center about the 35s. level but show prolonged swings between the mint par ratio of 36.59 Fl. s. and the approximate specie point for export from London, 34.76s. In the period 1698–1722 the pound fell relative to the guilder during the War of the Spanish Succession, and the fluctuations reflected accurately and promptly the exigencies of war finance. Note the especially low levels of the British pound during the crisis years of 1709–10. The South Sea Bubble shows up as a period of sharp fluctuations reflecting first capital inflows and then capital flight. In the next period, 1723–50, the fluctuations were much smaller, especially in the 1720s and 1730s. The War of the Austrian Succession had a similar but less pronounced depressing effect on the pound as the War of the Spanish Succession did in the earlier period. This reflected well the relatively smaller scale of the British effort in the latter war.

The foreign exchange markets operated on a larger scale and with a broader range of more experienced participants than the stock markets of either Amsterdam or London, so the reliability of these market prices is much greater. However, they reflect different and broader economic forces. Obviously, the balance of total trade between the two countries can affect the relative demand for their currencies in the foreign exchange markets. But more generally, it will be changes in the *relative* trade balances of the two countries with the rest of the world, not just with each other, that will change the exchange rate of their currencies.

Particularly interesting in the 1720s and 1730s is the possibility of capital movements affecting the exchange rates. In analyzing the price differences for EIC stock between the Amsterdam and London markets over the entire period 1723–94, I have found that only in the period 1723–38 was a higher price in Amsterdam than in London strongly associated with a higher value of the pound sterling in terms of Dutch currency.[22] In the rest of the periods, higher prices in Amsterdam were strongly associated with a higher value of the Dutch

---

[22] Neal, "Integration and Efficiency," 112.

currency. This suggests that in 1723–38 Dutch demand for English securities drove up the value of the English currency, whereas in succeeding periods a rise in the English exchange rate would drive up the value of English securities held in the Netherlands. It is interesting that it is precisely this period that P. G. M. Dickson has identified as the most important period for foreign investment, especially Dutch, in the English public securities, including stock of the EIC.[23]

These ideas can be formalized in the following way, using the data available from the financial press of the time. Periodically, shares of the VOC would lose value as the financial markets reevaluated its competitive standing in the Asian trade with Europe. Investors, whether Dutch or foreign, would move out of VOC stock. They or other investors in Amsterdam would switch to the more successful competitor, the EIC. This would drive up the price of EIC stock in Amsterdam, where the initial purchases by Amsterdam-based investors would be made, relative to its price in London. It was normal for all English stocks to be a bit higher in the Amsterdam market, since Amsterdam prices were time prices and London prices were spot prices. But an unusual drop in VOC stock might create an unusual rise in the Amsterdam price. If so, this would induce a change in the exchange rate in favor of London, since buyers of EIC stock located in Amsterdam would find it cheaper to buy in London, whereas sellers of EIC stock located in London would find it more profitable to sell in Amsterdam. In equation form:

$$dXR = a_0 + a_1 (dAgio) + a_2 (dSil_{AL}) + a_3 (dVOC) + a_4 (ALd); \tag{1}$$

where dXR is the change in price of pound sterling in Flemish shillings; dAgio is the change in the premium of bank money (used for bills of foreign exchange); $dSil_{AL}$ is the change in the ratio of silver prices in Amsterdam and London; dVOC is the change in price of VOC stock in Amsterdam; and ALd is the difference in the price of EIC stock between Amsterdam and London. The expected signs of a_1 and a_2 are positive, and those of a_3 and a_4 are negative.

The second relationship can be expressed

$$ALd = b_0 + b_1 (DIVPAY) + b_2 (ExDiv) + b_3 (dVOC) + b_4 (dXR); \tag{2}$$

where DIVPAY is the number of months to payment of the next dividend, and ExDiv is a dummy set to 1 in months when London is

[23] Dickson, *Financial Revolution*, 312 and 321.

Table 6.2

Regression Results on Amsterdam-London

Asset Price Differences and Exchange Rates,

Monthly Data 1723-44.

Variables in Regressions

CONSTANT

dXR   change in price of pounds in terms of Flemish s.

ALd   difference in price of EIC stock in Amsterdam and London

ExDiv   1, when London price quoted ex dividend

DIVPAY   number of days to next dividend

dVOC   change in price of VOC stock

dSil$_{AL}$ change in silver prices, Amsterdam/London

dAgio   change in agio rate in Amsterdam

Panel A. Ordinary Least Squares Regressions

Equation 1. dXR (change in London-Amsterdam exchange rate)

Indep. var.	coeff	std. error	t-value	sig.level
CONSTANT	-0.001	0.007	-0.16	0.88
dAgio	0.059	0.046	1.29	0.20
dSil$_{AL}$	0.358	0.214	1.68	0.09
dVOC	-0.000	0.000	-0.94	0.35
ALd	-0.003	0.004	-0.78	0.44

R^2(adj.) = 0.007   SE = 0.104   MAE = 0.081   DW = 2.01

257 observations fitted

Equation 2. ALd (Amsterdam-London difference in EIC share price)

Indep. var.	coeff	std. error	t-value	sig.level
CONSTANT	0.240	0.206	1.16	0.25
DIVPAY	-0.085	0.062	-1.37	0.17
ExDiv	2.242	0.286	7.83	0.00
dVOC	-0.004	0.007	-0.55	0.59
dXR	0.965	0.778	1.24	0.22

R^2(adj.) = 0.342   SE = 1.280   MAE = 0.88   DW = 1.91

257 observations fitted

Table 6.2. (*Cont.*)

Panel B. Two-Stage Least Squares Regressions

Equation 1. dXR (change in London-Amsterdam exchange rate)

Indep. var.	coeff	std. error	t-value	sig.level
CONSTANT	0.005	0.007	0.72	0.47
dAgio	0.073	0.045	1.61	0.11
dSil$_{AL}$	0.439	0.213	2.06	0.04
dVOC	-0.001	0.000	-1.36	0.18
ALdHat	-0.018	0.007	-2.58	0.01

R^2(adj.) = 0.030   SE = 0.103   MAE = 0.080   DW = 1.99

257 observations fitted

Equation 2. ALd (Amsterdam-London difference in EIC share price)

Indep. var.	coeff	std. error	t-value	sig.level
CONSTANT	0.288	0.204	1.41	0.16
DIVPAY	-0.121	0.063	-1.93	0.05
ExDiv	2.862	0.364	7.86	0.00
dVOC	0.013	0.010	1.38	0.17
dXRHat	17.871	6.307	2.83	0.01

R^2(adj.) = 0.36   SE = 1.26   MAE = 0.889   DW = 1.83

257 observations fitted

quoted ex dividend as dividends are being paid and 0 otherwise. The expected signs of b_1 and b_2 are positive, and those of b_3 and b_4 are negative.

Table 6.2 shows some regression results that try to capture these possibilities for the period 1723–44. The *Amsterdamsche Courant* is especially rich in Amsterdam stock market quotes for this period, reporting the chief stock prices in virtually each issue. These quotes have been averaged monthly, as well as the daily exchange rates and EIC stock prices reported in the London *Course of the Exchange*. Panel A shows the results of doing ordinary least squares regressions for each equation, while Panel B displays the results of two-stage least squares regressions, in which the feedback effect of the two dependent variables on each other is taken into account.

The ordinary least squares regression for equation 1 seems to explain very little. The only cause for encouragement is the marginally significant coefficient on the silver price ratio and the appearance of the expected sign on each variable. The one for equation 2 does considerably better in terms of overall explanation, but still only one variable seems to be significantly different from zero, the dummy term for ExDiv. Worse is that the signs on DIVPAY and dXR are opposite of what is expected. The opposite sign on dXR, however, is consistent with our earlier results and may simply indicate the power of feedback influences running from differences in share prices between Amsterdam and London to changes in the exchange rate between the two cities. The two-stage least squares estimates in Panel B are designed precisely to take this feedback into account.

For the exchange rate equation, the feedback adjustment does improve the quality of the coefficient estimates. It is especially satisfying that each estimated coefficient continues to have the correct sign. Except for the constant term, which is close to zero and insignificantly different from zero as we would hope, each coefficient is different from zero with a reasonably low level of significance. For the EIC price difference equation, however, the results are a bit embarrassing since the signs are now "wrong" in three of the four cases, instead of just two, and the level of significance is even better than in the exchange rate equation.

Despite these disappointing results for the thesis that capital movements accounted for much of the exchange rate fluctuations in this period, it remains the case that the Amsterdam–London exchange rate data show an unusual relationship to the mint par ratio during the 1730s, just as the price deviations from trend of the English and Dutch companies show an unusual divergence from each other during the 1730s. What could have caused this disturbance in the foreign exchange markets and the offsetting price movements in the shares of the two companies given the absence of war or major economic policy change?

TREASURE AND TEA

The explanation of the dramatic rise of the fortunes of the English company and the equally dramatic decline in the anticipated fortunes of the Dutch in the 1720s and 1730s lies, according to both Glamann and Chaudhuri, in the way each handled the tea trade with China. Glamann notes that the Dutch had the favored position until 1718, based on selling in European markets the tea brought to Batavia by Chinese junks. In that year, the VOC's governor general and council in Batavia decided to offer the Chinese fixed prices much lower than previously. This appears to have been a response by Batavia to orders from the Netherlands to charge higher prices to the Chinese for pepper (so they would not be able to resell at a profit to European competitors of the Dutch). The Chinese were outraged and refused to come to Batavia at all for the next five years. The net result was that the European competitors of the Dutch now bought tea directly from the Chinese instead of buying black pepper from them. Moreover, they found an exploding market in Europe for the better varieties of tea that were available to them in Canton. By the time the junks finally resumed voyages to Batavia in 1723, the market for their traditional green teas had been surpassed in Europe by the demand for black teas.[24] The EIC began importing tea directly from Canton on a regular basis in 1717, and each succeeding decade until 1760 saw an accelerating rate of growth in the volume of its imports.[25] The Dutch eventually adjusted to the new marketing situation generated by European demand and different conditions of supply from China, but at a distinctly inferior position to that of the English.[26]

Tangible evidence of the relative failure of the Dutch in the new tea trade was the rise in bullion shipments relative to total exports that occurred in the 1720s and 1730s. Glamann does not give annual figures of shipments from the Netherlands to Batavia in the way that Chaudhuri does for the English company, because by this time an

[24] Glamann, *Dutch-Asiatic Trade*, 216–43.
[25] Chaudhuri, *Trading World of Asia*, 388.
[26] An excellent summary of the successful rise of the English tea trade and the failure by the Dutch is given by Holden Furber, *Rival Empires of Trade in the Orient, 1600–1800* (Minneapolis, 1976), 129–35; 140–4.

increasing amount of bullion could come on private account with passengers. This was especially so in the period 1724–35, when the turnover of ducatons (the Dutch-minted silver trading coin) in the general commerce ledgers of the VOC in Batavia shows a remarkable increase from 948,739 fl. in 1724/25 to over 7 million in 1733/34. Much of this arose from ducatons being shipped on private account by Dutch money dealers to Batavia and there turned into the VOC to purchase bills of exchange payable in bank money in Amsterdam. Since the VOC in Batavia was paying a premium for ducatons in order to ship them to Canton or Bengal, speculators in the Netherlands could realize a profit of over 20 percent plus a 4 percent premium that the VOC regularly gave on bills of exchange for the interest lost during the time of transfer from Indonesia to Europe.[27] In sum, the VOC began in the eighteenth century to ship enormously larger sums of silver and (to a lesser extent) gold to Asia, both directly on its own account and indirectly by encouraging smuggling out of silver coins by their passengers to Batavia. Nevertheless, it appears from the analysis of Gaastra that it was not so much the increase in demand for silver by tea merchants in Canton that accounted for this rise but the drying up of Asian sources of bullion that the Dutch had been able to tap in the seventeenth century. Preeminent was the loss of Japanese silver, but Spanish silver was no longer available to the Dutch from Manila, being used directly in Chinese trade, and even the northwestern Indian and Persian supplies were lost in the eighteenth century.[28]

By contrast, the EIC was shipping ever smaller amounts of bullion, both in absolute quantities and relative to commodity exports, during the 1730s (see Fig. 6.8). The apparent reason for the success of the English company relative to the Dutch was the salability of Indian goods transported by the English (mainly cotton textiles but apparently also some opium even at this early date) in the Chinese market. By contrast, the Dutch no longer had the textiles of the Coromandel Coast of southeast India to ship to China, due to the increasing success of the French East India Company in that region. The encroachment of the English and others in the Spice Islands trade meant that fine spices could be provided in China by Dutch competitors. In sum, it was not so much the loss of the tea trade in the early 1720s that damaged the Dutch relative to the English. The Dutch recovered from that setback rather quickly. But it was significant in foretelling the

---

[27] Glamann, *Dutch-Asiatic Trade*, 72.
[28] F. S. Gaastra, "The Exports of Precious Metal from Europe to Asia by the Dutch East India Company, 1602–1795," in J. F. Richards, ed., *Precious Metals in the Later Medieval and Early Modern Worlds* (Durham, N.C., 1983), 447–76.

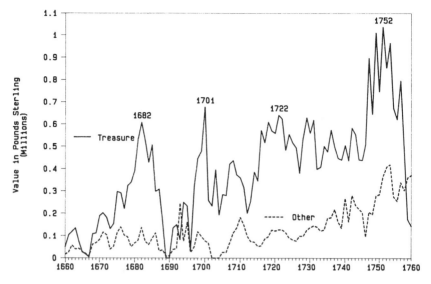

Figure 6.8. English East India Company exports of treasure and other goods, 1660–1760

greater difficulty faced by the VOC compared with the EIC in adjusting to competition from new companies, particularly the French. (See Chapter 4, where Butel discusses the growing success of the French company in the 1730s and 1740s.)

Our stock prices, it should be recalled, are from the Amsterdam market for both the VOC and the EIC, so they show that the Dutch merchant community was well aware of the implications of these movements of bullion by each company from Europe to Asia and of the sale of each company's goods in China. The exchange rate movements between London and Amsterdam indicate a strengthening of the pound due to the favorable effects on English trade balances of English success in the China–Europe tea trade and the India–China textile trade. This movement of the pound encouraged and abetted financial adjustments that led to a sharp fall of VOC equity valuation and a corresponding rise in the valuation of the EIC in the early 1730s and again in the early 1740s.

CONCLUSION

This exercise in the statistical analysis of the financial data left in the historical record of northwest Europe in the eighteenth century should increase our appreciation, first, of the modernity of the financial markets of that time; second, of the rationality of the merchant community, which, for the first time, was trading and investing on a European-wide scale and responding to global economic developments; and third, of the possibilities of using this overwhelming data legacy to illuminate other episodes in the course of trade and empire during this pivotal epoch.

For example, it is now known that each company relied primarily upon the shipment of bullion and specie, especially silver specie, to the Far East in order to effect payment for the Asian products they brought back to Europe. It appears from our stock market data that whichever company had the best access to sources of silver specie in a particular period also enjoyed at that time the greatest returns upon its investments in Europe. The disturbances to trading opportunities and profits of each caused by the repeated outbreaks of war in Europe and Asia seemed to affect each company's profitability much the same way. The major exceptions are the early years of the War of the Austrian Succession and the French revolutionary wars at the end of the century. Both the Dutch and the English profited from the defeat of the French in the Seven Years' War.

The institutional structure that linked the home merchants in control of the finances of the overall enterprise with the merchants stationed in the East in control over the trading activities of the respective companies differed greatly between the two companies. This structural difference reflected the distinctive strategies of each company in dealing with "country," or intra-Asian, trade.[29] The Dutch controlled these activities strictly from the headquarters in Batavia, whereas the English were much looser. The Dutch company was rigidly divided into six chambers, with Amsterdam providing half the capital but only eight of the seventeen *heren* (directors) who directed the overall affairs of the united company. The remaining *heren* were divided as follows: four from Zeeland, one each from Delft, Rotterdam, Hoorn, and Enkhuizen, with the final member rotated among the last four chambers. The charter of the English company, by contrast, was up for renewal at relatively short intervals, although these became increasingly longer as time went on. Even when the charter was not in question, stockholder revolts could easily occur, for ex-

---

[29] The inference of corporate strategies from their organizational structures is now standard procedure in business history but was pioneered by Alfred D. Chandler, *Strategy and Structure: Chapters in the History of Industrial Enterprise* (Cambridge, Mass., 1962).

ample, in 1732 and again in 1763.[30] Since stockholders in the VOC delegated their powers to the Heren XVII, their only effective means of influence was exit, rather than voice. The charter of the VOC did come up for renewal at intervals of twenty to forty years, and at those times powerful stockholders could assert more influence. But in the Nine Years' War (War of the League of Augsburg, 1689–97) the charter due to expire in 1700 was extended to 1740 in return for a one-time payment of three million guilders.[31] For that critical period during which the value of the VOC declined markedly relative to the EIC, there was no threat of stockholder revolt or state control. It was perhaps this protection from internal innovation that made the VOC more vulnerable than the EIC to the external encroachment of competing European enterprises in Asia.

The greater rigidity of the VOC also held true in the organization of shipping. The Dutch ships were built and owned by the respective chambers. The EIC, by contrast, hired their ships each year until the large buildup of their own fleet during the Seven Years' War, when the Royal Navy was occupied in the Atlantic and Mediterranean war of blockade with the French navy. J. R. Bruijn argues that one cannot tell which of the two systems was more expensive. The English system appeared more flexible in form, but in fact "hereditary bottoms" appeared that were owned by a self-perpetuating shippers' group. This group exercised monopoly power over ships suitable for the East India trade and enforced it by using their large holdings of EIC stock to elect a significant number of directors. The modal number of voyages for the English ships was four; for the Dutch it was six to seven.[32] Nevertheless, it is clear that the English led in innovations in navigation and construction (especially copper sheathing), resulting in shorter trips and fewer losses en route. The Dutch chambers, by contrast, were prevented from adopting foreign innovations because of the requirement for shallow-draft ships to gain access to their increasingly silted ports.[33] So although shipping prime costs per voyage may well have been less for the Dutch due to tight internal controls, it appears the English likely enjoyed superior profits per voyage, especially after the mid–eighteenth century, when the pace of shipping innovation began to quicken.

The marketing areas of the VOC were always continental Europe,

---

[30] For 1732 see Chaudhuri, *Trading World of Asia,* 448. For 1763 see Sutherland, *East India Company in Politics,* 141–91.

[31] Bruijn, Gaastra, and Schöffer, *Dutch-Asiatic Shipping,* 1:7.

[32] Ibid., 94–5. See also Chapter 5 in this volume.

[33] Bruijn, Gaastra, and Schöffer, *Dutch-Asiatic Shipping,* 1:105–6.

whereas the EIC concentrated on its growing home market, and re-exports of its imports were directed increasingly to the growing Atlantic empire of the British. Country trade within Asia was undoubtedly more important in quantity and value for each company than the intercontinental trade, however. The Dutch dominated the southern Asian seas and the trade in exotic spices, whereas the English developed trade at the very edge of the Muslim world, where religious wars were always a possibility even in the absence of Christians. Finally, it is interesting to note the rallying of the VOC relative to the EIC in the peacetime period (in Europe) of the early 1770s. This was clearly due to the increasing control of the English company by its home government and its continued obligation to remit large sums as tax revenues.

The greater success of the English company in meeting the economic competition of the French, Austrians, and Scandinavians during the 1730s and 1740s enabled them eventually to achieve military victories over the French in India as well as in the Atlantic during the course of the Seven Years' War. It is ironic, but in accord with Steensgaard's thesis, that it was precisely the military success of Clive that in the next twenty years enabled the Dutch company to become a free rider. Until the fourth Anglo-Dutch war in the 1780s, the Dutch enjoyed the protection of the English from the competition of the French and other upstarts without paying nearly as much as the English were paying to maintain their military gains. And the stock and foreign exchange markets of the time reflected this turnabout.

CHAPTER 7

World bullion flows, 1450–1800

WARD BARRETT

THE purpose of this essay is to review published accounts of bullion flows in the early modern period in order to estimate the magnitude of the flows between sources and sinks of precious metal, and to see if they can yield estimates of flows and balances that are reasonably consistent and coherent. Because the data are so spotty for most of the flows that annual or other short-term figures cannot be obtained, estimates will instead be presented by periods a quarter of a century in length, thus yielding twelve such periods between 1500 and 1800 (Table 7.3). Because Europe was the major region of transshipment from dominant source (the Americas) to principal sink (Asia), the major focus will be on shipments to and from that region. The result will be a brief assessment of the current state of our knowledge of these flows, in the broadest and simplest terms possible. We begin with the sources of precious metal.

PRODUCTION OF SILVER AND GOLD IN THE AMERICAS

The overwhelming dominance of the New World in the production of precious metals in early modern history is illustrated in Table 7.1. It shows that from 1493 to 1800, 85 percent of the world's silver and over 70 percent of its gold came from the Americas. In each century both absolute production and the relative share of the Americas in world production increased, with gold showing the greatest rate of increase in the eighteenth century owing to continued Colombian production and a great increase in Brazilian production. The decline of gold production in Africa and Europe, like the considerably greater drop in production of silver in the latter, was an effect of the import of large quantities of more cheaply produced American precious metal.

The principal producing regions of the New World include, for sil-

Table 7.1

Production and European Imports of Precious Metals in Tonnes, or Metric Tons

	Silver			Gold				
	World	Americas	Americas'% of World	World	Americas	Americas'% of World	Africa	Europe
1493-1600	23,000	17,000	74	714	280	39	255	148
1601-1700	40,000	34,000	85	900	590	66	200	100
1701-1800	57,000	51,000	90	1900	1620	85	170	108
TOTALS	120,000	102,000	85	3514	2490	71	625	356

Sources and notes: Silver: C. W. Merrill et al., Summarized Data of Silver Production, U.S. Dept. of Commerce, Bureau of Mines, Economic Paper 8 (Washington, 1930), 3; gold: R. H. Ridgway et al., Summarized Data of Gold Production, U.S. Dept. of Commerce, Bureau of Mines, Economic Paper 6 (Washington, 1929), 6. H. E. Cross ("South American Bullion Production and Export, 1550-1750," in J. F. Richards, Precious Metals in the Later Medieval and Early Modern Worlds [Durham, N.C., 1983], 402) has adjusted Merrill's figures to take account of higher estimates of Japanese production recently advanced by Kozo Yamamura and Tetsuo Kamiki ("Silver Mines and Sung Coins--A Monetary History of Medieval and Modern Japan in International Perspective," in Richards, Precious Metals, 329-62); he has thus reduced the share of New World production of silver in the sixteenth and seventeenth centuries to 69 and 84 percent, respectively. These differences are scarcely more than those caused by rounding.

ver, the young Andean mountains of the Viceroyalty of Perú (where the principal mines were in present-day Bolivia) and the southern extension of the similarly young North American chain into New Spain. Gold was found in varying abundance within these silver deposits, but its principal colonial sources were alluvial or placer, in Colombia and Brazil. Production of gold in Brazil lasted only slightly more than half a century, from before 1700 to the 1750s, but Colombian production was sustained throughout the colonial period. In the case of silver, in both Perú and Mexico by far most of the production was highly localized, being accounted for by a few mines or veins within a few regions of small extent. These few great mines did not all produce steadily at high levels throughout the colonial period but rather sustained high production over relatively short periods of several decades, although many of them produced at lower rates for much longer periods and some continue to produce today.[1]

Given the circumstance of highly localized, concentrated production of silver at a few, perhaps only several dozen, mines within the Spanish Empire, combined with a bureaucratic effort to measure production in order to tax it, one might suppose that developing a time-series of production is an easy matter, but such is not the case for two principal reasons: (1) the records of individual major mines are either incomplete or missing, and (2) the operators and owners of the mines failed to register some unknowable part of total production at local Crown offices.

The first of these reasons is self-explanatory and cannot be overcome unless records turn up. The second obstacle to full description has been dealt with by Latin Americanists in two ways in order to increase the accuracy of their estimates of production: the older method, probably as old as the inception of mining and the problem itself, has been to rely on estimates of unregistered production by colonial observers; the newer method, developed only recently, consists in attempting to find a ratio between the consumption of mercury (indispensable to the principal method of silver production in the New World) and the production of silver of specified fineness.

Many colonial observers put forth many estimates of unrecorded production of precious metals, and I have the impression that many or most of these fall between a quarter and a half of total production. Many of these observers were officials newly appointed to the duties

---

[1] Alexander von Humboldt was the first to determine systematically that production was highly concentrated spatially in the New World, which he recognized to be the case in Europe as well (*Political Essay on the Kingdom of New Spain*, trans. John Black, 4 vols. [London, 1811], 3:136–9).

and inexperienced in both mining and local affairs; on the other hand, more experienced observers arrived at uncertain conclusions as well.[2] Hernandez, who was familiar with the mines of Perú and visited one or more in Mexico in mid–eighteenth century, wrote that the amount of unregistered silver produced in Perú was "commonly very considerable," concluding that it might range from a third to a half of total production. Humboldt stated that if the amount of silver registered in Mexico were increased by 20 percent, the result would yield total production; this means that he estimated that only 17 percent of total Mexican production was unregistered, and in his final summary of total production in both Spanish and Portuguese America he used the same ratio of 17:83.[3] This seems very low in relation to many other colonial estimates.

A newer method relies on the observation that the so-called patio process of extracting silver from the low-grade ores common in the New World required the use of mercury to amalgamate with silver in the ore and thus extract it from its matrix; the mercury was then evaporated by heating the amalgam and was lost in large part, so not all of it was reused. Mercury was obtained from only a few sites – Huancavelica in Perú, Almadén in Spain, Idria in Slovenia – and was distributed by a Crown monopoly in the New World. Records were kept by officials of amounts of mercury distributed in the New World, and many of these records have survived. Because mercury was consumed in proportion to the richness or poverty of the ore, and the ratio of consumption to production for the few important mines is approximately known, it is possible to estimate silver production from mercury consumption, and indeed this relationship was known to colonial officials and observers.[4]

---

[2] Ann Twinham, *Miners, Merchants, and Farmers in Colonial Colombia*, Latin American Monographs, vol. 57 (Austin, 1982), 19, cites the case of the new governor Silvestre, who wanted to estimate gold production in Antioquia in 1775 but could not even determine the number of gold mines there. A characteristic of the Colombian industry was the large number of small operators.

[3] James Hernandez, *A Philosophical and Practical Essay on the Gold and Silver Mines of Mexico and Peru* (London, 1755), 12–13, 22; he visited and described the mines at Pachuca, 50. Humboldt, *Political Essay*, 3:251; he also (3:389–93) described high estimates (a third to a half of all production) of unregistered gold and silver as being "very exaggerated ideas" and insisted that the amounts not registered varied considerably from place to place. His ratio for the value of unregistered to registered gold and silver is found in 3:418 and applies to all the Americas; thus in the end, he used the assumed Mexican ratio (17% unregistered) even for places where he described contraband shipments as greater than in Mexico, which lacked sufficient ports to make this activity easy.

[4] The matter was discussed by Humboldt in various places; for examples see *Political*

Table 7.2

Production of Silver and Gold in Spanish and Portuguese America (Tonnes)

	Sixteenth Century			Seventeenth Century			Eighteenth Century			Total		
	Silver	Gold	Silver equivalent	Silver	Gold	Silver equivalent	Silver	Gold	Silver equivalent	Silver	Gold	Silver equivalent
Humboldt[a]			17,563			42,040			73,971			133,574
Soetbeer[b]	17,128	327	20,823	34,008	606	42,431	58,530	1,614	84,354	109,666	2,547	147,608
Merrill and Ridgway[c]	16,925	280	20,089	34,435	590	42,636	51,080	1,620	75,380	102,440	2,490	138,105
Morineau[d]	7,500	150	9,120	26,168	158	28,459	39,157	1,400	61,417	72,825	2,708	98,996
Slicher van Bath[e]	11,175	628	18,544	27,640	420	33,734	58,366	1,485	81,970	97,182	2,587	13,247

a 1500–1800: Humbolt, Political Essay on the Kingdom of New Spain, trans. John Black, 4 vols. (London, 1811).

b 1493–1800: Adolf Soetbeer, Edelmetall-Produktion und Wertverhältnisse zwischen Gold und Silber seit der Entdeckung Amerikas bis zur Gerenwart : Petermanns Mittheilungen, suppl. 13, no. 97 (1880).

c 1493–1800: Merrill et al., Summarized Data of Silver Production, and Ridgway et al., Summarized Data of Gold Production.

d 1500–1800: Michael Morineau, Incroyables gazettes et fabuleux métaux (London, 1985).

e 1503–1820: B. H. Slicker van Bath, "Het Latijins-Amerikaanse gold en zilver in de kolonial tijd," Economisch- en Sociaal Historisch Jaarboek 47 (1984). These are not production figures; see text.

But the method can provide only estimates, whose error of estimation cannot be assessed. Ore from the same mine was not uniform in silver content; the experience of the operators played a role; some mercury condensed in the process and could be reused; and some unknown part of the silver was produced without mercury by a process of smelting. Furthermore, interannual fluctuations in mercury supplies and stocks in the mining areas make estimates of annual production obtained by this method less reliable than estimates of, say, quinquennial production. Its use provides, nevertheless, a welcome check on figures arrived at by other means.[5]

To arrive at a first approximation, we review the estimates of American production of gold and silver (Table 7.2) made by six authors for three successive centuries, using centuries as units of time because three of the authors give production by century only (Merrill, Ridgway, and Slicher van Bath). Although estimates cannot be presented for shorter units of time, it is nevertheless useful to see how closely they resemble each other at this scale. Before discussing this table, it is necessary to describe the works from which these figures were taken. The earliest, the work of Humboldt, is the first comprehensive overview of the mining economy of Spanish America, based both on personal observation and on documentary sources, not all of which were fully identified or described by him, which is a source of doubt concerning the value of his conclusions. Criticizing the "vague and imperfect data . . . in several recent works," he wrote that he would "discuss only what I have been able to procure from official papers communicated to me," which included, among other documents, "the registers of the mints of Mexico, Lima, Santa Fe, and Popayan." In another place, he wrote of a table he presented that it was "drawn up from the valuable information which I obtained more recently from

---

Essay, 3:265, 281–2, 284–9. See also F. de Solano, *Antonio de Ulloa y la Nueva España* (Mexico City, 1979), 75, for Ulloa's observation.

[5] The most useful survey of the method, as well as of colonial silver mining generally in Perú and Mexico, is given by D. A. Brading and Harry E. Cross, "Colonial Silver Mining: Mexico and Peru," *Hispanic-American Historical Review* 52 (1972): 545–79, who describe the problems associated with it. Cross has used the method more recently ("South American Bullion Production and Export, 1550–1750," in J. F. Richards, *Precious Metals in the Later Medieval and Early Modern Worlds* [Durham, N.C., 1983]). It has also been used by P. J. Bakewell ("Registered Silver Production in the Potosí District, 1550–1735," *Jahrbuch für Geschichte von Staat, Wirtschaft, und Gesellschaft Lateinamerikas* 12 [1975]: 81–3), who offers as well a survey of the problems of unregistered production, concluding (p. 85) that there is no evidence of illegal traffic in mercury sufficient to justify high estimates of unregistered production. It should be noted that according to Brading and Cross ("Colonial Silver Mining," 556) nearly half of all silver produced at Zacatecas from 1685 to 1705 was obtained by smelting, because of a shortage of mercury.

Spain, and the kingdom of New Granada," but in this case, as in so many others, he did not give detailed information concerning the sources of his data. For this reason, it is not possible to identify the sources of the data presented in this graph entitled "Produce of the Mines of America since Its Discovery." This graph is the only continuous and comprehensive set of such data. In some cases where he did identify the documentary source, its current location is unknown.[6]

Faced with the fact that this rather casual documentation is a pervasive feature of Humboldt's famous work, we have two choices: We can discard or ignore much of it as insufficiently documented, or we can accept it at least provisionally on the basis of the great deal that is known of his character, his scholarly reputation, and his experience. Humboldt dedicated his adult life to the systematic collection of scientific information, including the measurement of many features of the physical world, to which end he carried with him into the Spanish Empire the finest scientific instruments available. A partial witness to his diligence in their use are the countless barometric estimates of altitude that are scattered throughout his work, along with many other measurements. There can be no doubt that it was his wish to be equally precise and correct in his statements of social and economic facts and quantities. In these matters, he had to rely on data given to him by local authorities or on his own estimates. In the case of his statistics of precious metal production, we are on ground made very solid by the fact of his preeminent expertise: a geologist and mining engineer by training and experience, he was one of the Western world's foremost authorities on the mining of precious metals. In this he followed a long-established German tradition that included the sixteenth-century masterpiece of Georgius Agricola on mining and metallurgy. In his official and practical work in German mines, including such important silver mines as those at Freiberg, where he attended the Mining School (a large part of whose curriculum consisted of experience in the local mines), he was concerned with quantities of many substances, a concern expressed throughout his many works and in many fields of inquiry. Thus his extended description of the mining of precious metals in Spanish America, forming a large part of his report on New Spain and one of its most valuable features, is a substantial expression of professional interests and experience in the mining and

---

[6] Humboldt, *Political Essay*, 3:336, 287, 388. The graph is part of the frontispiece of the same volume. D. A. Brading (*Miners and Merchants in Bourbon Mexico* [Cambridge, 1971], xi) regarded Humboldt's *Political Essay* as still "the best account" of eighteenth-century New Spain.

processing of ores of precious metals. He was not an amateur in these matters. He was, rather, in a position to give us, through the unique combination of his knowledge, interests, and unmatched access to information, the best estimates anyone could have made at the time of the production of precious metals in Spanish America.

Humboldt's estimates were followed by Soetbeer's in 1880. Humboldt's work is listed in the bibliographies that precede each section of Soetbeer's discussion of production in the Americas, except the parts dealing with the West Indies and Brazil, where he relied on other sources. Soetbeer appears to have accepted Humboldt's estimates as minimum amounts and added greater values for unregistered production subject to fraud and smuggling to arrive at a total some 13 percent greater than Humboldt's.[7]

The estimates of production in the reports of Ridgway and Merrill on gold and silver, respectively, are derived to some unknowable extent from the work of Soetbeer, although theirs differ somewhat from his. Ridgway's "brief bibliography of the more important references to gold production" includes Soetbeer's work but not Humboldt's, and his summary Table 5 has no estimate of production in Central America and the West Indies, both places where gold was produced.[8] This omission, as well as the fact that his summary goes only to 1800 whereas Soetbeer's extends to 1810, may explain some of the differences between his and Soetbeer's figures. Merrill noted that his estimates of production before 1877 were "largely taken" from Soetbeer's works, and the only significant difference between the two occurs in the estimates for the eighteenth century, where Merrill's is 13 percent lower than Soetbeer's.[9] Ridgway's estimates are also close to those of Soetbeer, except for the sixteenth century, where Ridgway's is 14 percent less than Soetbeer's.

Cross believed that the Merrill and Ridgway reports for the U.S. Bureau of Mines formed "one of the most comprehensive collections of bullion production ever assembled."[10] Like Soetbeer's, both of these reports contain regional breakdowns, but Soetbeer's discussion of the mining districts within the regions is fuller; Ridgway gave little subregional description, and Merrill's is summary, without estimates of

---

[7] See, for example, his treatment of the Mexican values; Adolf Soetbeer, *Edelmetall-Produktion und Wertverhältinisse zwischen Gold und Silber seit der Entdeckung Amerikas bis zur Gegenwart: Petermanns Mittheilungen,* supplement 13, no. 97 (1880), 59–60.

[8] Robert H. Ridgway et al., *Summarized Data of Gold Production,* U.S. Department of Commerce, Bureau of Mines, Economic Paper 6 (Washington, 1929), 62–3, 12.

[9] Charles W. Merrill et al., *Summarized Data of Silver Production,* U.S. Department of Commerce, Bureau of Mines, Economic Paper 8 (Washington, 1930), 2.

[10] Cross, "South American Bullion Production," in Richards, *Precious Metals,* 402.

production from individual mines or mining districts. Unlike Soetbeer's work, which contains summary regional tables divided into
twenty-year periods, Merrill and Ridgway give data of production
only for periods a century in length.

One may agree with Cross that the two reports are comprehensive,
but the fact remains that they are not detailed, and thus one cannot
determine how the regional totals were estimated. On the other hand,
Cross noted that the estimates made by the bureau's researchers for
production in seventeenth-century Mexico are within 10 percent of
his own, an amount regarded by him as "an acceptable tolerance."[11]
Because his estimates and the bureau's were arrived at by different
methods, his conclusion is plausible: the estimates reinforce one another. At the same time, Merrill's and Ridgway's estimates appear to
me to be variations on Soetbeer's, and because the major purpose of
their reports was to review production of precious metals since 1800,
they probably relied heavily on Soetbeer's comprehensive coverage
of the centuries before 1800 for their own estimates.

The work of Morineau has provoked far more controversy than all
of the others, and this in spite of the fact that his totals are a full 25
percent less than those nearest his, Humboldt's and van Bath's. It
should be kept in mind, of course, that Morineau has provided estimates of *arrivals* of gold and silver from the Americas, not figures of
total production as have the others; his figures must therefore be lower
than theirs, if only because some unknown part of American production went to Manila. Most interestingly, a "reasonable" estimate of
unregistered production and imports might be about 25 percent, and
yet increasing Morineau's figures by only 10 percent would convert
them to the same order of magnitude as the rest.

The great value of Morineau's estimates lies in the fact that they are
based on sources different from those used by anyone else, including
the authors listed in Table 7.2. His are independent estimates of the
amounts of American gold and silver arriving in Europe, including
unregistered, smuggled bullion, because these amounts were described in Dutch corantos, or gazettes, of the seventeenth and eighteenth centuries. The earliest known Dutch coranto was issued on
June 14, 1618, and large numbers of various series of them were published in the Netherlands in the seventeenth century. They contained
commercial reports, news of shipping, reports from the East and West
Indies and other places of current interest, and, above all, reports of
the arrival of American treasure ships and their cargoes of bullion,

---

[11] Ibid.

news picked up at dockside in many places. Through many examples of sharply contrasting reports of treasure brought by particular ships and fleets in the official registers, on the one hand, and the gazettes, on the other, Morineau has constructed a plausible and most persuasive case that discredits the official statistics, which in any case have been known for many years to be incomplete on the basis of a multitude of remarks from as many sources.[12]

Morineau's statistics of arrivals of precious metals have had considerable impact because they controvert important and long-held beliefs, assumptions, and conclusions concerning European economic and social history of the sixteenth, seventeenth, and eighteenth centuries. The work of E. J. Hamilton seemed to have established as fact that European imports of American bullion rose to a peak in the late sixteenth century and then began to fall; the rise in imports produced inflation, it was thought, and the fall a drop in economic activity, which revived with the renewed influx of American treasure in the eighteenth century. The works of Chaunu, along with many others, have affirmed this monetarist model, which was based on and confirmed by a wide range of official statistics other than those used by Hamilton, whose thesis relied on the official accounts of the arrival of registered bullion at the House of Trade (Casa de Contratación) in Seville, which reflect the course Hamilton described.[13] The continuing reception of greatly reduced amounts was demonstrated by García Fuentes, who extended Hamilton's work from 1650 to 1700 by using more of the same data from the House of Trade.[14] With unofficial sources and an abundance of data and examples, Morineau has shown that far more treasure was arriving from America, and at places

---

[12] F. Dahl, *Dutch Corantos* (The Hague: 1946), 17, 25–6. This work contains facsimiles of many corantos and a descriptive introduction concerning them. See also Michel Morineau, *Incroyables gazettes et fabuleux métaux* (London, 1985); and D. O. Flynn's review in *Journal of Economic History* 47 (1987): 799–801.

[13] Pierre Chaunu, with Huguette Chaunu, *Séville et l'Atlantique (1504–1650)*, 8 vols. (Paris, 1955–9); Earl J. Hamilton, *American Treasure and the Price Revolution in Spain, 1501–1650* (Cambridge, Mass., 1934).

[14] L. García Fuentes, (*El comercio español con America, 1650–1700* [Seville, 1980], 382, 414) made only two references to the work of Morineau, noting in the last that whereas the statistics of the House of Trade showed about 44 million pesos were imported in the entire last half of the seventeenth century, Morineau claimed that over 46 million pesos arrived in the last five years alone, from 1696 to 1700. García Fuentes concluded that the difference could be explained only by "large and frequent exemptions . . . granted by the Crown and that doubtless they hid enormous inflows of unregistered bullion." A most interesting discussion of smuggling was given by Jorge Juan and Antonio de Ulloa, *Discourse and Political Reflections on the Kingdom of Peru*, trans. J. J. Te Paske and B. A. Clement (Norman, Okla. 1978), 42–68.

other than Seville, than was revealed by the documents in the House of Trade and other official records. Thus were confounded both the accepted data as indicators of bullion shipments from America and the monetarist model they supported: the price inflation of the sixteenth century abated in the seventeenth, when even more treasure arrived; nor did it return to persistently high levels in the eighteenth century, which saw far greater inflows than ever of bullion in the form of Brazilian gold and Mexican silver. In spite of these empirical achievements, Morineau's work is often described as superficial; but these descriptions lead one to ask, if mere superficial analysis can inflict such severe damage on a ruling paradigm, what are we to think of the paradigm?

The explanation of the decline in receipt of registered American treasure has to do with the replacement of Seville by Cadiz as the terminus of American shipping and with an increase in smuggling in the seventeenth century. The former process began in the 1630s and ended with a royal decree in 1679 establishing Cadiz as the terminus, without protest from the House of Trade of Seville, which accepted the change as already-accomplished fact.[15] In 1717 the House of Trade itself was moved to Cadiz. Because these changes reflect the reality that more and more American trade was being diverted from Seville to Cadiz, including the unloading of bullion, the records of the House of Trade at Seville cannot possibly include all the bullion that arrived in Spain or elsewhere in Europe.

The increase in smuggling was the result not only of greed but also of necessity, caused by the rule that those who registered freight had to share the costs of the convoy. This meant that an increase in smuggling was almost inevitable, because those who registered their freight had to pay more and more of the costs of those who smuggled, and thus themselves felt pressure to smuggle. This vicious circle was described as early as 1634 in an unpublished Royal Order of 18 March, which stated that the king and a few others who could not evade registration had to bear a disproportionate amount of the costs of the convoy, adding that it was rumored that the previous convoy had carried more unregistered than registered bullion. After 1660, according to Domínguez Ortiz, the official registers do not show total arrival of bullion but only the royal treasure, although some private shippers preferred for reasons of security to declare their shipments rather than

---

[15] García Fuentes, *El comercio español con America*, 57–63, contains a useful account of the causes for the change of terminus.

to smuggle them. He concluded that by mid–seventeenth century the registered bullion was far less than the unregistered.[16]

Slicher van Bath's work, like Morineau's, is valuable because his sources are different from those of the others, and therefore his are also independently derived estimates. They are aggregates of recent regional estimates of production, such as those made by Bakewell and Brading and Cross.[17] For the entire period, his totals are very close to Humboldt's, keeping in mind that Slicher van Bath has included the years from 1800 to 1820, as Humboldt did not, and that some of those twenty years saw high production in Mexico, at least. For the three years from 1801 through 1803, for example, Humboldt estimated that some 1,400 tonnes of silver equivalent were produced there, but Brading showed a sharp decline in mintage of silver and gold in Mexico after 1810 at the beginning of the War for Independence, and similar declines occurred elsewhere.[18] Thus, given that the Mexican mines were the major producers, the addition of two decades more of estimates means a difference of less than 5 percent, which would put Slicher van Bath's total near 130,000 tonnes. Interestingly, then, of all the estimates, the earliest and the latest are closest to each other.

The estimates in Table 7.2 of total American production of silver equivalent from 1500 to 1800 do not differ greatly from one another. We have three independently derived estimates, if Soetbeer's figures are taken as independent of Humboldt's, and if we view the Merrill and Ridgway values as qualified endorsements of Soetbeer's. Rounded, the four estimates range from 130,000 to 150,000 tonnes. The difference between Morineau's total and the others is roughly 40,000 tonnes, or about 135 tonnes per year, an amount less than 5.5 million pesos in value. This sum is reasonably close to total estimates for the cost of the two main uses of silver other than that of export to Europe: the

---

[16] Antonio Domínguez Ortiz, "Las remesas de metales preciosos de Indias en 1655," *Anuario de Historia Economica y Social* 2 (1969): 563–4.

[17] Bakewell, "Registered Silver Production in the Potosí District"; Brading and Cross, "Colonial Silver Mining."

[18] B. H. Slicher van Bath, "Het Latijns-Amerikaanse gold en zilver in de koloniale tijd," *Economisch- en Sociaal-Historisch Jaarboek* 1984 (47): 181; Humboldt, *Political Essay*, 3:291; Brading, *Miners and Merchants in Bourbon Mexico*, 131. Slicher van Bath's estimates of American production have been used by Artur Attman in his recent review entitled *American Bullion in the European World Trade, 1600–1800* (Acta Regiae Societatis Scientiarum et Litterarum Gothoburgensis, Humaniora vol. 26 [1986], 19–20). Although Attman treated seriously these and other estimates not based on official statistics, including Morineau's, he concluded that "for the time being estimates must still be based on official fiscal records," while recognizing that both Portuguese and Spanish records yield only minimum estimates (pp. 21, 25, 27).

Philippine trade and its subsidies, which might have taken half of the missing 40,000 tonnes, and other expenses of empire in the Americas. Some of the latter could have found its way eventually to Europe by means that enabled it to escape Morineau's net, whereas the silver equivalent that went directly to the Philippines was forever lost to Europe. In this way, his estimates can be reconciled with the others. Therefore, the most complete estimates we have of American production of silver equivalent from 1500 to 1800 range from about 130,000 to 150,000 tonnes.

Although the estimates for the entire period show substantial agreement, those for centuries within it differ, in some cases markedly. The two most recent sets of figures, Morineau's and Slicher van Bath's, assign much lower values to the sixteenth and seventeenth centuries than do the others, but they differ sharply in estimates of silver (although not of gold) in the eighteenth; for the latter, Slicher van Bath's estimate of silver production is identical to Soetbeer's. Soetbeer's, Merrill's, and Ridgway's estimates differ substantially only in regard to silver production in the eighteenth century, with Merrill's values much lower than Soetbeer's. On one important point, made so frequently as to have become a commonplace by now, there is agreement: whether or not there was a drop in production of precious metals in the seventeenth century, total production in that century increased greatly over that of the sixteenth.

Some estimates of production of precious metals in the Americas during the colonial period are shown graphically in Figure 7.1. Five different sets of data are displayed. The reasons why these were chosen will be discussed in turn, beginning with the oldest set, furnished by Humboldt.

Humboldt's graph is the only continuous source of annual data of production in the Americas from 1500 to 1800 and beyond. It was first published as part of the frontispiece of volume 3 of his *Political Essay on the Kingdom of New Spain*. To make the data of his graph usable, I have converted them to quinquennial data by estimating at five-year intervals the value of production and then taking the average of each pair of successive five-year intervals to establish the average annual production for each quinquennium of the entire period covered by the graph. These figures have been used to draw curve 1 of Figure 7.1. Humboldt's tabulated estimate of the total value of gold and silver exported from the Americas to Europe from 1493 to 1803 is roughly equal to 134,500 tonnes of silver equivalent; my estimate of the total produced from 1500 to 1800, as read from Humboldt's graph, is 133,574 tonnes, which is nearly equal to his tabulated total. His tabulated total

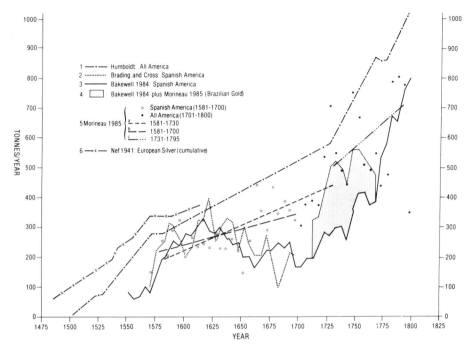

Figure 7.1. Production and European imports of precious metals

is included in a table confirming the trend of his graph, but having periods of various numbers of years and thus lacking the usefulness of annual estimates.[19]

In contrast to the continuously rising production of bullion shown in Humboldt's graph, many works of this century have emphasized a late sixteenth-century boom in production followed by a seven-

---

[19] Humboldt, *Political Essay*, 3:431, 433–4. Humboldt's estimates would be more useful had he separated them into gold and silver produced rather than presenting the combined value of production of both because as D. Flynn has pointed out, they may move in different directions ("The Microeconomics of Silver and East–West Trade in the Early Modern Period," in Wolfram Fischer, R. Marvin McInnis, and Jürgen Schneider, eds., *The Emergence of a World Economy, 1900–1914* [Wiesbaden, 1986], 38). There is, however, no way to remedy this. To convert Humboldt's values (in pesos) of total production, I have used the following numbers of grams of pure silver contained in the peso: 25.56 (1500–1728); 24.81 (1728–71); 24.43 (1772–1800). For the ratio of value of silver to gold, I have used the values given by F. Gil y Pablos, *Estudios sobre el credito publico y la dueda publica español* (Madrid, 1900), 360; these are, for the sixteenth century, 11.3; for the seventeenth, 13.9; for the eighteenth, 15.0. The values differ slightly from those used by, for example, Slicher van Bath ("Het Latijns-Amerikaanse gold en zilver," 180): 11.2, 13.9, 15.4. The problem of which to choose has no easy solution.

teenth-century bust; this gave way near 1700 to a Brazilian gold rush that faded after about half a century and was replaced about the same time by the beginning of the famous Mexican silver boom. The most influential boom–bust cycle of this model was established by Hamilton, who used official Spanish records of annual silver imports into Spain to delineate the part of it that ran from 1501 to 1650.

The reliance on official records has been the major feature of this group of estimates of production, export, and import of bullion. The official records are of four kinds, and all four are only indirectly related to production: (1) records of the royal share, or tax, on production (mostly 20 percent in Perú and 10 percent in New Spain; these records reflect the willingness of miners to reveal to the royal authorities the yield of their mines); (2) records of the royal mints, to which buyers or producers of refined silver were to bring their refined ingot silver for assay and mintage; (3) registers of silver shipments into Spain, where for long there was a single official port of entry; (4) records of the official monopoly of the supply of mercury, necessary to the production of most silver. In addition to official sources, there are also extant private records of individual mines, which are incomplete and always raise questions of representativeness.

Whatever may be said for the efficacy of internal checks within the system or the comparison of one of these sets of records with another, nearly everyone agrees that all the records are incomplete because of failure to register production and because of smuggling, the two most important sources of understatement. The problem then becomes one of estimating these quantities.

Hamilton's model was supported by the Chaunu study of transatlantic shipping and trade and by many others. Subsequently, Bakewell's study of Zacatecas, based on official records, moved the peak of the boom to the 1620s, but still yielded a cycle. Brading and Cross estimated production by employing the ratio of mercury use to production of silver. Their results, covering the period from 1571 to 1700, have been included in Figure 7.1 and show a cycle with a peak near that of Zacatecas.[20] They have also estimated gold production and the amount of silver produced by smelting rather than amalgamation, making theirs the first attempt since Humboldt's to estimate for short periods of time the total production of bullion in the Americas. To be sure, this was Spanish America, and their series stopped in 1700, at about the time Brazilian gold production began; nevertheless, the

[20] Pierre Chaunu et Huguette Chaunu, *Séville et l'Atlantique (1504–1650)*, 8 vols. (Paris, 1955–9); Bakewell, "Registered Silver Production in the Potosí District"; Brading and Cross, "Colonial Silver Mining," 579.

method of estimation was useful, although it yielded results essentially similar to Hamilton's.

In 1983 Cross presented new estimates of South American bullion production from 1556 to 1760, using a variety of methods of estimating silver production. For Potosí, he used official records of the royal tax on production plus an estimate of unregistered production and of smuggled (also unreported) silver. Cross pointed out that the results "closely parallel" those obtained by Bakewell from different records of registered production in the same mining district. For Charcas, the other principal producing area, he again used the mercury ratio (1611–50) together with an estimate (20 percent of total production) of smelted silver, still important among Indians. Cross's estimates of Brazilian gold exports (1699–1755) were derived from those of Godinho.[21] Although they do not cover all of the eighteenth century, they do represent the first attempt to provide a comprehensive account of all of South America; however, I have not included his data on this graph because they do not include New Spain and, more important, their cyclical course produces a curve very similar to that of the other two curves based on official records (Figure 7.1, curves 2 and 3).

Finally, I have included in the group of studies based on official records a recent work by Bakewell that contains the latest comprehensive statement of American bullion production, in this case of Spanish America, from 1551 to 1800. This includes both Colombian placer gold and gold derived from silver deposits elsewhere, but not Brazilian gold, for which reason I have added to it estimates of the latter offered by Morineau (curve 4).[22] Bakewell's latest statement is based on records of the royal tax offices, which he considers "the most reliable source for gold and silver production" figures.[23] However, what is new here is the addition of data from the royal tax offices not previously studied and, in addition, the data run to the end of the eighteenth century.

In sharp contrast to these works based on official records, and much closer to the estimates of Humboldt, stands the work of Morineau. Because Morineau's estimates concern imports of bullion into Eu-

---

[21] Cross, "South American Bullion Production," in Richards, *Precious Metals,* 408, 427; Bakewell, "Registered Silver Production in the Potosí District"; V. Magalhães Godinho, "Le Porfugal, les flottes du sucre et les flottes de l'or," *Annales* 5 (1950): 184–97.

[22] P. J. Bakewell, "Mining in Colonial Spanish America," in Leslie Bethell, ed., *The Cambridge History of Latin America,* vol. 2 (Cambridge, 1984); Morineau, *Incroyables Gazettes,* 139.

[23] Bakewell, "Mining in Colonial Spanish America," 138.

rope, they must be less than Humboldt's, who estimated production of bullion in the Americas. Because some of the bullion was diverted to the Philippines, a considerably lesser amount to Africa, the West Indies, and the Atlantic colonies, and some other part was retained in Spanish and Portuguese America, imports into Europe must have been less than total production. Another major difference between the two sets of estimates is the contrast between the more or less continuous growth of production shown by Humboldt and the wildly fluctuating quinquennial averages of imports presented by Morineau. However, there is no reason at all why even a quinquennial average of deliveries should match a schedule of production: they are not wholly unrelated, but neither need they be closely matched. In the case of Mexican mining, production depended on delivery of imported mercury and Mexican salt; exports to Spain depended on overland transport to Veracruz and a long sea voyage to Cadiz. Smelting could be and was substituted for amalgamation when mercury was short; delivery of salt was not a major problem, but the delivery of bullion was, on the record, much more erratic.[24]

There are two important similarities between Humboldt's estimates and Morineau's unofficial data: (1) Over a long range of time (from 1576 to 1790) they approach each other more frequently than do any other sets; (2) although the inflection point at about 1575 is the most important one of Humboldt's graph, it does not presage a seventeenth-century depression but rather merely precedes a period of reduced but steady growth for nearly 150 years, and if Morineau's data show a seventeenth-century decline, it was over by about 1660.

Comparisons of other details of the curves show that the seventeenth-century decline of production is the major point at issue. For example, the closest agreement among all the curves occurs between about 1575 and 1630, and were Cross's data included, the case would be even stronger because his data on South American production alone exceed Humboldt's for three decades (1581–1610) in that period. Humboldt's estimates for the period from 1500 to 1575 yield a rate of growth similar to that of curves 2 and 3 (Figure 7.1) beginning fifteen to twenty-five years earlier. In addition, Humboldt's and Bakewell's data show similar rates of growth, but at any particular date Humboldt's estimates far exceed those of Bakewell's. We may conclude that there is fairly general agreement on the amount of bullion pro-

---

[24] Brading and Cross, "Colonial Silver Mining," 556; Ursula Ewald, *The Mexican Salt Industry, 1560–1980* (Stuttgart and New York, 1985), 59; Humboldt, *Political Essay*, 3:354, 259–60 (Humboldt inspected salt mines in Germany).

Table 7.3

Average Annual Estimates (in Tonnes) of

Production and Movement of

Silver and Silver Equivalent, 1501–1800

	1 American production (Humboldt)	2 European arrivals (Morineau)	3 Col. 1 minus col. 2	4 Exports from Europe	5 Net balance col. 2 minus col. 4
1501–1525	45	40[a]	5		
1526–1550	125	105[a]	20		
1551–1575	240	205[a]	35		
1576–1600	290	205	85		
1601–1625	340	245	95	100	145
1626–1650	395	290	105	125	165
1651–1675	445	330	115	130	200

1676–1700	500	370	130	155	215
1701–1725	550	415	135	190	225
1726–1750	650	500	150	210	290
1751–1775	820	590	230	215	375
1776–1800	940	600	340	195	405

Sources: Col. 1, Humboldt, Political Essay, vol. 3, fig. 2 of frontispiece. Col. 2, Morineau, Incroyables gazettes, 250, table 42; 40, table 1; 483–4, tables 72–3. Col. 4, See Table 7.5.

a Humboldt's Estimates minus 15%.

duced in Spanish America from about 1575 to 1625; however, there is less certainty concerning what happened to production, exports, and imports after about 1625.

Thus, the major difference concerns the decline registered in official statistics, from whatever cause. One may draw either of two conclusions: either these statistics are correct, or nearly so, or systematic underreporting began or intensified about 1625 or 1630, and the decline and its amount are of doubtful status. It seems obvious, given that a variety of official records have already been exhaustively analyzed, that any further work with such data will produce only similar results and we will perhaps never arrive at a firm conclusion about the truth of the matter. For this reason and because I find the conclusions of Humboldt and Morineau persuasive and mutually reinforcing, I am going to use their two sets of data as the primary ones in attempting to calculate the magnitude of world bullion flows from 1500 to 1800.

Curve 5a shows the trend of Morineau's data of European imports from 1581 to 1730, and curve 5b depicts the shorter period from 1581 to 1700; the difference in slope between the two is caused by the inclusion in curve 5a of Brazilian gold from 1700 to 1730 and its absence before 1700. I shall use curve 5a rather than curve 5b as a basis for calculations because it is more nearly parallel to Humboldt's curve and because its end corresponds to the date (1726–30) of the second most important inflection of his curve.[25] Thus, the fitted curve 5a represents average annual deliveries to Europe, and Humboldt's curve represents total American annual production of bullion; the difference between these two curves must therefore represent retention of bullion within America and deliveries elsewhere than to Europe and smuggled European deliveries.

Curve 5c shows Morineau's estimates of European imports of New World silver and gold from the quinquennium 1731–5 to 1790–5. I have omitted from it his estimate for the last quinquennium of the eighteenth century (1796–1800) because it is very low and would skew the trend line; however, I have used this low estimate for the five-year period 1795–1800 in calculating the quarter-century totals in Table 7.3.

To supply estimates for the years from 1501 to 1575, after which Morineau's data begin, I have assumed that 85 percent of Humboldt's estimated production of these years arrived in Europe. This may be reasonable in light of the fact that shipments to the Philippines, which received the major secondary flow from the Americas, did not begin

---

[25] Curve 5a: $Y = 186.6 + 8.431\ X$; curve 5b: $Y = 219.75 + 5.14X$; curve 5c: $Y = 747.5 + 16.5X$.

until the 1570s or 1580s. Thus the remaining 15 percent may be assigned to retention in the Americas or to losses. This is about half of the difference between production and European arrivals in subsequent years, which generally ran between 20 and 30 percent.

NON-AMERICAN PRODUCTION OF SILVER AND GOLD

In addition to the Americas, we shall consider silver production only in Europe and Japan, because there were no other major producers.

Production in Europe

Curve 6 of Figure 7.1 shows European silver production according to Nef (1941). Nef wrote his article in partial reaction against the oft-quoted work of Soetbeer, which had dominated thinking about precious metal production for over half a century. Nef suggested that Soetbeer's conclusions understated peak production and were incorrect regarding the timing of it. According to Nef, the European peak came in the decade 1526–35, just before the flood of American silver began, when the mines of Germany produced about 35 tonnes annually and those of the rest of central Europe about 53 tonnes; for Europe as a whole, the peak may thus have been about 100 tonnes annually in this decade. Nef placed the period of growth of output from 1460 to 1530, with little growth before 1450 and considerable variation among mines as to time and rate of growth and time of peak.

By the first two decades of the seventeenth century, production had fallen to about 30 tonnes. I have drawn curve 6 accordingly, with an arbitrary end to it in 1620–5.[26] This curve is cumulative in the sense that it represents the combined values of European and American production.

Production in Japan

It is clear that Japan was a major producer and exporter of silver during much of both the sixteenth and the seventeenth centuries and that both activities fell off in the late seventeenth century. The Japanese export trade began to flourish shortly before the arrival of the

---

[26] John U. Nef, "Silver Production in Central Europe, 1450–1618," *Journal of Political Economy* 41 (1941): 577–8, 584–5, 590–1.

Table 7.4

Silver Exports to China

(in Tonnes per Year)

	1560-99	1600-40	1601-94
From Japan	34-49	150-187	40
From Spanish America	10	22	--

Source: Yamamura and Kamiki, "Silver Mines and Sung Coins," 351-3.

Portuguese in the early 1540s and continued despite official restrictions through the efforts not only of European but also of Chinese and Japanese merchants. We know most about the European side of the trade, but the volume of non-European trade also appears to have been considerable, with the result that in this limited time Japan was second only to Spanish America in silver production and export.

The peak of the Japanese–Chinese trade is said by Yamamura and Kamiki to have occurred in the years from 1560 to 1640; their data are shown in Table 7.4.[27]

For the period 1695–1709 they estimated average annual exports from Japan to have been about 7.5 tonnes, representing a continuing decline owing in large part to an exclusionary policy adopted by Japan in the 1630s. These figures may seem high, but they are supported by other recent and by older estimates, including those of Kobata, who has suggested that around 1600 the "total amount exported from Japan, calculated in chogin (a coin of 80 percent silver) may have been 150–200 tons/year."[28]

We may conclude that Japan was a significant producer of silver in the sixteenth century; however, because the market for Japanese sil-

[27] Kozo Yamamura and Tetsuo Kamiki, "Silver Mines and Sung Coins – A Monetary History of Medieval and Modern Japan in International Perspective," in Richards, *Precious Metals*, 351–3. The authors' data come from eighteenth- and nineteenth-century official estimates (p. 344), and they state that they are also supported by contemporaneous observations, although the latter appear to be of a lower order of magnitude than the official estimates. Recent work by Kazui Tashiro, which I have not yet seen, suggests higher figures; I thank Dennis Flynn for this information.

[28] Atsushi Kobata, "Production and Trade in Gold, Silver and Copper in Japan, 1450–1750," in Hermann Kellenbenz, *Precious Metals in the Age of Expansion* (Stuttgart: 1981), 273.

Table 7.5

Gold Exports from West Africa

by Land and Sea, Tonnes

	Total Gold	Annual Average	Silver Equivalent
1471–1500	17	0.6	192
1501–1550	19	0.4	215
1551–1600	17	0.3	192
1601–1650	46	0.9	639
1651–1700	46	0.9	639
1701–1750	37	0.7	555
1751–1800	25	0.5	375

Source: T. F. Garrard, Akan Weights and the Gold Trade (New York, 1980) 152, 156-8.

ver was limited to East and Southeast Asia, I have not included Japanese production in Figure 7.1, which shows silver and gold that either passed through Europe or was produced in its colonies.

Non-American production of gold

For western Europe, West Africa was the principal source of gold in Africa. Before the mid–fifteenth century, West African gold had been important in the mintage of the Arab states in North Africa, and it was a major source of the metal for them. Exports to western Europe continued for several centuries, but by the 1760s West African gold became too expensive for Europeans, and exports fell off, with the result that West Africa may have become a net importer of gold. Even earlier in the eighteenth century, Brazilian gold was imported into Africa to pay for slaves; Curtin gives the example of the year 1721, when about 480 kilograms of gold were shipped there from Brazil, an amount far greater than that exported from West Africa to Europe at the same time. West African exports of gold to Europe in tonnes of silver equivalent were apparently not large: the average annual figures do not exceed in any half-century 640 tonnes of silver equivalent (about 920 kilograms of gold, or less than 1 tonne per year in the peak seventeenth century) and thus cannot be considered important except in regional trade (see Table 7.5). These estimates from the work of Garrard are similar to, but higher than, those reviewed by Curtin.[29] In Chapter 10 Austen shows that for the period 1480–1720 average annual West African gold exports via trans-Saharan and coastal routes were roughly 1–2 tonnes.

Export of bullion to the Philippines

It is generally thought that Manila was the principal non-European destination for New World silver, and it may be true that it was, but the assumption is exceedingly difficult to verify because of lack of documentary evidence and the possibility of smuggling on a grand scale; available estimates cover a wide range and are less complete than New World production figures. Table 7.6 summarizes recent data of official records concerning shipment of public and private silver to the Philippines.[30] According to TePaske, the data on private revenue shipped to the Philippines yield underestimates and, in any case, do not go beyond 1660 in his table. The annual average shipments at no time exceeded 17 tonnes, which means that well under a million pesos annually have been accounted for (1 million pesos equaled about 25.6 tonnes before 1728). Thus, high estimates of annual shipments (2–3 million pesos) are not supported by documentary evidence, and Humboldt insisted that the amounts were small. He estimated that on average only 600,000 pesos were shipped annually to the Philippines in the seventeenth and eighteenth centuries and that the trade at this time did not exceed 800,000 pesos.[31] As was the case with

---

[29] Timothy F. Garrard, *Akan Weights and the Gold Trade* (New York, 1980), 163; see Curtin's table 7 in "Africa and the Wider Monetary World, 1250–1850," in Richards, *Precious Metals*, 245–6.

[30] In John J. TePaske, "New World Silver, Castile, and the Philippines, 1590–1800," in Richards, *Precious Metals*, 425–46, data are presented by decades; to make Table 7.6 consistent with the others regarding the use of quarter-century periods, I have assigned half of his values for the twenties, fifties, and seventies of each century to successive quarter-centuries. Neither W. L. Schurz (*The Manila Galleon* [New York, 1939]) nor Carmen Yuste López (*El comercio de la Nueva España con Filipinas, 1590–1785* [Mexico City, 1984]) attempted to estimate long-term flows.

[31] Humboldt, *Political Essay*, 3:430. Many other contemporaneous estimates are higher. One anonymous letter from Manila dated January 8, 1780, stated that in some two hundred years, 300 million pesos had been imported from the Americas (meaning obviously for the China trade alone and not for government expenses in the islands); this is 1.5 million pesos per year, about 38 tonnes. (Anon., *Varios comercio y fábricas,*

Table 7.6

Shipment of Silver (Tonnes)

to the Philippines

	1	2	3	4
	Public	Private	Total	Annual
	revenue	revenue		average
1581–1600	44	15[a]	59	2.4
1601–1625	141	289	430	17
1626–1650	196	205	401	16
1651–1675	95	52[b]	147	6
1676–1700	113	262	375	15
1701–1725	82	293	375	15
1726–1750	105	270	375	15
1751–1775	135	240	375	15
1776–1800	211	289	500	20

Sources for col. 1 and col. 2, 3, and 4, 1581–1675, see J. J. TePaske, "New World Silver, Castile, and the Philippines (1590–1800)," in Richards, Precious Metals, 444–5. For col. 4, 1676–1800, see Humboldt, Political Essays, 3:430. I have calculated figures for cols. 2 and 3, 1676–1800, by subtracting entries in col. 1 from entries in col. 4 multiplied by twenty-five years, 1676–1800.

[a] 1591–1600 only.

[b] 1651–1660 only.

smuggling of bullion, he regarded accounts of large amounts of money in the Philippines trade as greatly exaggerated. Even so, by his estimate of 600,000 pesos, the annual shipment to the Philippines was

James Ford Bell Library, University of Minnesota, catalog no. 1715 f. Va). I thank Abby Sue Fischer for bringing this to my attention.

equal to about 15 tonnes of silver from 1601 to 1800. This estimate agrees with the early annual average for 1591–1600 in Table 7.6.

Public revenue was shipped to the Philippines to cover the expenses of government, including defense, in the islands. The course of these shipments follows a familiar one in official records: an increase up until the early seventeenth century and then a fall, followed by recovery in the eighteenth century, with a record amount shipped in the late eighteenth century. The figures for average annual shipments in column 4 of Table 7.6, which are a mixture of TePaske's figures (1581–1675) and Humboldt's (1676–1800), show much less variation. Even if these figures were doubled, they would remain secondary in relation to the different flows of bullion from Europe, shown in Table 7.7. Furthermore, they cannot begin to account for the net balances shown in column 3 of Table 7.3, the difference between American production and European arrivals, which are mostly of a different order of magnitude from exports to the Philippines, even when the figures of column 4, Table 7.6, are doubled.

EXPORT OF BULLION FROM EUROPE

Western Europe had chronic trade deficits with three areas, the Baltic (East Prussia, Poland, and Russia), the Levant, and the Orient. The purpose of this section is to present estimates of payments to cover these deficits, assuming that such payment was made in bullion.

The Baltic trade

From the Baltic came the necessities of life of western Europe: grain (wheat and rye), lumber, hemp, hempseed, flax, flaxseed, bar iron, tallow, wax, leather, skins, furs, potash, ash, and naval stores. Because these were basic commodities not available elsewhere, this trade was fundamental to western Europe and commonly ran a deficit that, in the case of Russia, was about twice the value of imports from western Europe. It is assumed that the deficit was made up by importing bullion, largely silver coins. In the late sixteenth century and certainly by 1600, the Dutch were dominant in this trade, but they were displaced by the English about 1700, and this meant that large amounts of specie flowed to the east to settle the Baltic accounts. Settlements were effected through Holland in both centuries.[32]

---

[32] Artur Attman, *Dutch Enterprise in the World Bullion Trade, 1550–1800*, Acta Regiae Societatis Scientiarum et Litterarum Gothoburgensis, Humaniora, vol. 26 (1986), 84.

Table 7.7

Average Annual Estimates (Tonnes) of

Exports of Silver and Silver Equivalent

from Europe

	1	2	3	4	5
	To	Via	Via	To	Total
	Levant	VOC	EIC	Baltic	
1601–1625	50	8	--	43	101
1626–1650	50	9	10[a]	56	125
1651–1675	50	10	10[a]	59	129
1676–1700	50	21	32	53	156
1701–1725	50	43	42	53	188
1726–1750	50	45	56	59	210
1751–1775	50	51	50[a]	65	216
1776–1780	50	34	40[a]	71	195

Sources: Col 1., A. Attman, Dutch Enterprise in the World
Bullion Trade (1985) 95. Col.2, Dutch East India Company (VOC),
F. S. Gaastra, "The Exports of Precious Metals From Europe to
Asia by the Dutch East India Company, 1062-1795," in Richards,
Precious Metals, 451. Col. 3, English East India Company (EIC),
K. N. Chaudhuri, The Trading World of Asia and the English East
India Company, 1660-1760 (Cambridge,1978) 177. Col. 4, Attman
Dutch Enterprise, 78.

[a] My estimates based on A. Attman, The Bullion flow between
Europe and the East, 1000-1750. Acta Regiae Societatis
Scientiarum et Litterarum Gothoburgensis, Humaniora 20
(Göteborg, 1983).

Attman has insisted on the continuing importance of this trade from medieval times through the early modern period. He has provided a summary of it from 1600 to 1800, which I have used in Table 7.7. According to him, the annual deficits were approximately as follows, in millions of rix-dollars: 1600, 1.5; 1650, 2.5; 1700, 2.0; 1750, 2.5; 1800, 3.0. I have interpolated estimates from these data for both quinquennia and quarter-centuries for these two hundred years, using a value of 24.38 grams of pure silver per rix-dollar.[33]

The Levant trade

In spite of the nearness of the Levant to Europe and its great cultural and economic importance, the magnitude of its trade with Europe is the most difficult to document or to estimate; there are, according to Attman, "only isolated figures" from the sixteenth through the eighteenth centuries and no "invoice values" to serve as the basis of estimates, as in the Baltic and East Indian trades.[34] Of France, perhaps the most important trader there in the seventeenth and eighteenth centuries, it can be said only that its balances or deficits were "significant," with payment requiring "considerable" sums of bullion. Attman estimated that the Dutch Levantine trade required 1 million rix-dollars annually in the seventeenth century and concedes that this was probably true for the eighteenth, as well; however, since the Dutch may have covered English deficits there also, as in the Baltic trade, it is possible that they supplied 1 to 1.5 million rix-dollars per year in the eighteenth century. Given the "considerable" deficits of the French, we may assume that these three nations alone had average deficits of 2 million rix-dollars (about 50 tons of silver) and that these were settled with bullion. This annual figure has been used in Table 7.7.

The Orient trade

Although trade with the Orient is generally agreed to have been the most important of the flows from Europe, information about its size is scanty and spotty, as with the others. To provide a minimum esti-

---

[33] *Ibid.*, 78. The value of 24.38 grams is given by John J. McCusker, *Money and Exchange in Europe and America, 1600–1775* (Chapel Hill, 1978), 9. Attman (*Dutch Enterprise in the World Bullion Trade*) arrives at a "conservative calculation" for "around 1600" of a deficit of 2 million rix-dollars (p. 89) and of another 2 million for 1750 (p. 91); the figure of 3 million on p. 91 corresponds to 1790, and the year 1640 is used instead of 1660. It might be noted that the deficits were met by "Dutch precious metals" (p. 91) and "precious metals from Western Europe" (p. 78).

[34] Attman, *Dutch Enterprise in the World Bullion Trade*, 92–3.

Table 7.8

Average Annual Net

European Balance per Capita

	Population of Europe (millions)	Net annual balance, from Table 7.1 (tonnes)	Grams of Silver and Equivalent/ European
1600	100	145	1.45
1700	120	220	1.82
1800	180	405	2.25

mate of its size, I have used only data of the bullion exports of the English and Dutch East India companies, as shown in Table 7.7. These are therefore underestimates of the flow to the Orient, because other European countries traded with the East, but these two companies were the most important entities in the trade.

OBSERVATIONS

All columns in Table 7.3 show increases from 1501 to 1800 except in the case of exports of bullion from Europe in the quarter-century from 1776 to 1800, which registered a slight decrease. However, the rates of increase were not steady.

In light of the size of American production (column 1) and of European arrivals (column 2), the major flows of bullion from Europe (column 4) were not large: Not only were they easily covered by European arrivals from the New World alone, but if the latter had been only half of Morineau's estimates, there would still have been a surplus (compare column 5, showing net European balances, with column 4, exports from Europe).

Thus, neither exports to the Philippines (Table 7.6) in the case of the Americas nor exports through any of the four major flows identified in Table 7.7 could extinguish these surpluses unless in the case of the latter, the flows were increased by half or doubled. Since these are generally agreed to have been the five major flows, no lesser ones could, if added to these others, extinguish the surpluses, either. This is especially the case in the last half of the eighteenth century.

The estimates of Humboldt and Morineau yield large surpluses at both ends, both in the producing areas and in Europe. But the surplus in Europe was much greater than that in the Americas in absolute terms, although this was not the case with net balance per capita. Table 7.8 shows only the balance per capita for Europe, which was a very small annual amount of silver and its equivalent, not reaching at its peak in the late eighteenth century even 10 percent, or a dime, of the common silver coins containing abut 25 grams of silver, such as the peso or the rix-dollar. The balance per capita in Spanish America differed from the European balance by an order of magnitude, as did the population.

CHAPTER 8

Merchant communities, 1350–1750

FRÉDÉRIC MAURO

THE study of "merchant communities" represents the sociological dimension of research on "merchant empires." Apart from the geography of trade and commercial mechanisms, institutions, techniques, commercial doctrines, and politics, merchant community is the social base of the merchant universe. It would be beneficial if beyond that social base we could reach the mental base. Unfortunately the latter, despite the classic works of authors such as Werner Sombart and Max Weber, still remains largely unknown. This paper will therefore put emphasis on the former.

The first difficulty one encounters in approaching the subject is that of periodization. Merchant communities, as we will see, existed before 1350. Well before 1750, moreover, they no longer played the role that they had in the sixteenth century, at least if we use the term "merchant communities" in its most precise sense. In fact, the boundaries of merchant communities are to be found not so much in space as in the definition itself. The term "merchant community" could be loosely used to describe various forms of merchant gatherings or groupings that are not exactly the "merchant communities" I will be discussing. At the outset of merchant activities, merchants in towns formed a sworn association, or one or more guilds, in the same way as artisans or specialists of all kinds. They had nothing in common with a *prêt à la grosse*, a union of at least two partners, or a *commenda*, ancestor of the modern limited partnership company, or even a company of equal partners gathered for either a specific trade operation or a series of operations. Insofar as these communities of merchants were based on the principle of solidarity and mutual aid and often formed alien minorities – isolated "nationals" in a port or a country that was sometimes friendly and sometimes hostile – they often ap-

Translated by Seong-hak Kim and John Wrathall, University of Minnesota.

pear almost as social organizations. This being the case, what about those communities that developed into real trade companies or that gave birth to them, such as the *Companie Française des Cent Associés* and the various East and West India companies? To some extent, the great charter companies, the joint-stock companies, and the precursors of the modern limited partnership companies are extensions not only of the medieval trade companies but also of merchant communities.

THE HANSEATIC LEAGUE

To avoid falling into generalizations, we can perhaps begin with the concrete case of the Hanseatic League, one of the oldest, most complete and complex merchant organizations of the Middle Ages. In analyzing the history of its functioning from its birth to its decline, we will establish a basis of comparison for other merchant communities that existed during the time period 1350–1750.

We should remember that northern Europe, by the end of the early Middle Ages, had already enjoyed a privileged position for several centuries as a result of the rise in global temperature. Warmer temperatures made northern Germany and Scandinavia much more suitable for habitation, and this climatic change doubtless explains the flowering of a dazzling civilization in that region and even the daring naval adventures that brought the Viking *drakkars* to the coasts of America.

The Baltic Sea, in the eyes of the people of that time, was not a blind alley surrounded by frozen rivers: it was a trade route, wide open to rivers in Russia, to the large markets of Novgorod and of Smolensk. Rare and precious goods flowed into those markets coming through long caravan routes from the most remote regions like the Muslim or Byzantine Orient along the White Sea.[1]

The history of the Hanseatic League can be summed up as follows. In the fourteenth century, to resist competition from Hollanders and southern Germans, many north German towns signed treaties of mutual protection and formed the Hanseatic League, an association of northern German merchants pitted against the Holy Roman Empire. This association of towns was more capable of protecting the interests of its merchants abroad. Despite some striking successes, however, its political as well as economic plans failed to check the progress of its competitors. By the beginning of the sixteenth century, the decline

[1] Translated from Philippe Dollinger, *La Hanse* (Paris, 1964), 8.

of the league was apparent; yet its member cities continued to develop. The Hansa organization was no longer useful to them. The Hanseatic League disappeared in 1630 and was replaced by a limited alliance between Lübeck, Hamburg, and Bremen. The last official meeting of the Hanseatic Diet (Hansetag) took place in 1669.[2]

The merchant communities of the Hanseatic League established trading posts abroad. The trading post was a merchant community of the German Hanseatic League. The term *kontor* did not come into common use until the sixteenth century. There were many trading posts but there were four pillars of Hanseatic trade: Novgorod, Bergen, London, and Bruges. Why were there no large trading posts in Denmark, Sweden, or Poland? It was because the development of a large trading post depended on certain conditions: the existence of an important commercial center relatively distant from northern Germany with products in great demand as well as privileges granted by local authorities. These conditions were not realized in Denmark, Sweden, and Poland.

The internal organization of the trading posts was much more rigorous than that of the individual Hansas. Each had its leaders, its tribunal, its bank, and a legal personality (which the Hanseatic League did not have). Strict discipline regulated the merchants. Each year, the general assembly of merchants elected the elders, who had heavy responsibilities and no compensation. We will not go into the details of the daily life of the four large trading posts. The trading post in London was called the Stahlhof, or steelyard; the merchants were divided into geographical sections according to the three zones of the Hanseatic League. Bruges was the most important of the four trading posts. Besides those four, other factories were scattered throughout all the countries bordering on Germany. After 1350 they were, like trading posts, controlled by the cities, and each country had one of them. In the west, they were subordinated to large trading posts.

It is striking to contrast the volume of trade of the Hanseatic League and its weak structure. The Hanseatic League had neither legal personality nor its own seal, and the only common body, the Hansetag, had no staff, at least not before 1550, and no regular financial resources, fleet, or army. The fact that the Hanseatic League had no responsibility for the acts of its members was an embarrassment for jurists accustomed to Roman law. Attempts were made to strengthen the Hanseatic League by creating "leagues" with specific financial and military obligations for a certain number of years, often renewed. The

[2] Ibid., 9.

first was the League of Cologne, created in 1367 to intensify the war effort against Denmark. In the fifteenth century, under pressure from the princes, new leagues, the *tohopesate*, appeared (the word meaning "to hold together"). One of these leagues was created by Lübeck in 1418 and was renewed in 1430. Its success was modest. Lübeck would have liked to transform the Hanseatic League into such a binding league but it did not succeed. The Hanseatic League had other means to implement its decisions. With its members, it used persuasion, arbitration, and sanctions. It could pronounce the exclusion of a city or a merchant that did not follow its rules. With foreign countries, it had three means: negotiation, possibly with the dispatch of a diplomatic mission, cessation of trade or blockade, and war.[3]

Within the structure of the Hanseatic League existed associations of merchants that were at once professional, religious, choral, and recreational. The center of each association was a house with at least one big meeting room administered by the elders elected by the general assembly of the members. These associations could be of different types. In certain cities, there was an association of oceangoing merchants, and in other cities there were groups specializing in a certain country or a certain port. From the end of the fourteenth century, these merchants were called the *Fahrer*, or travelers; for example, *Bergenfahrer* and *Schoenenfahrer*. Of course, these merchants could also organize into trade companies that were comparable to the general or limited partnership companies of modern times. Every great merchant was a member of several trade companies at the same time.

THE FLOWERING OF THE GUILDS

If the Hanseatic League could develop in this way from the thirteenth century through the sixteenth century, it was because the preconditions were in place: among the guilds and confraternities of the towns were those of merchants. Let us take the case of England.

The gild merchant came into existence in England soon after the Norman Conquest, as a result of the increasing importance of trade, and it may have been transplanted from Normandy. Until clearer evidence of foreign influence is found, it may, however, be safer to regard it simply as a new application of the old gild principle, though this new application may have been stimulated by Continental example. The evidence seems to indicate the preexistence of the gild merchant in Normandy, but it is not mentioned any-

[3] Ibid., 133–40.

where on the Continent before the 11th Century. It spread rapidly in England, and from the reign of John onward we have evidence of its existence in many English boroughs. . . . [In towns where the guild merchant existed], its chief function was to regulate the trade monopoly conveyed to the borough by the royal grant of *Gilda mercatoria*. A grant of this sort implied that the gildsmen had the right to trade freely in the town and to impose payments and restrictions upon others who desired to exercise that privilege.[4]

One special case is that of Venice, whose guilds were recently studied by Richard MacKenney.[5] He compares the guilds of Venice with those of other cities: Florence, Lyons, London, and Amsterdam. What strikes him in the case of Venice is the absence of a merchant guild. The *arti* were simply artisans and did not play any role in overseas commerce. But the economic life of the city revolved around what merchant guilds elsewhere attempted to promote and protect: the staple. From the fifteenth century the Rialto received goods coming from both the east and the west and exchanged them; this was the role of merchants. A historian's assertion that the Venetian merchants did not need guilds "because they all lived in one guild" is certainly an exaggeration, but it reveals one important truth about the Venetian economy. From the beginning Venetian merchants were essentially agents – "brokers" according to MacKenney – engaged in furnishing commercial services. The nature of goods hardly mattered to them. We can also presume that because large-scale trade was in the hands of the patricians – real urban aristocracy – who held the political power, the patricians did not need a defensive association to protect themselves from political power. This mercantile supremacy was accepted by the people because the patricians did not interfere in judicial matters and the magistrates remained entirely independent. Furthermore, a considerable part of the administration was reserved for participation by the plebeians.

Perhaps Venice is the key to understanding the evolution of the Hanseatic League. Trade was a business too serious to be left in the hands of merchants. Or, rather, the interests of merchants became so important that their corporate organizations were no longer adequate, and the state took charge of their protection; the state was a city-state such as Stralsund, Lübeck, or Venice or a federation of city-states such as the Hansa of Cities. It is important to remember that the phenomenon we are studying took place at a time when the large

[4] *Encyclopaedia Britannica* (1962), s.v. "Guilds."
[5] *Tradesmen and Traders: The World of the Guilds in Venice and Europe (c. 1250–c. 1650)* (Totowa, N.J., 1987), 304.

medieval cities were at their height and were becoming bases for large-scale trade and commercial capitalism, a system of production in which traders assumed the control and derived the profits.

Now let us leave behind the extreme case of Venice and also Italy, which has been studied elsewhere,[6] and take the case of France, exemplified in Toulouse in the province of Languedoc. Toulouse allows us to discover a new transformation that marked the merchant communities of the sixteenth century.

According to Philippe Wolff, between 1350 and 1450, merchants in Toulouse dealt in limited kinds of goods. The few trade goods they effectively controlled were those imported from distant regions: salt, spices, dry goods, silk, woolen cloths from the Netherlands and Normandy, certain metals, and so on. Wool cloth from England needs mentioning. These fabrics, which were brought by the merchants of Béarn to Toulouse and to the nearby markets of the Lauragais to be traded for woad, "passed through as many hands as were offering the precious local product. But a number of other Toulousains could, without going through them, procure several *cannes* of these fabrics coming from across the Channel, sometimes in sufficient quantity to resell them themselves."[7]

If the artisans were subjected to rather severe regulations, at least after 1450, the luxury trade and even some retail trade completely escaped regulation. "Grocers had statutes, but only to regulate the sales in stores; merchants selling salt or wine, and innkeepers had none. Likewise, merchant drapers, mercers, and silk merchants neither belonged to craft guilds nor were under the control of the municipality."[8]

Therefore, between 1350 and 1450, those who were engaged in long-distance trade were considered merchants and were not subject to the restraints of a guild or other regulations. It might seem, since they played a certain role in municipal affairs, that they dominated political matters as in Venice. This was not the case in Toulouse, however. The city remained dominated by the *noblesse d'epée* and the *noblesse de robe*. Insofar as the merchants were part of the *noblesse de cloche* – the lifetime nobility of the *capitouls* – they were preoccupied more with their offices and privileges than with business. In fact, the *capitouls*, by and large, supported the artisans against the merchants.

During the period 1450–1550 Toulouse was bustling with the woad trade. There appeared, then, a phenomenon reminiscent not of Ven-

---

[6] See Chapter 1.
[7] *Commerce et marchands de Toulouse vers 1350–vers 1450* (Paris, 1954), 537.
[8] Translated from ibid., 549, 544.

ice but rather of the trading posts of the Hanseatic League: the creation of a formal foreign colony in Toulouse for the purpose of the woad trade. This phenomenon was also to spread elsewhere. Commercial relations with the Spanish and the English markets quickly became quite active. Doubtless some merchants selling woad were Marranos. Jean Bernuy was a Marrano, whose mansion, built in the Renaissance style, still remains one of the most beautiful, if not the most beautiful, building in Toulouse today. Here, again, it does not seem that this burgeoning gave rise to any one particular type of trade association. On the contrary, various types of company associations existed in Toulouse between 1350 and 1560.

Everywhere, therefore, merchants enjoyed a privileged status in cities even if they did not dominate the city itself. Often the interests of a city and those of its merchants were closely intertwined. Hence the reactions of the artisan from the outset. Fernand Braudel explains:

The number of guilds nevertheless increased [in the thirteenth century]. But the economic upturn it brought was soon to threaten the very structure of the guilds, *now endangered by the triumph of the merchants*. From this violent opposition there naturally emerged a civil war for control of power within the city. German historians refer to the *Zunftrevolution*, with guilds rebelling against patricians. Behind this rather simplified schema, it is easy to recognize the struggle between merchant and artisan, punctuated by alliances and quarrels – a long class struggle waged to and fro over the years. But the age of violent clashes was comparatively short and in the undeclared war that was to follow, the merchant eventually emerged victor. Collaboration between merchant and guild could never be conducted on a completely equal footing, since what was at stake here was the conquest of the labour market and economic domination by the merchant, not to say by capitalism.[9]

THE CASE OF ANTWERP

In the sixteenth century, Antwerp took over from Bruges as the center of redistribution of goods from Mediterranean Europe and eastern European countries as well as from overseas to the northwestern part of Europe.[10] Antwerp was to exhibit the phenomenon already clearly

[9] *Civilisation matérielle, économie, et capitalisme,* vol. 2, *Les jeux de l'echange* (Paris, 1979), 275 (*Civilization and Capitalism,* vol. 2, *The Wheels of Commerce,* trans. Sian Reynolds [New York, 1981–4], 315); emphasis is mine.
[10] Raymond de Roover shows how the conservative attitudes of the merchants played a significant role in the decline of Bruges in favor of Antwerp, in *Money, Banking, and Credit in Medieval Bruges* (Cambridge, Mass., 1948). On Antwerp, see J. A. Goris, *Etudes sur les colonies Marchandes meridionales à Anvers, 1477–1567* (Louvain, 1925); and Herman van der Wee, *The Growth of the Antwerp Market and the European Economy,* 2 vols. (Louvain, 1963).

attested to in the cities of the Hanseatic League, and rather indirectly shown in cities like Toulouse: the development of foreign merchant communities. In contrast to local merchants, whose interests were identified with those of the city, the members of these communities were foreigners who formed the "nations," autonomous groups with their own privileges and rivalries.

The prosperity of these "nations" depended, above all, on the attitude of the city toward foreigners and on the legal status awarded to them by the city. In Antwerp the foreign merchants were treated very favorably, and the port was an islet of economic liberty in Europe, where economic conservatism was still prevalent. The attitude of the city was in turn influenced by the attitude of its prince, on whom the city remained dependent as a vassal town. In the sixteenth century, Maximilian I displayed a more conciliatory policy toward Antwerp than his predecessors had, and Antwerp in return supported the emperor despite his absolutist pretensions. As a result, Antwerp remained isolated. Neither the fifteenth nor the sixteenth century saw the emergence of a sense of kinship among the cities in the Low Countries.

At the beginning of the sixteenth century Antwerp's prosperity began to increase. This growing prosperity attracted young men who had little wealth and little intention to settle permanently on the banks of the Scheldt, unless they married a fortune. Most of them were less than twenty-two years old when they landed in Antwerp. Take the example of the factor of several Portuguese companies who was only eighteen years old. Most of them came between 1520 and 1530, and many stayed on thanks to the riches they made, by both audacity and luck.

Some merchants were interested in financial speculations. By 1550 speculation was taking place at the Bourse, not always with complete honesty. Many of these new bourgeois went bankrupt. But they formed an active minority, composed mainly of Italians. Between 1523 and 1600, for instance, 186 immigrants acquired the right of bourgeoisie: 123 were Italians, among whom 78 were merchants.

In fact, however, the majority came to be incorporated into the nations. What were these nations? During the fifteenth century, the term "nation" was used for the merchant association of a certain nationality. In legal matters, they occupied a place between the guilds or the corporations and lesser associations known as *eendrachtigheid*. A merchant nation was established with the tacit approval of the territorial prince and with the consent of the prince of the merchants' land. Since almost the entire southern part of Europe, except Portugal and some parts of Italy, came under the rule of Charles V in the first half of the sixteenth century, the term "nation" mostly applies to Portuguese merchants.[11]

It is necessary to emphasize that the Portuguese nation occupied a special place among the other nations, especially during the period before 1530, when the Portuguese exclusively controlled the pepper and spice trade. The privileges acquired by the Portuguese in Bruges served as the framework of the Portuguese nation. These privileges, of which the most important one was granted in 1411 by John the Fearless, were based on the reciprocity of favors and on the friendship that existed between the princes of Portugal and those of Flanders. The relationship between them, dating back to the early Middle Ages, was of a dynastic and religious nature. The king of Portugal, for those reasons, always treated well the Flemish merchants, who began settling in Lisbon in 1452. Philip the Good granted the same privileges to the Portuguese in Bruges. Nevertheless, notes Goris, there seemed to be more freedom in Portugal than in Flanders.[12]

THE CASE OF LYONS

Just as Antwerp was developed by foreign nationals, so was Lyons. Lyons, however, was not a seaport, and its commercial role was quite different from that of Antwerp.[13]

Lyons assumed an important role in trade during the Middle Ages because of its geographic situation. The association of the "merchants frequenting the Saône River" was famous. According to Gascon, transporters on the Saône River, as on the Loire River, banded together to better protect themselves against abusive tolls.[14] From 1504 they shared toll expenses. The idea of reforming the system came from Lyons, which invited other cities to join. In 1513 an "assembly of the merchants frequenting the Saône River" examined the possibility of dissolving the common account. The majority of the merchants were in favor of retaining it, because common action had brought results; that is, the tolls had already decreased. In 1575 the same merchants were to start the proceedings against the tolls of Trévoux.

By the first half of the sixteenth century, local merchants were supplanted by foreign merchants and merchant-bankers, of whom the

---

[11] Goris, *Colonies marchandes meridionales*, 33.

[12] Ibid., 38.

[13] The basic work on Lyons is still Richard Gascon, *Grand commerce et vie urbaine au XVIᵉ siècle: Lyon et ses marchands (1520–1580)*, 2 vols. (Paris, 1971).

[14] Ibid., 178; see also Henri Dubois, *Les foires de Châlon et le commerce dans la vallée de la Saône à la fin du Moyen Age (vers 1280–vers 1430)* (Paris, 1976).

Italians were the majority, drawn to Lyons by the fairs held there four times a year. Here, again, the nations, the foreign colonies, predominated. Five to six thousand people, many French merchants among them, came to visit each fair. In 1569 there were more than five hundred foreign importers, excluding Germans, and of them only a few dozen were wholesale merchants. With the German merchants included, there were about a hundred wholesale merchants at most.

It appears that, within a foreign colony, there existed an actual hierarchy between groups of different geographical origins. Important groups took the name "nation." A nation could be a legal, administrative, and even religious entity – this was the case of the Florentine nation, which had a consul and two councillors and kept archives in a chest at the church of the convent of the Franciscans, which was its church. It was an old organization established in 1447 in Geneva. Only the Florentines had their own consul, who represented them at the exchange market or before the communal authorities.[15] Other nations were, it appears, nothing more than simple gatherings of merchants. They designated a representative only when contact was necessary with the consulate of Lyons, or the king of France. The consulate made the final selection of brokers among the nations. We have a list of the nations present in Lyons in 1483: Savoyards, Germans, Milanese, Florentines, Genoese, and Venetians.

Richard Gascon gives us the statistics of the foreigners in 1571:

Florentines	42	Bolognese	1
Milanese	36	Other Italians	14
Lucchesi	27	Germans	22
Genoese	27	Portuguese	4
Piedmontese	5	English	1
Romans	1	Flemish	1
Mantuans	1	Spanish	1

It is noticeable that the Italians dominated the fairs of Lyons: the Florentines, the Milanese, the Lucchesi, and the Genoese. In 1571, bankers (nine) and big merchants (thirteen) made up a little over half the Florentine contingent. Among the Lucchesi, there were more bankers than merchants: twelve against five. For the Milanese, there were nineteen merchants and two bankers. Among the Germans, there was only one banker. Among the Italians could also be found commercial or exchange brokers and artisans. The Italian artisans were mostly silk workers and tailors; there were also a barber, a physician, a surgeon, and a famous painter, Corneille de La Haye. As for the

---

[15] Gascon, *Grand commerce et vie urbaine*, 359.

other foreigners – the Germans, the English, the Spanish, the Flemish, and the Portuguese – they were all merchants. Their fortunes were much smaller than those of the Italians, according to fiscal sources. Some of them reached the level of well-to-do Lyonese merchants, but they were still far behind when compared with the richest. The income of the Italian artisans also remained modest.

Within each nation, powerful houses, virtual dynasties, stood out. Among the forty-two Florentines, the nine most powerful controlled one-fourth of the estimated total assets of the Florentine nation. Among the twenty-seven Lucchesi, six accounted for 84 percent of the estimated assets, two of them together holding more than 50 percent. The concentration of wealth is less conspicuous within the Genoese nation because the most important Genoese bankers attended the fair in Chambéry and what was called the Besançon fair instead of the Lyons fairs. The distribution of wealth was also relatively even within the Milanese nation, where trade prevailed over banking. In addition to the concentration of wealth, the permanence of the large companies justifies the use of the term "dynasty." The same families were still operating in the sixteenth century, although the "corporate names" or the nominal heads might have changed.

On the whole, only a small number of foreigners were really integrated into Lyonese society. Some – the Gadagnes, the Scarrons, the Henrys, the Panses – contributed to the restoration of the old stock of local families. Others dispersed throughout the kingdom. Some people reached the top, obtaining royal or ecclesiastical offices.

According to Richard Gascon, however, most foreigners retained their vocation in external trade. Let us take the example of the Bonvisi family, who had come from Lucca. They were citizens of Lyons probably from as early as 1466 to at least 1629. They remained loyal to their new country even during the difficult time of the Catholic League, when many others went back to their original homes. They successfully played the role of great seigneurs and patricians, receiving Cardinal Carrafa and Marshall Strozzi. But their ties to Lucca remained solid: They rented, not bought, homes in Lyons; and they married within the circle of Italian merchants. They were dedicated to trade as most Lucchesi were. When they traveled in Europe it was to visit the colonies of their city. From the economic point of view, in the sixteenth century, other parts of Europe were no less important than France.

Local merchant families of Lyons played an equally important role in the economic life of their city. A document of the mid–sixteenth century shows a list of 3,644 taxpayers divided into a scale from 12 to

1,500 livres according to the amount of their income.[16] Among them, those whose income was more than 800 livres were all merchants, representing 0.27 percent of the taxpayers and 6.9 percent of the total income. There was no merchant whose income was below 100 livres.

Can we draw some conclusions from the case of Lyons? A favorable geographic situation – two important rivers flowed through Lyons, and it was the contact point for France, Burgundy, Switzerland, Italy, and the Holy Roman Empire – made it a commercial city, even before the coming of the foreigners. Among foreign merchants, the Italians were predominant, along with some Germans. These merchants were also bankers, and they financed other merchants, such as the merchants of Toulouse. But Lyons was a city in France, a nation-state and already a strong and expansive monarchy – in the eyes of the contemporary people the equivalent in territory of China today. The Italians of Lyons were tempted to become citizens of Lyons and subjects of the king of France, which would give them a source of power. They were restrained from doing so only by other potential loyalties: to Europe, on the one hand, which was a real economic entity in the sixteenth century, and to their home country of Italy, on the other, which was divided into city-states on their way to becoming territorial states. Therein lay the originality of the merchant community in Lyons: in the balance between the temptation of assimilation and other appeals.

AN ETHNOLOGY OF MERCHANT COMMUNITIES

The case of Lyons illustrates the importance of geographical origins in merchant communities. Merchant communities and nations retained their own culture, and strong ties of solidarity existed within each nation. Powerful internal solidarity was most conspicuous among large ethnic formations of eastern origin, which stood out against the purely European western background. Let us first take two typical cases: the Jews and the Armenians.

The Jews

The Jewish Diaspora was very significant for the whole Mediterranean basin, for eastern as well as western Europe. The Jews in the Iberian Peninsula played an important role in world trade, one of the few high-level activities permitted to them. The Ashkenazi Jews of

---

[16] The "*Nommées*" for the *taille* in 1545.

northern Europe were violently persecuted during the Crusades and were forced to be baptized to avoid massacres, and the Sephardic Jews of Spain suffered periodic persecutions and were the object of a systematic policy of conversion by the king and the Church. Such a policy resorted not only to terror and physical compulsion but also to peaceful evangelization and moral persuasion. The converted Jews were called Marranos in Spain and New Christians in Portugal. In Spain as well as Portugal, the Church, although in theory opposed to violent conversion, considered all kinds of baptism to be indelible and irrevocable, including conversion by force. In these two countries, the Inquisition would be in charge of keeping the New Christians and their children loyal to the faith.

From the end of the fifteenth century, the persecution of the Jews developed in different directions in Spain and in Portugal. In Spain, the dreadful repression of the Inquisition swept over Marranos, whether they were Jewish sympathizers or not. They were given a choice between emigration and auto-da-fé. Portugal, on the other hand, accepted the Jews expelled from Spain in 1492, and they joined the Portuguese New Christians. In principle, all were to be baptized according to the royal order of 1497. In fact, no one was persecuted before 1536. In that year, King John III obtained permission from the pope to create an Inquisition in his kingdom. The ravages caused by the Inquisition in Portugal in fact turned out to be more severe than those of its Castilian counterpart. In Spain, the activities of the Inquisition against the Marranos significantly diminished after the initial fervor. Meanwhile, during the period 1497–1536, the New Christians in Portugal had time to expand their economic activities. Documents of the sixteenth and the seventeenth centuries, even official ones, indicate that finance and international trade were completely monopolized by the New Christians. Pleas and royal edicts in favor of the descendants of converts most often referred to *homens de negocios, homens da nação*, and *Cristãos-Novos*, three expressions considered equivalent in that era. The establishment of the Portuguese New Christians, whether Jewish sympathizers or not, in finance and international trade at the beginning of the sixteenth century was to determine the historical role of New Christians and Marranos in the world history of the seventeenth century. Their role in world trade became particularly significant when Philip II of Spain became the king of Portugal in 1580 and the New Christians, who already had the monopoly of trade in their empire, burst into major commercial cities in Spain as well as into Spanish overseas territories. In those regions, the name "Portuguese" became synonymous with "New Christian" or even

"Crypto-Jew." Either as a result of persecution or for the purpose of trade, many New Christians settled down in big ports or important commercial cities across Europe. The Portuguese nation in Antwerp, at the height of the spice trade, was mostly composed of these New Christians. What, then, was the daily life in the New Christian or the Jewish communities that were scattered in different cities of Europe and America? A series of studies has appeared on the subject, using the proceedings of the Inquisition in particular, in which are included the property inventories of the accused, and the archives of synagogues as well as various local archives. Trade registers and the correspondence of merchants have also been discovered.[17] On the advice of the Jesuit Antonio Vieira, and thanks to the capital of the New Christians, the king of Portugal created the General Company of the Trade of Brazil. The company, which was established in 1648–9, was in charge of protecting vessels on the Lisbon–Brazil route from piracy and privateering. The cultural role of these communities was also considerable. The Dutch philosopher Spinoza was a member of the Portuguese Jewish community in Amsterdam. Proceedings of the Inquisition, meanwhile, reveal that the communities continued to practice their religion even in the countries where Judaism was prohibited, secretly observing its rites and interdicts. It would be an interesting project to reconstruct the commercial and financial networks of the Jews or the New Christians and to draw up a prosopography of their families, already begun by many researchers.

To take an example, the studies of Jean-Pierre Filippini have shed some light on the Jewish community in Livorno, at least during the eighteenth century.[18] Livorno had long attracted Jewish merchants. As a result, it had become an important nucleus of Hebrew culture and one of the largest Hebrew book-publishing centers in the Mediterranean basin. Commercial motives also deserve mention. Livorno was, in fact, one of the largest commercial and financial centers in the Mediterranean, especially the western Mediterranean region. It was a redistribution point for goods coming across the Atlantic Ocean. Neither xenophobia nor restrictive legislation that might have hindered the immigration of Jewish merchants was found in Livorno. Jewish merchants even came from North Africa; they were to come

---

[17] There is a vast literature on this subject. See, for example, I. S. Revah, "Les Marranes," *Revue des Etudes Juives* 1 (1959–60): 29–77.

[18] Filippini, "Il posto dei negozianti ebrei nel commercio di Livorno del Settecento," *Rassenga Mensile di Israel*, 3d ser., 50 (1984): 633–49; "La ballottazione a Livorno del Settecento," ibid. 49 (1983): 199–268; and "Les Juifs d'Afrique du Nord et al communauté de Livourne au XVIIIᵉ siècle," *Relations Intercommunautaires*, Centre National de la Recherche Scientifique (Paris, 1984), 60–9.

in large numbers and settle in the city in the eighteenth century, sheltered from the Muslim tyranny of the Maghreb. The "Livournine" of 1593 (a law of the Tuscan state organizing the harbor of Livorno), still in force in the eighteenth century, furthered their settlement. Common people also benefited from it. "One could settle in Livorno without the fear of being expelled as long as one did not threaten public order," wrote Filippini.[19] A Jew who came to Livorno was called *ballottato* ("registered") and became a subject of the Grand Duke of Tuscany. They all kept their previous status; even the nonregistered were protected in person and property by law.

Some of them were refugees, taking shelter in Livorno not so much from religious persecution as from creditors. This strengthened the ties between Livorno and other countries. They knew very well the commercial situation in their countries; most of them served in Livorno as representatives for their relatives who remained in the homelands. All these factors furthered not only the immigration to Livorno but also the emigration from this Tuscan port. A certain number of immigrants stayed there only as long as was necessary to obtain the status of *ballottato* and then went somewhere else to settle, for example, to Smyrna. This explains the solid commercial links with North Africa and with the Levant, where the Livornese traders played a relay role in the trade with England.

The commercial activities of the Jews in Livorno were promoted by their knowledge of advanced commercial techniques, such as bills of exchange and double-entry bookkeeping, as shown in inventories after death. Nevertheless, the Jewish nation in Livorno is not fully understood, even during the eighteenth century, because there remain few lists of the merchants of this nation. Even the list of 1799, the most complete one, has many shortcomings, besides being beyond our period. By 1733 there were 55 Jewish trade firms. In 1793 the number decreased to 44 among 143 foreign companies in all, and in 1796, 46 among 199. However, the numbers of merchants were higher because a single trade firm could consist of several merchants. Most of the firms were family enterprises. The capital was mobilized within the family and when it was necessary to expand the financial base of a company, the family was asked for a supplementary contribution. This was also the situation at Marseille and, in fact, throughout the Mediterranean world. The ties in family companies remained close even when their numbers were scattered in several places.

Without going into the strategy of business, which is not the sub-

[19] Filippini, "Les Juifs d'Afrique du Nord," 60.

ject of this paper, let us examine the Jews of North Africa who came to settle in Livorno. Their number appears to have increased in the eighteenth century. The censuses conducted in Livorno early in the eighteenth century show that there were few Jews from the Maghreb. In contrast, by the beginning of the nineteenth century, they represented about 13 percent of the Jewish community, or 176 persons. The majority of the community was composed of Tunisians and Tripolitans. Some immigrants came to Livorno to escape their unstable countries, while others were drawn by the influence of Hebrew culture. Most people were looking for a job or, at least, an opportunity to master commercial techniques before going somewhere else to settle down. Among all the Jews who came to Livorno, the most successful were traders and brokers who decided to stay in the city. They were easily integrated into the Livornese society, mostly by marriage. They even invested in land, thus conforming to the Livornese inclination in that epoch to buy villas rather than to invest in profitable business. Like other Jews, they moved up various steps on the "career of honors" (*massaro, camerlinque,* deputy, and so on) of the Jewish nation of the city.[20]

The Armenians

Armenian trade, a very ancient trade, extended in several directions: to the Levant, Europe, India, and the Far East. Its redeployment on a vast scale, which occurred between the sixteenth century and the eighteenth century, corresponded to a combination of new political and economic circumstances. In the seventeenth century, the main Armenian trade center was the suburb of New Julfa, near Isfahan, which was the headquarters of an Armenian trade company. With New Julfa as its core, the Armenian trade network covered, beyond the seaports in the Levant and the cities in Europe, a large area in Asia, extending from Bandar ʿAbbās to Manila.

Much research remains to be done on Armenian trade.[21] There are many sources available. In addition to travelers' accounts of all kinds, one finds the archives of the great companies and a certain number of manuscripts as well as printed documents. Specialists have worked

---

[20] See ibid. passim.
[21] On Armenian merchant communities, there are two essential articles: Keram Kévonian, "Marchands arméniens au XVIIᵉ siècle: A propos d'un livre arménien publié à Amsterdam en 1699," *Cahiers du Monde Russe et Soviétique* 16 (1975): 199–244; Michel Aghassian and Keram Kévonian, "Le commerce arménien dans l'océan Indien aux XVIIᵉ et XVIIIᵉ siècles," in J. Aubin and D. Lombard, eds., *Marchands et hommes d'affaires asiatiques dans l'océan Indien et la mer de Chine XIII–XXᵉ siècles* (Paris, 1988).

hard to enumerate the distinctive characteristics of this commerce. Who were the merchants who practiced it, and from what period? Why does it fall off in the eighteenth century?

The Armenians are sometimes thought to have been traders since the classical era. This misperception is due to the fact that Armenia was a crossroads of land and sea routes linking Europe and Asia. It is, however, possible to substantiate the fact that beginning in the ninth century A.D., the Armenians played an important role in the commerce of the north of Russia and of Bulgar, a Bulgarian colony on the Volga. During the early Middle Ages, they were middlemen in the trade between Italy and Mongolia. In the sixteenth century, their activities were concentrated along the axis of the Araks River, which now forms part of the border between the U.S.S.R., Turkey, and Iran. A number of small, prosperous trading villages flourished there, among which the village of Julfa attained particular distinction. The Armenians had outposts all over the Ottoman Empire and particularly in Constantinople. But they were also to be found in Europe – in Amsterdam; in Venice, where there was an important community of Armenian merchants; and in Livorno, where there were a dozen Armenian trading establishments at the end of the sixteenth century. Trading colonies also existed in the Ukraine, in the Crimea, in Moldavia, and in Persia. In the sixteenth century, Akbar the Great was encouraging traders to settle in India.

By the beginning of the seventeenth century, however, Shah ʿAbbās I of Persia had the inhabitants of the trading villages along the Araks deported during his campaign of 1603–5 against the Turks. Many Armenians were unable to resist deportation, were victims of epidemics, or were sold as slaves. Thousands of families were settled against their will in the region south of the Caspian Sea. Only the nobility were treated by the shah with some respect; they were settled near Isfahan, where they founded the suburb of New Julfa. Their commerce was once again encouraged and they were granted numerous privileges. Abbas wanted to enrich Persia through the silk trade with Europe, which was to bring its science and technology to Persia. The Armenian commercial nobility understood that they had everything to gain by these measures and eventually felt more secure than they had in the border region of the Araks valley. The nobility elected a *kalentar,* a sort of mayor, local district leaders, and a council of prominent citizens.

Under the impulse of Safavid power, of whose protection it was assured, New Julfa did not take long to enter into a period of remarkable prosperity. This rapid rise was to be the decisive factor in the integration of Armenian commerce in the seventeenth century. From that time on, there was a general redeployment of commercial activity on a vast scale and in regions greatly separated from one another. Simultaneously stimulated and limited by European expansion, this activity maintained itself for two centuries before being absorbed into other trade spheres, or converted (notably in Transcaucasia) into industrial capitalism, to give birth to the twentieth century.[22]

In the immense Eurasian landmass covered by the commercial system of New Julfa, commercial traffic was based on the provision of Asian goods to European cities and the provision of European goods to Asian cities. This new system made use of old local networks in widely scattered places, relics of the activity of the merchants of the Araks. These old connections were often enlarged, complemented, or given new life. New Julfa was not the only center of Armenian commerce, but it was the most important one, and used the others as relay stations. It was a center for all types of commerce, some long or very long distance with large profits, some more modest, but all dominated by a number of large transactions between Europe and Asia.

Michel Aghassian and Keram Kévonian have provided a list of the key points of this system in Asia, excluding the Near East:

—Basra and Baghdad first, as gates of the Ottoman Empire.
—At the entry of the Persian Gulf: Hormuz and Bandar ʿAbbās.
—Agra, where there was already a church in 1567 (which would be rebuilt in 1636) and an Armenian carvanserai; further north, Delhi and Lahore; in the northwest, Diu, Cambay, and Bombay. Commercial activities were constantly moving from one city to another, depending on the situation.
—In southern India, the Malabar and Coromandel coasts, notably at Madras, where they played a very important role from the sixteenth to the eighteenth century.
—In the east, in Bengal at Saidabad, Chinsura, Hugli, and Calcutta, where there is a tomb dating from 1630.
—In Burma (at Pegu, Ava, Syriam, and Rangoon) their presence extends very late into the nineteenth century. From these lands, they developed a trade with Madras and Calcutta. They also entered into the service of local lords as counselors (and as such were influential), interpreters, and tax collectors.
—In Siam (the land of Sornan), and on the Malayan coast, where they settled during the sixteenth century.
—In Batavia, where they appeared in 1636, attracted by the spice trade.
—At Manila, in the seventeenth century, they sold their cloth from Madras

---

[22] Translated from Aghassian and Kévonian, "Le commerce arménien dans l'océan Indien."

for gold and silver and benefited from the embargo that afflicted the Protestants and the Muslims by obtaining navigation rights from the Spanish.
—At Canton, where they appeared after 1720, involved in the tea trade.[23]

Aghassian and Kévonian add that there existed even in the seventeenth century an important Armenian community in Lhasa, Tibet, which disappeared, it seems, around 1717–20, with the invasion of the Jungars. In general, Armenian merchants in Asia practiced all forms of commerce (caravans, peddling, large-scale retailing, large-scale trading). They even embarked in maritime trade when they realized that it was the only way to fight European competition.[24] They used the same commercial techniques as the Europeans. And when they felt it necessary, they did not hesitate to embark on a coordinated political and commercial strategy directed by the leading citizens of New Julfa. They prospected new markets and new trade circuits. They took advantage of competition or rivalry that arose between their European partners. In 1667 an agreement was concluded in Moscow with the czar, and in 1688 in London with the British sovereign. In 1692 the Swedes granted Armenians the right to bring their goods through the port of Narva to the Baltic, and in 1696 Livonia and Courland granted them the right to use the port of Libau.

One of the reasons for the success of the Armenians was the atmosphere that prevailed at the heart of this merchant community: a great sense of solidarity based on kinship ties or marriage and on contractual relations, especially relations of trust, which did not exclude recourse in case of disputes to an informal system of arbitration and, more rarely, to systems of local justice. It is possible to see therein several of the factors that brought about the remarkable rise of Armenian commerce in the seventeenth century:

There were reasons for its success: the relative emancipation of an elite group due, in part, to the rise of the Safavid and the Mughal empires; good knowledge of the "land," itineraries, sources of goods, and conditions of sale; continuous exchange of information regarding the fluctuation of European demand and Asian supply; capability of immediate adoption to the *conjoncture* and the crises caused by the shifting of trade to new circuits; absence of religious persecution or proselytism. Historians of New Julfa, meanwhile, emphasize a certain number of qualities: experience, mastery of accounting, stubbornness and courage, solidarity and constant inclination to unite together; and they note in passing the existence of proclivity for commercial adventure, which was less apparent with the Persians. . . . In this merchant

[23] Ibid.
[24] Their ships bore a red-yellow-red flag marked with the Lamb of God.

world, which was geographically extended but socially integrated, and which was established without the direct support of the state, the framework of commercial capitalism was still largely based on family structure. Not only the ties of kinship and marriage but also patronage created solid relationships. The community was composed of virtual merchant dynasties, the transmission of wealth being often assured by the marriages between great families. . . . Even though the network was composed of a minority in each region, the network as a whole was not a mere chain of minorities, or a "diaspora," because there existed a country, that retained its spirit as well as the collective destiny of a nation, one of the major concerns of the elite. This particularly was to give the Armenian community an economic advantage, from which it obviously knew how to draw the best part.[25]

The Armenian merchant community dedicated a considerable part of its profits to the activities of piety or charity. It was for some people a means of demonstrating their position, while fulfilling their obligations to the church and the nation. Thanks to the donations, a cathedral and twelve churches were built in New Julfa, and in 1638 the first printing house in Persia was established. In 1656 a merchant council took control of a lawsuit that threatened the patrimony of the Armenian patriarch in Jerusalem. The enormous wealth accumulated in India played an essential role. Gregory Mikaelian financed the establishment of the first printing house in Armenia in 1771, and a papermill was soon added. In 1790 a rich Armenian from Surat funded the building of two schools and a printing house in the Armenian colony of Nakhitchévan-on-the-Don, and an Armenian from Calcutta bequeathed his fortune to the colony of Grigoriopol. These two cities were located in Russia. There are many other examples.

Is lavish patronage one of the reasons for the decline of Armenian trade after 1760? Were there any other intervening factors? What about weakening kinship ties and community cohesion, growing rivalries between great families, or accelerating social assimilation? External forces should also not be overlooked, such as deterioration of political situations, challenges from European powers, and integration of international exchange. The shifting trend of European demand, as a result of industrialization, from manufactured products and precious goods to raw materials also hurt Armenian trade.

---

[25] Translated from Aghassian and Kévonian, "Le commerce arménien dans l'océan Indien." I wish to thank Mr. Kévonian for his excellent advice.

ANTHROPOLOGY CONTINUED: THE INDIAN
OCEAN AND THE CHINA SEA

Merchant communities in the areas of the Indian Ocean and the China Sea are discussed in Chapters 12 and 13. Here it may be useful to summarize the results of a roundtable discussion in Paris on "Asian Merchant Milieus."[26] Before the Europeans arrived, the maritime space from the east of Africa to Japan constituted a trade zone dominated by Muslim merchants. Their commercial networks over the area were only partially destroyed during the early seventeenth century, when the great trading companies arrived, and colonial systems were launched. We have already examined the role of the Armenians in the Indian Ocean. The activities of other communities also need to be studied, such as those of Parsees, Hadrami, Isma'ilis, Chetti, and overseas Chinese.

The Muslim merchant societies of the western Indian Ocean (the Red Sea, the Arabian Sea, the Persian Gulf) in early modern times have not yet been dealt with as a whole in any research, and only a few regional studies have appeared. Jean Aubin has specified a number of issues to be clarified by future study:

1. A transformation of the merchant societies was in progress at the time of the arrival of the Portuguese in India; this transformation was neither triggered by the interference of the Europeans nor interrupted by it.
2. The growth of Iranian emigration to the Deccan was accompanied by the hegemony of Persian merchants.
3. In the colonial countries, merchants acceded to political roles denied to merchants in the lands where Islam was long established, where they could exercise influence only from behind the scenes.
4. International merchants in these societies did not have a complete monopoly on the economic exchanges. Besides the princes (through the mediation of the so-called royal merchants), the clerical classes also had some power in this realm.
5. The culture of the merchants appears to have been predominantly religious, but this impression may be exaggerated by the nature of biographical accounts, which tend to focus on individuals.
6. We have yet to understand adequately the evolution of merchant classes between the sixteenth and the nineteenth centuries.[27]

---

[26] Typewritten summary of the roundtable discussion on "Les milieux marchands asiatiques." Here I would particularly like to thank Denys Lombard and Jean Aubin, the organizers of this roundtable, for their invaluable collaboration. The proceedings of the conference have been published in Aubin and Lombard, eds., *Marchands et hommes d'affaires asiatiques* (see n. 21).
[27] Roundtable discussion on "Les milieux marchands asiatiques," summary, 2.

Jean Calmard has studied Iranian merchants between the sixteenth and the nineteenth centuries and emphasizes their power as a pressure group. It is necessary to distinguish between big merchants, who, along with bankers, jewelers, and so on, tended to assimilate with the upper echelons of society (military, tribal, or bureaucratic aristocracy), and numerous artisan-traders of the *bâzâr* and various intermediaries.

Merchants occupied a separate place in the midst of "corporations" (approximate translation of *sanf/asnaf*), which were belatedly formed by the combined forces of the socioprofessional groups wishing to unite together and the state wishing to achieve centralization. At the top of the hierarchy was the *malek-ot-tojjar* (literally "king of merchants"), who was not appointed by the state. Various representatives of power exercised the control over commercial activities.[28]

Completely integrated into the socioreligious milieu, these merchants (in Persian, *bâzargân*, in the singular) were seriously challenged, in international trade and in Iranian trade as well, by Europeans, pirates, minorities, their colleagues who had political backing, and even princes or bureaucrats, who were more and more interested in trade profits. They showed, and were to show, a remarkable power of adaptation as late as the nineteenth century. But their tendency to invest in real property and in agricultural products for export, such as cotton or opium, obstructed the development of local industry. It was a situation that could be called the new "betrayal of the bourgeoisie." Finally, the great geographical and social mobility of the *bâzargân* allowed them to exercise an influence on politics that could still be felt in the late nineteenth and early twentieth centuries.

Merchant communities in Yemen and Hadramaut were studied by R. B. Sergeant, but otherwise we do not have much information about them.[29] Better known is an important community in Calicut, studied, for the sixteenth century, by Geneviève Bouchon.[30] On arrival in Calicut, the Portuguese found powerful merchant groups. The Chinese, who had regularly loaded their ships with pepper in Calicut in the fourteenth and fifteenth centuries, had gradually abandoned the port for Malacca. Around 1500, the merchant society of the city was composed of three major groups: (1) merchants of the Malabar Coast,

---

[28] Ibid., 3.
[29] Ibid., 4. In his summary, Sergeant comments: "Information on early Hadrami merchants is sparer but they had links with Rasulid and Ayyubid Aden and many settled in Yemeni ports and migrated to East Africa."
[30] Ibid., 6.

most of whom were Muslims (Mapilla); (2) foreigners (Pardesi) – Arabs, Persians, Turks, Somalians, Maghrebians – mostly composed of merchants from the Near East and the Middle East; and (3) merchants who came from other regions in India – the Bengalese, the Deccans, and the Chetti of the Coromandel Coast – among whom the merchants from Gujarat played a predominant role. Similar analyses could be made of other ports of the Indian Ocean.

For the sixteenth century, Malacca has been studied by Luis F. Thomaz, using several narratives like the *Suma oriental* by Tomé Pires and the archives in Lisbon. Thomaz was struck by the ethnic diversity among the urban population and the importance of foreign minorities in political, economic, and social domains. These minorities were under the systematic protection of the sultans at first and then the Portuguese.

The foreign communities in Melaka formed four major ethnic groups, each not only retaining its own manners and customs but also observing its own law.

The two richest and most influential communities of the time of the Sultanate were the Gujarati Muslims and the *keling* (Tamil) Hindus. The former specialized in trade with the Near East, and the latter with eastern Indonesia where they traded their cotton fabrics for spices. After the Portuguese conquest, the Gujaratis virtually deserted the port. The Hindus, on the other hand, became the privileged business partners of the Portuguese Crown.

There were also the Javanese merchants, specialized in regional trade, and the Chinese as well as the Luzonese merchants. There are few extant documents for the period following the Portuguese conquest through 1580, and we almost lose track of these communities. It seems that the foreign colonies were founded in the Mestizo society of Melaka during the last half-century of the Portuguese domination. Doubtless the intensification of evangelical activities during the sixteenth century, and the increasing number of Portuguese who married native women and settled there furthered the establishment of the foreign colonies. It was henceforth they who dominated the scene.[31]

Malacca was not the only large trading city in the Indonesian archipelago. The trade center shifted from Pasay (in the thirteenth century), to Gresik (in the fourteenth century), to Malacca (in the fifteenth century), and thereafter a series of city-ports rapidly developed, located on the coast of the archipelago: Aceh and Bantam in the sixteenth and the seventeenth centuries, Macassar in the seventeenth century, and so on. They became more important than the agrarian centers in the interior when a merchant sultanate essentially turned

[31] Ibid., 7.

away from the agricultural zone in favor of long-distance trade. An extensive trade network was built and used by the Portuguese.[32]

Meanwhile, China experienced an economic revival and went through a substantial structural transformation on the eve of the arrival of the Europeans. Thanks to Chen Dasheng, we have some knowledge of the Muslim merchant community established in the port of Quanzhou, on the southeastern coast of the Fujian province.[33] The case of Japan is quite different; can we speak of merchant communities there? The relationship with China had been growing since 1400, and relations with the Europeans had also been expanding from 1543, the year when the Portuguese arrived, until 1610, the year when Japan closed its door. It seems that the merchants were strictly controlled by the *daimyo* until 1610 and, after that, by the *shogun*. The *shogun* exercised a complete monopoly of trade.[34]

It is time to draw some conclusions on the merchants of the East. "Eastern merchants" is used here to cover all those who traded around the Indian Ocean and the China Sea and who mostly came from the Middle East. What is most remarkable, first of all, is their similarity to the merchants of the West. They had almost the same organization, problems, and difficulties. Merchant communities were cosmopolitan, and tended to identify themselves as foreign "nations" abroad. Everywhere special attention was given to precious goods. Everywhere the importance of maritime transport was emphasized. Everywhere solidarity existed within merchant communities, and they attempted to achieve prestige as well as cultural influence. The commercial and financial techniques of the East, to be sure, were not always as advanced as those of the West. Much can be said about that subject; however, it is not our focus here.

AFTER THE EAST, THE WEST

With the discovery of America, a new world was opened to trade. Because of the colonial monopolies, trade in the new territories of Spain, Portugal, England, France, and the Netherlands was allowed only by their own nationals. It should be noted, nevertheless, that the Portuguese Jews were firmly established in the Castilian Indies during the period of the "union of two crowns" (1580–1640) and played an important role in trade. In the Spanish Indies, a class of Creole

[32] Ibid., 8, comments of Denys Lombard. See also p. 18, the study of G. Hamonic, "Les réseaux marchands Bugis-Makassar."
[33] Ibid., 5.
[34] Ibid., 10, comments of Paul Akamatsu.

merchants developed; it is noteworthy that such a class did not appear in Brazil to any great extent. In the colonies of England, France, and the Netherlands, the activities of traders were soon to be limited or directed by the great companies of commerce and navigation. As for England, its traders were often transformed into trade-agents. New England was soon to have its autonomous merchant group.

For these reasons, we should go back to the ports in Europe that controlled the trade with the colonies. We will confine ourselves to Seville, because merchant communities in Europe have already been well-researched. In Spain, Seville, along with Cadiz, enjoyed the privilege of trade with the West Indies almost continuously until the second half of the eighteenth century.

The studies by Albert Girard are essential. He emphasized the changes that took place in Seville: Seville, which had been sending its merchants out to other parts of Europe in the fifteenth century, now received, in the sixteenth century, foreign merchants from throughout Europe. First came the Genoese, the Flemish, and the Germans, and then came the Portuguese. Most of the Portuguese were New Christians, often descendants of Spanish Marranos. The Dutch and the English showed up later. One of the reasons for this major influx of foreign merchants was the extensive privileges awarded to them by the city. Girard explains how the French benefited:

> The more powerful, economically and politically, the people of a country, the more they sought to gain important privileges. Any countries that managed to change the European balance of power to their advantage sought accordingly to enjoy the same privileges as others and to expand them. This was the case of the French. The growth of their power in the seventeenth century seemed to entitle them to as privileged a position in the Iberian Peninsula as that of any nation.[35]

The consuls of the foreign countries were responsible for protecting their nations. Some were named by the merchants in Seville, and others by their king with the ratification of the king of Spain. After 1578, the kings of France tended to designate the French consuls in Spain themselves. The number of merchants who were under the jurisdiction of the consul of France was not very large, if we exclude those who were naturalized. But it is not correct, Girard points out, to count only those who were not naturalized, because the legal concept of nationality at that time was still very ambiguous. In Spain, foreigners wanted to acquire the letters of naturalization in order, above

---

[35] *Le commerce français a Séville et Cadix au temps des Habsbourg* (Paris, 1932): the quotation is translated from pp. 89–90.

all, to obtain the right to trade with the Indies. There are many indications of French traders residing in Spain during the reign of Henry IV.

By 1589, some inhabitants of Vitré, thrown out of their homes by the Huguenots, went to settle in Spain, with which they had long business relations. In the instructions to Sieur de Sancerre, who was going to Spain as the ambassador of France in 1598, Henri IV referred to the "communities of Seville and Saint-Lucca." He also mentioned three merchants from Bayonne, Arnaud du Fau, Bertrand Jardin, and Pierre de Harambur, who had been established in France. Frain, in his book *Les Vitréens et le commerce international* and in his pamphlet *Le commerce des Vitréens en Espagne, 1629–1630*, gives many names of merchants who had long resided in Andalusia and were even married to Spaniards. Contrary to what Montchrestien asserts, they were commissioned traders.[36]

By 1625, the number of French traders rose to about twelve, and by 1670, about twenty. Twenty-seven names are found during 1682–5, twenty-nine in 1700. The fact that the lists we have almost always give the same names allows us to assume that the composition of the French colony was fairly stable.[37] According to Savary, the agents whom the French traders delegated to Cadiz were generally their sons or other members of their family. They were often young bachelors, who were learning commercial skills so as to eventually take charge of their parents' firms in France. Sometimes, however, when a young merchant stayed in Seville long enough, he married a local woman and settled down in Spain.

A study by two Spanish scholars provides us with more general information on the merchant communities in Seville.[38] From the fourteenth to the sixteenth century, merchants showed the most notable growth among the different socioeconomic groups and became increasingly specialized. There were only six people who were called merchants (*mercaderes*) in 1384, thirteen between 1426 and 1451, and twenty-six between 1480 and 1490. Their number reached 353 in 1533, due to the rise of American trade. Their social origins were quite varied, but the merchants were traditionally linked to the urban nobility even before the discovery of America. The trade with America created a special type of merchant class, *el cargador a Indias*. Some of them were called *hacendados-cargadores*, or *cosecheros*, who were large rural

---

[36] Translated from ibid., 547–8.

[37] Ibid., 551.

[38] Antonio Miguel Bernal Rodriguez and Antonio Collantes de Teran Sanchez, "El puerto de Seville, de puerto fluvial medieval a centro portuario mundial (siglos XIV–XVII)," in *I porti como impresa economica* (Prato, 1988), 779–824.

landowners exporting their crops. The *hacendados-cargadores* were merchants who were also engaged in some agricultural activities. Finally, there were *artesanos-cargadores*. All these three groups were wholesale merchants and were necessarily engaged in the import and export business. Aside from the *mercaderes*, there were the *comerciantes*, dealing in wholesale or retail, and the *corredores* in credit or insurance, who served as intermediaries.

What is probably more important is the merchant-banker community. Due to the trade with America, Seville became a large financial center through which gold and silver from Mexico and Perú passed. Already in the fourteenth and fifteenth centuries, two groups distinguished themselves in financial activities: the Jews, who soon became *conversos*, and the Genoese. The Jews were money changers and bankers. The Genoese more and more stood out as bankers: Pinelo, Gentil, Grimaldo, Centurion, and Merlesin were already well established before America was discovered. According to Jacques Heers, it was from Seville that the Genoese oversaw the trade throughout southern Spain and even Castile. By the sixteenth century they were leading the trade with America, and the Genoese families such as the Spinolas, the Grimaldis, the Centurions, and the Mortelos were engaged in all kinds of financial operations, including money exchange and the gold, silver, and pearl trade. According to the study of Santiago Tinoco on the Bank of Seville in the sixteenth century, the Genoese families made Seville the leader in international finance.[39]

Of course, there were other Italians in Seville: the Florentines, studied in part by Federigo Melis (Pedro Dolfo, Carcedonia, Talento Tedale, Baroncheti, Nicolen, Rondenelli, etc.); bankers from Piacenza who kept their own stock market until the end of the fifteenth century; the Piedmontese; the Milanese; the Lombards; and the Venetians. The Venetians experienced various successive setbacks in their relations with Seville. The English and the French, already examined above, should also be mentioned.

The situation in Seville confirms what we had presupposed in the case of the French. With the discovery of America, there was a considerable increase in the number of foreigners in Seville, but in order for them to be "naturalized," that is, to obtain the right to trade with the Indies, they had to have resided in Castile for at least twenty years and to own a house in the city. The Catalans, the Portuguese, the Genoese, the Flemish, and, in general, all the subjects of the Holy Roman Empire and the subjects related to the Empire by alliance found

[39] Quoted in ibid.

it was relatively easy to obtain naturalization. Francisco Morales Padron, for the sixteenth century, and Dominguez Ortiz, for the seventeenth century have studied the process of the integration of foreigners in Seville. Bernal and Collantes de Teran note that the city had the reputation of a "Republica de mercaderes." Naturalizations continued even when Seville was no longer the center of trade, after 1650 (fifty-three naturalizations between 1650 and 1700). Cadiz was more or less transformed into a residential city. But some merchants remained in Seville, such as the Genoese Bocardo and Viganego, the Milanese Visca, the Flemish Mestre and Ness, and the Germans like Conique.[40]

THE EARLY EIGHTEENTH CENTURY

Before we discuss the eighteenth century, it is helpful to summarize the evolution of merchant communities and the changes that occurred.

1. The struggle between local artisan guilds and native and foreign merchant corporations proceeded in a direction advantageous to the latter. In the era of commercial capitalism, it is logical that capitalist merchants should triumph. They were the final winners, and they controlled and profited from this economy.

2. Their power is revealed in the creation of chambers of commerce in large cities or seaports during the Age of Enlightenment. In France, the first chamber was established in Dunkirk in 1700. They did not appear in Venice until 1763, or in Florence until 1770. These chambers, according to Fernand Braudel, attempted to reinforce the authority of big merchants at the expense of others. As a merchant in Dunkirk remarked in 1770: "All those chambers of commerce . . . simply destroy the general structure of trade, bringing the absolute control of navigation and trade of the area into the hands of five or six individuals." The importance of this new institution varied depending on the location. In Marseille, Braudel writes, quoting the works of Carriére and Rambert, that it was "the heart of the merchant activities." In contrast, at Lyons, everything was decided in the *Echevinage* and the chamber of commerce ended up falling into desuetude. Saint-Malo petitioned the king in 1728 to create a chamber in the city, but they did not succeed.[41]

3. It is not the purpose of this paper to discuss either commercial techniques or the various trade companies that appeared during and

---

[40] Ibid.

[41] F. Braudel, *Civilisation matérielle*, 2:63 (*Civilization and Capitalism*, trans. Reynolds, 2:81). On Marseille, see Charles Carrière, *Négociants merseillais au XVIIIᵉ siècle*, 2 vols. (Aix, 1973); and, of course, *L'histoire du commerce de Marseille*, ed. G. Rambert (Paris, 1949).

after the Middle Ages and were still prosperous and expanding in the eighteenth century. The seventeenth century saw the success of the greatest companies. The life of merchant communities, however, cannot be understood without considering the overlapping network of diverse relations within them, including family relations and the relations between factors, branches, subsidiaries, and brokers. The network reinforced solidarities between merchants and mitigated the competition and rivalry between clans and families. All those complicated relations persisted and expanded in the eighteenth century. As in the sixteenth century, the number of merchant communities rose rapidly in the eighteenth century. New cities began to receive foreigners. One of them was Salonika, which was studied by N. G. Svoronos.[42] Svoronos examined, for example, the case of the French. French merchants began to establish themselves in Salonika in the late seventeenth century; the first four settlers were Damiras, Espanit, Roubaud, and Granier. Wars had interrupted the Levant trade. The French consuls complained about the absence of French agents in Salonika when its trade was yielding more profits than that of Smyrna. Other foreign traders who were already established there were enjoying profits. By 1698, in fact, the only Frenchmen residing in Salonika were the consul, a surgeon, and a man who stayed with the consul. A merchant had come in 1691 but had been sent back to France for misbehavior. The small trade colony continued to grow, despite the war, the lack of credits, and the plague. About ten French companies existed there by 1740. The consul of France was the only foreign consul present in Salonika at the beginning of the eighteenth century, and foreign traders depended upon his protection. Before long England and even Venice posed a serious challenge to France, and the English consul at last took the place of the French consul. The French consul, nevertheless, continued to protect Greek and Jewish barrators and dragomen who escaped from the tyranny of the Turks.

4. In the European context, Portugal was the center of a world economy in the sixteenth century. Portugal successfully resisted the vicissitudes of the seventeenth century, thanks to sugar from Brazil, and was to resume a new importance in the eighteenth century with the gold from Minas. Many studies have appeared on the Italian, German, and even French foreign merchant communities in Lisbon.[43] In particular, the English community has been of great interest to histo-

---

[42] *Le commerce de Salonique au XVIIIe siècle* (Paris, 1956).

[43] V. Rau, *Estudos de historia economica* (Lisbon, 1961); F. Mauro, *Le Portugal, Le Brésil et l'Atlantique* (Paris, 1983). On the Germans, read the bibliography provided in H. Kellenbenz, "Lisboa nos negocios da casa Hasenclever de Remscheid," in *Estudos de Historia de Portugal 2, Mélanges Olivera Marques*, vol. 1 (1983), 243–72.

rians since the publication of the classic work by Shillington and Chapman. The most recent critical discussion of its role during the eighteenth century was made by the English historian Stephen Fisher.[44] Fisher describes the development of English merchant communities throughout Europe, and in the Mediterranean area in particular, and examines the role Lisbon played as an intermediary in English trade in the Mediterranean. Portuguese trade with Europe and the Mediterranean was in the hands of foreign merchants, whose factories invaded the city. Among those factories, the most important by far in the eighteenth century was the factory of Britain. English trade in Portugal was the most considerable, and it was England that benefited the most from the gold of Brazil.

5. London and other ports in England began to emerge in the eighteenth century, following the upsurge of the English economy since the Elizabethan era. Even if we accept the revisionist views of some historians, for whom England's pre–Industrial Revolution of the seventeenth century was only a dream of John U. Nef,[45] the seaports in England became so important in the eighteenth century that many European merchants rushed into those cities. Among the vast bibliography on the subject, two or three recent studies need mentioning: that of Carla Rahn Phillips on Spanish merchants, that of Stephen Fisher on Jewish merchants, and that of Sarah Palmer on London and Liverpool.[46]

6. In the eighteenth century, merchant communities were no longer of the same nature as in the fourteenth or the fifteenth century. They were more numerous, larger, and more securely established in the cities in which they settled. But they enjoyed less autonomy in relation to their mother cities. The advances in communications, the development and the diffusion of commercial techniques and different forms of partnership, the development of trade networks, and the emergence of the great trading companies and important firms all combined to limit and diminish the role of common individual traders. Finally, it was now maritime cities that controlled trade. As a consequence, it was the cities that dominated their resident merchant nations, no longer the other way around.

[44] Fisher, "Lisbon, Its English Merchant Community and the Mediterranean in the Eighteenth Century," in *Shipping Trade and Commerce: Essays in Memory of Ralph Davis* (Leicester, 1981), 23–43; idem, "Lisbon as a Port Town in the Eighteenth Century," in *I porti como impresa economica*, 703–31; idem, *The Portugal Trade* (1971).

[45] Nef, *The Rise of the British Coal Industry*, 2 vols. (London, 1952).

[46] Phillips, "Spanish Merchants and the Wool Trade in the Sixteenth Century," *The Sixteenth Century Journal* 14 (1983): 259–82; Fisher, "Jews in England the Eighteenth-Century English Economy," *The Jewish Historical Society* (1982): 156–65; Palmer, "The Eighteenth Century Ports of London and Liverpool," in *I porti como impresa economia*, 381–99.

CONCLUSION

Now it is necessary to draw some tentative conclusions from the preceding analysis, which I tried to make concrete and empirical, using the examples of relatively limited cases.

1. Merchant communities were at first not different from other sworn merchant associations established within cities. Very rapidly, however, some communities became so powerful that they were confused with the government of the city, generally a powerful city-state.

2. Local communities quickly extended abroad, where they created "nations," or merchant colonies. By the fourteenth or the fifteenth century, the terms "merchant community" and "community of foreign merchants" were often considered synonymous.

3. There are thus two different ways to approach merchant communities: studying every colony sent out by a city-state, a group of city-states, or a large territorial or even national state; or studying one or all foreign nations represented in a city. Ugo Tucci employed the first method, and Goris, Girard, and Svoronos used the second approach.

4. Cities that either sent out or received merchants were not necessarily seaports. The role of seaports became essential only with the emergence of the economy centered on the Atlantic Ocean. And from the first, merchant cities could conclude alliances or form a federation as the cities of the Hanseatic League.

5. The existence of merchant communities created ties of solidarity and fraternity. Within such a framework sound commercial competition could still persist. Since the time of Savary, however, and throughout the eighteenth century, merchant communities were subjected to the same criticism as the guilds, that is, that they limited economic liberty, created monopolies, and caused a rise in prices through the monopolies they enjoyed.

6. Merchant communities facilitated the development and the diffusion of new commercial techniques: the bill of exchange and its attendant financial developments (guarantee, endorsement, discount), double-entry bookkeeping, interest loan, transmission of news, and so on. Merchant communities adapted themselves to the emergence of the state monopolies (the king-merchant in Portugal), to the great privileged companies, and to other forms of companies, described in the trade manuals of that time. They often participated in the great companies, as did the New Christians in the General Company of the Trade of Brazil in 1648.

7. The legal and institutional structures of foreign merchant communities come into focus on occasion, as in those of Islamic countries,

but the details of daily activities are rarely visible. We have information about the role of the consul, various incidents such as disputes of precedence, cultural influence, and patronage exercised by these foreigners. We can assume that the merchants more or less accepted certain local customs of the region of the world where they were established. Many details remain unclear. For example, how common was it for a merchant to change his nationality and marry a local woman?

8. Documents dealing with the problems of merchant communities are very scattered. They are found in various sources such as notarial records, correspondence, travelers' narratives, legal or financial archives, and registers of municipal proceedings, or sometimes in books that devote but one chapter to this aspect of their topic. It would, therefore, be desirable to compile a dictionary of commercial cities, classify the characteristics of the merchant communities of these cities using different variables, and enter the information into a computer. Also, one could construct a prosopography of merchants of those communities. Then, all the tentative conclusions we have made in this study, largely based on an intuitive and qualitative analysis, would become working hypotheses that could be quantitatively verified.

9. There remains a final question, one that many historians and especially many nonhistorians are likely to ask: are these merchant communities closely related to the development of world-economy, the notion presented by Immanuel Wallerstein? Wallerstein conceived of the concept of world-economy as opposed to an "empire," or rather like an empire without a head, which avoids the heavy expenses of central government and the revolts and wars imposed on its subjects by an empire. If such a world economy existed, the harmony in that order must have been created by a system that took the place of a central authority, political and religious, which was more and more contested. To this question, we can answer in the affirmative. It can be said that the network of merchant communities continually established or reestablished the equilibrium of the world economy, by the means of brokerage and feedback.

One can thus understand that both the world economy and the merchant communities were unable to withstand the rise of "hegemonic empires."[47]

---

[47] It is not possible for me to give a bibliography on a subject so vast and for which the documentation is scattered throughout works on commerce, cities, ports, social structures, mentality, and the daily life of Europeans and others. But at least the references in the notes can serve as a beginning.

CHAPTER 9

Economic aspects of the eighteenth-century Atlantic slave trade

HERBERT S. KLEIN

In recent decades there has been a fundamental change in the study of the Atlantic slave trade. From almost total neglect, the trade has become an area of major concern to economists and historians who have dedicated themselves to analyzing the African experience in America. Especially since the publication by Philip Curtin of his masterly synthesis *The Atlantic Slave Trade: A Census* in 1969, a massive amount of archival research has resulted in publications both of collections of documents from all the major archives of Europe, America, and Africa and of major works of synthesis on the demography, politics, and economics of the slave trade.[1]

[1] Curtin's book was published by the University of Wisconsin Press. Much of the archival material remained unpublished until quite recently. The major printed collection until the 1920s was the listing that the Foreign Office published for the trade from 1817 to 1843, to be found in *Parliamentary Papers*, 1845, xlix (73), 593–633. The first scholarly collections were published in the 1920s and 1930s by Dieudonné Rinchon, *La traite et l'esclavage des Congolais par les européens* (Brussels, 1929); Elizabeth Donnan, *Documents Illustrative of the History of the Slave Trade to America*, 4 vols. (Washington, D.C., 1930); and Gaston Martin, *Négriers et bois d'ébène* (Grenoble, 1934). Recent publications of new archival materials include the monumental study of the French slave trade by Jean Mettas, *Répertoire des expéditions négrières françaises au xviiie siècle*, 2 vols. (Paris, 1978–84); and a more complete listing for Virginia by Walter Minchinton et al., *Virginia Slave Trade Statistics, 1698–1775* (Richmond, Va., 1984). Recent monographs on the economic aspect of the trade include Roger Anstey, *The Atlantic Slave Trade and British Abolition* (London, 1975); Herbert S. Klein, *The Middle Passage: Comparative Studies in the Atlantic Slave Trade* (Princeton, 1978); Colin Palmer, *Human Cargoes: The British Slave Trade to Spanish America, 1700–1739* (Urbana, 1981); Jorge Palacios Preciado, *La trata de negros por Cartagena de Indias* (Tunja, Colombia, 1973); Robert Louis Stein, *The French Slave Trade in the Eighteenth Century: An Old Regime Business* (Madison, 1979); Jay Coughtry, *The Notorious Triangle: Rhode Island and the African Slave Trade, 1700–1807* (Philadelphia, 1981); David W. Galenson, *Traders, Planters, and Slaves: Market Behavior in Early English America* (Cambridge, 1986); and David Eltis, *Economic Growth and the Ending of the Transatlantic Slave Trade* (New York, 1987). For a survey of the bibliography on the noneconomic aspects of the

287

In this essay, I would like to concentrate on those aspects of the trade most directly related to its economic organization and impact on world trade and markets, including that of the international market in labor. This will involve a study of such questions as the relative importance of the trade in African slaves within the total movement of goods and services across international frontiers; the relative costs and benefits of the trade in slaves to its various national participants; and the mechanics of the trade in terms of goods exchanged and routes developed. Finally, given the unique commodity being shipped by the slave traders, it is essential to examine the demographic characteristics of the trade and its impact on American and African labor markets.

Though the Atlantic slave trade officially dates its origin from the 1440s and does not end until the 1860s, both the mass of documentation and the period of its greatest importance were in the eighteenth century. Even though over a million and a half Africans had been brought to America before 1700, over six million arrived in the period 1701–1810, or 63 percent of the total who ever landed in the Western Hemisphere.[2] The eighteenth century also marks the definitive shift among all traders from an era of largely monopoly company activities to that of a free trade organization.[3] The trade ends for most Europeans by the last quarter of the eighteenth century and first decades of the nineteenth century, and it officially disappears from the public records of the remaining traders after 1830. For these reasons, the eighteenth century is the best studied of all centuries and the one most representative for almost all trading nations.

Though the slave trade was a concern for scholars, moralists, and politicians from the late eighteenth century and was one of the major areas of activity of British diplomacy and the British navy in the nineteenth century, the systematic study of the trade only dates from the twentieth century. A combination of late nineteenth-century European racism and imperialism and early twentieth-century unease with these concepts led to an era of scholarly neglect in which popular

trade, Herbert S. Klein, *African Slavery in Latin America and the Caribbean* (New York, 1986).

[2] Curtin, *Atlantic Slave Trade*, 268.

[3] On the history of these trading companies see, e.g., Johannes Postma, "The Dimensions of the Dutch Slave Trade from West Africa," *Journal of African History* 13 (1972): 237–48, on the Dutch West India Company; for the very late development of limited Iberian monopoly companies see António Carreira, *As Companhias Pombalinas de navegação, comércio e tráfico de escravos . . .* (Porto, 1969); and Bibiano Torres Ramirez, *La compañia gaditana de negros* (Seville, 1973). On the French and British Chartered Trading Companies, see Abdoulaye Ly, *La Compagnie du Sénégal* (Paris, 1958); and K. G. Davies, *The Royal African Company* (London, 1951).

writers dominated the analysis of the trade with their limited and highly emotional accounts based on few observations and a lack of awareness of the realities of African history or society. This rather uncritical literature created a whole set of untested hypotheses about the costs of the trade, the pattern of shipping slaves across the Atlantic, the mortality they suffered, and the ultimate gains and benefits to the Europeans. "Tight packing" and "astronomic" mortality rates were tied to the concept of virtually costless slaves.[4] This model of the trade, which still pervades much of the popular literature on the subject, also assumed a totally passive and dependent role of Africans. Research since the beginning decades of this century has shown this model to be badly flawed, and it is with this newer research and its implications with which I am concerned in this essay.

By the eighteenth century, the Atlantic slave trade had become one of the most complex international trades developed by European merchants. It involved the direct participation of East Indian textile manufacturers, European ironmongers, African caravan traders, European shippers, and American planters in the purchase, transportation, and sale of the largest transoceanic migration of workers known up to that time in recorded history. At its peak in the last quarter of the nineteenth century, Europeans were moving some 90,000 Africans per annum to America in some 200 to 300 ships under the flag of every major maritime power of western Europe.

To begin with, it should be stressed that the trade in African slaves long preceded the European development of an Atlantic route. From known historical times African slaves had been shipped across the Sahara to the Mediterranean world and had also gone by sea and land routes to Asia Minor. Secondly, the slave trade was only one of several important exports from Africa to the rest of the world, with gold being the primary product until well into the eighteenth century. The Atlantic slave trade thus initially fitted into traditional trading networks and was but an extension of both the internal and the external slave trade markets already existing in Africa. Equally, this particular trade, even for Europeans, was initially not the most important product that they brought out of Africa. The Atlantic trade in slaves, which began in the mid–fifteenth century, was initially only a minor trade associated with the Portuguese exportation of gold, and to a lesser extent of ivory, from the western shores of sub-Saharan Africa. Since Europe was well populated with a growing peasant labor force at this

---

[4] See, e.g., D. P. Mannix and M. Cowley, *Black Cargoes: A History of the Atlantic Slave Trade, 1518–1865* (New York, 1962); and James Pope-Hennesey, *Sins of the Fathers: A Study of the Atlantic Slave Traders, 1441–1807* (London, 1967).

time, the demand for slaves within Europe itself was small, and most of the Africans shipped to the Iberian peninsula were used in domestic or urban artisanal tasks. Few were brought into agriculture or even into the production of sugar, which was then of major importance in the local economies. For this reason, the export of slaves remained a minor part of the European trade with Africa at least into the middle decades of the sixteenth century, or some one hundred years after the first slaves were carried aboard Portuguese vessels. Even with the opening up of the eastern Atlantic islands (e.g., the Canaries) and their exploitation as sugar colonies in the last decades of the fifteenth and early decades of the sixteenth centuries, Africans were a minor element in the local labor force.

It was, of course, the opening up of America that finally guaranteed an expanding and seemingly limitless market for African slave labor. But even despite the ever-growing transportation of Africans to America in the first two centuries of American colonization, slaves did not surpass the value of all other African exports until 1700.[5] Thus European trade with Africa remained a multifaceted experience until some two and a half centuries after the first slave shipments. All of which meant that a whole range of commercial contacts not directly related to slaves had been developed alongside the slave trade. It also meant that African consumers had been well integrated into the European trading networks well before slaves became their chief export. It was only the decline of their own gold production (which peaked in the 1680s), and the entrance of American gold on the European market that finally forced them and their European contacts to turn more heavily toward shipments of slaves.[6] Whereas in the 1680s it has been estimated that gold and to a lesser extent ivory and other products made up over 50 percent of the value of exports from Africa, by the 1780s, these nonslave items had fallen to only an estimated 8 percent of the total value of goods exported from this region.[7]

It was this relatively sophisticated African consumer market and its basic needs that in many ways explains the geographic specialization that emerged in the European trading communities. It was no accident that by the mid–eighteenth century the two leading centers of Asian textile importers – the ports of Nantes and Liverpool – were to

---

[5] Richard Bean, "A Note on the Relative Importance of Slaves and Gold in West African Exports," *Journal of African History* 15 (1974): 351–6.

[6] Philip D. Curtin, "Africa and the Wider Monetary World, 1250–1850," in J. F. Richards, ed., *Precious Metals in the Later Medieval and Early Modern Worlds* (Durham, 1983), 245–7.

[7] David Eltis, "African Trade with the Atlantic World before 1870: Estimates of Trends in Value, Composition, and Direction" (unpublished paper, 1987).

emerge as the two biggest ports in France and England of African slave traders.[8] African demand for East Indian textiles was so high that there soon developed a close link between East Asian traders and African slave traders. Though the two trades were so complex that specialization was the norm for most merchant companies, slave traders found it convenient to be close to the single most important and expensive item used in their trade to Africa.

The role of East Indian products is well revealed in the French trade with Africa in 1775 and 1788, which showed a constant and dominant role for Indian cloths, representing 54 and 57 percent respectively of the total value (10.5 million livres tournois in 1775 and 14.7 million in 1788) of goods used to purchase slaves. With the addition of a small quantity of European cloths, the total value of all textiles represented 59 and 64 percent respectively of all goods shipped, with the second most important product, which was brandy, being a poor second at 12 and 7 percent respectively.[9] In comparing the West Indies trade – which exclusively consumed French-produced goods – with the African trade, the historian of French colonial commerce, Jean Tarrade, noted that the African consumers became very knowledgeable about general European and Asian products. Thus, "the Africans are accustomed to furniture coming from England or Holland and they refuse to accept merchandise of which the quality is not in conformity with acquired tastes. This explains why the principal articles used in the slave trade are of extra-metropolitan origin."[10]

The same trends produced at the national level were evident in detailed listings of the goods carried by outbound slave ships outfitted in the port of Rouen. In five selected years (1767, 1769, 1771, 1774, and 1776) the total value of all goods shipped was 3.9 million livres tournois. Of this total 1.4 million livres consisted of East Indian textiles. Not only were these cloths the single most valuable commodity shipped – representing 36 percent of the value of all trade goods – but they also represented 63 percent of the value of all cloths, European and East Asian combined (with the total textile figure representing 56 percent of all goods).[11] The reason for this African demand for

---

[8] Jean Tarrade, *Le commerce colonial de la France à la fin de l'Ancien Régime*, 2 vols. (Paris, 1972), 1:126.

[9] The third most valuable export of the French in 1788 was tobacco (at 5 percent), which the French had to import from Brazil (Ibid., 125).

[10] Ibid., 126.

[11] Pierre Dardel, *Navires et marchandises dans les ports de Rouen et du Havre au XVIIIe siècle* (Paris, 1963), 141. Gaston Martin, summarizing his research on this question, estimated that East Indian cloths (and their counterfeits made in Europe) made up between half and two-thirds of the value of exports to Africa for shipping from the

East Asian textiles had a great deal to do not only with the brilliance and quality of the colors but also (as a French commercial text of the eighteenth century noted) with the durability of the cloths, which retained their brilliance through numerous washings.[12] The trade was also an important stimulus to the textile industry within Europe itself, especially in the last decades of the eighteenth and throughout the nineteenth centuries.[13]

All studies of the combination of goods making up the bundle of products that Africans demanded in payment for their slaves also show a very high proportion of Indian goods listed for the English trade in the eighteenth century. Marion Johnson has reconstructed British exports to Africa in the eighteenth century. Between 1699 and 1800 textiles accounted for 68 percent of all goods shipped from England to Africa, and among these textiles, East Indian goods accounted for 40 percent of all textiles and were the single largest item in the entire trade (27 percent of the value of all goods shipped from 1699 to 1800). Moreover, despite the steady growth of English cotton exports after 1750, Indian textiles continued to maintain their relative importance until the end of the century. Next in importance after textiles were metal products, with bar iron being the crucial element in this category. Guns and gunpowder represented only 5 percent, and alcohol just 4 percent of the total value of goods shipped.[14]

Between them, the French and the British in the late eighteenth century moved about two-thirds of the slaves being shipped to America, with the Brazilian and Portuguese traders transporting most of the rest. It should be stressed that the Portuguese traders, though they exported more foodstuffs, tobacco, and American-produced rum from Brazil, did introduce both re-exported East Asian textiles and English manufactured cotton cloths to Africa for purchasing slaves. Thus 41 percent of the value of Brazilian exports to Angola in 1812 were made up of European and Asian textile re-exports, with East Asian cloths making up 15 percent of the total value of textiles.[15] Rum,

---

port of Le Havre from 1767 to 1777 (*Nantes au xviiie siècle, l'ère des négriers [1714–1774]* [Paris, 1931], 47ff).

[12] See M. Chambon, *Traite général de comerce de l'Atlantique pour Marseille*, 2 vols. (Amsterdam and Marseille, 1783), 2:389.

[13] See Pierre H. Boulle, "Marchandises de traite et développement industriel dans la France et l'Angleterre du XVIIIᵉ siècle," *Revue Française d'Histoire d'Outre-Mer* 62 (1975): 76ff.

[14] H. A. Gemery, Jan Hogendorn, and Marion Johnson, "A Tentative Terms of Trade for Africa and England in the Eighteenth Century" (paper presented at the Nantes Colloquium on the Slave Trade, 1985), tables 1–4 (papers from this conference are to be edited by Serge Daget).

[15] Because of the special trading relations of the British with Brazil after 1808 and the

though the single most valuable item shipped from Brazil, made up only 14 percent of the total value of goods imported into Angola and with re-exported European wines accounted for only 19 percent of all imports. The rest of the imported goods was made up of foodstuffs (and tobacco) produced in Brazil.[16]

It is this high percentage of manufactures and imported (and thus re-exported) goods in the trade of Africa that explains the consistent finding for all the European slave trades that the goods used by the Europeans to purchase the slaves on the African coast were their single largest cost. Thus, from the earliest studies of Rinchon and Gaston Martin, through the recent detailed analyses of provisioning costs, it is evident that slaves purchased in Africa were not a low-cost item.[17] The goods exported to Africa to pay for the slaves were costly manufactured products and were the single most expensive factor in the outfitting of the voyage, being more valuable than the ship, the wages for the crew, and the food supplies combined. Two-thirds of the outfitting costs of the French slaves in the eighteenth century, for example, came from the goods used to purchase the slaves.[18]

Along with the myths about the cheap cost of slaves, the traditional literature stressed the dependent position of the African merchants in the trade. It was thought that prices demanded for slaves were low and invariant, that the trading was all dominated by the Europeans, and that the Africans were passive observers to the whole process. But in fact, all studies show that the mix of goods that went to make up the price in each zone tended to vary over time and reflected changing conditions of demand and supply. Thus African merchants adjusted their demands for goods in response to market conditions.

---

increasing African acceptance of British manufactured cloths in the nineteenth century, the relative weight of East Asian- and European-produced cloths had probably shifted substantially from the norms of the eighteenth century. On the nineteenth-century shifts in African consumption of Asian cloths and British textiles, see Eltis, *Economic Growth and the Ending of the Transatlantic Slave Trade*, 59–60.

[16] Manuel dos Anjos da Sila Rebelo, *Relações entre Angola e Brasil, 1808–1830* (Lisbon, 1970), quadro no. 1. In the period from 1796 to 1811 Brazil itself was a heavy importer of European textiles, which made up 26 percent of the value of all imports, with Asian products adding another 17 percent. Thus a good portion of its exports to Africa were made up of these re-exported European and Asian cloths. See José Jobson de A. Arruda, *O Brasil no comércio colonial* (São Paulo, 1980), table 21.

[17] Dieudonné Rinchon, *Les armements négriers au xviiie siècle* (Brussels, 1956); Jean Meyer, *L'armement nantais dans le deuxième moitié du xviiie siècle* (Paris, 1969); Anstey, *Atlantic Slave Trade*; Stein, *French Slave Trade*; Coughtry, *Notorious Triangle*; and finally Carreira, *As Companhias Pombalinas*.

[18] Meyer, *L'armement nantais*, 161–3. Two independent sources (as presented in Klein, *Middle Passage*, 169) show that the outbound cargo for Africa on late eighteenth-century ships amounted to 65 percent of total costs.

Moreover, two recent studies of the eighteenth- and early nineteenth-century trade have shown that the terms of trade between Africa and Europe were progressively moving in favor of the Africans as the price of slaves rose and the price of European textiles (which by the end of the trade were of equal quality to the East Asian products and were replacing them) steadily fell, along with the price of all European manufactures.[19] Though the two studies differ somewhat on the timing and intensity of the trends, both are in total agreement that the barter terms of England in its trade with Africa dropped by over 50 percent from 1701 to 1800. This same trend was also repeated in the nineteenth century between the 1810s and the 1840s.

Not only was there a trend in favor of the African sellers of slaves throughout the eighteenth and nineteenth centuries, but in all their dealings with Europeans the multiple groups of African traders did everything possible to prevent the Europeans from monopolizing any one source of slaves or any one route. Although Africans could not prevent the Europeans from eliminating each other from a given region – usually through armed conflict – they could prevent the victors from exercising exclusive control on the coast itself. This was a consistent response to European monopoly efforts over all regions of western Africa. The European forts in West Africa and even the Portuguese coastal and interior towns in southwest Africa were ineffective in excluding competing buyers from entering the local market. The forts exercised dominion for only a few miles inland and were more designed to fend off competitors than to threaten suppliers. As for the unique Portuguese settlements, these were unable to prevent the French and English from obtaining Congo and Angolan slaves on a massive scale. Yet these supposedly were domains totally monopolized by the Portuguese.

It should be stressed that trading was a complex affair, involving everything from fixed coastal fort or port locations to open boat traders who sailed the rivers and coastal waters. African traders up and down the coast also varied considerably, from mulatto middlemen, to state trading monopolies, to noble or royal trading arrangements. Some states were strong enough to tax the trade heavily; in other areas a free market existed. But everywhere it was the Africans who controlled the volume of slaves and determined the type of slaves who would be offered. And it was they who determined the prices.

---

[19] See David Eltis and Lawrence C. Jennings, "Trade between Sub-Saharan Africa and the Atlantic World in the Pre-Colonial Era: A Comparative Overview" (unpublished paper, 1987); and Gemery, Hogendorn, and Johnson, "A Tentative Terms of Trade for Africa and England in the Eighteenth Century."

Some economists have even gone so far as to argue that the resulting market was open, with little effective monopoly activity over a long period of time even on the part of sellers.[20] Although this seems a more questionable proposition given the need for a strong military establishment to be able to capture or tax for slaves, it is possible that the existence of so many competing sources may have created some local free market conditions in terms of even suppliers of slaves in some of the more heavily exploited regions.

Although trading was profitable at the microlevel of the individual, group, or class doing the trading, the question remains of the societal costs of the trade. The slave raids against agriculturalists and subsequent abandonment of good croplands, the stress on defense or militaristic activity, and the draining of young adults from the labor force, all had their long-term economic costs. But for those engaging in the trade and for the vast majority of Africans who consumed the imported Asian and European goods, the trade was a profitable development.[21]

Another major area where Africans dominated the structure of the trade was in terms of the selection of persons offered for sale in the Atlantic market. As studies from all trades have shown, there was a consistent bias against women and children among the slaves offered for sale on the Atlantic coast. Women represented on average a third to a quarter of the Africans forced to migrate, and children represented on average less than 10 percent. Though there were fluctuations over time and space, in general it would appear that these figures were surprisingly consistent. To many researchers this suggested special American demand factors to explain this lack of random selection. Support for this view was found in the contemporary discussions, quite extensive in the eighteenth- and nineteenth-century literature, about the good or bad qualities of different African groups in terms of working habits. But just as the perception of European dominance has been challenged in terms of purchasing slaves and their cost, so too have recent studies questioned American demand factors

[20] Two attempts to provide a model for estimating the profits of the trade in relation to Africans are those by H. A. Gemery and J. S. Hogendorn, "The Atlantic Slave Trade: A Tentative Economic Model," *Journal of African History* 15 (1974): 223–46, and Robert Paul Thomas and Richard Nelson Bean, "The Fishers of Men: Profits of the Slave Trade," *Journal of Economic History* 34 (1974): 885–914.

[21] John Thornton, "The Slave Trade in Eighteenth Century Angola: Effects on Demographic Structures," *Canadian Journal of African Studies* 14 (1980): 417–27; and the two studies of Patrick Manning, "The Enslavement of Africans: A Demographic Model," ibid., 15 (1981): 499–526; and "The Impact of Slave Trade Exports on the Population of the Western Coast of Africa, 1700–1850," (paper presented at the Nantes Colloquium).

as the primary influence in determining the type of slaves transported.

Clearly the timing of the migration of these Africans and the places to which they were delivered were determined to a significant extent by American conditions. An American region, even with the credit universally supplied by all traders, could not enter the trade without a crop marketable in Europe. Equally, the actual movement of slaves across the Atlantic was seasonal in nature, owing both to prevailing currents and winds that influenced the crossing and to the seasonality of American demand considerations. Though the sailings from East Africa around the Cape of Good Hope were more dependent on local weather conditions, the West African routes seemed to respond to planters' harvesting needs in America.

If seasonality in the movement of slaves was influenced by American demand factors, the nationality, sex, and age of the slaves entering the transatlantic trade were primarily determined by African conditions. All studies show that except for the Portuguese in Angola and Mozambique, Europeans had little idea of the nature of the societies they were dealing with. In most cases Africans were simply designated by the ports from which they were shipped rather than by any truly generic language, group, or national identity. Most traders had no conception of what went on even a few miles inland from the coast, and even those who established forts and fixed settlements essentially dealt with only local governments. While Europeans fought among themselves to protect a special section of the West African coastline, interlopers from both other European and other African groups went out of their way to guarantee that no monopolies were created. Attempts by any one African group to monopolize local trade often led to the opening up by their competitors of new trading routes. Some American planters may have thought "Congolese" hardworking, and others thought them lazy, but it made little difference what they wanted. They got whatever group was then entering the market in Africa. A few American ports had close contact with a given region of Africa over a long period of time, the connection between Salvador in Bahia and the Bight of Benin being the best known. On a few occasions, such as the collapse of a large state or after a major military defeat, whole nations of well-defined and clearly delineated groups entered the slave trade and were known by their proper names in America. But these cases were the exception rather than the rule.

The sexual imbalance in the departing Africans was also more determined by African supply conditions than by American demand. Though there was a price differential between males and females in

America, this was insufficient to explain the low ratio of females in the slave trade.[22] Women performed almost all the same manual tasks as men on the plantations of America and in fact made up the majority of most field gangs in sugar, coffee, and cotton fields.[23] Nor did they experience any differences in mortality in the Atlantic crossing than men, which might have explained European reluctance to ship them. The answer appears to be that Africans simply presented far fewer women for sale in the coastal slave markets than they did men.

African women, both free and slave, were in high demand locally, and it was this counterdemand that explains why fewer women entered the Atlantic slave trade. In some African societies women were highly valued because they were the means of acquiring status, kinship, and family. One of the distinguishing features of West African societies was their emphasis on matrilineal and matrilocal kinship systems. Since even female slaves could be significant links in the kinship networks, their importance in the social system was enhanced. Also slave women were cheaper to acquire than free local women in polygynous societies and were therefore highly prized in societies that practiced this marriage arrangement. Even more important was the widespread West African practice of primarily using women in agricultural labor. For all of these reasons women had a higher price in local internal African markets than did men.[24]

Aside from the high incidence of males, the trade also exhibited a very low incidence of children. Although children suffered no higher mortality rates in crossing than any other group of slaves, their low sale prices and their costs of transportation (equal to adults) discouraged slave captains from purchasing them. Also it seems that children were more prized than adult males in the internal slave trade and may not have appeared on the coast in great numbers because of local supply considerations.

The demographic makeup of the Africans transported to America had a profound impact on both African and American labor market conditions. Clearly the high retention of women and children in Af-

---

[22] For a survey of American slave prices by sex see Manuel Moreno Fraginals, Herbert S. Klein, and Stanley L. Engerman, "Nineteenth Century Cuban Slave Prices in Comparative Perspective," *American Historical Review* 88 (1983): 1201–18.

[23] For nineteenth-century Jamaica see Barry W. Higman, *Slave Population and Economy in Jamaica, 1807–1834* (Cambridge, 1976), 161, 194, 197; for eighteenth-century Saint Domingue see Gabriel Debien, *Les esclaves aux Antilles françaises (xviie–xviiie siècles)* (Basse-Terre and Fort-de-France, 1974), chap. 8.

[24] Herbert S. Klein, "African Women in the Atlantic Slave Trade," in Claire Robinson and Martin A. Klein, eds., *Women and Slavery in Africa* (Madison, 1983), 29–38; and David W. Galenson, *Traders, Planters, and Slaves: Market Behavior in Early English America* (Cambridge, 1986), 105ff.

rica tended to reduce the long-term negative impact of the loss of so many young adults to the Atlantic trade. The retention of women guaranteed higher birthrates for the remaining cohorts than for those who left. Thus the overall population growth rate in Africa suffered less than it would have had this massive out-migration been more sexually balanced. But at the same time, the immediate impact on the African work force was negative because of the withdrawal of so many adult males of working age. This drain on active workers would have tended to increase the dependency ratios and decrease the productivity of the population as a whole, as fewer workers had to provide for more dependents.[25] There were also many negative consequences due to the internal traders carrying disease across epidemiological frontiers and thus often causing epidemics in previously protected populations. At the same time the high incidence of the use of force in the trade tended to significantly influence settlement patterns in western Africa. Thus much fertile but unprotected and open farmland was abandoned by peasant populations unable to defend themselves from slave raiders. This in turn must have had a long-term negative impact on regional economic growth. Given the poor quality of precolonial African population and economic statistics, it is difficult to fully evaluate all of these factors, though recently a number of imaginative reconstructions have been carried out.[26]

As much as the new scholarship has concerned itself with the economic impact of the trade for the Africans, equally pervasive have been the new debates about the overall economic benefits of the slave trade to the Europeans themselves. These debates began with Eric Williams and have continued on into the most current journal articles.[27] The discussion can be divided into two general questions. Was the slave trade profitable at the firm level and were these profits ex-

---

[25] One estimate on the productivity lost because of the workers forced to leave Africa in the eighteenth century finds it equal to, if not greater than, the gains made by Africans from the sale of slaves (Henry A. Gemery and Jan S. Hogendorn, "The Economic Costs of West African Participation in the Atlantic Slave Trade: A Preliminary Sampling of the Eighteenth Century," in H. A. Gemery and J. S. Hogendorn, *The Uncommon Market: Essays in the Economic History of the Atlantic Slave Trade* [New York, 1979], 143–61).

[26] A useful set of papers on this topic by Joseph Inikori (pp. 283–314), Patrick Manning (pp. 371–84), and John Thornton (pp. 691–720) is found in Christopher Fyfe and David McMaster, eds., *African Historical Demography, II* (Edinburgh, 1981). Also see the interesting computer simulations of population loss and models of regional settlements and abandoned villages in the recent work of Manning, "Enslavement of Africans"; and his essay "The Impact of Slave Exports on the Population of the Western Coast of Africa, 1700–1850" (paper presented at the Nantes Colloquium).

[27] Eric Williams, *Capitalism and Slavery* (Chapel Hill, 1944).

cessive; and what impact did the slave trade and its profits have on the economic growth of Europe?

From the work of the European economic historians, it is now evident that slave trade profits were not extraordinary by European standards. The average 10 percent rate obtained in studies of the eighteenth-century French and English slave traders was considered a good profit rate at the time but not out of the range of other contemporary investments.[28] From a recent detailed study of the nineteenth century, it would seem that profits doubled in the next century largely as a result of rising slave prices in America, which in turn were due to the increasing suppression of the trade by the British navy. On average (except for some extraordinary voyages to Cuba in the 1850s), the rate of profit for nineteenth-century slavers was just under 20 percent.[29] Thus, while profits in the special period of suppression in the nineteenth century were quite high, even these profits were not astronomic.[30]

But if presuppression trading profits were not extraordinary, was the trade an open one or a restricted one that created concentrated oligopolistic profits that could then possibly serve as a fundamental source for capital investments in the European economy? It has been suggested that high initial costs of entrance plus the long time period needed to fully recover profits (up to five years on some slaving voyages) meant that only highly capitalized firms could enter the trade. Most merchants spread their costs around by offering stock in slaving voyages and otherwise trying to insure themselves from catastrophic loss on one or more lost voyages. But the costs of entrance, the experience of contacts, and the international nature of the complex negotiations suggest that there were limits on the number of merchants who could enter the trade. Although this specialization seems to have taken place (and there are cases of quite major houses operating in

---

[28] Anstey, *Atlantic Slave Trade,* chap. 2; David Richardson, "The Profits in the Liverpool Slave Trade: The Accounts of William Davenport, 1757–1784," in R. Anstey and P. E. H. Hair, eds., *Liverpool; the African Slave Trade and Abolition* (Liverpool, 1976); Stein, *French Slave Trade,* 137ff.; Meyer, *L'armement nantais,* 204ff.

[29] Eltis, *Economic Growth and the Ending of the Transatlantic Slave Trades,* appendix E.

[30] One of the most difficult problems related to profits was the long-term payoff in the trade. A very high percentage of all sales in America were for credit, and though a markup on the price occurred, the long repayment period and the resulting discounting of notes and failed installment payments reduced profits or drew out the completion of a sale for two to three years. On the selling of slaves, the best single study is Galenson, *Traders, Planters, and Slaves;* and for an interesting document of price differentials on credit sales see António Carreira, *O tráfico portugues de escravos na costa oriental africana nos começos do século xix* (Lisbon, 1979), 40ff.

both England and France),[31] it is also impressive just how many independent merchants participated in the trade and how many ships were outfitted for the trade in any given year.[32]

This debate on the relative rates of merchant participation and control has generated a lively analytical literature.[33] In this debate, however, no current scholars have been able to show that the gains from the trade were directly invested in the earliest industrial enterprises of Great Britain. All the studies of the sources of industrial capital in England suggest local origins from agriculture or European commerce or both.[34] Nevertheless, the Williams thesis has come in for some support on the question of Africa as a market for European manufactures, especially of the more basic sort. It has been suggested that the French armaments industry was completely dependent on the African trade (which was paid for by slave exports) during times of European peace. Several other industries on the Continent and in England can also be shown to have been highly dependent on the African market. Because much of early industrial activity involved production of crude and popularly consumed products, it has been argued that the African market played a vital part in sustaining the growth of some of Europe's newest infant industries.[35] This part of the trade has yet to be fully studied, but recent work does suggest a need to reevaluate the role of European exports to Africa in this crucial period of the early Industrial Revolution.

A subtheme of this debate about the use of slave trade profits has

---

[31] See, e.g., the studies on the house of Walsh by Jean Suret-Canale, "De la traite négriere a l'aristocratie foncière: Les Walsh-Serrant" (paper presented at the Nantes Colloquium); Gomer Williams, *A History of the Liverpool Privateers . . . with an Account of the Liverpool Slave Trade* (London, 1897); Richardson's study on Davenport ("Profits in the Liverpool Slave Trade"); and James Rawley, "Humphry Morice: Foremost London Slave Merchant of His Time" (paper presented at the Nantes Colloquium).

[32] Thus, e.g., to move the estimated 90,000 slaves per annum in the 1780s (the highest decadal figure of the trade) required the use in any year of between 180 and 360 ships, assuming a 2.5 slaves per ton average and ships ranging from 100 to 200 tons.

[33] See Joseph E. Inikori, "Market Structure and the Profits of the British African Trade in the late Eighteenth Century," *Journal of Economic History* 41 (1981): 745–76. A critique of this position is found in two articles by B. L. Anderson and David Richardson, "Market Structure and Profits of the British African Slave Trade in the Late Eighteenth Century," *Journal of Economic History* 43 (1983), and ibid. 45 (1985).

[34] Stanley L. Engerman, "The Slave Trade and British Capital Formation in the Eighteenth Century: A Comment on the Williams Thesis," *Business History Review* 46 (1972): 430–43.

[35] Pierre H. Boulle, "Slave Trade, Commercial Organization, and Industrial Growth in Eighteenth Century Nantes," *Revue Française d'Histoire de Outre-Mer* 59, no. 214 (1972): 70–112; and idem, "Marchandises de traite et développement industriel dans la France et l'Angleterre du XVIIIe siècle."

only just been suggested in the literature. This concerns the role of profit for American merchant participants in the trade: the West Indians, the North Americans (above all, the New Englanders), and especially the Brazilians. In terms of volume and capital generated, there is little question that few regions compare to those of Bahia, Rio de Janeiro, and Rhode Island. The number of ships provisioned for the African trade in these areas suggests a major growth of local capital. Who these merchants were and what their relationship was to both the plantation economy and the new industrial mills are still to be determined.[36]

In terms of the larger patterns of Europe's international trade, the role of the Atlantic slave trade can be analyzed with a bit more precision. In general, in terms of volume of shipping and relative exports, the trade absorbed at most a fifth of any major European nation's ships or resources. Among the French, for example, exports to Africa amounted to 25 percent of total exports to the colonies in the 1770s and 20 percent in the 1780s.[37] They took up 15 percent of the ships and 13 percent of the tonnage devoted to these trades in 1788.[38] If all foreign trade were included, the relative importance of the trade to Africa would drop by over half, though it would still represent a substantial 10 percent of the value of all French intracontinental and overseas foreign trade.[39]

Among the British the same general pattern held true. We know, for example, that British exports and re-exports to Africa averaged around 4.5 percent of total British exports in the last quarter of the eighteenth century.[40] In terms of the number of ships employed, the African trade was even more important. Thus at the height of its slave trade, Bristol slavers accounted for 14 percent of all ships cleared from that port, whereas a third of the Liverpool ships clearing port were

[36] The best study to date is that of Coughtry, *Notorious Triangle.* Nothing comparable yet exists for Brazil, though there are some suggestive ideas given in Luiz Felipe de Alencastro, "Le commerce des vivants: Traite d'esclaves et 'Pax Luistana' dans l'Atlantique sud" (doctoral thesis, University of Paris X, 1986).

[37] Tarrade, *Commerce colonial,* 2:740.

[38] Ibid., 1:654.

[39] An estimate for all French Foreign Trade in the 1770s is given by Paul Butel, "French Foreign Trade from 1359 to 1750" (paper presented at the Minnesota Conference on "The Rise of Merchant Empires," October 1987), 38 (Editor's note: Professor Butel has not included this table in the revision of his paper published in Chapter 4, but cf. his Table 4.2). It should be stressed that when the African trade is combined with that of the French West Indian trade, they together form a very substantial 42 percent of the total trade figure.

[40] Phyllis Deane and W. A. Cole, *British Economic Growth, 1688–1959* (Cambridge, 1967), 87.

slavers in the 1770s.[41] Finally, from contemporary figures provided by Bryan Edwards it would appear that slaves represented just under a fourth of the value of all persons and goods imported into the British West Indies.[42]

In the case of Brazil the value of slave imports did not differ that much from the British West Indies. In the period from 1796 to 1808 slaves represented between 23 and 33 percent of the value of all imports into the colony.[43] Although the trade was a crucial component of Brazilian imports as it had been in the West Indies, it played a much lesser role in the trade accounts of Portugal itself because of the Brazilian control over a large percentage of the carrying trade.

To make a definitive judgment of the relative weight of the Atlantic slave trade in the total picture of Europe's overseas trade would require a full estimation of the value of slave imports, slave-produced colonial exports, and European consumption and re-exportation of these slave-generated products. This is a difficult set of calculations. The few attempts to undertake such an estimate have led to lively debate among scholars of the West Indian economy but have resulted in no definitive conclusions.[44] Though there is considerable debate about the meaning of the numbers and which estimates to accept or reject, both major authors in this debate agree that the profits of the slave trade are rather a small part – less than 10 percent – of the entire wealth generated from Britain's possession of its American sugar colonies.[45] Furthermore, a recent attempt to estimate the impact of Great Britain's relations with the non-European world and its influence on British capital formation has suggested (again, with some controversy) that only 15 percent of Britain's gross investment capital ex-

[41] Walter Minchinton, "The British Slave Fleet, 1680–1775: The Evidence of the Naval Office Shipping Lists" (paper presented at the Nantes Colloquium).

[42] Edwards gives an estimate of 21,023 slaves imported into the British West Indies in 1787 and estimates the value of all goods imported into the islands at £3.1 million, excluding the African slaves. If one uses an average price of £35 per slave (taken from estimates of slave values in Richard Sheridan, "The Wealth of Jamaica in the Eighteenth Century," *Economic History Review*, 2d ser., 18 [1965]: 303), the relative importance of slaves runs from 19 to 24 percent of the value of all goods, including slaves, entering the islands in 1787 (Bryan Edwards, *The History, Civil and Commercial, of the British West Indies*, 2 vols. [London, 1793], 2:55, 365).

[43] See Klein, *Middle Passage*, 62–3, for the details of these calculations. During the height of the European trade crisis of the Napoleonic wars in 1807, the value of slave imports jumped to 64 percent.

[44] See Sheridan, "The Wealth of Jamaica in the Eighteenth Century," 292–311; R. P. Thomas, "The Sugar Colonies of the Old Empire: Profit or Loss for Great Britain?" *Economic History Review*, 2d ser., 21 (1968): 30–45; and P. R. Coelho, "The Profitability of Imperialism: British Experience in the West Indies, 1768–1772," *Explorations in Economic History* 10 (1973): 253–80.

[45] Thomas, "Sugar Colonies," 36.

penditures during its Industrial Revolution could have come from the profits on all Great Britain's overseas trades, including that of the Atlantic slave trade.[46]

Though clearly the slave trade was in all respects a profitable and important trade, it evidently was not the single largest capital-generating trade of the Europeans even within the context of their American empires. Even if the part of the Asian trade that went to Africa is added to these calculations, along with the value from slave-produced American goods, the figures are still not a significant addition to potential European savings available for investment in the Industrial Revolution, nor do they match the figures for the most economically profitable of Europe's overseas trades, at least according to recent macroeconomic calculations of the New Economic Historians. If these estimations hold up under critical review, they will be a significant challenge to an important element in the Eric Williams thesis on the importance of the slave trade and American slavery in providing the capital savings for the Industrial Revolution in England.

The Atlantic slave trade was unique in the product it transported and in its impact on labor market conditions on several continents. In this last section of this essay, I would like to examine these two issues: the economics of shipping slaves and the impact that the demographic characteristics of the transported slaves had on the makeup of the American and African labor markets.

The conceptions prevalent in the popular literature about the relative costs of African slaves have their corollary hypotheses about the economics of their transportation. It was assumed that the low cost of the slaves made it profitable to pack in as many as the ship could hold without sinking and then accept high rates of mortality during the Atlantic crossing. If any slaves delivered alive were pure profit, than even the loss of several hundred would have made economic sense. But if the slaves were not a costless or cheap item to purchase, then the corresponding argument about "tight packing" also makes little sense. In fact, high losses on the crossing resulted in financial loss on the trip, as many ship accounts aptly prove.[47]

Even more convincing than these theoretical arguments against

---

[46] See Patrick O'Brien, "European Economic Development: The Contribution of the Periphery," *Economic History Review*, 2d ser. 35 (1982): 1–18. This conclusion is in sharp contrast to the recent restatement of the Williams hypothesis by Joseph E. Inikori, "Slavery and the Development of Industrial Capitalism in England," *Journal of Interdisciplinary History* 17 (1987): 771–93.

[47] Robert Stein estimated that "the death of each slave on a 300-slave expedition theoretically cut profits by .67 percent, and the average mortality rate of 10 to 15% reduced gains by 20 to 30 percent" (*French Slave Trade*, 141–2).

reckless destruction of life is the fact that no study has yet shown a systematic correlation of any significance between the numbers of slaves carried and mortality at sea. Thousands of ship crossings have now been statistically analyzed, and none show a correlation of any significance between either tonnage or space available and mortality.[48]

This does not mean that slaves were traveling in luxury. In fact, they had less room than did contemporary troops or convicts being transported. It simply means that after much experience and the exigencies of the trade, slavers only took on as many slaves as they could expect to cross the Atlantic safely. From scattered references in the pre-1700 period it seems that provisioning and carrying arrangements were initially deficient. But all post-1700 trade studies show that slavers carried water and provisions for double their expected voyage times and that in most trades they usually carried slightly fewer slaves than their legally permitted limits.

This increasing sophistication in the carrying of slaves was reflected in declining rates of mortality. In the pre-1700 trade, mean mortality rates over many voyages tended to hover around 20 percent. In turn this mean rate reflected quite wide variations, with many ships coming in with very low rates and an equally large number experiencing rates of double or more than double the mean figure. But in the post-1700 period the mean rates dropped, and the variation around the mean declined. By midcentury the mean stood at about 10 percent, and by the last quarter of the century all trades were averaging a rate of about 5 percent. Moreover the dispersion around these mean rates had declined, and two-thirds of the ships were experiencing no more than 5 percent variation above or below the mean rate.

These declines in mortality were due to the standardization increasingly adopted in the trade. First of all there developed a specialized and specifically constructed vessel used in the slave trade of most nations. By the second half of the eighteenth century slave ships were averaging two hundred tons among all European traders, a tonnage that seemed best to fit the successful carrying potential of the trade. Slave traders were also the first of the commercial traders to adopt copper sheathing for their ships, which was a costly new method to prolong the life of the vessels and guarantee greater speed. It should be stressed that these slave trade vessels were much smaller ships than Europeans used in either the West Indian or East Indian trades. This in turn goes a long way to explaining why the famous model of

---

[48] For the most recent survey of this question see Charles Garland and Herbert S. Klein, "The Allotment of Space for African Slavers Aboard Eighteenth Century British Slave Ships," *William and Mary Quarterly* 42 (1985): 238–48.

a triangular trade, long the staple of western textbooks, is largely a myth. This myth was based on the idea that the slave ships performed the multiple tasks of taking European goods to Africa, transporting slaves to America, and then bringing back the sugar or other slave-produced American staple for Europe all on the same voyage. In fact, the majority of American crops reached European markets in much larger and specially constructed West Indian vessels designed primarily for this shuttle trade; the majority of slavers returned to Europe with small cargoes or none at all; and in the largest slave trade of them all – that of Brazil – no slavers either departed from or returned to Europe.

All traders carried about two and a half slaves per ton, and although there was some variation in crew size and ratios, all slave trade ships carried at least twice the number of seamen needed to man the vessel, and thus double or more than that of any other long-distance oceanic trade. This very high ratio of sailors to tonnage was due to the security needs of controlling the slave prisoners. All the European slave traders were also using the same provisioning, health, and transportation procedures. They built temporary decks to house the slaves and divided them by age and sex. Almost all Europeans adopted smallpox vaccinations at about the same time, all carried large quantities of African provisions to feed the slaves, and all used the same methods for daily hygiene, care of the sick, and so on. This standardization explains the common experience of mortality decline, and it also goes a long way to rejecting contemporaneous assertions that any particular European trader was "better" or more efficient than any other.[49]

Although these firmly grounded statistics on mortality certainly destroy many of the older beliefs about "astronomic" mortality and tight packing, there does remain the question of whether a 5 percent mortality rate for a thirty- to fifty-day voyage for a healthy young adult is high or low. If such a mortality rate had occurred among young adult peasants in eighteenth-century France, it would be considered an epidemic rate. Thus, although Europeans succeeded in reducing the rate to seemingly low percentages, these rates still represented extraordinary high death rate figures for such a specially selected population. Equally, although troop, immigrant, and convict mortality rates in the eighteenth century approached the slave death numbers, in the nineteenth century they consistently fell to below 1 percent for transatlan-

[49] For a detailed discussion of these questions see Klein, *Middle Passage*, chap. 4, 7, and 8.

tic voyages. For slaves, however, these rates never fell below 5 percent for any large group of vessels surveyed. There thus seems to have been a minimum death rate caused by the close quarters during transport, which the Europeans could never reduce.[50]

Death in the crossing was due to a variety of causes. The biggest killers were gastrointestinal disorders, which were often related to the quality of food and water available on the trip, and fevers. Bouts of dysentery were common and the "bloody flux" as it was called could break out in epidemic proportions. The increasing exposure of the slaves to dysentery increased both the rates of contamination of supplies and the incidence of death. It was dysentery that accounted for the majority of deaths and was the most common disease experienced on all voyages. The astronomic rates of mortality reached on occasional voyages were due to outbreaks of smallpox, measles, or other highly communicable diseases that were not related to time at sea or the conditions of food and water supply, hygiene, and sanitation practices. It was this randomness of epidemic diseases that prevented even experienced and efficient captains from eliminating very high mortality rates on any given voyage.

Although time at sea was not usually correlated with mortality, there were some routes in which time was a factor. Simply because they were a third longer than any other routes, the East African slave trades that developed in the late eighteenth and nineteenth centuries were noted for overall higher mortality than the West African routes, even though mortality per day at sea was the same or lower than on the shorter routes. Also, just the transporting together of slaves from different epidemiological zones in Africa guaranteed the transmission of a host of local endemic diseases to all those who were aboard. In turn, this guaranteed the spread of all major African diseases to America.[51]

Along with the impact of African diseases on the American populations, the biases in the age and sex of the migrating Africans also had a direct impact on the growth and decline of the American slave populations. The low ratio of women in each arriving ship, the fact that most of these slave women were mature adults who had already

---

[50] This may explain the recent findings from some ninety-two selected voyages in the 1790s showing a correlation between "crowding" and mortality due to gastrointestinal diseases (Richard H. Steckel and Richard A. Jensen, "New Evidence on the Causes of Slave and Crew Mortality in the Atlantic Slave Trade," *Journal of Economic History* 46 [1986]:58–78).

[51] See, e.g., Kenneth F. Kiple and Virginia H. King, *Another Dimension to the Black Diaspora: Diet, Disease, and Racism* (Cambridge, 1981); Kiple, *The Caribbean Slave: A Biological History* (Cambridge, 1984); and Frantz Tardo-Dino, *Le collier de servitude: La condition sanitaire des esclaves aux Antilles françaises du XVIIe au XIXe siècle* (Paris, 1985).

spent several of their fecund years in Africa, and the fact that few children were carried to America were of fundamental importance in the subsequent history of population growth. It meant that the African slaves who arrived in America could not reproduce themselves. The African women who did come to America had lost some potential reproductive years and were even less able to reproduce the total numbers of males and females in the original immigrant cohort, let alone create a generation greater than the total number who arrived from Africa. Even those American regions that experienced a heavy and constant stream of African slaves still had to rely on importation of more slaves to maintain their slave populations, let alone increase their size. Once that African migration stopped, however, it was possible for the slave populations to begin to increase through natural growth, so long as there was no heavy out-migration through emancipation.

It was this consistent negative growth of the first generation of African slaves which explains the growing intensity of the slave trade to America in the eighteenth and early nineteenth centuries. As the demand for American products grew in European markets because of the increasingly popular consumption of tobacco, cotton, coffee, and above all sugar, the need for workers increased and this could be met only by bringing in more Africans. It was only in the case of the United States that the growth of plantation crop exports to Europe did not lead to an increasing importation of African slaves. This was largely due to the very early North American experience of the local slave population achieving a positive growth rate and thus supplying its increasing labor needs from the positive growth of its native-born slave population.[52] Although most demographic historians have shown that

---

[52] There is a major debate about the relative impact of "treatment" of slaves and the causes for the extraordinary growth rates achieved earliest by the slaves in the United States. Although the relative marginality of North American exports to European markets prior to 1800 explains the low volume of migration of African slaves and the consequent earlier domination of native-born slaves in the work force, the ultimate population explosion can be explained only by more complex demographic variables. Since the period of potential fertility of slave women in all America has been found to be approximately the same, and since the length of fertility is directly related to differing health conditions, food supplies, and work experience, the fact that there was no difference leads to a rejection of the argument for better treatment. Recent scholars have argued that the primary difference is to be explained by shorter periods of lactation, with the U.S. slaves adopting the northern European practice of breast-feeding children for only one year, while the slaves of the rest of the Americas maintained traditional African practices of on-demand breast-feeding for two years. The contraceptive affects of breast-feeding in turn explain the longer child spacing of the non-U.S. slaves and thus their lower reproduction rates (Herbert S. Klein and Stanley L. Engerman, "Fertility Differentials between Slaves in the United

the creole slave populations had positive growth rates from the beginning and that it was the distortions of the African-born cohorts that explain overall decline, more traditional historians have tried to explain the increasing demand for slaves as due to the low life expectancy of the Afro-American slave population. Much cited is the contemporary belief found in the planter literature of most colonies that the Afro-American slave experienced an average working life of "seven years." This myth of a short-lived labor force was related to the observed reality of slave population decline under the impact of heavy immigration of African slaves. Observers did not recognize the age and sexual imbalance of these Africans as a causal factor for the negative population growth of the slave labor force. Rather, they saw this decline as related to a very high mortality and a low life expectancy. Yet all recent studies suggest both a positive rate of population growth among native-born slaves and a life expectancy well beyond the so-called average seven working years in all American societies.[53]

The average life expectancy of slave males was in the upper twenties in Brazil, for example, and in the midthirties for the United States, which might suggest an average working life of at least twenty years in Brazil and twenty-five years in the United States. But this average figure, of course, takes into account the very high infant mortality rates. For those slaves who survived the first five years of life – and these are the only ones we are concerned with here – the comparable life expectancies was in the midthirties for the Brazilians and lower forties for the U.S. slaves. This suggests that the average working life was, at a minimum, twenty-five years for Brazilian slaves and thirty years for the U.S. ones – both figures far from the supposed seven-year average postulated in most histories.[54]

A final aspect of the trade worth considering is the debate about its abolition. Though having most of its impact in the early nineteenth

States and the British West Indies: A Note on Lactation Practices and Their Implications," *William and Mary Quarterly* 35 [1978]: 357–74).

[53] See Jack E. Eblen, "On the Natural Increase of Slave Populations: The Example of the Cuban Black Population, 1775–1900," in Stanley R. Engerman and Eugene D. Genovese, *Race and Slavery in the Western Hemisphere: Quantitative Studies* (Princeton, 1975), 211–47; and Barry W. Higman, *Slave Populations of the British Caribbean, 1807–1834* (Baltimore, 1984).

[54] At first glance the difference in life expectancies might appear to support the argument for the "better treatment" of U.S. slaves. But in fact, it appears that the same difference in life expectancies could be found among free coloreds and whites in all American societies. That is, white Brazilians lived comparatively shorter lives than white North Americans. Thus it was the general differences in overall health conditions that explain the differences in life expectancies and not special treatment afforded slaves.

century, the abolitionist movement began in the last quarter of the eighteenth century, and in both its causes and consequences it would have a profound economic impact on American, African, and European trade. A major literature has appeared that has tried to examine the economic background to abolition as well as its economic impact. It is well known that the campaign to abolish the Atlantic slave trade, which began in the last quarter of the eighteenth century, is considered to have been the first peaceful mass political movement based on modern political propaganda in English history, if not for Europe as a whole. The traditional literature viewed this campaign as a moral crusade that was successful at the economic cost of profits and trade.[55] Once having abolished this trade to the English colonies in 1808, the British then attempted to force all the other major European slaving countries to desist from the trade. This campaign in turn was a costly one in terms of lost trade, alienation of traditional allies, and the very high costs of naval blockade.[56]

Though English statesmen and writers portrayed their campaign as a moral one from the beginning, there was a large contemporary literature attacking their motives. Cubans, Spaniards, and Brazilians, the objects of most of the post-1808 attacks by the British abolitionists, argued that the nineteenth-century campaign was motivated by fears of competition, especially after the abolition of slavery in 1834, when sugar became a free labor crop in the British West Indies. Later historians went even further and argued that the British West Indies plantations by the last quarter of the eighteenth century were in decline, and that it was economic motivation which explained the wellsprings of the British abolition campaign against the foreign slave traders, because the British West Indian plantations could not compete with the French, Spanish, and Brazilian ones.[57]

In contrast to this economic causal model, recent scholars have argued that the late eighteenth- and early nineteenth-century economy of the British West Indies was in fact a thriving one. Even after aboli-

[55] The standard works include F. J. Klingberg, *The Anti-Slavery Movement in England* (New Haven, 1926); and R. Coupland, *The British Anti-Slavery Movement* (London, 1933).

[56] Phillip LeVeen, *British Slave Trade Suppression Policies, 1821–1865* (New York, 1977), examines the economic costs of this effort. For detailed recent analyses of the complex maneuverings of the Brazilian and Spanish governments to defend their trades see David R. Murray, *Odious Commerce: Britain, Spain, and the Abolition of the Cuban Slave Trade* (Cambridge, 1980); Arturo Morales Carrión, *Auge y decadencia de la trata negrera en Puerto Rico (1820–1860)* (Rio Piedras, 1978); and Leslie Bethell, *The Abolition of the Brazilian Slave Trade* (Cambridge, 1970).

[57] L. J. Ragatz, *The Fall of the Planter Class in the British Caribbean, 1763–1833* (New York, 1928).

tion of the trade, the older and newer islands were competitive on the European market, and it was only slave emancipation itself that sent a shock wave through the local economy. Though the campaign for abolition is no longer seen as simply a great moral crusade by any major group of scholars, the economic determinism argument of Williams and his supporters is being challenged.[58]

It should also be stressed that many of the issues that I have presented in this preliminary essay are far from resolved in one way or another. A lively industry has developed critiquing even the numbers provided by Curtin.[59] Nevertheless enough of the basic economic structure of the trade is known to disprove many of the long-held assumptions about the trade. There are, of course, numerous areas that still need to be explored. Little is known about the economics of the Brazilian trade or about the patterns of investment of slave trade profits. Long time series of trade accounts, on the order of those developed by a Marion Johnson, must also be constructed for the other slave trades. Finally more work must be done on placing the slave trade in the context of all trades and alternative investments in the eighteenth century to be able to prove or disprove the famous Williams thesis. But whatever the current state of the debate, or the degree to which any particular argument may be considered closed, it is obvious that our understanding of the scale, importance, and impact of the Atlantic slave trade has been profoundly changed by the recent massive research effort that has taken place in the past twenty-five years.[60]

---

[58] See Anstey, *Atlantic Slave Trade;* the two works by Seymour Drescher, *Econocide: British Slavery in the Era of Abolition* (Pittsburgh, 1977) and *Capitalism and Anti-Slavery* (New York, 1986); and David B. Davis, *Slavery and Human Progress* (New York, 1984). The most complete restatement and reanalysis of this aspect of the problem is contained in the new work of David Eltis, *Economic Growth and the Ending of the Transatlantic Slave Trade* (New York, 1987).

[59] Much of this new literature is summarized in Paul E. Lovejoy, "The Volume of the Atlantic Slave Trade: A Synthesis," *Journal of African History* 23 (1982): 473–501; and in David Eltis, "The Nineteenth Century Transatlantic Slave Trade: An Annual Time Series of Imports into the Americas Broken Down by Region," *Hispanic American Historical Review* 67 (1987): 109–38.

[60] Though no definitive study has yet appeared covering all of these topics, recent surveys of the trade have finally begun to incorporate much of this new research. See Hubert Deschamps, *Histoire de la traite des noirs* (Paris, 1971); Pierre Pluchon, *La route des esclaves, négriers et bois d'ébène au xviiie siècle* (Paris, 1981); James A. Rawley, *The Trans-Atlantic Slave Trade* (New York, 1981); and Françoise Renault and Serge Daget, *Les traites négrières en Afrique* (Paris, 1985).

CHAPTER 10

Marginalization, stagnation, and growth: the trans-Saharan caravan trade in the era of European expansion, 1500–1900

RALPH A. AUSTEN

OF the two great Afro-Asiatic caravan systems that were the targets of Renaissance European maritime ventures, the trans-Saharan route appeared to be both less commercially significant and more vulnerable to competition from the sea. The most important commodities that the desert route brought to the Mediterranean, gold and slaves, both derived from regions in West Africa not too far from the Atlantic Ocean. Once Europeans established direct maritime contact with the Guinea coast, it appeared that neither the Saharan caravans nor the Sudanic empires built up around the entrepôts between desert and forest would survive in anything but very attenuated form.

Many of the major developments after 1500 both within North and West Africa and in their external relations seemed to confirm just such an outcome. Gold and slaves were exported via the Atlantic in quantities that seemed to leave little over for northern trade routes. In an effort to regain control of West African gold sources at the end of the sixteenth century, the Moroccan sultan Ahmad al-Mansūr dispatched a military expedition across the desert; the only lasting result was the destruction of Songhai, the last of the great medieval Sudanic empires, leaving political chaos and economic hardship in its place. The focus of West African state building and commerce now seemed to shift to the Guinea forest around such centers as Asante, Benin, Oyo, and Dahomey, while the Sudan reasserted itself only in the apparent

I want to thank the following colleagues for their comments on this essay: Stefano Feneoaltea, Jan Hogendorn, and the late Marion Johnson.

desperation of Islamic religious revivals. On top of all this, the Saharan caravan system still functioned, although reduced, scholars asserted, to "but a fraction of its former volume."[1]

More recent historiography, without denying either the technological stagnation of trans-Saharan trade nor the irreversible fall of its position within the world economy, suggests that the absolute quantity of goods passing annually across the desert was actually greater in the eighteenth and nineteenth centuries than in the pre-European era. Moreover in this same period the Sudanic region of West Africa also appears to have experienced a more dynamic and particularly a more integrated growth pattern than the neighboring Guinea forest zone.[2]

What do these new findings tell us about the relationship between transport costs and economic development in the early modern world economy? One hypothesis might be that as in the Europe-centered economies discussed by Russell Menard, transport costs were much less important than other factors in determining growth patterns.[3] It is also possible to see some cases of stagnant transport development (i.e., "natural protection") as promoting autonomous growth in otherwise disadvantaged regions of international trading systems. Finally, we may still find evidence of development within Saharan transport reflecting in some way the more obvious economic dynamism of at least its southern trading partners.

Despite the elegant proofs presented in Menard's paper, no student of the African past will find it easy to minimize the significance of transport for economic change. The very pattern of Africa's unique development within the Old World depends to a great extent upon the barriers to easy transport presented by such factors as the desiccation of the Sahara, the disrupted flow of the continent's great riv-

---

[1] E. Adu Boahen, "The Caravan Trade in the Nineteenth Century," *Journal of African History* 3 (1962): 349–59; for the classic general account of this decline, see E. W. Bovill, *The Golden Trade of the Moors* (London, 1968).

[2] On the Sahara, the key revisionist works are C. W. Newbury, "North African and Western Sudan Trade in the Nineteenth Century: a Re-evaluation," *Journal of African History* 7 (1966): 233–46; Marion Johnson, "Calico Caravans: The Tripoli–Kano Trade after 1880," *Journal of African History* 17 (1976): 95–117; Ralph A. Austen, "The Trans-Saharan Slave Trade: A Tentative Census," in H. Gemery and J. Hogendorn, *The Uncommon Market: Essays in the Economic History of the Atlantic Slave Trade* (New York, 1979), 23–76; Stephen Baier, *An Economic History of Central Niger* (Oxford, 1980). For more detail on Sudanic economic history and historiography see Ralph A. Austen, *African Economic History* (London, 1987), 31–55.

[3] Russell R. Menard, "Transport Costs and Long-Range Trade: Was There a European 'Transport Revolution' in the Early Modern Era?" in *The Political Economy of Merchant Empires* (New York, forthcoming). In the conference at which it was originally delivered, this essay functioned as a specific response to Menard's argument.

ers, tropical disease ecology, and the relative absence of large indentations in its oceanic coastline. Moreover, in every instance when new transport technology breached these obstacles, as with the introduction of camels into the Sahara, the opening of South Atlantic sailing routes, and the mechanized rail and road vehicles of the twentieth century, major market expansion has followed. For African economic historians, the prevailing argument is perhaps the reverse of that among Europeanists such as Michael Postan: efficiency in the production of goods has tended to lag far behind – indeed, resist linkage to – the cost effects of transport innovations.[4]

If transport is therefore critical to African economic development, the persistence and growth of trans-Saharan trade after 1500 must be understood primarily in terms of the two alternative hypotheses presented above: that the Saharan–Sudan zone benefited from the protection of continuing transport barriers between itself and the Atlantic Ocean and that somewhere in this interregional economy there may be transport innovations not evident in the simple examination of technology and commercial organization. The main body of this paper will deal with these hypotheses, although I will return to the Postan–Menard argument in the conclusion.

CARAVAN AND OCEAN: COMPETITION VERSUS NATURAL PROTECTION

Trans-Saharan commerce in the postmedieval/precolonial era operated simultaneously under the shadow of a European-dominated world economy and within its own closed inland enclave. Wherever the caravans competed directly with European shipping, they lost out and found their trading position considerably diminished. However, in trade between North Africa and the Sudan, caravan enterprise benefited from the fact that the alternative was not maritime transport but rather overland carriage through the West African forest. The absence of navigable waterways between the Sudan and the Guinea coast and the presence in the forest of disease parasites fatal to pack animals meant that goods had to be conveyed by very expensive human porterage.

The comparative cost factors of camels and ships are shown in Ta-

---

[4] This argument, including the very critical retarding role of factors outside transport, is developed throughout Austen, *African Economic History* (see particularly pp. 122–46); for Postan's views (the basis for Menard's general argument) see his "The Trade of Medieval Europe: The North," in M. Postan and E. E. Rich, eds., *The Cambridge Economic History of Europe*, vol. 2, *Trade and Industry in the Middle Ages* (Cambridge, 1952).

ble 10.1. The inferences from these data are confirmed by the experience of a Muslim merchant facing the two alternatives in about 1905 who calculated "that his 40 camel loads had cost £240 by sea as against £400 by desert."[5] On a broader historical scale, the shipping advantage is reflected in the total value of goods carried from West Africa during the nineteenth century (the only period for which we have comparable figures) by sea and by land (see Table 10.2). There are no quantitative data of even this level of reliability for comparing the scale of the trans-Saharan trade before 1500 with that of the eighteenth and nineteenth centuries. However, we can assume that the commerce in the latter period was probably larger than in the former from three sets of data: first, the accounts of the size and frequency of caravans in both periods (see Table 10.6); second, the changes, however loosely measured, in movements of similar commodities from the sixteenth through the nineteenth centuries; and last, the addition of new export commodities to the caravan system after 1500, particularly in the nineteenth century.

The examination of trade goods both leaving and entering West Africa after the arrival of European seagoing merchants not only tells us about the effect of maritime competition upon caravan trade but also reveals something of the relationship between transport and other factors in determining the nature of such trade. The following discussion will deal with two commodities that did shift significantly from desert to oceanic routes (gold exports and cowrie shell imports), two items continuing and even increasing as caravan cargoes (slave exports and cotton cloth imports), and a variety of items (gum, hides, ivory, and ostrich feathers) that emerged as newly significant Sudanic exports.

Gold

For the medieval world economy gold was clearly the most important product to come out of West Africa, and its diversion from desert to oceanic routes marked a critical decline in the international significance of Saharan trade (Table 10.3). By the fifteenth century the main source of West African gold lay in the middle Volta region (present-day Ghana). This area is a good deal closer to the Atlantic coast than to the Sahelian entrepôts of trans-Saharan trade but somewhat less

---

[5] Naruf, a Kano Arab cited from the 1905 northern Nigeria *Annual Report* in Johnson, "Calico Caravans," 111; other North African traders in Nigeria even shipped Sudanic ostrich feathers to Libya by sea around this time (Baier, *Economic History of Niger,* 87–8).

Table 10.1

Comparative Productivity: Camel Caravan and Sailing Ship

	Caravan[a]	Ship[b]
Ton/man ratio	0.05-0.09 tons/1 man (4 camels/man, 120-200 kg./camel)	3.3-13.9 tons/1 man
Miles per hour	2.5-5	1.5-3
Miles per day	20-40 (8-12 hours/day)	36-72 (24 hours/day)
Days to traverse	40-70 (N. Sahara[c] to Sudan) 10-12 (Med. to N. Sahara)	70-80 (Europe to W. Africa)
Freight cost per ton (in £)	35-40 (N. Sahara to Sudan) 5-6 (Med. to N. Sahara)	39-40 (tobacco) 22-32 (sugar) 1-6.5 (rice)

[a] Sources for this column are listed in Table 10.6; see also Table 10.5 and J. Rennell, "On the Rate of Travelling, As Performed by Camels," Philosophical Transactions of the Royal Society, (abridged edition) 17 (1791):38-43.

[b] The source for this column is R. E. Menard, "Transport Costs and Long-Range Trade" (paper presented at the "Rise of Merchant Empires" conference, Minneapolis, 1987); a revised version of this paper will appear in The Political Economy of Merchant Empires.

[c] For a breakdown of the caravan routes from the Mediterranean coast to the northern edge of the desert and then across the Sahara, see pp. 331-332 below.

Table 10.2

Trans-Saharan and West African Coastal Trade: Export Values

(Units of £1,000)

	Trans-Saharan[a]		Coastal[b]		Ratios
1875[c]	Morocco	160	Britain	2,559	
	Libya	347	France	2,136[d]	
			U.S.A.	833	
	Total	507[e]	Total	5,528	1:11
1879[c]	Morocco	40	Britain	2,054	
	Libya	583	France	1,735[d]	
			U.S.A.	1,354	
	Total	623	Total	5,143	1:8

a P. E. Lovejoy, "Commercial Sectors in the Economy of the Sudan: The Trans-Saharan Trade," African Economic History 13 (1984): 23-55; J. L. Miège, Le Maroc et l'Europe, 4 vols. (Paris, 1962), 3:358-60; Lovejoy's evaluation of slave imports into Libya (£20,000 per annum) is probably an overestimation, but it has been retained so as to shift any possible bias toward the Sahara; there are no estimates in this period for independent trans-Saharan trade into Algeria and Tunisia (both generally agreed to be small) or the southern regions of Libya (a significant transit zone for slaves and other goods going to Egypt). There is also no calculation of Libyan consumption of trans-Saharan goods, although this value cannot have been great given the very small Libyan population. In any case, these omissions are more than compensated for by the Libyan slave trade evaluations and the absence in the coastal figures of Dutch and other minor European coastal trade.

b Annuaire statistique de la France; George E. Brooks, Jr., Yankee Traders, Old Coasters, and African Middlemen: A History of American Legitimate Trade with West Africa in the Nineteenth Century (Boston, 1970), 300-10; Statistical Abstract of the United Kingdom.

c The years used here have been chosen, first, because relatively reliable trade statistics for the two routes out of West Africa are available and, second, because they represent a high point in the value of postmedieval trans-Saharan trade, mainly due to a boom in the ostrich feather market. By contrast, West African coastal trade was in somewhat of a depression during the 1870s because of a major decline in vegetable oil prices.

d The French statistics are not as precise as the British because for 1875 they are not broken down by African region, and in both years cited, an estimate had to be made of the West African component of "English African Possessions."

e According to C. W. Newbury, "North African and Western Sudan Trade in the Nineteenth Century," Journal of African History 7 (1966):241, ostensibly based on the same evidence as used here, this figure is about £1,500,000. Using this figure would make the ratio of the export values of the trans-Saharan trade to the coastal trade about 1:4.

Table 10.3

West African Gold Exports

(in Metric Tons)

Period (A. D.)	Routes	Annual average
800-1480	Trans-Saharan	0.5-1.5[a]
1480-1720	Trans-Saharan	0.2-0.3[b]
	Guinea coast	0.7-1.7[c]
1720s-1820s	All	"smaller"[d]
1825-1900	Trans-Saharan	0.1-0.2[e]
	Guinea coast	0.8[f]

[a] Philip D. Curtin, "Africa and the Wider Monetary World, 1250-1850," in J. F. Richards, ed., Precious Metals in the Later Medieval and Early Modern Worlds (Durham, N.C., 1983), 238-41 (based on twentieth-century productivity estimates and sixteenth-century European exports).

[b] M. Abitol, Tombouctou et les Arma (Paris, 1979), 196-218; Elizabeth Hodgkin, "Social and Political Relations on the Niger Bend in the Seventeenth Century" (Ph.D., University

of Birmingham, 1987), 377–406; Terrence Walz, "Gold and Silver Exchanges between Egypt and Sudan, Sixteenth-Eighteenth Centuries," in Richards, Precious Metals, 308–19. The statistical data in these sources are neither very reliable nor fully worked out by the authors, but the evidence does point to slightly higher rates of gold trade than for the better-measured nineteenth century.

c Curtin, "Africa and the Wider Monetary World," 241–50.

d There are no general estimates of Guinea coast gold exports for this period. However, evidence of various kinds, e.g., the import of Brazilian gold, indicates that West African gold exports had diminished considerably during the eighteenth century, probably due to the competing commercial and manpower demands of the expanded slave trade (see Richard Bean, "A Note on the Relative Importance of Slaves and Gold in West African Exports," Journal of African History 15 [1974]:351–6, and idem, The British Trans-Atlantic Slave Trade, 1650–1775 [New York, 1975]). British Gold Coast (Ghana) customs records for the early 1800s, although clearly not applicable to the region or even the Gold Coast as a whole, suggest a rather small trade for this period, as do Curtin's figures for Senegambia (Alfred Soetbeer, Edelmetall-Produktion [Gotha, 1879], 46; G. E. Metcalfe, Great Britain and Ghana: Documents of Colonial History, 1805–1957 [London, 1964], 110; Curtin, "Africa and the Wider Monetary World").

e Miège, Le Maroc et l'Europe, 3:361–2; Newbury, "North African and Western Sudan Trade"; Soetbeer, Edelmetall-Produktion, 47.

f Curtin, "Africa and the Wider Monetary World," 239, 250–2; Metcalfe, Great Britain and Ghana, 110, 115, 168; Soetbeer, Edelmetall-Produktion, 46–7.

separated from the latter points by the forest lands, which, as already noted, constituted the main factor in determining transport costs within West Africa. In the absence of real price data we can thus assume that the key advantage enjoyed by Europeans in bargaining for West African gold supplies was the lower cost of oceanic over desert transport once the expense of bringing goods to the respective ports was discounted.

Gold, it should be noted, is an item of very small bulk in relation to value. Thus the principal European transport advantages lay in their ability to bring barter goods to West Africa rather than in the carriage of gold itself. Desert traders dealing mainly in gold tended, according to at least one thirteenth-century source, to return to North Africa from the Sudan in very small caravans.[6] If the trans-Saharan trade was to continue on any significant scale in an era when it procured relatively little gold, the bulk in return cargoes and thus the size of caravans had to be larger, implying some shift in market factors that will be examined below.

Cowries

Cowries, highly valued in both forest and Sudanic zones of early modern West Africa for local monetary use, are a more complex matter.[7] Both European and Muslim merchants initially brought these shells by sea from the Maldive Islands in the Indian Ocean to a secondary distribution point, after which they were carried by ship or camel to West Africa. If we assume that the Muslim shipping costs from the Maldives to the Red Sea are somewhat lower than European costs from the Maldives to the North Atlantic, but that European shipment back to West Africa was cheaper than Muslim caravan carriage from the Red Sea to the northern edge of the Sahara, we would expect a division of markets: Europeans enjoying a monopoly of the Guinea coast and Muslim caravaneers continuing to supply the Sudan.

In fact the competition was not this straightforward. Muslims appear to have ceased carrying cowries to the Red Sea by the mid–seventeenth century, possibly because the comparative cost to European

[6] Al-Sharisha, cited in J. F. P. Hopkins and N. Levtzion, *Corpus of Early Arabic Sources for West African History* (Cambridge, 1981).

[7] Jan Hogendorn and Marion Johnson, *The Shell Money of the Slave Trade* (New York, 1986); this work incorporates all the references I have found independently on Saharan cowrie traffic. I am ignoring major changes in the nineteenth-century cowrie market following the European exploitation of cheaper shell sources on the East African coast.

competitors was based less on the immediate capital and labor inputs than on the function of cowrie cargoes going to the Atlantic as ballast. Such evidence as we do have of continuing cowrie trade by caravans indicates that shells were sometimes purchased from European merchants in Morocco or even acquired by arbitrage in the Sudan itself from shipments that had obviously arrived first on the Guinea coast. For cowrie imports the competitive advantage of Europeans thus appears to have derived less from the technological efficiency of shipping than from the internalization of this commodity into an entire commercial system that brought overall costs well below the price at which Muslims could deliver shell money even to the protected (and flourishing) market of the Sudan. Cowries, unlike gold, are a bulky item with relatively low value per unit. Although we have no precise idea of the quantities imported across the desert at any time, their disappearance from camel baggage might conceivably have shrunk total caravan volume. However, as will soon be seen, imports across the desert to West Africa in the eighteenth and nineteenth centuries did include other items with high bulk-to-value ratios.

Slaves

By the late seventeenth century slaves had replaced gold as the export commodity most purchased by Europeans in West Africa. Given the great numbers of Africans who fell victim to forced Atlantic emigration, it has surprised many scholars to be confronted with evidence that the trans-Saharan slave trade continued during this same period at an increasing rate, even if a much lower one than that of the Europeans (see Table 10.4).

Given both its steady volume and high profit rate, the slave trade was a major basis for the vigor of postmedieval trans-Saharan commerce. But this enterprise also reveals the degree to which African desert commerce functioned as a protected enclave rather than as a direct competitor with European oceanic trade.

Internal West African carriage factors do not explain much of this protection, since slaves transported themselves by foot from their areas of initial acquisition to both the northern and southern exit points from the region. It is true that the trans-Saharan markets placed a higher value on women than on men, thus possibly capturing a residue from slaving ventures oriented toward the larger, male-preferring European market (except that Guinea forest and Sudanic exporters tended to keep slaves of the less salable sex for their own uses). Some part of the lower Saharan price probably did derive from the fact that

Table 10.4

Saharan and Guinea Coast Slave Trades

A. Quantities (units of 1,000)[a]

	Trans-Saharan		Guinea/Atlantic	
	Total	Per annum %	Total	Per annum %
700-1400	2,000+	3.0+		
1401-1500	260-	2.5+	41.9	0.8 (50 years only)[b]
1501-1600	300+	3.0+	324.9	3.2[c]
1601-1700	300+	3.0+	1,868.0	18.7
1701-1800	550+	5.5+	3,455.6	34.6
1801-1867	425	6.5-	1,286.0	19.2
1868-1900	110+	3.5	—	
Total	3,945+	3.3	6,976.4	14.9

B. Prices (units of pounds sterling unless otherwise specified)

Source	Sudan	N. Africa	Markup	Guinea	New World	Markup
1445, Malafante[d]	2 dinars (6 liras)					
1445, Cadamosto[e]	1 horse = 10-15 slaves					

1456-7, Gomes[f]	1 horse = 7 slaves		1 horse = 6 slaves		
1768-72, Bean[g]			17	39	124%
1773-5, Bean			16	43	169%
1780, Leveen[h]			16	38	138%
1787, Lucas[i]	3-4 (male) 2.5 (female)				
1789, Jackson[j]	2.5-5	15-25	18	39	117%
1790, Leveen		400%-500% (Morocco)			
1790, Venture[k]	10-12 livres	High[l] (Morocco)			
1800, Leveen			19	40	111%
1810, Leveen			19	40	111%
1818-20, Tambo[m]		12-22.4 (Tripoli)			
1815-20, Eltis[n]			5.2	53.2 (Cuba)	923%
1822, Leveen			15.6	58 (Brazil)	272%
1821-5, Eltis			6.7	53.2 (Cuba) 75 (Brazil)	381% 699%
1823, Tambo	7.5 (Tripoli)	12.7 (Tripoli) 69%			
1826-30, Eltis			10.4	22.1 (S. Brazil) 34.7 (Bahia) 56.3 (Cuba) 30.7	230% 418% 441% 195%

Table 10.4. (*Cont.*)

Source	Sudan	N. Africa	Markup	Guinea	New World	Markup
1826–7, Tambo	3–3.7				(S. Brazil) 34.7 (Bahia)	234%
1830, Leveen				14	71	407%
1831–5, Eltis				7.5	59 (Cuba)	607%
					27.6 (S. Brazil)	230%
					37.9 (Bahia)	405%
1830s, Tambo	3.7–4.5					
1836–40, Eltis				10.2	59 (Cuba)	687%
					34.4 (S. Brazil)	238%
					37.9 (Bahia)	405%
1840, Leveen				12	65 (Cuba)	442%
					70 (S. Brazil)	483%
1841–5, Eltis				6.4	64 (Cuba)	900%
					41.7 (S. Brazil)	552%
					40.7 (Bahia)	536%
1845, Tambo	2.2–3	10.4–12 (Tripoli)	298%–373%			
1846–50, Eltis				13.4	89.7 (Cuba)	569%
					41.9 (S. Brazil)	212%
					49.5 (Bahia)	269%

Year, Source						
1850, Tambo	4.8	14.9 (Tripoli) 19.4 (Turkey)	213% 306%	11	80 (Cuba) 84 (Brazil)	627% 664%
1850, Leveen						
1851–5, Eltis				8.6	107.1 (Cuba) 63.2 (S. Brazil) 59.8 (Bahia)	1,145% 634% 595%
1856–60, Eltis				7.6	164.9 (Cuba) 96.2 (S. Brazil)	2,070% 1,166%
1860, Leveen				10	100 (Brazil) 170 (Cuba)	900% 1,600%
1861–5, Eltis				7.6	104.5 (Cuba)	1,275%
1862, Tambo	3–4.5					
1866, Tambo	4.5–9	30–45 (Egypt)	400%–567%			
1872–3, Tambo	6–15					
1890s, Tambo	3–20	15–18 (Morocco)	100%–400%			

a R. A. Austen, "The Mediterranean Islamic Slave Trade Out of Africa" (paper presented at Workshop on the Long-Distance Trade in Slaves, Bellagio, Italy, December 1988); Paul E. Lovejoy, "The Volume of the Atlantic Slave Trade: A Synthesis," Journal of African History 23 (1982):473–501.

b Includes west central African slave exports.

Notes to Table 10.4. (*Cont.*)

c British West Indies up to 1810; Brazil and Cuba afterward.

d A. Malafante, "Lettre écrit du Touat," in C. de la Roncière, La découverte de l'Afrique au Moyen Age, 3 vols. (Cairo, 1925), 1:155.

e Alvise Ca da Mosto, "Voyage [1455]," in G. R. Crone, The Voyages of Cadamosto and Other Documents on Western Africa in the Second Half of the Fifteenth Century (London, 1937), 17.

f Diego Gomes, "Voyage [1468]," in Crone, Voyages, 101.

g Bean, The British Trans-Atlantic Slave Trade, 72–77.

h E. Phillip Leveen, "British Slave Trade Suppression Policies, 1821–1865: Impact and Implications" (Ph. D. diss., University of Chicago, 1971), 10.

i Simon Lucas, "Communications [1789]," in Association for Promoting the Discovery of the Interior Parts of Africa: Proceedings, 2 vols. (London, 1810), 1:172–3.

j James Grey Jackson, An Account of Timbuctoo and Housa . . . by El Hage Abd Salam Shabeeny (London, 1820), 27–8, 219–20.

k Jean-Michel Venture de Paradis, "Route de Tafilet à Tounbouctou," Raynal Papers, ms. fr. 6430, fol B8, Bibliothèque National, Paris.

l Venture notes that although many slaves die during the desert passage, the price in Morocco is still sufficient to provide a comfortable profit.

m David A. Tambo, "The Sokoto Caliphate Slave Trade in the Nineteenth Century," International Journal of African Historical Studies 9 (1976):210–17.

n David Eltis, Economic Growth and the Ending of the Transatlantic Slave Trade (New York, 1987), 263. These figures are far better documented than those of Leveen, but the consistently lower prices for Africa probably reflect the fact that they are not all derived from the Guinea coast, as Leveen's apparently are.

Sudanic slave sellers were often military elites who had actually captured their victims, as opposed to the chains of middlemen involved in coastal human exports. However, as indicated in the Gomes account cited in Table 10.4, the major cause of higher prices on the Atlantic was competitive bidding among a multitude of buyers, whose presence is, in turn, a function of the lower entry (mainly transport) costs of this route.

The failure of Europeans to use their maritime advantage to enter the Mediterranean as well as the Atlantic slave market seems to be explained sufficiently by the evidence in Table 10.4 of lower prices in North Africa than in the New World. Despite the lower initial purchase costs and higher markup rates, the price differential might be ascribed to the relative efficiency of caravan versus oceanic transport in this particular trade, since a large portion of the slaves were also made to walk across the desert rather than riding on camels. However, the provisioning costs for such individuals were not negligible, and death rates were also significantly higher than on the Atlantic.[8] Thus, it is hard to imagine any expansion of the trans-Saharan slave trade beyond the scale reached in the early nineteenth century.

What ultimately kept European ships out of the Mediterranean slave market, therefore, was probably not so much price by itself (lower transport costs to North Africa as opposed to crossing the Atlantic would have made such transactions theoretically profitable in some periods) but rather the combination of small scale and high transaction costs. It was simply not worth extending to the different route and commercial culture of North Africa the kind of credit and payment arrangements that existed on the Atlantic system, particularly when piracy survived so much longer in North Africa than it did in the Caribbean. Culture does not imply much about moral issues in this situation. During the Middle Ages Europeans regularly supplied Slavic, Balkan, and Caucasian slaves to the Islamic world.[9] In the nineteenth century, when Muslim demand was at its peak and the price differential between the Guinea coast and the Sudan had shrunk

---

[8] James Richardson, "Report on the Slave Trade of the Great Desert," *Anti-Slavery Reporter* 1 (1846): 154–5, provides some figures, including both provisioning and customs payments, for this cost (see Table 10.7); on death rates in the central Saharan slave trade, see Ralph A. Austen, "The Mediterranean Islamic Slave Trade out of Africa: Toward a Census" (paper presented at Workshop on the Long-Distance Trade in Slaves across the Sahara and the Black Sea in the Nineteenth Century, Bellagio, Italy, December 1988).

[9] Robert Brunschvig, *Encyclopedia of Islam*, new edition, vol. 1 (Leiden, 1960), s. v. "Abd"; in 1754 the French government sought to *buy* black slaves in Libya, but was frustrated by local restrictions on the trade (Mark Dyer, "The Foreign Trade of Western Libya, 1750–1830" (Ph.D. diss., Boston University, 1987), 122–3.

considerably, there was a legal injunction against European slave trading. However, as shown in Table 10.4, the rewards for violating this law became so much greater in the Atlantic than the Mediterranean that we need not inquire further why this was the route taken by contraband shippers.

In short, the survival of the trans-Saharan slave trade resulted from neither competitive efficiency nor the natural protection of the African landscape. Instead, it depended upon the structural protection of an enclave North African market too small and too costly for Europeans to enter.

Cloth

Throughout the history of the Saharan caravan trade, cotton cloth was one of the major items brought southward. Despite the development (see next section) of a competitive cotton handicraft industry within the Sudan itself, the proportion of cottons in caravan cargoes appears to have increased during the nineteenth century.[10] The vast majority of this cloth was European so, on the supply side, we may explain this shift as the result of the Industrial Revolution, which generally increased cotton textile consumption throughout the world. Given the European origin of the goods, it might be expected that the savings in direct shipment from country of manufacture (particularly Britain) to the West African coast might overcome even the forest barrier protection of trans-Saharan commerce. However, it appears that common European "calicoes" could also be delivered to North Africa more cheaply than in the past, so that the nineteenth-century Sudan cloth trade involved a very direct competition between desert caravans and carriage through the Guinea forest.

The surprising persistence of caravan cloth imports right into the early years of colonial rule in West Africa inspired a number of European officials to undertake studies of the comparative costs of various overland transport systems within the region (see Table 10.5). Initial inroads into the desert traffic were made by colonial government-organized oxcart and river systems, which minimized the role of expensive human porterage.[11] The true returns on these ventures are

---

[10] Johnson, "Calico Caravans"; in the eighteenth century, trans-Saharan caravans also carried large quantities of cloth, but more surprisingly, they continued to transport equal values of brass, a commodity with a very high weight-to-value ratio; brass transport across the desert declined in the 1800s largely because of its replacement by silver in Sudanic currency systems (Dyer, "Trade of Western Libya," 191, 361–2).

[11] Baier, *Economic History of Niger*, 87.

Table 10.5

Comparative Efficiency of Overland Transport:

Desert, Savannah, Forest

	Camel	Donkey	Ox	Porter
Load per unit (kg)	120-150	70	55-120	25-40
Man/ton ratio	0.5-0.7	0.4	0.1-0.3	0.03-0.04
Miles per day	20-40	15-20	20	15-28
Cost per ton/mile	10.5 d	1.6 d	2-9 d	5.5-29.2 d[a]
Purchase cost (£)	4.8-8	1-1.4	2.4-3.2	
Limits of tolerance (south latitude)	14.5° (dry season)	5°	12° (wet season) 10° (dry season)	

Sources: Jacques Meniaud, Haut-Sénégal-Niger (Soudan Français): Géographie économique (Paris, 1912), 118-19; Gabriel Ogundeji Ogunremi, Counting the Camels: The Economics of Transportation in Precolonial Nigeria (New York, 1982), 182; see also, Table 10.1.

[a] Ogunremi, Counting the Camels, 83-6, notes that costs moved toward the higher end of this scale as a function of distance as well as climate, thus reaching their peak when porters carried goods from the dry savannah to the humid coast.

difficult to measure, but it seems clear that the definitive breaking of the natural protection of the forest barrier came only with the construction of railroads. The case of the cloth trade suggests rather complicated relationships between the role of transport factors and external commodity production costs in determining African economic change. I will take up these issues more fully in the conclusion.

New exports

Among the caravan-borne cargoes from West Africa after 1500 both gold and slaves were eventually superseded in value by an entire range of commodities that are seldom mentioned in the records of earlier periods: particularly, ivory, leather hides, ostrich feathers, and gum arabic. As with cloth imports, the engine driving the trade in these commodities was located in the expanding economies of Europe and North America, which again found it more convenient to deal with the Sudan through North Africa. Most of the growth in the export of these goods appears to have occurred in the nineteenth century, but at least gum and hides had substantial European markets by the latter 1700s.[12]

The export of such bulkier items (along with slaves and their food supplies) produced much larger northbound caravans than those of the medieval gold-trading era.[13] Even the continuation of a diminished but regionally significant gold trade depended upon this traffic, because small amounts of gold (often carried in such receptacles as feather quills) could always be added to any existing transport system with no additional cost.

European calculations comparing West African transport economies were based on a bottom-line analysis of caravan costs without much concern about the relative weight of their various components or how any of these components could be made less expensive. The very reasonable assumption of colonialist observers was that the only significant regional transport changes would occur in the Sudanic–ocean routes through the Guinea forest; for practical purposes, the Saharan caravan system could be looked upon as historically static. However, the examination of desert–ocean competition in various commodities has already suggested that important changes did take place in trans-Saharan trade after 1500. To the extent that these shifts can be explained by developments in the world outside Africa, they

[12] We do not yet have a comprehensive assessment of the trade in these goods over extended time periods, but Dyer ("Trade of Western Libya," 90–2, 358–62) indicates that in the mid–eighteenth century hides were exported across the central Sahara, ostrich feathers came only from the northern desert, and ivory was not yet a significant export; for other useful accounts of specific times and places, see Michel Abitol, *Tombouctou et les Arma* (Paris, 1979), 196–218; Austen, *African Economic History*, 36, 38; Baier, *Economic History of Niger*, 39–41, 233–5, passim; Thomas S. Jago, *Parliamentary Papers: Tripoli Consular Report* (Great Britain, House of Commons, 1901), 103; Johnson, "Calico Caravans"; idem, "By Ship or by Camel: The Struggle for the Cameroons Ivory Trade in the Nineteenth Century," *Journal of African History* 19 (1978): 539–49; Jean-Louis Miège, *Le Maroc et l'Europe (1830–1894)*, 4 vols. (Paris, 1962), 3:87–90, 361–3; and Newbury, "North African and Western Sudan Trade." There is a good account of the European market for African gum and hides in Philip D. Curtin, *Economic Change in Precolonial Africa: Senegambia in the Era of the Slave Trade* (Madison, 1975), 215–21.

[13] See Daumas, 1840s, in Table 10.6.

are quite compatible with an assumption of unaltered costs in the desert transportation system itself. But the changes in the Sudan economy during this same period are more closely linked to the caravan system and its protected zone than are those in the wider economy. It is to this last relationship we must now turn in attempting to gauge whether there were any efficiency improvements in caravan trade during this period and what the relationship of this transport sector was to the world with which it was most intimately joined.

CARAVANS, DESERT, AND SUDAN: STASIS VERSUS TRANSFORMATION

In examining the historical economics of the Saharan caravan system from within, we are faced with severe data problems. There are no serial records of Muslim trading firms, which itself reveals something about the nature of these commercial institutions. As indicated in Tables 10.6 and 10.7, some valuable information on costs, profits, and organization of the trade can be gleaned from reports by European merchants, consuls, and colonial administrators from the late eighteenth to the early twentieth century. In addition, we have more anecdotal accounts of caravans accompanied by Arab and European authors or reported to them.

What we can infer generally from these records is that (1) caravans worked for the interests of professional North African merchants motivated to maximize their profits by whatever means available; (2) the technological resources for these efforts appear not to have changed during the entire period under study; and (3) at neither end of the Saharan trade routes were merchants able to integrate the transport factors of the desert routes into the economic systems prevailing in their home areas. The immediate impression is thus one of a transport system that contributed nothing dynamic to whatever economic development took place on its shores. A closer examination (to the extent that this is possible) of the various factors constituting caravan transport costs will not revise this picture very radically but does suggest some subtle modifications.

Caravan merchants

Although we lack any working records of Saharan commercial firms, considerable evidence about them can be found in the medieval Muslim as well as modern European travel literature, much of which drew upon oral information from active merchants. We thus know that

Table 10.6

Caravan Cost Factors

Date	Source	Route	Intermediate markets	Caravan size	Kilograms/camel	Days/route	Camels/man
Mid-800s	al-Yaqubi, H/L, 22	Morocco-W. Sudan	Awdaghast			50	
947-51	ibn Hawqal, H/L, 46,49	Morocco-Ghana	Awdaghast			70	
960s-1060	al-Bakri, H/L, 64	Zawila-Kanem				40	
960s-1060	al-Bakri, H/L, 64	Awdaghast-Morocco				51	
Mid-1100s	al-Idrisi, H/L, 107	Senegal-Morocco				40	
Early 1200	al-Sharisi, H/L, 152-3	Morocco-Ghana				90	
Mid-1200s	al-Qazwini, H/L, 177	Morocco-W. Sudan				90	
1353	ibn Battuta, H/L, 303-4, 418	Takedda-Morocco	Kahir			50	
1787	Jackson, "Timbuktoo"b	Morocco-Timbuktu	Salt (adds 150-200 camels)	350	200	43	1 (armed)

Date	Source	Route					
1780s	Emerit, "Liaisons,"[c]	Morocco–Timbuktu	Salt			55	
1789	Lucas, "Communications," 118–87	Murzuk–Borno, Katsina			150+		
1789, 1805	Jackson, Morocco,[d] 285–90	Timbuktu–Morocco		1,900			
1805	Jackson, Timbuktoo, 282–9	Morocco–Timbuktu	Taghaza salt	300		76	
1811	de la Porte[e]	Morocco–Timbuktu	Yes			113	
1828	Caillé[f]	Timbuktu–Morocco	Aruwun, al-Harib	1,400	225	67	3.5
1840s	Daumas[g]	Katsina–Insalah		2,600			
1840s	Daumas, 227	Sokoto–Ghadames		3,500			
1840s	Daumas, 227	Kano–Ghat		750			
1840s	Daumas, 230	Sokoto–Murzuk		750			
1840s	Daumas, 230	Insalah–Katsina	Agades	650		60	
1845–6	Richardson[h]	Ghat–C. Sudan					4

Table 10.6. (*Cont.*)

Date	Source	Route	Intermediate Markets	Caravan Size	Kilograms/ camel	Days/ route	Camels/ man
1850-4	Dickson[i]	Ghadames-Timbuktu			180	60	
1850-4	Dickson 259-60	Ghadames-Kano			180	40	
Early 1850	Mordekei[j]	Morocco-Timbuktu			150	66	
1854	Barth[k]	Morocco-Timbuktu		1,000			
c. 1861	Emerit, "Liaisons," 40	Ghadames-Kano	Ghat			75	
c. 1862	Emerit, 40	Ghadames-Timbuktu	Tuat			71	
1862	Mircher[l]	Ghadames-Kano		1,625	150	54	
1860s	Mircher, 159-64	Ghadames-Timbuktu	Ghat, Insalah	350		71	
1862	Mircher, 164	Morocco-Timbuktu		1,350			
1870s	Miège, Maroc, 3:85-6	Morocco-Timbuktu				63	
1876-7	Schirmer[m]	Ghadames-Ghat-C. Sudan	Ghat, Agades				

"before"	Lhote[n]	Hoggar	Amadror salt mines		2 (10 now)
Early 1890s	Moore[o]	Tripoli-Ghat-Sudan		600	77
Early 1900s	Etiévant[p]	Ghat-Kano	Agades, zinder + Bilma salt caravan	125	59
1930s	Lhote, 312-20	Insalah-Goa	focus = salt center	100+	

a Hopkins and Levtzion, Corpus of Early Arabic Sources for West African History.

b James G. Jackson, An Account of Timbuktoo and Housa (London, 1820), 1-22.

c Marcel Emerit, "Les liaisons terrestres entre le Soudan et l'Afrique du Nord au XVIIIe et au du XIXe siècle," Travaux de l'Institut de Recherche Saharien, Université d'Alger 11 (1954):31-2.

d James G. Jackson, An Account of the Empire of Morocco (London, 1820).

e I. D. de la Porte, "Itinéraire de Constantine à Tafilet et de Tafilet à Tombouctou (14 Août 1822)," Bullietin de la Société Royale de Géographie de l'Égypte 13 (1925):215-16.

Notes to Table 10.6. (*Cont.*)

f R. Caillé, Travels through Central Africa to Timbuctoo and across the Great Desert to Morocco, 2 vols. (London, 1830), 2:88-174.

g M. J. E. Daumas and A. de Chancel, Le grand désert (1856; Paris, 1985), 227.

h James Richardson, Travels in the Great Desert of the Sahara in the Years of 1845 and 1846, 2 vols. (London, 1848), 2:33.

i C. H. Dickson, "Account of Ghadamis," Journal of the Royal Geographical Society 30 (1860):259-60.

j Abyseru Mordekei, "Die Reisen des Rabbi Mordekei nach Timbuktu," Peterman's Mitteilungen 16 (1870):355-7.

k Heinrich Barth, Travels and Discoveries in North and Central Africa from the Journal of an Expedition Undertaken under the Auspices of H. B. M.'s Government, In the Years 1849-1855, 3 vols. (New York, 1859), 3:366.

l H. Mircher, Mission de Ghadames (Algiers, 1863), 44-51, 143ff.

m Henri Schirmer, Le dernier rapport d'un Européen sur Ghat (Journal de voyage d'Erwin de Bary) (Paris, 1898), 18.

n H. Lhote, "Le cycle caravanier des Touaregs de l'Ahaggar et la saline de Amadror," Bulletin de l'Institut Français de l'Afrique Noire 31 (1969):1024-5.

o T. Moore, Parliamentary Papers (Great Britain, House of Commons, 1892), 84, 411-15.

p J. Étiévant, "Le commerce tripolitain dans le centre Africain," L'Afrique Française 20 (1910):280-1.

substantial communities of literate Muslim merchants were established from the early Islamic period in North African coastal or near-coastal cities (Tripoli, Tunis, Fez, and so on), on the northern edge of the Sahara (Murzuk, Ghadames, Ghat, Wargla, Insallah), and eventually at the major Sudanic entrepôts (Wadai, Kukwa, Zinder, Katsina, Kano, Timbuktu). The relationship between these points was generally hierarchical; that is, capital was concentrated at the Mediterranean end of the system, where the most valuable import and export goods were purchased and sold; caravans for crossing the desert were organized at the northern desert centers, and Sudanic goods were brought back north by the same traders only after they had been paid for with imports.[14]

The caravan itself was not the central institution of commercial organization within this system; instead, it represented a temporary association of firms who happened to be bringing goods across the desert at the same time. A coastal entrepreneur or north Saharan often sent merchandise to the desert edge in his own small caravan, but before entering the Sahara these goods would have to be reloaded onto other camels (usually in smaller weight units), and then this group of animals would join the others being assembled for the same Sudanic destination.[15] During its collective existence, the caravan was subject to the authority (sometimes described as strict, other times as lax) of its guide, not usually himself a merchant.

The individual firms constituting the organizational core of the trans-Saharan caravan trade were held together by a series of formal and informal bonds. Islamic law provided the formal basis for drawing up written agreements of partnership in trading ventures or credit advances between independent merchants. At a minimal level, merchandise traveling across the desert seems almost always to have been accompanied by written documentation indicating the content of cargoes and their designated recipient. Historians of the medieval Sahara have sometimes made a great deal of a tenth-century "check" (actually a bill certifying indebtedness) for the huge sum of 42,000 gold dinars owed by a merchant at Awdaghast in the Mauritanian

---

[14] The best descriptions of caravan geography and organization are Boahen, "Caravan Trade," and Dyer, "Trade of Western Libya," 222–71.

[15] The process was frequently more complicated than this, since caravans and/or their component merchant units would often pass through several northern staging points before undertaking the main desert crossing; e.g., nineteenth-century Ghadames caravans went through either Ghat or Insallah (see Table 10.6) depending on whether their final destination was in the central or western Sudan, and the new merchants might join them at these intermediate points.

Table 10.7

Caravan Accounts

(in units of 1 French franc)

	itinerary	merchant	no. loads	goods	purchase price	selling price	transport[a] costs	net profit	transport % of sale	transport % markup
1845	Kano-Tripoli[b]	not given		female slave	65.3	280	13.4	256%	5%	6%
				male slave	41.0	233	13.4	328%	6%	7%
1861-62[c]	Tripoli-Kano	el-Haj Ahmed Mercrouen	1	cloth	743.8	1,500	(1) 178.1 (2) 210.3	see below	(1) 12% (2) 14%	(1) 24% (2) 28%
1861-62	Kano-Tripoli	Mercrouen	1	ivory	1,260	1,190	(1) 133.4 (2) 143.0	36.3%[d]	(1) 11% (2) 12%	none (-6%)
1861-62[e]	Tripoli-Timbuktu	Mohammad Babani	1	cloth	595	1,338.8	(1) 272 (2) 335.8	43.8%	(1) 20% (2) 25%	(1) 37% (2) 45%
circa 1906[f]	Tripoli-Kano	Mohammad ibn Saleh	4	mainly cloth	800	4,000	(1) 350 (2) 543[g]	see below	(1) 9% (2) 14%	(1) 11% (2) 17%
circa 1906	Kano-Tripoli	ibn Saleh	32	goat hides	4,000	16,000	(1) 4,160 (2) 4,768	125%	(1) 26% (2) 30%	(1) 35% (2) 40%

a (1)= freight costs alone; (2)= freight + protection/customs charges.

b Richardson, "Report on the Slave Trade," 154-5; idem, Travels in the Great Desert of the Sahara, 2:204; prices originally given in Maria Theresa dollars.

c Mircher, Mission de Ghadames, 52-3.

d This is calculated by Mircher (and presumably by the merchant himself) in terms of the Ottoman currency (mahboub) used in Tripoli; however, all of the transactions in the southern Sahara and Sudan are recorded in the local cowrie shell currency, with no indications of how the cowries were acquired. Mircher (and Newbury, "North African and Western Sudan Trade," following him) reports Mecrouren's profit on his original outlay without noting that at the cowrie-franc exchange rate used by Mircher (Newbury uses several different rates in his article without explanation) there is actually no profit on the importation of the ivory from Kano to Tripoli. One could redistribute the profit between the two portions of the round-trip by using a higher franc-to-cowrie rate, which is perhaps what Newbury means when he remarks that part of the profit in trans-Saharan trade came from manipulating currency exchanges. It would be necessary to look at trends in Tripoli ivory prices to see if the purchase in Kano was made in the expectation of adding profit or simply to transform a cowrie profit into an exportable value, even at a discount of 6 percent plus transport charges.

e Mircher, Mission de Ghadames, 54; in this case all transactions are presented in the same currency, but there is no record of purchases in the Sudan and their resale in Tripoli, although Mircher remarks that Ballani could have made an additional profit by converting his Timbuktu recipts into gold and feathers for import into North Africa.

f Etiévant, "Commerce tripolitain"; all prices here have been given in francs.

g This includes French- and British-administered tariffs that are several times higher than those levied previously by African authorities.

desert to a creditor at Sijilmasa in central Morocco.[16] The very high monetary level of this transaction undoubtedly reflects the differing value of gold at its source area in the western Sudan as opposed to the rest of the Muslim world. Moreover, not only are there no other accounts of such major credit arrangements, but evidence from numerous other medieval sources indicates that trans-Saharan trade was considered so risky as to be outside the jurisdiction of Islamic commercial law and even beyond the pale of general respectability.[17]

Instead of formal legal arrangements, the ties between participants in the various zones of the caravan trading system seem to have been based mainly upon various combinations of kinship, clientage, and slavery.[18] These arrangements could withstand the uncertainties of the trade, managed to incorporate not only major partners but also lesser attendants of camels on the journeys themselves (there was virtually no wage labor in the caravans), and also linked the desert system to the growing merchant network extending across the Sudan into the Guinea forest zone.

The high risk factor in the Saharan caravan trade is reflected not only in the problems of assimilating it to the commercial culture of metropolitan Islamic society but also, given the absence of any evidence of monopoly control within the trade, in the high profit rates shown in Table 10.7. It is striking that in all recorded cases these profits were shared on roughly a fifty/fifty basis between the owners of southbound goods (usually coastal entrepreneurs) and the intermediaries directly responsible for conveying goods across the desert.[19] The first European to observe this system from the desert edge, the fifteenth-century Genoese merchant Antonio Malafante, was shocked by what he perceived as an exorbitant 100 percent commission charged by desertside agents.[20] What Malafante failed to understand was seen

---

[16] Nehemiah Levtzion, "Ibn Hawqal, the Cheque, and Awdaghast," *Journal of African History* 9 (1968): 223–33.

[17] Hady Roger Idris, *La Berberie orientale sous les Zirides: Xe–XIIe siècles* (Paris, 1962), 675–6; Hopkins and Levtzion, *Corpus of Early Arabic Sources for West African History* 55, 60–1, 103, 382–3.

[18] Henri Peres, "Relation entre Tafilalet et le Soudan à travers le Sahara, du XIIe au XIVe siècle," in E. F. Gautier, *Mélanges de géographie et orientalisme* (Tours, 1937), 409–14; Baier, *Economic History of Niger*, 57–78.

[19] Melchior J. E. Daumas and Ausone de Chancel, *Le Grand désert: Itinéraire d'une caravane du Sahara au pays des nègres, royaume de Haoussa* (1856; Paris, 1985), 289; J. Etiévant, "Le commerce tripolitain dans le Centre Africain," *L'Afrique Française* 20 (1910); F. O. [British Foreign Office] miscellaneous series, Tripoli, 1902, in Johnson, "Calico Caravans," 112; Jago, *Parliamentary Papers* (1901); Temple Moore, *Parliamentary Papers: Tripoli Consular Report* (Great Britain, House of Commons, 1892).

[20] Antonio Malafante [1447], "Lettre écrit du Touat," in Charles de la Roncière, *La découverte de l'Afrique au Moyen Age,* 3 vol. (Cairo, 1925), 1:15, 157.

much more clearly by nineteenth-century European students of (and less-enthusiastic advocates of European participation in) the trans-Saharan trade: anyone entering it had to be willing to share the high risks involved, and the rewards for successful ventures also had to be divided between those whose capital was at peril and those who stood a great chance of losing their lives to the natural and human hazards of the desert.

Table 10.7 presents a few cases where we can measure transport costs as a proportion of total costs in the trans-Saharan trade. It would be useful to compare these figures with other preindustrial ventures, but even by themselves, they indicate a classic case of what Lopez calls a high-profit/high-risk "external" trade.[21] It is notable that not only transport but also protection costs play a relatively small role in these accounts. Apparently it was not easy to buy security (other caravans, particularly in the western Sahara, are reported as arming themselves or taking circuitous routes to avoid pillaging; see 1787, Jackson, in Table 10.6). To consider more directly the components of risk in caravan travel it will be necessary to examine the desert environment itself. But first we must look at the immediate determinants of productivity in trans-Saharan transport.

Caravan technology

If the risk factors in desert travel (and also, as will be seen, some cost-saving factors) remained both dominant and clearly external to merchant culture, the more immediate expenses of transport are not negligible in the Table 10.7 accounts nor are they so obviously outside the control of merchants. Yet it has already been stated that the technology of desert transport remained static during the period under examination here. How do we know that there were no productivity improvements in camel caravans and how do we explain the failure of the invisible hand to find devices for moving commerce more quickly across the African sands?

The one indicator of efficiency on which we have at least rough statistical evidence extending from the medieval to the modern period is the time it took caravans to travel from the northern to the southern end of the Sahara. As Table 10.6 indicates, this did not change for a period of over one thousand years.

The original introduction of camels into the desert around the first century A.D. did represent a major transport innovation, which stim-

---

[21] Robert S. Lopez, "The Trade of Medieval Europe: The South," in Postan and Rich, *Cambridge Economic History*, 2:333.

ulated the development of an urbanized export economy in the Sudan.[22] Camels were also developed in several varieties for such diverse purposes as plowing, speedy human travel, and goods carriage over diverse Sahelian and desert zones. However, it is a not insignificant comment on the enclave character of the Saharan economy that its major transport innovation contradicts the most basic Western metaphor of technological progress; here the wheel – present in North Africa and the Sahara from Phoenician times – had to be "disinvented" in order to make possible the linking of the Sudan and the Mediterranean.[23]

Caravan merchants depended upon camels for their transport, and many of them became skilled in managing the animals along the lengthy and dangerous routes across the Sahara. But the economy into which camels were ultimately "domesticated" was not that of the urban merchant but rather that of the desert nomad, whether indigenous North African Berber or immigrant (from another desert area) Arabian. Most accounts of caravan transactions refer to merchants renting animals or buying them on what amounted to a temporary basis from nomads. Once having crossed the Sahara, the animals had to be rested for several months, and most caravans returned from the Sudan with different camels than those with which they had arrived.

In some respects the limited commitment of the merchant to his transport vehicle provided a degree of flexibility not available to the owners of ships or wheeled vehicles: There was no "backhaul" problem of finding a cargo to meet full round-trip costs. As already seen, the size of southbound and northbound caravans could vary on the same venture, according to the carriage needs of goods available at each terminus. However, the inability of merchants to bring camel transportation under their direct control meant that its level of efficiency remained a fixed exogenous factor of desert commerce, irreplaceable by any substitute and subject to no improvement from within Islamic mercantile culture or from European examples.[24]

Given the frequent comparison of the Sahara to a sea (with its *sahel* [shore] at each edge) and the camel as the "ship of the desert," navigation is an area of caravan technology where one might look for innovation. Yet all descriptions of caravans agree that their highly

[22] Austen, *African Economic History*, 22–3, 32–4.
[23] Richard Bulliet, *The Camel and the Wheel* (Cambridge, Mass., 1975); John T. Swanson, "The Myth of Transsaharan Trade during the Roman Era," *International Journal of African Historical Studies* 8 (1975):582–600.
[24] For technological change in Muslim Indian Ocean seafaring, both before and after European contact, see Austen, *African Economic History*, 58, 64.

skilled guides never made use of the compasses and other devices familiar to Arab seafarers but rather navigated by a combination of astral-sightings (always possible in the cloudless Sahara, where much traveling was done in the cooler night hours) and landscape orientation.[25] It must be kept in mind, however, that the desert is unlike the sea precisely in the relationship between geometry and geography; the formal calculation of location would not necessarily reveal where a given oasis or foraging ground or safe route to the next stopping place might be in a given year.[26] The guide thus needed (also for political reasons) to be an inhabitant *of* the desert rather than an expert *on* it. In this sense the secondary technology of desert travel also remained alien to the culture of urban caravan merchants, who could never incorporate it directly into their own rationality of minimizing costs.

Internal economics of the desert

In all of the preceding discussion of caravan trade the unyielding physical qualities of the Sahara and the gap between major caravan merchants and their nomad collaborators have been presented as obstacles to improving the efficiency of camel transport. Nonetheless, it is evident that over time trans-Saharan trade was able to adapt to major changes in surrounding market conditions, including shifts in the commodities passing across the desert and new developments in the immediately adjacent Sudanic economy. Adaptation of this kind does not necessarily imply gains in the productivity of transport or any of its immediately associated mercantile enterprises. But it is at least necessary to examine the relationship between long-distance commerce and the internal desert economy from the fifteenth to the late nineteenth century to specify the limits and dynamics of this commercial system.

The paradoxical role of the Sahara as both medium of and obstacle to African economic integration is based primarily upon its arid physical landscape. This was and remains a very dangerous area to travel across; yet, unlike the forest, the desert allowed the utilization of animal transport. The desert environment was not unchanging; histori-

---

[25] The French explorer René Caillé was forced to conceal his compass to protect his disguise as a Muslim (*Travels through Central Africa to Timbuctoo and across the Great Desert to Morocco*, 2 vols. [London, 1830], 2:91).

[26] European experiments with compass navigation in eighteenth-century Middle Eastern caravan travel also indicated that such methods were not fully reliable; see James Rennell, "On the Rate of Travelling, As Performed by Camels," *Philosophical Transactions of the Royal Society* (abridged edition) 17 (1791):38–43.

cal accounts of caravan trade give considerable information about shifts in the routes used to enter, cross over, and stop in the desert.[27] But it is difficult to discern any long-term decisions about control over transport costs in these alterations. Instead they seem to reflect the cyclical perturbations in political circumstances and minienvironmental conditions reported by all travelers for the much shorter periods in the desert areas they visited. Rather than representing progressive transformations of the transport system, the route changes reveal a persistent characteristic of instability in the desert trade conditions, a characteristic over which merchants had no control other than that of substituting the costs of delay and extra caution for the risks of total loss.

The key to discovering any persistent pattern of development in the Saharan economy lies in the examination of its nomadic inhabitants and their links with the settled societies on either the north or, especially for our period, the south end of the desert.[28] Most observers have viewed the Berber and Arab camel herders of this region as an obstacle to the rationalization of caravan trade. Indeed, the introduction of the camel into the Sahara apparently had the effect of setting back Mediterranean economic penetration of the region, since it allowed desert populations to impinge upon settled frontier zones more effectively than in the era of horses and chariots. Even after the institution of commercial caravan traffic across the desert, the slow-moving animals used to carry merchandise were always threatened by attacks from nomads mounted on swift and lightly loaded mehari camels.[29]

If desert populations are simply seen as exclusive proprietors of camels who could use this resource (and control over desert water and fodder) either to provision or to pillage caravans, there would be little point in examining further the links between caravan trade and the internal Saharan economy. Yet the Sahara also contains resources with an immediate market value in surrounding areas, such as dates, salt, and senna (a local plant widely used as a drug in the Mediterra-

---

[27] This is a major topic of discussion for the period of most interest here in Abitol, *Tombouctou*, 185–94. For an earlier era see Jean Devisse, "La question d'Audagust," in Denis Robert, Serge Robert, and J. Devisse, *Tegdaoust*, vol. 1 (Paris, 1972).

[28] The logic of the available data has brought me to this argument, but readers should be warned that my present resources do not presently allow me to pursue it with the same degree of confidence as in what has preceded.

[29] Bulliet, *Camel and the Wheel*, 138–40; E. Carette, *Recherche sur la géographie et le commerce de l'Algérie méridionale* (Paris, 1844), 160–61; Emilienne Demougeot, "Le chameau et l'Afrique du Nord romaine," *Annales: Economies, Sociétés, Civilisations* 15 (1961): 209–47.

nean). Salt in particular was much in demand for human and cattle nutrition as well as artisanal purposes among the populations of the Sudan. Salt trade even appears to predate the establishment of camel transport across the desert.[30] Moreover, nomadic society in the desert was far from economically self-sufficient. In order to maintain their own basic nutrition, clothing, armament, and harness, along with a well-developed lifestyle, camel-raising Berbers and Arabs needed staple food supplies (especially cereals), luxury foods such as coffee, tea, and sugar, and a wide variety of handicraft goods from outside the Sahara.

The market needs of the Saharan peoples could be met in a number of ways, which were often combined. The first and oldest was to organize caravans of their own between the desert and the settled areas (particularly the salt-hungry Sudan), often timed to fit the cycle of seasonal pasturage migrations. A second was to provide services (camels, guidance, protection) to trans-Saharan merchants, who paid for these in both consumer goods and coinage. Finally, nomads could acquire control over sedentary populations, as either slaves or clients, to grow crops, tend cattle, manufacture goods, and mine salt at appropriate points in and around the desert.[31]

These nonpastoral nomadic activities were of great interest to caravan merchants, since they provided various means of increasing profits and reducing expenses. The most frequent and autonomous device for tapping the desert market was arbitrage: Caravans often traveled through the desert by way of major salt centers (see Table 10.6), where Mediterranean goods were used to purchase a Saharan product for ultimately more profitable sale in the Sudan. At other times trans-Saharan caravans joined with regional ones for lower-cost access to nomadic services.

Such maneuvers do not suggest actual control of the internal Saharan economy by Mediterranean merchants. Indeed, they often manipulated costs and benefits only in return for lengthening the period required to achieve a return on original investments. This kind of economizing is closely linked to the self-taxation of caravaneers, whose diet and general living comfort during the many months of desert travel were extremely spartan. Within a short time frame, the cost controls of caravan trade suggest less a dynamic of growth than a strategy of enclave survival in a marginalized sector of the world

---

[30] Devisse, "La question d'Audagust"; Patrick Munson, "Archeology and the Prehistoric Origins of the Ghana Empire," *Journal of African History* 21 (1980): 457–66.

[31] Paul E. Lovejoy and Steven Baier, "The Desert-Side Economy of the Central Sudan," *International Journal of African Historical Studies* 8 (1975): 551–81.

economy. The gains were not increased productivity but rather the maintenance of a way of life that would be altered only under the double pressure of direct intrusion by outside forces (using mechanized transport) and the possibility of increased income in the immediate locale (through the petroleum industry).[32]

Before reaching such a negative conclusion, however, it is necessary to consider the possibility that during the four centuries after 1500 there had at least been one historical process contributing to improved trans-Saharan transport productivity: the increasing integration of nomads into the economy of both caravans and surrounding settled populations. Given the available data, we cannot measure the relevance of such a change to the precise costs of transport, but we may assume that developments of this kind would provide greater predictability of even unaltered cost factors, thus enabling the system to adapt more effectively to market shifts. Even without significant technological innovations in either the transport or the production sectors, integration of the desert into the larger regional economy could be furthered by two means: extension of political control over nomadic violence by societies and states at either end of the Sahara, or growth within the desert of autonomous communities more committed to maintaining external economic ties.

In the northern desert, the political and economic solution to Saharan problems had been achieved to a considerable extent during the medieval period. Entrepôt communities in the Fezzan, the Mzab, or Tuwat, whether or not under the direct control of authorities nearer the coast, shared the same culture as the rest of the Maghreb and could be generally relied upon to provide effective support for caravan trade.[33] Indeed, we generally think of the trans-Saharan trade beginning at these points, although they are already inside the desert. The real problem lay farther south where the desert represented a frontier between Mediterranean culture and a *bilad es-Sudan* (land of the blacks), which, even in the 1800s, was only belatedly and very incompletely being assimilated to Islamic civilization.

As has already been suggested, despite difficulties in some regions, both Islamization and political development in the Sudan made con-

---

[32] Douglas A. Johnson, *Jabal al-Akhdar, Cyrenaica: An Historical Geography of Settlement and Livelihood* (Chicago, 1973), 197–212.

[33] Tadeusz Lewicki, "L'état nord-africaine de Tahert et ses relations avec le Soudan occidental à la fin du VIIIe siècle et au IXe siècle," *Cahiers d'Etudes Africaines* 2 (1962) 513–35; A. G. P. Martin, *A la frontière marocaine – Les oasis sahariennes: Gourara, Touat, Tidleket* (Algiers, 1908); B. G. Martin, "Ahmed Rasim Pasha and the Suppression of the Fezzan Slave Trade," in John Ralph Willis, ed., *Slaves and Slavery in Muslim Africa*, vol. 2 (London, 1985), 51–82.

siderable progress in the early modern period. However, power relations between the Sudanic rulers and desert nomads followed a reverse path. Before its defeat by Morocco we have some evidence that the Songhai empire had established dominion over salt-producing centers in the western Sahara. The sixteenth-century Borno kings likewise maintained hegemonic alliances with nomadic groups in the Kanem desert. During the ensuing centuries, it was the desert peoples (particularly Twareg Berbers) who periodically imposed themselves upon affairs in the former Songhai capital of Timbuktu while Borno, in the early nineteenth century, fell under the control of a new Kanemi (i.e., Saharan) dynasty. The most powerful of the new jihadist states, the Sokoto Caliphate, had its base away from the desert edge, well into the agricultural savannah, and never attempted to extend itself into the Sahara.[34] If political control from the south is to be an indicator of Saharan economic development, new consideration must be given to the thesis of postmedieval decline rejected at the beginning of this essay.

For economic historians it is perhaps not so surprising to discover that the basis upon which the central and southern Sahara became more effectively integrated into growing Sudanic and world economies was not the expansion of imperial states but rather the growth of more stable and autonomous communities within the desert itself. For the period after 1600 (mainly for the nineteenth century) we have information on such communities in four regions of the Sahara: Hoggar in the north central desert, Air in the south center, Cyrenaica in the northeast, and the Mauritania–Mali region of the southeast.[35] The last three of these zones became, in the course of the period under consideration, major centers of political–judicial authority, religious learning, and local commerce. Without going into extensive detail here, it should be noted that these desert communities not only provided more reliable support for trans-Saharan trade than had been the case earlier but also played an important role in religious/cultural transfor-

---

[34] Abitol, *Tombouctou;* Louis Brenner, *The Shehus of Kukwa: A History of the al-Kanemi Dynasty of Bornu* (Oxford, 1973); D. Murray Last, *The Sokoto Caliphate* (London, 1967); cf. the tenth–eleventh century struggles between ancient Ghana and the Sanhaja Berbers over the desert entrepôt of Awdaghast (Devisse, ''La question d'Audaghust'').

[35] Dennis D. Cordell, ''Eastern Libya, Wadai, and the Sanusiya: A Tariqa and a Trade Route,'' *Journal of African History* 18 (1977): 28–9; Henry Lhote, *Les Touaregs de Hoggar (Ahaggar)* (Paris, 1944); idem, ''Le cycle caravanier des Touaregs de l'Ahaggar et la saline de Amadror,'' *Bulletin de l'Institut Français de l'Afrique Noire* 31 (1969): 1014–27; Lovejoy and Baier, ''Desert-Side Economy''; Elizabeth Ann McDougall, ''The Ijil Salt Industry: Its Role in the Pre-Colonial Economy of the Western Sudan'' (Ph.D. diss., University of Birmingham, 1980); Charles C. Stewart, *Islam and the Social Order in Mauretania* (Oxford, 1973).

mation and capital concentration in the neighboring Sudanic regions. It was the Air and Mauritanian desert communities in particular that constituted the key export market for Sudanic textiles and manufactured leather goods. Moreover, the development of internal merchant networks within the Sudan depended more directly on the distribution of goods traded between the desert, forest, and savannah than upon trans-Saharan commerce.[36] Nonetheless, trans-Saharan trade benefited in indirect but, as already seen, critical ways from this internalization of the desert economy.

Hoggar, by contrast, is a good example of a more traditional desert community, interdependent with the trans-Saharan trade but unable to provide needed services on as reliable a basis as its southern and eastern counterparts and far less involved in such sedentary activities as religious learning, agriculture, and handicrafts. Hoggar thus represents a now-narrowed band of desert society that maintained only a minimal (albeit still considerable) interdependency with more densely settled areas and their commercial representatives. But the apparent fact that this zone of totally external desert society had shrunk in the course of the four centuries between European arrival on the coast and colonial conquest of the interior does explain at least some of the resiliency of the trans-Saharan caravan trade.

CONCLUSION

Two mutually compatible hypotheses were suggested at the beginning of this paper to explain the survival of trans-Saharan caravan trade after 1500. Most of the evidence presented has tended to support the first of these arguments: that the trade was conducted on an essentially unchanged basis and persisted mainly because it was protected from European oceanic competition by the natural barrier of the Guinea forest as well as the structural barrier between the Atlantic commercial circuits and North Africa. The only element of increased efficiency within the desert trading derived from the increased integration of southern Saharan nomadic societies into the growing economy of neighboring Sudan.

How do these conclusions relate to the broader and incompatible arguments concerning the relationship between transport innovation

---

[36] Louis Brenner, "The North African Trading Community in the Nineteenth Century Central Sudan," in Norman R. Bennett and Daniel F. McCall, eds., *Aspects of West African Islam* (Boston, 1971), 137–50; Paul E. Lovejoy, "Commercial Sectors in the Economy of the Nineteenth-Century Central Sudan: The Trans-Saharan Trade and the Salt Trade," *African Economic History* 13 (1984): 85–116.

and economic growth? Do they support Postan's Productivity Postulate (increased efficiency in agriculture and industry is more important than changes in transport) or Austen's Africanist Axiom (transport innovation is the overwhelmingly dominant engine of historical economic growth)?

Postan clearly wins out if we consider the trans-Saharan trade from an international perspective. It was a noninnovative transport system that nevertheless prospered from increases in supplies of manufactured goods and demand for raw materials generated by production innovations in the Atlantic economy. The Africanist argument is most valid for understanding the significance of the Guinea forest transport barrier (and its later penetration by railroads) for the survival and eventual demise of an archaic caravan economy.

The most interesting confrontation between these two positions occurs when we consider the role of Sudanic economic growth in creating a more stable environment for long-distance transport in the southern Sahara. Here Postan seems stronger in explaining the internal African factors, since such Saharan transport changes as did develop appear to be a function of innovations in other sectors. But if we look at development in those other sectors either more closely or at a greater distance, agricultural and industrial productivity seems less determinant. First of all, there were no technological changes in Sudanic production systems during this period, although we may consider the concentration of dependent cultivators and urban craftsmen a partial example of productivity gains.[37] Second, European trade with and through the even less innovative Guinea forest zone played a major role in Sudanic economic growth; thus the opening of new sea routes ultimately contributed as much to the preservation of their trans-Saharan "competition" as they did to drawing increased quantities of raw materials to the coast.

The ultimate issue in studying the role of transport systems in the immediately precolonial African economy is, of course, to comprehend the nature of that economy and the direction of its change under the impact of European expansion. Because it was both deeply involved with Europe and yet significantly insulated from European influence by internal transportation barriers, Africa is at once the great victim and the great survivor of the early modern world economy. It was victimized with respect to the many millions of its people who were forced into the Atlantic and Islamic slave trades, and it was a survivor because its internal economic life was far less radically trans-

---

[37] See Austen, *African Economic History*, 44–9, for a fuller discussion of this issue.

formed than that of much of Asia and native America. What Africa, largely for environmental reasons, could not and did not become was a competitor with Europe (except in the white settled areas at the southern end of the continent, to which West Africa is the classic and self-celebrated antithesis). Noncompetitiveness allowed a form of continued growth in the early modern period but may be linked to major economic crises in the less-insulated modern period, especially in the Sahelian regions central to the Sudanic–Saharan caravan system. Thus the historical paradox analyzed here may be the prelude to a contemporary tragedy.

CHAPTER 11

The "decline" of the central Asian caravan trade

MORRIS ROSSABI

THE central Asian caravan trade linking Europe, the Middle East, and China, which had developed as early as the Han dynasty (206 B.C.–A.D. 220), began to decline during Sung (960–1279) times and truly collapsed in the late sixteenth and early seventeenth centuries. It flourished during the Han and T'ang (618–907) dynasties, but the turbulence in northwest China during the Sung period disrupted trade along the so-called Silk Roads. In the Mongol era (midthirteenth to midfourteenth centuries), trade across Eurasia witnessed a resurgence that continued through the first century or so of Ming (1368–1644) rule. By the late Ming, however, the long-distance trade between China and the Middle East and Europe had dwindled to a trickle.[1]

Decline of this central Asian caravan trade has often been attributed to competition from the European oceangoing vessels that began to reach China in the sixteenth century. This new trade conveyed bulkier items, was less costly, and was freer of harassment and plunder. Such economic advantages, it has been asserted, enabled the sea trade to supersede the overland commerce, resulting ultimately in the collapse of the traditional caravan trade. This paper proposes, however, that though rising costs and competition from the oceangoing trade undermined land commerce across Eurasia, the political disruptions and the religious and social changes of the time must also be considered. These transformations were as critical as the economic pressures challenging merchants who were intent on maintaining the caravan trade.

An analysis of the reasons for the changes in the central Asian caravan trade in the sixteenth and seventeenth centuries needs to take

---

[1] For additional details on these developments, see Morris Rossabi's essay "Trade Routes in Inner Asia," in Denis Sinor, ed., *Cambridge History of Inner Asia,* forthcoming from Cambridge University Press.

351

into account two other considerations. First is that the short-distance caravan trade did not diminish. Commerce between the sedentary civilizations and the pastoral nomadic societies across Eurasia continued relatively uninterrupted even after the seventeenth century.[2] Second is the paucity of precise information about this commerce. The merchants who conducted the long-distance trade kept few records of their transactions nor did they wish to reveal what they perceived to be their commercial secrets. As Niels Steensgaard has observed in his study of the European–Asian trade: "Information concerning the costs of caravan transport is unfortunately extremely scanty. This is hardly an accident, since it was one of the peddlar's business secrets just like routes and prices. The information at our disposal is scattered and difficult to interpret precisely."[3]

DIFFICULTIES OF LONG-DISTANCE TRADE

Formidable obstacles had traditionally confronted long-distance trade across Eurasia. The caravan trade required an enormous investment of time and capital. Ghiyāth al-dīn Naqqāsh, who traveled in 1419 on an official embassy sent by Tamerlane's son Shāhrukh to the Ming court, wrote that the journey from Herat (in Afghanistan) to Peking took about a year.[4] In the same decade, the Chinese envoy Ch'en Ch'eng traveled for approximately the same length of time to reach Samarkand from Peking.[5] About nine to ten months elapsed between the papal legate John of Marignolli's departure from Constantinople and his arrival in central Asia in 1339.[6] Thus a trip from the Middle East to the Chinese capital might last a year and a half to two years. The individual states and papacy defrayed the costs of these aforementioned official embassies, but the expenses of most caravans were borne by merchants and other private individuals.

Since the caravans needed to obtain supplies and to rest their animals en route, a series of oases, free from bandit harassment, were essential if the caravan trade were to survive. The oases relied on a subsistence agriculture and generally had small populations, though the inhabitants were of diverse ethnic and religious backgrounds. They

---

[2] For the continuation of this trade, see Saguchi Toru, *Juhachi jukyuseiki higashi torukistan kenkyu* (Tokyo, 1963), and idem, "Kashgaria," *Acta Asiatica* 34 (1978): 61–78.

[3] *The Asian Trade Revolution of the Seventeenth Century: The East India Companies and the Decline of the Caravan Trade* (Chicago, 1973), 31.

[4] K. M. Maitra, *A Persian Embassy to China* (reprint, New York, 1970), 5–6.

[5] Ch'en Ch'eng, *Hsi-yü hsing-ch'eng chi* (reprint, Peking, 1937); Morris Rossabi, "Two Ming Envoys to Inner Asia," *T'oung Pao* 62, 1–3 (1976): 15–21.

[6] Henry Yule, *Cathay and the Way Thither* (reprint, Taipei, 1966), 3:190.

owed their significance to their fortuitous geographic locations, not to their resources or other economic advantages. Their hospitality to travelers was also as important as their fine geographic positions in the mostly bleak and desolate desert and mountainous regions of central Asia. Merchants and missionaries repeatedly referred to the friendliness and cordiality of the inhabitants of such oases and towns as Hami, Khotan, and Samarkand.[7] Since they could often find residents who spoke the same language, commercial transactions would in theory be smoother. The major Chinese and Persian dynasties sought to and at times actually did rule these areas, and it is no accident that the volume of trade during those periods was greater than at any other time. When the dynasties were weak, the oases and towns were unstable or were threatened by bandits, and long-distance trade was at a low ebb.

Yet the success of the caravan trade required measures other than the pacification of a few oases and towns. Defense against marauders was essential, and the great dynasties devised at least three institutions to safeguard travelers and caravans. The Chinese stationed garrisons and erected watchtowers beyond the Great Wall, seeking in this way "to provide a safe line of communications for the use of diplomats, trading caravans, and other travellers who were proceeding to the west."[8] The soldiers managed hostels, supplied water and other necessities, and used smoke and flag signals to warn of dangers or unusual occurrences. The Chinese and, in particular, the Mongols created the second institution, the postal station.[9] Though the primary objective of the postal stations was the speedy conveyance of government documents, they also benefited commerce, for they fre-

---

[7] On Hami, see M. C. Imbault-Huart, *Le pays de Hami ou Khamil* (Paris, 1892); Morris Rossabi, "Ming China and Central Asia" (Ph.D. diss. Columbia University, 1970); Edward Schafer, *The Golden Peaches of Samarkand* (Berkeley, 1963). On Khotan, see, among other sources, Roy A. Miller, *Accounts of Western Nations in the History of the Northern Chou Dynasty* (Berkeley, 1959), 11. Marco Polo tells us that the inhabitants of Hami were hospitable to the point of lending their wives to weary travelers. See Henry Yule, *The Book of Ser Marco Polo the Venetian concerning the Kingdoms and Marvels of the East,* 3d ed. revised by Henry Cordier (London, 1903), 1:209–10. On the trade routes in general, see Luce Boulnois, *The Silk Road,* trans. Dennis Chamberlain (New York, 1966), and L. Carrington Goodrich, "Trade Routes to China from Ancient Time to the Age of European Expansion," in Jean Labatut and Wheaton Lane, eds., *Highways in Our National Life* (Princeton, 1950), 16–32.

[8] Michael Loewe, *Records of Han Administration* (Cambridge, 1967), 1:48. For the argument questioning the existence of the so-called Great Wall, see Arthur Waldron, "The Problem of the Great Wall," *Harvard Journal of Asiatic Studies* 43, 2 (1983): 643–63.

[9] On the postal system at its height during the Mongol era, see Peter Olbricht, *Das Postwesen in China unter der Mongolenherrschaft im 13. und 14. Jahrhundert* (Wiesbaden, 1954), and Haneda Tōru, *Genchō ekiden zakkō* (Tokyo, 1930).

quently provided supplies and lodgings for merchants. The peoples
of the Middle East developed the caravanserai, the third such institution, to facilitate trade in much the same ways.[10]

Natural conditions also served as barriers to the caravan trade.
Sandstorms, accidental spillage or theft of water, loss of supplies and
inability to reach the next oasis, and sunstrokes and attendant hallu-
cinations were a few of the hazards of desert travel. The inhabitants
of Turfan, situated below sea level in one of the world's great depres-
sions, spent most of the summer in underground shelters in order to
escape the high temperatures of the surrounding desert.[11] Ava-
lanches, icy conditions, frostbite, and altitude sickness were deter-
rents and dangers in traversing the rugged mountainous terrain of
central Asia.[12] To assist in overcoming such obstacles, the caravans
often relied upon camels, which could carry more weight and required less water than any other available animals. They also needed
less pasture than horses or mules and were thus more suited to desert
and high-altitude travel.[13] Yet camel raising and maintenance required expertise. The gestation period for camels is long, many of the
beasts are sterile, and the death rate in infancy is high – all of which
makes camel rearing time-consuming and expensive. These conditions contributed to the risk and costliness of the caravan trade, and
abundant evidence of the dangers may be found in numerous travel
accounts describing the skeletons of men and animals observed en
route.

Bandit raids and customs duties added to the expense and occasionally led to the development of partnerships designed to reduce
the risks for the individual merchant. Looters roamed the steppe and
desert areas and preyed upon caravans loaded with valuable goods.
The various kingdoms and tribes en route demanded payment in return for permitting caravans to travel through their territories. These
expenses, which Steensgaard refers to as "protection costs," were
onerous and fostered unstable and unpredictable costs for merchants.
Some merchants responded by forming *commenda* or *ortogh*, associations of investors and traders who raised capital for and shared the

[10] Jean Sauvaget, "Caravanserails syriens du moyen-âge," *Ars Islamica* 4 (1937): 98–
121.

[11] Morris Rossabi, "Ming China and Turfan, 1406–1517," *Central Asiatic Journal* 16, 3
(1972): 206–7.

[12] Albert von Le Coq, *Buried Treasures of Chinese Turkestan*, trans. Anna Bartwell (London, 1928); and Ch'en Ch'eng, *Hsi-yü hsing-ch'eng chi*, 3–5a.

[13] Edward Schafer, "The Camel in China down to the Mongol Dynasty," *Sinologica* 2
(1950): 165–94, 263–90; Richard Bulliet, *The Camel and the Wheel* (Cambridge, Mass.,
1975).

risks of the caravan trade. Yet few such associations developed. The *ortogh*, for example, which were composed of Muslim merchants, were encouraged and promoted by the Mongol khans but they split apart once the Mongol empire declined.[14] Individual merchants and peddlars, by and large, conducted most of the trade and assumed most of the risks.

Taking into account the expenses, hazards, and insecurities of long-distance trade, its continuance throughout the centuries requires explanation. Short-distance trade between the sedentary agricultural civilizations and the neighboring pastoral nomadic societies was useful and profitable for both, and the commodities exchanged were often necessities. Long-distance trade, on the other hand, involved such luxury goods as silk and jade, for the economics of such commerce entailed the transport of articles of low volume but high value. Since these commodities were not essentials, it seems clear that caravans continued to convey goods across Eurasia because of the anticipated high profits. The elites in Europe and the Middle East were willing to pay vast sums for foreign luxury items. Though the Chinese, in theory, disdained commerce and professed a lack of interest in "exotic" products from abroad, their elites too coveted rare and precious goods from Persia and the Middle East. Despite disasters that might befall individual caravans, long-distance trade remained lucrative at least until the late sixteenth century.

CARAVAN TRADE AT ITS HEIGHT

Before we consider the forces leading to the decline of the caravan trade, we ought to examine the specific factors that contributed to its prosperity. The commercial handbook of Francesco Balducci Pegolotti, which was written in the fourteenth century, offers valuable insights into the operations and economics of the flourishing caravan trade. And the Chinese sources on trade and tribute of the fifteenth and sixteenth centuries yield data on the overland commerce with central Asia and the Middle East.

Pegolotti, who never personally undertook a journey across Eurasia but instead gathered information from other merchants, provided a guidebook for trading caravans planning the long trip to China. He sketched a route from Azov in southern Russia to Hang-chou, the

---

[14] On the *commenda*, see Abraham L. Udovitch, "Commercial Techniques in Early Medieval Islamic Trade," in D. S. Richards, ed., *Islam and the Trade of Asia* (Philadelphia, 1970), 47; and on the *ortogh*, see Weng Tu-chien, "Wo-t'o tsa-k'ao," *Yen-ching hsüeh-pao* 29 (June 1941): 205–9.

capital of the recently subjugated Southern Sung dynasty, and identified the modes of travel, be they by camel, boat, ass, or horse, from
the major halting places. Travel time was one of his concerns, and his
estimate of the length of the journey amounted to two hundred and
seventy days. His figure referred only to actual days of traveling and
did not include the lengthy intervals when journeys were delayed
due to inclement weather or other hazardous conditions, not to mention the need for rest and for additional supplies. Given these extra
days, our earlier estimate of approximately a year and a half for the
trip from the Middle East to China seems reasonable.

Pegolotti emphasized the security of the Eurasian trade route. He
sought to reassure potential traders by reporting that "the road you
travel from Tana [Azov] to Cathay is perfectly safe, whether by day
or by night, according to what the merchants say who have used it."[15]
The Mongol hegemony had fostered a relatively peaceful environment over much of Asia and had reduced bandit harassment of caravans. With less fear of plunder, the costs incurred by the merchants
were lowered and became more predictable. The so-called protection
costs thus were generally not oppressive, did not deter trade, and did
not add substantially to the merchants' expenses.

Neither were transport and customs duties, the other component
of protection costs, excessively burdensome. Pegolotti reckoned the
expenses of a caravan transporting goods that could be sold for 25,000
golden florins. Assuming that the merchant brought along a total of
sixty men and sufficient animals and supplies for that contingent, his
expenses would amount to 300 to 400 golden florins for the trip to
China. The return trip would cost about 25 golden florins per pack
animal. Since forty to sixty animals were needed for transport, the
expenditures would run to 1,000 to 1,500 golden florins. The merchant could count therefore on transport expenses of less than 2,000
golden florins. The customs charges for goods entering Azov varied
somewhat. Gold, silver, and pearls were not liable to any duty, but a
charge of 5 percent was imposed on wine, oxhides and tails, and many
other commodities. Assuming that officials demanded an average
payment of 5 percent on the caravan's goods, the total duty was no
more than 1,000 golden florins. The duties imposed en route to China,
even including "the exactions of the Moccols [Mongols] or Tartar
troopers along the road, [which] will amount to something like fifty
aspers [or slightly more than one golden florin] a load," would average 5 golden florins per load, or 200 to 300 florins for the total of forty

---

[15] Yule, *Cathay and the Way Thither*, 3:152.

to sixty pack animals.[16] The round-trip duties would cost 400 to 600 golden florins for the entire caravan, and the total expenditures on transport and customs duties would amount to about 3,500 golden florins.

Perhaps equally important as these moderate costs was their apparent predictability. A merchant could count on a set expenditure for each caravan. One of the uncertainties often confronting him was no longer as risk laden. The Mongols had not totally pacified the regions caravans traversed. In fact, much strife and even actual warfare still occurred among the various Mongol khanates, but the generally amicable relationship between the Yüan rulers of China and the Il-khanids of Persia ensured relatively safe passage for most caravans.[17] The major remaining variable for the merchant was the price he could obtain after conveying goods to market. Supply and demand, factors over which he did not have much control, determined the value of his goods. The element of risk was not dispensed with but was certainly reduced. Eurasian trade flourished as a result.

The Ming dynasty sources reveal that this commerce continued into the fifteenth and early sixteenth centuries. The Ming dynastic history as well as the *Shih-lu* (Veritable record), a more comprehensive record of court activities, attest to the lively interchange of official embassies and trade caravans between China and the Middle East.[18] The first emperor of the dynasty, in reaction to the bitterness engendered by Mongol rule over China, sought to restrict, if not eliminate, commercial relations with foreigners and foreign lands. His son and the third ruler of the dynasty, the Yung-lo emperor, reversed this policy and encouraged tribute and trade with neighboring and distant states. Later emperors did not share the Yung-lo emperor's desire for expansion of foreign commerce, but neither did they ban trade.

Simultaneously, the Islamic dynasties of that era coveted Chinese products. The Turkish and Persian rulers were eager to obtain Ming jades, porcelains, and textiles. It is no accident that two of the finest collections of Ming porcelains in the world are located at the Topkapi Museum in Turkey and at the Ardebil Shrine in Iran.[19] Since Chinese

---

[16] Ibid., 164.

[17] On these struggles, see Peter Jackson, "The Dissolution of the Mongol Empire," *Central Asiatic Journal* 22, 3–4 (1978): 186–244; Joseph F. Fletcher, "The Mongols: Ecological and Social Perspectives," *Harvard Journal of Asiatic Studies* 46, 1 (1986): 47–50; and Morris Rossabi, *Khubilai Khan: His Life and Times* (Berkeley, 1988), 54–5.

[18] Rossabi, "Ming China and Central Asia," offers a study of these relations based on the *Shih-lu*. The extremely useful *Mindai seiiki shiryō* (Kyoto, 1973) includes all the references to the Western Regions in the *Shih-lu*.

[19] John A. Pope, *Fourteenth-Century Blue and White: A Group of Chinese Porcelains in the*

Muslims and the Turks of central Asia also prized porcelains, several of the Ming ceramic workshops produced porcelains specifically for this market.[20]

The success of this trade depended upon the security of four areas – the oases south of the T'ien Shan mountains in the area known as Uyghuristan, the towns of Transoxiana, the cities of Persia, and the commercial centers of Turkey. The fifteenth century witnessed a resurgence of powerful rulers and dynasties in each of these regions. Early in the century, the Mughals, Muslim descendants of the Mongols, succeeded in supplanting the Uyghurs as the governors of Turfan, Hami, and the other towns south of the T'ien Shan.[21] They retained control through the middle of the sixteenth century. Transoxiana was dominated by the Timurids, with a capital first in Samarkand and then in Herat. These descendants of the conqueror Tamerlane fostered the development of a flourishing economy and encouraged a literary and artistic renaissance in their domains.[22] The Timurids also dominated the great cities of Persia, pacifying the land and offering important positions in government to its talented men. But the dynasty collapsed in the first decade of the sixteenth century. The Uzbeks, a group of nomadic Turks, conquered Transoxiana, imposing their rule on the towns and the surrounding countryside while the Kazakhs and the Kirghiz, less sedentary Turkic peoples, dominated the steppelands. With the decline of the Timurids, an indigenous dynasty, the Safavids, took power in Persia. Yet throughout the fifteenth century Transoxiana and Persia were stable. In the same century, the Ottoman Turks gradually occupied Turkey, with the final step being the seizure of Constantinople in 1453. Turkey was thus united and pacified.

With such stability in the key regions, it is no wonder that Eurasian trade grew dramatically during this period. I have already shown in my other writings that trade between the oases of the T'ien Shan region and China persisted and, in some cases, expanded during the fifteenth century. Turfan, for example, dispatched fifty-four official

Topkau Sarayi Muzesi, Istanbul (Washington, D.C., 1952), and idem, *Chinese Porcelains from the Ardebil Shrine* (Washington, D.C., 1956).

[20] Kamer Aga-Oglu, "Blue-and-White Porcelain Plates Made for Moslem Patrons," *Far Eastern Ceramic Bulletin* 3, 3 (1951): 12–16.

[21] E. Denison Ross, trans., and N. Elias, ed., *A History of the Moghuls of Central Asia, Being the Tarikh-i-Rashidi of Mirza Muhammad Haidar, Dughlat* (reprint, New York, 1970).

[22] V. V. Barthold, *Four Studies on the History of Central Asia*, vol. 2, *Ulugh-Beg*, trans. V. Minorsky and T. Minorsky (Leiden, 1963), remains a standard source on the Timurids.

tribute embassies, which were simply disguised trading missions, to China from 1407 to 1502.[23] This figure does not include various unofficial commercial missions that traded with merchants along China's northwestern frontiers. There were, to be sure, complaints by both Ming and Mughal merchants and officials and even some temporary suspensions of trade, but generally commercial transactions were maintained, with Turfan receiving silks, paper money, and clothing while the Chinese obtained horses and camels.

Similarly, the Timurid rulers of central Asia and Persia, after an initial contretemps with the Ming court, developed a healthy commercial relationship with China. Samarkand dispatched one official embassy every two or three years throughout the fifteenth century. Despite sporadic Ming court efforts to restrict missions from the Timurids, trade was rarely interrupted. Ming officials, on several occasions, urged the emperors to reject embassies that offered "useless" gifts such as lions, but their objections were ignored.[24] Trade and tribute missions from the Persian cities of Shiraz and Isfahan, controlled by the Timurids, also flowed into China. Ming sources reveal that a steady influx of merchants and officials from the two cities reached the court; however, fewer missions and caravans from Persia than from central Asia arrived at the Chinese frontiers.[25]

Arabs from the Middle East and the Ottoman Turks who had overrun Turkey also shared in the trade. Merchants from Mecca reached China starting in the middle of the fifteenth century. Bandits attacked one of these caravans, killed the chief envoy, and wounded the son of one of Mecca's rulers.[26] No other untoward incidents are mentioned in the sources, and missions from Arabia were not deterred from making the long trek to the East. Caravans and missions from Lu-mi (Turkey) and Egypt also arrived to trade for Chinese goods, though they did not reach China as frequently. All of these caravans and so-called embassies brought horses and camels, which they traded for Chinese textiles and porcelains.

Though precise statistics on Eurasian trade are unavailable, this commerce must have been extensive, judging from the Ming court's knowledge of conditions in the Middle East and central Asia. The sources are silent on the quantity of goods, the prices of commodities,

---

[23] Rossabi, "Ming China and Turfan," 211–22.
[24] Chang T'ing-yü et al., *Ming shih* (Yang-ming-shan: Kuo-fang yen-chiu-yüan yin-hang, 1962–3), 3825.
[25] Ibid., 3831.
[26] Ibid., 3833; E. Bretschneider, *Medieval Researches from Eastern Asiatic Sources* (reprint, New York, 1967), 295.

and the expenses incurred by the caravans. The information contained in the Ming dynastic history, though disappointing for the modern economic historian, indicates that the court was well informed about northern Asia and the Middle East. Ch'en Ch'eng's missions from 1414 to 1421 had provided valuable and detailed information on central Asia, which the court historians simply incorporated into the dynastic history. But the court's data on the more distant regions of Persia and the Middle East did not derive from any official embassies; most likely, information was elicited from Arab and Persian merchants who traveled along the caravan routes to China. The *Ta Ming I-t'ung-chih* (Imperial geography) and the Ming dynastic history, as well as other contemporary sources on foreign relations, describe the customs and products of Mecca, Medina, and Turkey, among other lands.[27] Indeed quite a few Ming texts yield information on conditions in the Middle East, an indication of China's continuing contacts with the region.

POLITICAL DISRUPTION AND THE CARAVAN TRADE

The middle of the sixteenth century ushered in a period of political instability in the core areas of the Eurasian caravan trade. This era of political disruption lasted for almost a century and undermined the long-distance trade that had been developing since the Mongol period. The turbulence led to greater unpredictability in costs for merchants. They could not easily estimate their "protection costs" – that is, their customs duties as well as losses incurred in passing through hostile and bandit-infested territories. There was still a market for Chinese goods in western Asia and Europe, but the chaos along the caravan routes threatened the profitability of such trade.

The first political development that harmed the caravan trade was the fall of the Timurid Empire. Plagued by dynastic struggles and the decline of their military, the Timurids were easy prey for the nomadic people, who throughout history had capitalized on any weaknesses of the central Asian sedentary dynasties. The Kazakhs expropriated Timurid lands in the steppes, while the Uzbeks, their most numerous and intimidating opponents, crushed the dynasty and swept through the capitals at Samarkand and Herat in the first decade of the sixteenth century. Many of the Uzbeks eventually settled in towns, but for now they simply plundered these towns and disrupted the com-

---

[27] Mao Jui-cheng, *Huang Ming hsiang-hsü lu* (reprint, Shanghai, 1937), 7, 25b–26b, and 34a–36b, for example.

merce that previously flowed through them. The Uzbeks were not averse to trade, but the initial turbulence they induced as well as the dissolution of an empire and the eventual creation of several Uzbek khanates temporarily subverted Eurasian commerce.

Persia, another vital link in the Eurasian commerce, underwent a dynastic change that caused even more dislocation for the caravan trade. Around 1500, the Safavid leader Ismāʿīl began to dislodge the influence and power of the Timurids and several minor dynasties in Persia. In 1501, he proclaimed himself shāh and set forth on a decade-long series of campaigns that ultimately produced unity in Persia under his rule. But Persian unification did not foster the stability needed for a flourishing caravan trade. Conflicts erupted along Persia's eastern frontiers, as the Uzbek confederation challenged the Persian dynasty throughout the sixteenth century. The Safavids captured Samarkand in 1511 but were compelled to withdraw by a powerful Uzbek force the very next year. The new dynasty in Persia also faced enemies to the west. The Safavid ruler Ismāʿīl had embraced the Shīʿite form of Islam and pronounced it to be the state religion, enraging the Ottoman Empire, the other great Islamic dynasty of the time. His efforts at proselytization exacerbated hostilities with the Sunnī Ottoman Turks and led to sporadic warfare for the remainder of the sixteenth century.[28] Despite this conflict the Persians continued to export silk to the Ottomans, but on a somewhat reduced scale. With conflicts both to the west and to the east, Persia could no longer be as usable a thoroughfare for caravans. Sunnī merchants could not count on a cordial reception when traversing the country. Even if they were admitted and assured of safe passage, their protection costs, in particular the customs duties levied upon their goods, would be increased by the stronger theocratic government, which favored Shīʿites. Overland trade through Persia thus diminished considerably. By the early seventeenth century, Chinese goods were no longer as readily available in the cities of Persia.

The Safavids also initiated a seaborne commerce that may have adversely affected the overland trade from China to the West. Under Shāh ʿAbbās I (1588–1629), they encouraged a silk trade with Europe, with the British taking part as early as 1616 and the Dutch participating in it by 1645. They sought, in this way, to bypass the hostile Ottoman Turks and provided silk while receiving woolen cloth and Indian cotton from Great Britain and a variety of spices from Holland.

---

[28] R. Savory, "Safavid Persia" in P. M. Holt, Ann K. S. Lambton, and Bernard Lewis, eds., *The Cambridge History of Islam* (Cambridge, 1970), 1:396–402, offers a useful, though somewhat dense, summary of events in the early Safavid period.

This trade may have contributed somewhat to the decline of the caravan trade, but the forces leading to the ultimate downfall of the commerce had been set in motion earlier.[29]

Uyghuristan too was unsettled during the late sixteenth century. The Mughals, who had ruled from Turfan, began to fragment. After the deaths of Saʿīd Khan in 1533 and Mansūr in 1543/44 (two brothers who had together governed the Tarim river basin), succession disputes afflicted the Mughals. One explanation for their difficulties lies in the leadership's ambivalence about changing from a nomadic to a more sedentary society. This tension caused rifts among the elite, with one group seeking to revert to the traditional pastoral heritage and another attempting to promote transformation to an oasis-and-town-based economy. Disaffection spread and permitted the nomadic Kazakhs, a Turkic-speaking people, to detach Ili, the steppelands just north of the T'ien Shan, from Mughal control. The Kazakhs also raided the towns of Uyghuristan and threatened caravans that journeyed along the oases south of the T'ien Shan in order to skirt the inhospitable Taklamakan desert. One of the major overland trade routes thus was jeopardized and made more insecure.

Perhaps as subversive of Mughal rule was the challenge of the Muslim religious hierarchy. The Mughals had converted to Islam but had not established a theocracy or accorded much secular authority to religious leaders. Noticing the increasing difficulties confronting the Mughals, Ṣūfī notables known as Khōjas took advantage of the rulers' vulnerability to assert their own policies.[30] By the early seventeenth century, the Khōjas themselves divided into two warring camps. The Aqtaghliq ("White Mountain") Khōja, based in Kashgar, and the Qarataghliq ("Black Mountain)" Khōja, residing in Yarkand, were the principal rivals for power. They both espoused the Naqsh-

---

[29] It would be of great use to have more precise information about this reduction in trade, but such data are unavailable. As Philip D. Curtin, *Cross-cultural Trade in World History* (Cambridge, 1984), noted in his preface, ix, "The overland trade routes across Asia, for example, or the overland trade between Russia and China are barely mentioned, not because they were insignificant, but because the evidence about these commercial practices is not as rich as other evidence about other times and places." On the Persian silk trade with Europe, see Roger Savory, *Iran under the Safavids* (Cambridge, 1980), 114, 119, 140–4.

[30] My late, esteemed friend and colleague Joseph Francis Fletcher, Jr., had been studying the Moghuls and the Khōjas for many years. Before his untimely death in 1984, he had completed two articles that offer a much more complex portrait than I can present here: "Western Turkestan: The Emergence of the Uzbeks," and "The Eastern Chaghadayid Realm from the Moghuls' Adoption of Islam to Their Loss of Moghulistan," both in Sinor, *Cambridge History of Inner Asia*. A brief discussion may be found in Morris Rossabi, "Muslim and Central Asian Revolts," in Jonathan D. Spence and John E. Wills, Jr., eds., *From Ming to Ch'ing* (New Haven, 1979), 172–4.

bandiyya order of Sufism, but their shared religious views did not translate into common political views. Each sought to be the wielders of power in Uyghuristan. Uyghuristan became a battleground first between the Mughals and the Khōjas and then between the Aqtagh-liq Khōja and the Qarataghliq Khōja. The Khōjas were by no means opposed to trade; in fact, they often acted in the interests of the merchant class. Yet the warfare in which they engaged disrupted long-distant commerce.

The resulting political and military turbulence dealt a devastating blow to the caravan trade. Official missions from Turfan to China, for example, declined drastically. In the late sixteenth and early seventeenth centuries, only one Turfanese embassy every five to six years reached the Ming capital. The more distant towns of the Tarim basin sent even fewer missions. Only two embassies arrived in China from central Asia between 1600 and 1630.[31] Caravans, fearful of the banditry and the unsettled conditions along the Tarim basin did not venture to travel through Uyghuristan. The political chaos with the attendant unstable costs deterred merchants from undertaking the journey. Protection costs could be extorted from them by local rulers who had capitalized on the conflicts among the Mughals, the Aqtaghliq Khō-jas, and the Qarataghliq Khōjas to assert their own dominance over individual towns south of the T'ien Shan.

CHINA IN CRISIS: LATE SIXTEENTH AND SEVENTEENTH CENTURIES

The instability in Transoxiana, Persia, and Uyghuristan was matched by the social and political unrest that prevailed in China in the late sixteenth and early seventeenth centuries. The Ming dynasty was in dire straits. Fiscal difficulties emerged; corruption was rampant; and rebellions began to erupt. The emperor and the court were either unable or unwilling to address these problems.[32]

The northwest corridor through which caravans traveled to the West

---

[31] Based on my studies of the *Ming Shih-lu*. On the effects of this turbulence, Ronald Ferrier observes that "as a result of the gradual fragmentation of the Timurid legacy, the increasing isolationism of the Chinese behind the Great Wall and the rising power of the Uzbeks, the full flow of trade through northern Persia and Central Asia from east to west began to lessen" ("Trade from the Mid-fourteenth Century to the End of the Safavid Period," in Peter Jackson and Laurence Lockhart, eds., *Cambridge History of Iran*, vol. 6, *The Timurid and Safavid Periods* [Cambridge, 1986], 416).

[32] For the difficulties of the late Ming, see James B. Parsons, *The Peasant Rebellions of the Late Ming Dynasty* (Tucson, 1970); Larisa Simonovskaia, *Antifeodal'naia bor'ba kitaiskikh krest'ian v XVII veke* (Moscow, 1966); and Li Wen-chih, *Wan Ming min-pien* (Hong Kong: Yüan-tung t'u-shu king-ssu, 1966).

was economically troubled. The region that now comprises the provinces of Shensi, Ninghsia, and Kansu was not particularly fertile. Nor was it blessed with good communications or good opportunities for trade with the more prosperous areas of China. The peasants barely scratched out a living in ordinary times. The early seventeenth century was an extraordinary time for the northwest, for it was devastated by a disastrous and seemingly interminable drought. The threat of famine galvanized many of the peasants and those on the fringes of peasant society to rebel against the Ming. A key region in the operation of the caravan trade was thus in turmoil.[33]

Starting even earlier, in the late sixteenth century, the Ming court had been compelled to divert its focus from the northwest. The northern and northeastern frontiers riveted the attention of policymakers because of the growing number of confrontations with the non-Chinese groups across those borders. The Mongols had become dissatisfied with Chinese commercial and diplomatic policies, and in a raid in 1550 led by a charismatic and ambitious leader named Altan Khan had reached the gates of Peking before signing an agreement with the Chinese.[34] In the northeast, the Manchus, a new group composed principally of the Jurchen people, who had ruled north China in the twelfth and thirteenth centuries, gradually arose to challenge Ming forces.[35] The Chinese court, barely having the resources to cope with these serious threats to its survival, could not concern itself with the caravan trade. It could not squander resources to safeguard the routes to the West. Survival dictated concentration on the Mongols and the Manchus.

These political considerations had a devastating effect on the caravan trade. The unrest in northwest China, which eventually erupted into full-scale rebellion against the Ming, was not conducive to the growth and prosperity of Eurasian commerce. It deterred many merchants from undertaking the journey, and those who were not daunted faced possible bandit raids and probable exorbitant protection costs. The government's concern about the north and northeast also forestalled attempts to cope with the serious impediments to Eurasian trade.[36] Commerce via northwest China declined considerably.

The decline of the Ming dynasty in the early seventeenth century

---

[33] Rossabi, "Muslim and Central Asian Revolts," 187–9.
[34] Henry Serruys, "Four Documents Relating to the Sino-Mongol Peace of 1570–1571," *Monumenta Serica* 19 (1960): 2–11.
[35] See Morris Rossabi, *The Jurchens in the Yüan and Ming* (Ithaca, 1982).
[36] Joseph F. Fletcher, "China and Central Asia, 1368–1884," in John K. Fairbank, ed., *The Chinese World Order* (Cambridge, Mass., 1968), 217.

became even more of an impediment to the continuation of Eurasian trade. Rebellions under the leadership of Li Tzu-ch'eng broke out in the 1630s in northwest China. Much of the northwest was in turmoil and would remain unsettled for more than a decade. Li captured Peking in 1644 but was compelled to withdraw and was killed by Manchu forces. The Manchus quickly occupied the capital and established the Ch'ing dynasty later that year. The new dynasty was not, however, in full control of the territory of China. Its authority within the country would be challenged until 1681, and along its borders it faced grave threats as late as 1696.

The northwest, in particular, continued to disrupt the stability that the early Ch'ing wished to impose. Ting Kuo-tung and Mi La-yin, two Chinese Muslims, organized their coreligionists in the northeast into a force of approximately one thousand men and began a campaign in 1646 to oust Ch'ing forces from Lan-chou and the other towns along the silk route westward.[37] The rebels made steady progress with the help of fellow Muslims from Uyghuristan. The princes of Hami and Turfan offered supplies and a few reinforcements to the Chinese Muslim rebels. The Ch'ing court, concerned about this challenge, moved decisively to suppress the Muslims. It dispatched a large force, led by the Chinese governor-general of Shensi province, to destroy the rebel enclaves and to pacify the northwest.[38] He accomplished his mission in the most brutal way and by 1650 had crushed the Muslims with great loss of life on both sides. Tens of thousands died, and the bitterness engendered by these campaigns did not dissipate. Relations between the Chinese Muslims (or *Hui*, in Chinese) and the Ch'ing government deteriorated throughout the remainder of the dynasty.[39]

The oases of Uyghuristan too were hostile to the newly founded dynasty in China. Their hostility stemmed, in part, from the commercial disputes that flared up between them and the Ch'ing court, which sought to restrict trade. The Muslim merchants of Uyghuristan were determined to increase, rather than contract, trade with China and resented Ch'ing efforts to limit tribute and trade missions. In the 1640s, nine of the most important towns were briefly united, making them more potent adversaries of the Ch'ing. 'Abd Allah of Yarkand and his eight younger brothers dominated Uyghuristan, and they responded to Ch'ing policy by supporting the Chinese Muslim dissidents.[40] Even

---

[37] Chung Fang, comp., *Ha-mi chih* (reprint, Taipei, 1967), chap. 3.
[38] Arthur W. Hummel, ed., *Eminent Chinese of the Ch'ing Period* (reprint, Washington, D.C., 1943–4), 572.
[39] *Tun-huang hsien-chih* (reprint, Taipei, 1967), 91.
[40] Tseng Wen-wu, *Chung-kuo ching-ying Hsi-yü shih* (Shanghai, 1936), 242–3.

after the suppression of the Muslim rebels, Turfan, Hami, Yarkand, and the other oases continued to battle the commercial restrictions of the Ch'ing. In 1656 they began once again to send tribute missions to China, but they continued to chafe at the limitations arbitrarily imposed by the Ch'ing.

This turbulence in the northwest in the middle of the seventeenth century made merchants wary of dispatching caravans across Eurasia. The fear of attacks by one protagonist or another and of extortion by rapacious leaders and states deterred traders despite the prospects of sizable profits if the goods they transported reached the Middle East or Europe. Protection costs and other losses simply cut sharply into profits, and merchants found it impractical to convey products across these treacherous, unstable regions.

The rise of the Zunghar Mongols exacerbated the political and military tensions along China's northwestern border. Starting as pastoral nomadic people, the Zunghars made strides in the early seventeenth century toward the creation of a more sedentary society.[41] Their leaders encouraged crafts and industries, promoted agriculture, embraced Lama Buddhism, developed a new, more precise written script for Mongol, and made a concerted effort to establish the first powerful confederation among the Mongols since the time of the Yüan dynasty. In the middle of the seventeenth century, they moved from modern western Mongolia westward into the steppelands north of the T'ien Shan. From there, they learned of the lack of unified leadership in Uyghuristan and sought to capitalize on the unsettled conditions in the area. Their ruler Galdan had the grandiose ambition of founding a great Mongol empire in the manner of Chinggis Khan. The first target in his plans for expansion was Uyghuristan. He cleverly avoided full-scale warfare by shrewd manipulation of the divisions within the enemy camp. Allying himself with the Aqtaghliq Khōja, he moved against Hami and Turfan in 1679. He occupied those vital oases within a few months. Shortly thereafter, he marched toward and compelled the surrender of Kashgar and Yarkand. Yet peace eluded Uyghuristan, for two years later the Qarataghliq Khōja, taking advantage of Galdan's absence during a return to Zungharia, challenged the Zunghars' authority.[42] They did not oust Galdan's forces, but the continual raids and attacks by both sides disrupted commercial networks and, as a result, the caravan trade.

---

[41] On the Zunghars, see I. Y. Zlatkin, *Istoriya dzhungarskogo khanstva (1635–1738)* (Moscow, 1964), and C. R. Bawden, *The Modern History of Mongolia* (New York, 1968), 50–1.

[42] *Ch'ing Shih* (Taipei: Kuo-fang yen-chiu-yüan yin-hang, 1961), 1004–5.

All of inner Asia was in turmoil until the middle of the eighteenth century. Because Galdan was unable to unify the Mongols, he eventually succumbed to the Ch'ing Empire. In 1696 Manchu armies decisively defeated him in the steppelands, and the following year, he died or committed suicide. His nephew Tsewang Rabtan and his successors continued to threaten China's frontiers until 1757, when a Ch'ing army finally defeated and annihilated the Zunghars.[43] Most of the Zunghars were massacred; a few fled to Russia, but the Zunghars as a distinct people disappeared. Yet they had wreaked havoc on the central Asian trade. Commerce across the traditional routes in central Asia reached a virtual standstill.

From the early seventeenth century until the middle of the eighteenth century, China's northwest was chaotic. Chinese tea, porcelain, silk, and medicines were still in demand in the West, and Chinese merchants clearly prized the horses, wool, and silver bullion that they had received from abroad in the sixteenth century. They had traded for horses and wool for centuries, but silver had started to arrive, via Europe, only in the sixteenth century. Much of the bullion was transported by ship to China, but some had come along the caravan routes.[44] Silver had made a dramatic impact on China, leading to more commercialism in the economy. With the decline of the central Asian caravan trade and with less silver reaching the country, China's economy suffered some reverses.

The common assumption that the seaborne commerce superseded the caravan trade needs qualification. The political disruptions that afflicted most of the Asian regions through which caravans traveled were major causes for the decline of the central Asian overland trade. Protection costs were too expensive, and plundering of cargo was a real concern. The economies to be gained from ship transport dampened still further the merchants' plans for overland trade, but a major motive for not dispatching caravans stemmed from the military and political conditions to be faced along the Asian landmass.

---

[43] Morris Rossabi, *China and Inner Asia from 1368 to the Present Day* (London, 1975), 143–9.

[44] S. A. M. Adshead, "The Seventeenth Century General Crisis in China," *Asian Profile* 1, 2 (October 1973): 275–6. See also Frederic E. Wakeman, Jr., "China and the Seventeenth Century Crisis," *Late Imperial China* 7, 1 (June 1986): 1–26, and William S. Atwell, "Setting the Stage: Notes on Bullion Mining, Monetary Policy, and Foreign Trade before the Coming of the Portuguese" (paper presented at the Conference on the International History of Early-Modern East Asia, Kauai, January 1988). Jack Goldstone, "East and West in the Seventeenth Century: Political Crises in Stuart England, Ottoman Turkey, and Ming China," *Comparative Studies in Society and History* 30, 1 (January 1988): 108–9, disputes the significance of foreign silver for the Chinese economy.

The clearest indication that political considerations, not simply cheaper transport costs via seaborne commerce, were important considerations in the decline of the central Asian trade was that the caravan trade did, in fact, prosper in the late seventeenth and eighteenth centuries. But this new commerce did not traverse northwest China, Uyghuristan, Persia, and the Middle East. All of these areas were bypassed, and their economies, without exception, declined. The caravans traveled north through southern Siberia and northern central Asia, as Russian merchants dominated the trade. Russians, with the help of peddlars from Bukhara, revived the caravan commerce.

The Russians negotiated the Treaty of Nerchinsk (1689) and the Treaty of Kiakhta (1728), which permitted them to trade with China.[45] Russian merchants streamed into China during the eighteenth century to trade for cotton, silk, tea, tobacco, and rhubarb. In return, they exported furs, leather, woolens, and, to a lesser extent, iron axes, knives, and shears.[46] Though the trade experienced fluctuations throughout the eighteenth century, the volume of Chinese exports and imports increased dramatically. In 1755 the total volume of trade amounted to 837,066 rubles; by 1800 it had grown to 8,383,846 rubles.[47] Clearly a market for Chinese goods existed in the West, and one for Russian products in China. The new routes taken by the tsarist caravans were all within Russian territory until they reached the frontiers of China. The principal route originated in Moscow and, by both water and land, reached Verkhotur'e, which lay across the Urals, and then Tobol'sk, the capital of Siberia. From there, caravans continued to the city of Yeniseisk and via the Yenisei River to Irkutsk, and then across Lake Baikal toward the Selenga River, arriving at Kiakhta, where trade was conducted.

The success of the Russian–Chinese caravan commerce was due to the lack of turmoil on the northern trade routes. Banditry was virtually nonexistent, and customs duties were minimal, as the caravans merely traveled across one country instead of many disparate petty kingdoms and tribal units. The protection costs that plagued the central Asian caravan trade did not afflict this northern route. Merchants were not deterred by the expenses of the trip, and they did not need to fear attacks on their caravans by unruly vagabonds or rebels. That

---

[45] Numerous books have dealt with early Sino-Russian relations. A useful summary is Mark Mancall, *Russia and China: Their Diplomatic Relations to 1728* (Cambridge, Mass., 1971).

[46] Clifford M. Foust, *Muscovite and Mandarin: Russia's Trade with China and Its Setting, 1727–1805* (Chapel Hill, 1969), 344–60.

[47] Ibid., 332.

clearly was the difference between the traditional central Asian route and the newly developed paths to Russia. The route to Russia was much more secure, and merchants could be assured of profits since the danger of their cargoes being ransacked was limited. The competition from seaborne commerce certainly did not affect this Russian–Chinese trade. The transport costs were manageable, and trade was conducted.

Similarly, the central Asian caravan trade was not initially subverted by seaborne commerce. Instead, it was the rise in transport costs that undermined and finally ruined the overland trade. The arrival of the European merchants on the southeast coast of China accelerated the process of decline, but the underlying causes could not simply be attributed to seaborne commerce. Unsettled political conditions along the southern Eurasian routes precipitated the fall of the traditional caravan trade, but Russian–Chinese commerce replaced it. Trade between the tsarist empire and the Ch'ing dynasty continued concurrently with European sea commerce. To assert that ships were solely responsible for the end of the caravan trade is misleading.

Nonetheless, the central Asian caravan trade did decrease in the seventeenth century, and one indication is the mutual ignorance of China and central Asia, Persia, and the Middle East. The central Asian and Middle Eastern states often had distorted views of China. One bizarre misconception was that China desperately needed trade with central Asia. A central Asian source notes: "It is from Kashgar that jade stone comes. . . . Most of it shipped to China. . . . Without jade, which keeps off lightning, China would be devastated."[48] On the other hand, China during the Ming dynasty was at least somewhat informed about the rest of Eurasia. By the Ch'ing, however, relations with the Middle East and Persia were minimal, and knowledge of the Islamic world was sketchy. The dynastic history of the Ch'ing, unlike the Ming history, yields few details about the states and kingdoms west of China except for the central Asian regions directly adjacent to the Ch'ing dynasty's borders.[49] This is additional proof of China's limited contacts with western Asia during the Ch'ing.

In sum, the decline of the central Asian caravan trade cannot be attributed solely to economic considerations. The political changes in the late sixteenth and seventeenth centuries were at least as impor-

[48] Cited in Fletcher, "China and Central Asia," 358.
[49] Based on a perusal of *Ch'ing shih*, chaps. 517–23. For Ming knowledge of the Islamic world, see Morris Rossabi, "Two Ming Envoys to Inner Asia," 1–34, and J. V. G. Mills, trans., *Ma Huan: Ying-yai Sheng-lan: The overall survey of the ocean's shores* (Cambridge, 1970).

tant in reshaping the course of commerce. Much of the growth in transport costs was the result of political turbulence rather than inefficiencies or new costs in the long-established caravan trade. Neither did seaborne commerce, as is commonly assumed, spell the doom of overland trade across Eurasia.

CHAPTER 12

Merchant communities in precolonial India

IRFAN HABIB

If it were possible to have statistics of the volume of internal and external commerce around the year 1600 for different regions of the globe, it is fairly certain that India, with an estimated population of from 125 to 150 million, would at least have claimed a share proportionate to its population. The land-tax accounted for the larger portion of the surplus in India, and in most areas taxes were collected in money. This alone generated extensive trade in agricultural produce. The ruling classes were largely town-based, and an urban economy flourished, with craft production for both local and distant markets. India was undoubtedly the greatest cotton-textile producer of the world, and the finer qualities of cotton cloth sustained brisk long-distance commerce. The country exported calicoes, indigo, pepper, silk, and numerous other commodities over sea and over land, in return for which it absorbed large quantities of silver. The coinage of the Mughal Empire, issued from numerous mints all over India, was of wonderful fineness and uniformity.

These facts should be sufficient to persuade us of the importance of studying how commerce in India was conducted just at the time that the merchant empires of western Europe had begun their progress toward a worldwide hegemony. The present effort focuses on the merchants and selects two major mercantile communities, the Banjāras (long-distance transporters) and Banyas (village and town merchants), for description. The sketches of the two communities are followed by a discussion of the forms of mercantile organization and commercial and financial techniques of the Banyas. Financially, there will be a provisional attempt to evaluate some of the theories that have been advanced concerning precolonial Indian commerce.

371

THE BANJARAS

We may assume as a universal fact that as an agrarian society develops, interregional exchanges in certain agricultural products begin, and on this basis and, still more, on the basis of extraction of surplus from the countryside, an urban economy at last emerges. Commerce then assumes a number of varied forms depending upon the nature and scale of the exchanges between various communities and regions. Corresponding to such varied forms, there can be levels of organization, and so a hierarchy of mercantile communities, from the seemingly barbarous or nomadic to the patrician or aristocratic. At the lowest levels we come across communities that one would have readily assigned to a very primitive social stage until one realizes that the functions they performed could only have come about when social development had left prehistoric conditions far behind.

Writing in 1634, the author of a Mughal "gazetteer" of Sind tells us that

hill-people such as the Nahmardīs do not engage in agriculture, but possess capital *(māl)* and flocks of large numbers of animals, like camels, horses, sheep, and oxen, and their sustenance is obtained from [sales made in] the subdistricts *(parganas)* of Sehwān and Chakarhāla. Thus they bring and sell here camels, horses, sheep, felt, carpets, and other hill-products, and take away from here food grains, weapons, and cloth. (My translation)[1]

Such hill-tribes thus maintained a pastoral life, supplying cattle to the agricultural communities and distributing products of the plains in the hills. The author considered them a lawless, troublesome lot, for he urged the governor of Thatta (Sind) to forbid their trade altogether in order to prevent the thieving or marauding activities with which they apparently combined their commerce.[2]

The Bhotiyas of the central Himalayas offer a parallel to the nomadic Nahmardī traders of Sind and Baluchistan. Here too we have the same combination of pastoralism and commerce, which is possible only when advanced agricultural communities exist between which the nomads can act as carriers and to which they supply pastoral products.[3]

---

[1] The author adds that merchants from the plains also went into the hill-country, taking cloth, food grains, and weapons and bringing back camels, horses, and sheep. So the hill-tribes did not monopolize the commerce. See Yūsuf Mīrak, *Mazhari-i Shāhjahānī*, ed. Sayyid Husamuddin Rashidi (Karachi, 1962), 239.

[2] Ibid., 239–41.

[3] "At the highest level [in the Himalayas] live the Bhotiyas, among whom pastoralism and trading are more important than agriculture" (O. H. K. Spate and A. T. A. Learmonth, *India and Pakistan: A General and Regional Geography*, 3d ed. [London, 1967], 462).

The Bhotiyas still display these characteristics, because modern means of transport have not yet been fully extended into the Himalayas.[4] When the railways had not yet spread their network over the Indian plains, there were also large communities in the plains that performed the same functions as the Nahmardīs and Bhotiyas – that is, combining pastoralism and the carrying trade. They were known collectively as Banjāras; and their role in Indian agrarian commerce was far more important than that of the hill-tribes on the margins of the subcontinent.

The basis for the trade and, indeed, for the existence of the Banjāras lay in conditions of inland transport. Goods were carried on boats and carts and by camels and bullocks. A bullock could travel quite fast, but it would normally be more expensive than a cart. However, when the pack-oxen traveled slowly, grazing as they went, and were assembled in herds so as to reduce the cost of watching and guiding them, the expenses of transport were so greatly reduced as to make it the cheapest form possible.[5] Here was, then, the opportunity for groups of cattle breeders, who had large herds of oxen; they could travel with their herds over long distances, moving slowly and having their beasts graze directly off the land. They had to move in large groups for safety, and were kept together by strong clan ties and subordination to headmen.

Such carriers are first described in any detail in a historian's account of the price-control measures of Sultan ʿAlāʾ-ud-Dīn Khaljī (1296–1316). On the one hand, the sultan tried to ensure that the peasants sold food grains at low, fixed rates to the *kārwānīs* (literally, people of the caravans); on the other hand, the headmen (*muqaddam*s) of the *kārwānīs* were put in chains until they agreed to bind themselves "like one" and establish encampments for their "women and children, oxen and cattle" on the banks of the Yamuna, as hostages for their good conduct. So food grains began to be brought to Delhi in large quantities, enabling the sultan to have grain sold at approved prices.[6] Another account (c. 1355) calls the carriers *nāyak*s:

---

[4] Where modern transport and commerce disrupted traditional trade, the Bhotiyas had to leave their age-old occupation. Already by 1896, Bhotiyas in the Kumaun district of Uttar Pradesh were reported to be tenant-cultivators and field laborers and to be in the midst of a process of Brahmanization (W. Crooke, *Tribes and Castes of the North-western Provinces and Oudh* [Calcutta, 1896], 61–3).

[5] From data for the seventeenth century presented in my *Agrarian System of Mughal India* (Bombay, 1963), 63 (and nn. 8, 9).

[6] Ziāʾ Baranī, *Tārīkh-i Fīrūz Shāhī*, ed. Saiyid Ahmad Khan, Bibliotheca Indica (Calcutta, 1862), 305–7.

These are people who bring food grains to the City [Delhi] from various parts. Some bring ten thousand [laden] oxen, others twenty thousand. (My translation)[7]

The name Banjāra is not used by either Ziā' Baranī or Naṣīruddīn, our two informants. But their descriptions make any argument against such an identification superfluous. Kabīr's allegorical verse (c. 1500) about "one *nāyak*, five Banjāras with twenty-five oxen laden with bauble" shows that Naṣīruddīn's *nāyak*s were really the chiefs or headmen *(muqaddam)* of the Banjāras.[8] The Banjāra headmen are still called by that name.[9]

The name Banjāra, first used apparently in the sixteenth century, is derived from Sanskrit *vanij* (also the source of the name for the Indian mercantile caste of Banyas).[10] Its universal employment for the various communities of carriers of this kind is noteworthy, the name occurring unaltered in most regions of India, despite their different languages. In Karnataka it is varied to Banijagaru.[11]

It is possible to construct a fairly detailed description of the Banjāras from seventeenth-century sources. The Mughal emperor Jahāngīr (1605–27) noted in his memoirs:

In this country the Banjāras are a fixed class of people, who possess a thousand oxen, or more or less, varying in numbers. They bring grain from the villages to the towns and also accompany armies. With an army [like the one then being prepared for Qandahār], there may at least be a hundred thousand oxen, or more. (My translation)[12]

Among European travelers, Peter Mundy (1632) took a great deal of interest in them. He calls the moving assemblage of the Banjāras a "Tanda," which is in accordance with the surviving terminology.[13]

---

[7] Shaikh Naṣīruddīn's conversations recorded by Hamid Qalandar, *Khairu'l Majālis*, ed. K. A. Nizami (Aligarh, 1959), 241.

[8] *Guru Granth Sāhib*, Devanagari text, Gurudwara Prabandhak Committee (Amritsar, 1951), II, 1194; *Kabīr Granthāvaliī*, ed. Shyamsundardas, Kashi, V. S. 2008/1951, 300. The Urdu poet Naẓir Akbarābādī (d. 1830), in his popular poem "Banjāranāma," using the terms and idioms familiar to Banjāras, employs the word *nāyak* in the sense of "possessor, master."

[9] "Each community has a chief or Naik, whom all implicitly obey" (Henry M. Elliot's note on Banjāras in his *Memoirs on the History, Folklore, and Distribution of the Races of the Northwestern Provinces of India*, ed. J. Beames [London, 1869], I, 56). The same usage in the Panjab: "The headmen of the Banjara parties are called *naiks* and Banjaras in general are not uncommonly known by this name" (Denzil Ibbetson, *Panjab Castes* [1883; Lahore, 1916], 254). The Banjāra headmen were similarly called *nāiks* in central India and the Deccan (R. V. Russell and Hira Lal, *Tribes and Castes of the Central Provinces of India* [reprint, Delhi, 1975], II, 188).

[10] Elliot, *Memoirs*, I, 52.

[11] F. Buchanan, *A Journey from Madras through the Countries of Mysore, Canara and Malabar* (Madras, 1807), I, 205.

[12] *Tuzuk-i Jahāngīrī*, ed. Syed Ahmad (Ghazipur and Aligarh, 1863–4), 345.

[13] According to Captain Mackenzie (1881), a *ṭānda* means "a large caravan of laden

Theis Banjaras carrie all their howsehold along with them, as wives and children, one Tanda consisting of many families. Their course of life is somewhat
like Carriers, continually driveing from place to place. . . . There may bee in
such a Tanda 6 or 700 persons, men, women and children. There men are
very lustie, there weomen hardie, whoe in occasion of fight, lay about them
like men. Theis people go dispersedly [i.e., well spread out], driving their
laden Oxen before them, their Journey not above 6 or 7 miles a day att most,
and that in the Coole.[14]

Tavernier makes a similar statement about these carriers, whose
name is misprinted in his text as "Manaris":

They never dwell in houses and they take along with them their women and
children. Some of them possess 100 oxen, others have more or less, and they
all have a Chief, who acts as a prince.[15]

Mundy further noted that they normally traded on their own account:

Their Oxen are their own. They are sometymes hired by Merchants, but most
commonly they are the Merchants themselves, buyinge of graine where it is
Cheape to be had, and carryinge it to places where it is dearer, and from
thence again relade themselves with anything that will yield benefitt in other
places as Salt, Sugar, Butter, etts.[16]

But it seems that the Banjāras did often depend on credit: hence
their fear of doing business "where the capital *(mūl)* diminishes, while
the interest *(biāju)* ever increases" (Kabīr).[17] Certain verses in the *Guru
Granth Sāhib* (c. 1600) picture the Banjāras as factors of a great merchant-
banker *(sāhu)*, obliged to buy only such goods as would have his approval. God is likened to a *sāhu*, dwelling in a palace, served by millions of Banjāras.[18] The dependence of the Banjāras upon credit from
big merchants was also noticed by early nineteenth-century observers.[19]

bullocks" (quoted in Crooke, *Tribes and Castes of the Northwestern Provinces*, I, 159).
See also Russell and Lal, *Tribes and Castes of the Central Provinces*, II, 186. The term
ṭānda was also applied to customary encampments of the Banjāras; hence many place-
names bearing the word (cf. Beames's note in Elliot, *Memoirs*, I, 53).

[14] "Travels in Asia," *The Travels of Peter Mundy, in Europe and Asia, 1608–1667*, ed. Richard Carnac Temple, 5 vols. (Cambridge, 1907–36), II, 95–6.

[15] Jean Baptiste Tavernier, *Travels in India*, trans. V. Ball, 2d ed. revised by W. Crooke
(London, 1925), I, 33.

[16] *Travels of Peter Mundy*, II, 95–6.

[17] *Kabīr Granthāvali*, 300.

[18] *Guru Granth Sāhib*, I, 22, 180–1, 430.

[19] "The monied men . . . make the Brinjarrees [Banjāras] advances at high interest,
and then monopolize the power of employing them; rendering by this process, the
recovery of their money secure, and the carriers dependent" (John Malcolm, *Memoir
of Central India*, 2d ed. [London, 1824], II, 96). Cf. also Elliot, *Memoirs*, I, 56.

It is difficult to estimate the quantities involved in the trade carried on by the Banjāras. Roe (1615) met on his journey from Surat into Khandesh as many as "10,000 bullocks in one troupe laden with corne, and most days, others, but lesse."[20] Mundy (August 1632) once met "a Tanda or Banjara of Oxen, in number 14,000, all layden with graine as wheat, rice, etts."; two days later he encountered another "Tanda of oxen, number 20,000 (as themselves said) laden with Sugar."[21] Tavernier spoke of the "astonishing sight of 10,000 or 12,000 oxen together, for the transport of rice, corn and salt."[22] A Banjāra headman at Aurangabad (August 1661) submitted to the authorities a complaint, in the course of which he stated that he had gone to Burhanpur with about 1,000 bullocks to sell millet and was returning from there with his animals "unladen" to Jālna.[23] Aurangzeb (1659–1707) says in a letter from the last years of his reign that large numbers of Banjāras had gone to Gujarat but, failing to find food grains (to sell in the Deccan), had loaded their bullocks with salt and dispersed to other parts. Yet Banjāras with "a hundred thousand oxen" still remained in that province trying to buy grain and return to the Deccan across the Narbada.[24]

According to Mundy each ox in a Banjāra convoy carried between 265 and 280 lb. av.; a little larger load is reported by Tavernier.[25] Mundy, as already noted, stated they traveled at the most six or seven miles a day.[26] Fitzclarence, writing of his observations in 1817–18, explains that the Banjāras could not move at above two miles an hour, as "the cattle are allowed to graze as they proceed on the march."[27]

In spite of the slow speed, the quantities of the relatively cheaper goods they moved, essentially for the mass market, must have been considerable. Tavernier tells us that there were four tribes of the "Manaris" (Banjāras), each (doubtless according to popular belief) of a hundred thousand souls. This would give a total Banjāra population of 400,000; and if, as Tavernier says, each family had about a hundred oxen to load, we get a total ox population of about 9 million (assum-

[20] Thomas Roe, *The Embassy of Sir Thomas Roe, 1615–19*, ed. W. Foster (London, 1926), 67.
[21] *Travels of Peter Mundy*, II, 95–8.
[22] *Travels in India*, I, 32–3.
[23] *Selected Documents of Aurangzeb's Reign*, ed. Yusuf Husain Khan (Hyderabad-Deccan, 1958), 18.
[24] "Aḥkām-i ʿĀlamgīrī," India Office MS., 1.0.3887, fol. 83a.
[25] *Travels of Peter Mundy*, II, 95, 98; Tavernier, *Travels in India*, 32. Cf. Irfan Habib, *Agrarian System of Mughal India*, 378, n. 6.
[26] *Travels of Peter Mundy*, II, 96.
[27] Quoted in William Irvine, *The Army of the Indian Moghuls* (reprint, New Delhi, 1962), 192.

ing the conventional ratio of 4.5 persons to a family).[28] Even if an ox carried loads for only a third of the year, at six miles a day, the Banjāras should have annually conveyed on their cattle 1.14 million metric tons each year over an average of 720 miles, or a total of 821 million metric ton-miles a year. Even for so large a country as India, this would be a massive volume of goods transported. (In 1882 Indian railways handled about 2,500 million metric ton-miles.)

From our sources of the Mughal Empire we get little information about the structure and customs of the Banjāra communities. Tavernier seems to be the sole exception. He tells us that they were "idolaters" (Hindus), and their "four tribes" were distinguished by the goods they carried, namely, corn, rice, pulses (legumes), and salt. Their women tattooed their skin from the waist upward. They had priests and had a serpentlike idol carried on a staff placed on a special ox.[29]

There is no doubt that Tavernier's account, though essentially correct, has many inaccuracies. Not all Banjāras were Hindus. Muslims constituted an important segment of the Banjāras in northern India. Although some Banjāra communities were traditionally associated with trade in certain commodities, like the Labanas with salt, the Multānīs with grain, and the Mukeris with wood and timber, it is clear that most of them had no inhibitions about carrying anything that yielded a profit.[30]

Nineteenth-century British anthropological research has provided us with much information about the Banjāras. The tendency to accept a common origin for all Banjāra communities – for example, from the Bhats and Chārans of Rajasthān – may, however, invite skepticism.[31] Their origins were, perhaps, various, the Banjāras being divided among

---

[28] Tavernier, *Travels in India*, I, 33–4. Tavernier's estimate of the Banjāra population is not implausible. In 1911 there were as many as 174,000 Banjāras in Hyderabad State, 136,000 in Central Provinces and Berar, and a slightly smaller number in the Bombay Presidency (Russell and Lal, *Tribes and Castes of the Central Provinces*, II, 162). The North-West Provinces (present Uttar Pradesh) contained 66,828 Banjāras in 1891 (Crooke, *Tribes and Castes of the Northwestern Provinces*, I, 166–7). The 1881 census in the Panjab recorded 59,706 Banjāras, of whom 48,489 were Labanas (a subcaste) (Ibbetson, *Panjab Castes*, table, 256–7).

[29] Tavernier, *Travels in India*, I, 33–5.

[30] In 1891 in the North-West Provinces (Uttar Pradesh) there were 26,953 Muslims in a total of 66,828 Banjāras: For the Labanas, see Crooke, *Tribes and Castes of the Northwestern Provinces*, I, 159. For the Mullānīs and Mukeris, see Russell and Lal, *Tribes and Castes of the Central Provinces*, II, 172.

[31] Russell and Lal, *Tribes and Castes of the Central Provinces*, II, 163. James Skinner (1825) in his Persian work "Tashrīhu-l Aqwām" (British Museum MS, Add. 27,255, fols. 142b–43b) also gives this traditional derivation and says that all Muslim Banjāras were Chārans who had become Muslims "either voluntarily or by force."

different endogamous communities (castes) with different traditions, customs, beliefs, and rites. Elliot (1844) recorded five large castes in what is now Uttar Pradesh, and Cumberlege (1869) distinguished four such in Berar.[32] The communities were regarded by the settled population as of low status, though Elliot, writing before the railways deprived the Banjāras of their occupation, noted that "men of all tribes [castes] are constantly deserting their homes and joining the Banjara fraternity."[33] To European observers, the Banjāras often seemed to recall the Gypsies, and there was even a claim that a Hungarian nobleman had conversed with them in the "Zingari" tongue![34] Superstitions of all kinds, including suspected witch killings and sacrifices, reinforced the Gypsy image of the class.[35] The similarities stemmed from the conditions in which the Banjāras lived; but unlike the Gypsies, there was nothing primitive in the work they did, which, as we have seen, was to undertake as both carriers and merchants the transport of food grains and other bulk goods.

John Malcolm, in his *Memoir on Central India*, written immediately after British occupation, noted that the Banjāras "often engage in great speculations on their own account," though, being illiterate, "few keep accounts." Yet "habit has made them very acute, and their memory is, from continual exercise, extremely retentive of the minutest particulars of their extended transactions." Over fifty years later another observer offered similar testimony.[36]

At first sight, the operations of the Banjāras' might seem to be those of the "peddlers" of Van Leur's definition. No trace of communal possession of cattle has been found among the Banjāras, and Mundy and Tavernier refer to their being owners as individuals. Their joining in large groups led T. Raychaudhuri to comment that "here we have an instance of peddling trade organised on a massive scale."[37] But it is disputable whether just anyone could join a *ṭānda* at his own discretion. The headman's authority over the members of the *ṭānda* extended to what goods they were to carry and where – otherwise 'Alā'-

---

[32] Elliot, *Memoirs*, I, 53–55; Russell and Lal, *Tribes and Castes of the Central Provinces*, II, 163.

[33] Elliot, *Memoirs*, I, 53.

[34] Crooke, *Tribes and Castes of the Northwestern Provinces*, I, 166.

[35] Russell and Lal, *Tribes and Castes of the Central Provinces*, II, 179–82.

[36] Malcolm, *Memoir of Central India*, II, 152–3; Russell and Lal (*Tribes and Castes of the Central Provinces*, II, 191) quote Colonel Mackenzie (1881): "A Banjara who can read or write is unknown. But their memories from cultivation are marvellous and very retentive. They carry in their heads, without slip or mistake, the most varied and complicated transactions and the share of each in such, striking a debitor and creditor account as accurately as the best kept ledger."

[37] *Cambridge Economic History of India* (Cambridge, 1982), I, 342.

ud-Dīn Khaljī's measures of controlling the Banjāras' trade through their headmen would be hard to explain. Such unified operations would enable the Banjāras' trading to be conducted on more informed lines and with much greater effect than would have been the case if each individual made decisions on the basis of rumor or intelligence available to him. One begins to think of the *ṭānda*, then, not only as an instrument of security for its members but also as a primitive substitute for a joint-stock company.

When the Banjāras acted on behalf of large merchant-bankers (evidenced as early as the sixteenth century), their position as peddlers would be still more radically modified when the *sāhu* (merchant-banker), who gave them capital, did so on a large scale. All this should warn us that van Leur's thesis of peddling trade being the principal form of "traditional" Asian commerce needs to be scrutinized even with regards to a sector that, at first sight, looks most primitive and so seems to be an ideal ground for such commerce.

THE BANYAS: THE CLASS

Important as the "primitive" merchants like the Banjāras were for inland trade, they represented only a subordinate sector in the Indian commercial world. Precolonial India had a very large mercantile class, the bulk of it composed of castes, or endogamous communities, which have been so marked a feature of Indian society. Among these communities, the subcastes grouped under the name Banya or Bāniyā were preeminent. When Kabīr (c. 1500) saw the Lord as a Merchant, he saw him as a Bāniyā:

> "My Lord is a Bāniyā. He conducts His commerce righteously.
> Without scales and balances, He weighs the entire universe."[38]

The traditional view of the Banya caste was concisely stated by Abū'l Faẓl (1595):

"One caste of the Bais [Vaishyas], which is designated Banik, is called Banya in ordinary usage and *Baqqāl* in Arabic. It is divided into 84 sub-castes."[39]

The Sanskrit word *banik* or *vanik* meant merchant, and the dictionaries too agree that the name Banya comes from this word.[40] The Arabic

---

[38] *Kabīr Granthāvalī*, 62. Bāniyā, Banyā, Bānyā, etc., are various forms of the same word, Banya.

[39] Abū'l Faẓl, *Āʾīn-i Akbarī*, ed. H. Blochmann, Bibliotheca Indica (Calcutta, 1867–77), II, 57. For the use of the word *baqqāl* for Banya, see also ʿAlī Muḥammad Khān, *Mirāt-i Aḥmadī* (1761), ed. Syed Nawab Ali (Baroda, 1930), suppl., 132, 138.

[40] John Thompson Platts, *A Dictionary of the Urdu, Classical Hindi, and English* (London, 1930), s.v. "Bāniyā, Banyā."

word *baqqāl*, used in Indo-Persian writing as a synonym for Banya, meant "grain merchant" in India and "greengrocer" in Iran.[41] The fact is that trade of almost any kind has been the proper occupation of the Banya, and more so and far longer than any other caste, the Banyas have remained loyal to their traditional occupation. As late as 1911 in the Central Provinces, 60 percent of the Banyas were found to be engaged in trade, whereas only 19 percent of the Brahmans had any religious occupation.[42]

When one speaks of the Banya one means everyone who describes himself as such. Though there are some exceptions, the claim of one group to this status is generally recognized by other Banya subcastes – a situation rarer in other castes.[43] The recognition transcends religious affiliation to the extent that a large section of the Banyas in Gujarat and Rajasthān have professed Jainism for centuries.[44] The Banyas are spread over most of northern India and a large part of the Deccan, where they have dominated the commercial world. Only in Panjab proper did the rival caste of the Khatrīs keep them at bay; and they did not penetrate southern India.[45] But the Komatis ("Committeys") in the Golkunda kingdom seemed to an observer (1618–22) to be "Banians transplanted and grown up in this country by another name."[46]

The subcastes of the Banyas were defined by endogamy and restrictions on dining with members of different subcastes, as seen with some acuteness by Ovington (1696).[47] However, whereas Ovington

---

[41] Tek Chand Bahār, *Bahār-i ʿAjam* (1739–40) (litho., Lucknow, 1916), 153, s.v. "baqqāl."

[42] Russell and Lal, *Tribes and Castes of the Central Provinces*, II, 114.

[43] Cf. Ibbetson, *Panjab Castes*, 243; Russel and Lal, *Tribes and Castes of the Central Provinces*, II, 112–14.

[44] The celebrated anonymous work on the religions of the world *Dabistān-i Mazāhib* (c. 1655) says that "many of the Banyas and Bohras belong to this (Jain) community. Most of them sell grain, and some live by service" (Bombay ed., AH 1292, 166). The Baqqāls (Banyas) following the Jain religion are known as Sarāvags, and the others, mainly Vaishnavites, are known as Maishrīs. *Mirāt-i Aḥmadī* (suppl., 136–7, 139–40), making this statement, gives, first, a list of eighty-four Jain subcastes and, then, eighty-four subcastes of "Maishrī and Sarāvag (or Sarāog) Baqqāls"; this implies that the Hindu and Jain Banyas had common subcastes. This remains true at present (Russell and Lal, *Tribes and Castes of the Central Provinces*, II, 120).

[45] Ibbetson, *Panjab Castes*, 247–50; Sinnappah Arasaratnam, *Merchants, Companies, and Commerce on the Coromandel Coast, 1650–1740* (Delhi, 1986), 213, 220.

[46] Methwold's "relation" (report) in *Relations of Golconda in the Early Seventeenth Century*, ed. and trans. W. H. Moreland (London, 1939), 16–17. For a detailed description of the Komatis, "the great trading caste of the Madras Presidency," see E. Thurston and K. Rangachari, *Castes and Tribes of the Madras Presidency* (Madras, 1909), III, 306–48.

[47] "Among the Bannians are reckoned 24 Casts, or Sects, who both refrain from an indiscriminate mixture in marriages, and from eating together in common" (John

spoke of twenty-four subcastes, the more traditional figure was eighty-four, as given by Abū'l Faẓl. The *Mirāt-i Aḥmadī* (1761) actually gives us the names of eighty-four subcastes of the Maishrī and Sarāvag *baqqāls,* that is, the Hindu and Jain Banyas of Gujarat.[48] In fact, throughout the country, the Banya subcastes are far more numerous than eighty-four, and the major subcastes are much fewer than twenty-four.

There probably have been considerable movements of the sub-castes over time. The author of the *Mir'āt* correctly noted that they were "mostly named after places, villages and settlements."[49] The Agarwāl, which is widely dispersed today, is said to have originated in Agroha in Haryana, and the Oswāl, with perhaps even a larger spread, in Osi in Marwar.[50] Thirteenth- and fourteenth-century Sanskrit inscriptions in Delhi left by rich Hindu merchants show that they remembered the original seats of their families: Uchh (near Multan) in one case; Rohtak (Haryana) in two; and Agroha in one.[51] Banārasīdās (writing in 1641), who was of the Srīmāl subcaste, traced his sept *(gotra)* Biholia to Biholi (near Rohtak), was himself born at Jaunpur (eastern Uttar Pradesh), and married into a family of Srīmāls settled at Khairabad (central Uttar Pradesh).[52]

Undoubtedly, in the course of time certain subcastes became more prosperous than others. In the thirteenth and fourteenth centuries, the Multānīs (from Multan in Panjab) were the richest merchants and bankers of Delhi, as one can see from the observations of Ziā' Baranī, the contemporary historian.[53] But now we cannot even say for certain whether they were Banyas or Khatrīs.[54] Subsequently, there is no

---

Ovington, *A Voyage to Surat in the Year 1689,* ed. H. G. Rawlinson [London, 1929], 168).

[48] *Mirāt-i Ahmadī* suppl., 138–9.

[49] Ibid., 137 (cf. Russell and Lal, *Tribes and Castes of the Central Provinces,* II, 115); F. Buchanan (c. 1810) in *History, Antiquities, Topography, and Statistics of Eastern India,* ed. Robert Montgomery Martin (London, 1838), II, 465.

[50] James Tod (1832), *Annals and Antiquities of Rajasthan, or the Central and Western Rajput States of India* (London, 1914), II, 127.

[51] These are the Palam Baoli (1276), Delhi Museum (1291), Naraina (1327), and Sarban (1328) inscriptions. Their texts and translations, with annotation, are being published in Pushpa Prasad, *Nagari Inscriptions of Delhi and Uttar Pradesh under the Delhi Sultanate* (Delhi: Oxford University Press, forthcoming).

[52] Ramesh Chandra Sharma, "The *Ardha-Kathānak:* A Neglected Source of Mughal History," *Indica,* Bombay, 7 (1970): 52, 57–8. One could not marry within one's *gotra;* so each subcaste consists of a number of *gotras,* or septs.

[53] *Tārīkh-i Fīrūz Shāhī,* 120, 284, 311.

[54] Thevenot (1666), doubtless on hearsay, reports that Multan contained a large number of "Banians," but also that the city was, "properly," the original seat of the "Catry," who had spread all over India from there (*The Indian Travels of Thevenot and Careri,* trans. S. N. Sen [New Delhi, 1949], 77–8).

mention of the Multānīs as being important merchants at Delhi. In
the eighteenth century, the name came to stand for Hindu merchants
trading in Islamic countries and, presumably thence, for a community
of Sindi Lohana shroffs (bankers) settled at Bombay.[55]

The emergence of the Mārwārīs, a major group of Banya subcastes
tracing their origins to Marwar in Rajasthān, has been attracting some
attention.[56] In 1832 Tod claimed, with obvious exaggeration, that "nine-
tenths of the bankers and commercial men of India are natives of
Maroodes [Marwar]" and that of these the Oswāls alone numbered a
hundred thousand families.[57] The Oswāls were already widely dispersed more than two hundred years earlier. Banārasīdās not only
reports them at Agra, the Mughal capital, but also tells us that even
in a small city like Fatehpur, west of Allahabad, there was, around
1598, a quarter inhabited by the Oswāls.[58] Sāntīdās Sāhu, the great
merchant of Ahmadabad (Gujarat) and jeweler to Emperor Shāhjahān
(1628–58), was an Oswāl.[59] Clearly, then, the eminence of the Mārwārīs among the Banyas of northern and western India long predates
the colonial conquest.

It is possible that a sense of solidarity among members of a subcaste
may have helped in maintaining its prosperity, whereas another similar group might decline for lack of it. In the original settlement of the
Agarwāls at Agroha, so the tradition went, if a member of the community failed, each of the other members came forward with a brick
and five rupees to enable him to reestablish his shop.[60]

The subcaste identity existed alongside a very real sense of oneness
of the entire Banya caste. There was, first of all, no bar to members of
different subcastes of Banyas forming close business relations. Thus
Kharagsen, a Srīmāl and a Jain, had a partnership with Rāmdās, an
Agarwāl and "a worshipper of Siva," for conducting jewel trade at
Jaunpur (1576). Kharagsen's son Banārasīdās had a partnership at Agra
with Dharamdās, an Oswāl, and later worked as a factor for a *sāhu* of
the Mauthia subcaste.[61] Thus in addition to subcaste solidarity, there
was a larger sense of fraternity among the Banyas, enabling them to

[55] Tek Chand Bahār, *Bahār-i ʿAjam,* s.v. "Multānīo." See references given by Rajat K.
Ray, "The Bazar: Indigenous Sector of the Indian Economy," in *Business Communities
of India,* ed. Dwijendra Tripathi (New Delhi, 1984), 244, 253–4.
[56] A rather inadequate sketch is furnished in Thomas A. Timberg, *The Marwaris, From
Traders to Industrialists* (New Delhi, 1978), 41ff.
[57] *Annals and Antiquities of Rajasthan,* II, 127.
[58] Sharma, "The *Ardha-Kathānak,*" 60.
[59] Dwijendra Tripathi, *The Dynamics of a Tradition* (New Delhi, 1981), 9, 22ff.
[60] Reported by Buchanan (Martin, *History, Antiquities, Topography, and Statistics of Eastern India,* II, 465).
[61] Sharma, "The *Ardha-Kathānak,*" 56, 71, 108, 114–15.

join together in commercial enterprises irrespective of sect or sub-caste. In the same spirit, certain codes had been developed by which bargains could be made among the Banyas secretly from others – like the communication of bids through hidden pressures of fingers de-scribed by Carletti (1599–1601) and other foreign observers.[62] It was also reflected in common action by members of the entire Banya caste in the form of closure of shops or even departure from a place, when roused by a grievance. At Surat in 1616,

through some vyolence done by him [the judge of the customs house] to a chiefe Bannyane, the whole multitude assembled, shutt up their shopps, and (as their custome), after a generall complaynt to the Governor lefte the cittie, pretendeing to goe to the courte for justice.[63]

At the same city, in 1669, after a dispute with the *qāzī* (Muslim judge),

the Bannians having bound themselves under severe penalties not to open any of their shops without orders from their Mahager or Generall Councill, there was not any provisions to be got; the tanksall [mint] and customshouse shut; no money to be procured.[64]

"Mahager" is *mahājan* ("great men"), the rather shadowy and often ad hoc body of leading men of the caste.[65] Here, obviously, it repre-sented all the subcastes. The Hindi word for a general closure for shops was *hattāl* (now, *hartāl*); the occurrence was common enough for the word to be used to explain a Persian word of the same mean-ing in Bahār's great Persian dictionary (1740).[66]

The control the Banyas exercised over commerce was certainly aided by such actions of solidarity. But the major reason for their success surely lay in the training they received from early childhood in arith-metic, accountancy, and methods of business, sharpened by con-stant, acute competition with their peers.

They are most subtill and expert in casting of accounts and writing, so that they do not only surpass and go beyond all other Indians and other nations thereabouts, but also the Portingales [Portuguese], and, in this respect, they

---

[62] Francesco Carletti, "Regionamenti," translated by Herbert Weinstock as *My Voyage around the World* (New York, 1964, and London, 1965), 205–6. Cf. M. J. Mehta, "Some Aspects of Surat as a Trading Centre in the Seventeenth Century," *Indian Historical Review* 1, 2 (1974): 251–2, citing other sources.

[63] William Foster, *A Supplementary Calendar of Documents in the India Office, &c., 1600–1640* (London, 1928), 68.

[64] William Foster, ed., *English Factories in India* (Oxford, 1927), 1668–69 volume, 192.

[65] See Ashin Das Gupta, *Indian Merchants and the Decline of Surat, c. 1700–1750* (Wies-baden, 1979), 87, 87–8n. The evidence on the Banya *mahājan* is regrettably scanty.

[66] Tek Cahdn Bahār, *Bahār-i ʿAjam*, s.v. *dar-bandān*.

have much advantage, for that they are very perfect in the trade of merchandise, and very readie to deceive men.[67]

The members of this caste are so subtle and so skilful in trade that . . . they could give lessons to the most cunning Jews. They accustom their children at an early age to shun slothfulness, and instead of letting them go into the streets, teach them arithmetic which they learn perfectly, using for it neither pens nor counters, but the memory alone, so that in a moment they will do a sum however difficult it may be. They are always with their fathers, who instruct them in trade, and do nothing without at the same time explaining it to them. These are the figures [omitted] which they use in their books, both in the Empire of the Great Mogul, as well as in other parts of India, although the languages may vary.[68]

Single-minded acquisition of the capacity for acquisition was the cornerstone of the Banya's traditional outlook. Banārasīdās (1641) quotes the practical counsel of the elders of his family: "Too much study was meant for a Brahman or Bhat. The son of a Banik [Banya] should sit in the shop."[69]

In this outlook were married two Calvinistic virtues, namely, thrift and religious spirit. The Banyas would carefully refrain from display of wealth and not spend lavishly on anything, except jewelry for their womenfolk (which was a form of saving). They were equally careful in points of ritual and prescribed diet.[70] They, therefore, seemed to constitute with the Brahmans the twin pillars of orthodox Hinduism.[71] It is, incidentally, interesting to remember that their religious affiliation to Hinduism (and Jainism) when "Mohometan religion" was the "authorised" faith in India served for William Petty (1676) as an illustration of how trade was "most vigorously carried on in every state and government by . . . such as profess Opinions different from that are publickly established."[72]

---

[67] *The Voyage of John Huyghen van Linschoten to the East Indies*, from the old English translation of 1598, ed. E. C. Burnell (London, 1885), I, 252–3. I have modified the English translation according to corrections suggested by the editor.

[68] Tavernier, *Travels in India*, II, 143–4. Cf. Niccolao Manucci (1699–1709): "If the talk is of business, they [Banyas] give a ready answer and are such strong arithmeticians that in the shortest time they can make any sort of calculation, never making a mistake of a single figure" (*Storia do Mogor*, trans. W. Irvine [London, 1970], I, 156).

[69] Sharma, "The *Ardha-Kathānak*," 64.

[70] Both qualities are described in detail in J. Ovington, *Voyage to Surat*, 168–72, 184–8. Surely, there is nothing in polytheism or image worship that is less or more rational than monotheism. But see K. N. Chaudhuri, who seems to treat monotheism as an index of "rational thinking minds" among the Banyas (*The Trading World of Asia and the English East India Company, 1660–1760* [Cambridge, 1978], 151).

[71] When the fourteenth-century radical monotheist Nāmdev went into a Vaishnavite temple, he was expelled by "the Brahmans and Bānyas . . . since he was not acceptable in their assembly" *Dabistān-i Maẕāhib*, 160–1.

[72] *Political Arithmetick* (London, 1691), 25–6. His other example is that of Jewish and

Clearly, the Banyas were well placed to command a very large part of Indian commerce, although we have no evidence that they enjoyed any exclusive legal rights or officially sanctioned privileges, let alone monopolies.

The world of trade that the Banya was master of began with the village. The Indo-Persian name *baqqāl* for him suggests a popular picture of the Banya as a grain merchant. The "village Banya," later to be a familiar figure in official British writing, bought grain from the peasants as well as from the state (when it collected its tax in grain). This is fairly well brought out in S. P. Gupta's analysis of agrarian trade in eastern Rajasthān, on the basis of the relatively richer sixteenth- and seventeenth-century documentation we have for the area.[73] He was also the local moneylender *(mahājan, bohra)* and advanced loans to peasants at 1.5 to 2 percent per month.[74] Model village accounts reproduced in a textbook of the late seventeenth century, without any indication of locality, show a *mahājan* receiving the repayment of a loan of Rs. 80 from the village as a whole, the original loan presumably taken to meet the land-tax, which in that year amounted to a fraction over twice the sum of the loan.[75] Money was also advanced to the landholders. A judicial decision of 1611 recites that an earlier group of Muslim "owners" of a village near Shamsabad (district of Farrukhabad, Uttar Pradesh) had mortgaged their rights with the *baqqāl* of a neighboring village some time before 1530, the redeemed mortgage deed being still in existence in 1611.[76]

In the towns, the Banyas could be found hawking cloth, cowries, or even salt.[77] More characteristic, however, was the Banya shopkeeper, commonly selling rice and ghee (Indian butter) to a poor

---

Christian merchants in the Ottoman Empire. His conclusion: "Trade doth not flourish (as some think) best under Popular Governments."

[73] *The Agrarian System of Eastern Rajasthan (c. 1650–1750)* (Delhi, 1986), 92–115, 140–3.

[74] Ibid., 142. Gupta takes *mahajan*s, or Banyas, as grain merchants and *bohra*s as moneylenders.

[75] Nandrām, *Siyāqnāma* (Lucknow, 1879), 1694–6, 77–9.

[76] See my calendar of this collection of documents in "Aspects of Agrarian Relations and Economy in a Region of Uttar Pradesh during the Sixteenth Century," *Indian Economic and Social History Review* 4 (1967): 230–2.

[77] J. Ovington (*Voyage to Surat*, 130) describes how near the marketplace at Surat "tis not very easie to pass through the multitude of *Bannians* and other Merchants that expose their Goods. For here they stand with their Silks and Stuffs in their Hands, or upon their Heads, to invite such as pass by to come and buy them." Banārasīdās hawked cowries, when a boy, at Shahzadpur near Allahabad (Sharma, "The Ardha-Kathānak," 60). Abū'l Fazl in the *Akbarnāma* (ed. Agha Ahmad Ali and Abdur Rahman, Bibliotheca Indica [Calcutta, 1873–87], 337) alleges that Hemūn (killed, 1556) belonged to the lowly Baqqāl (Banya) subcaste of Dhūsar and early in life sold "salt in the by-lanes with a thousand indignities."

clientele, who often had to ask for credit and expected harsh conditions in return.[78] Such shops in a large city like Delhi vastly outnumbered shops selling the finer commodities, though Banyas must have been prominent in keeping shops of the latter kind as well.[79]

Shopkeepers are naturally to be distinguished from merchants proper. Among these, first there were the true peddlers. Tapan Raychaudhuri aptly compares the Banya jewelers Kharagsen and his son Banārasīdās to the Armenian Hovhannes, Steensgaard's typical peddler of the Asian markets.[80] Banārasīdās himself was sent by his father from Jaunpur in 1610 to Agra with jewels, ghee, oil, and cloth, all worth Rs. 200, some of the capital having been borrowed. Banārasīdās sold the goods gradually by going to the market, but, alas, at a loss. Then he went round Agra with a partner, buying and selling jewels (1611–13), with an initial capital (borrowed) of Rs. 500. In his subsequent operations at Jaunpur (1616), Banārasīdās again started with a capital of Rs. 500, borrowed against a bill *(hundī)*, which he used to purchase cloth.[81]

Above such peddlers stood the larger Banya merchants, respectfully styled *sāh*s. Through advances, they committed artisans as well as peddlers to work in their interest. The system of advances to artisans, binding them to work on orders of the merchant and sell at his price, was an established system and has been discussed often, though as yet mainly from information in the commercial records of the European companies.[82] Could it be that in the following allegorical verses, addressed to himself, Kabīr, the weaver, has this relationship in mind?

[78] See the story of Kabīr, his wife, and the Baqqʿal shopkeeper "in their lane" at Banaras, in *Dabistān-i Mazāhib*, 160.

[79] Bernier (1663) speaks of shops at Delhi "where nothing is seen but pots of oil or butter, piles of baskets filled with rice, barley, chick-peas, wheat and an endless variety of other grain and pulse." These outnumbered the shops selling fine cloth and other fine stuffs by twenty-five to one (*Travels in the Mogul Empire*, trans. A. Constable, ed. V. A. Smith [London, 1916], 248–9).

[80] *Cambridge Economic History of India*, I, 341–2. Cf. Niels Steensgaard, *The Asian Trade Revolution of the Seventeenth Century* (Chicago, 1974), 22ff. The ledger of Hovhannes Joughayetsi is described in an instructive paper by Levon Khachikan, "The Ledger of the Merchant Hovhannes Joughayetsi," *Journal of the Asiatic Society of Bengal*, 4th ser., 8, 3 (1966): 153–86. Steensgaard has used the French version of the same paper: "Le registre d'un marchand arménien en Perse, en Inde et au Tibet (1682–1693)," trans. Nina Godneff, *Annales* 22, no. 2 (1967): 231–78.

[81] Sharma, "The *Ardha-Kathānak*," 67–71, 111.

[82] See, e.g, Irfan Habib, "Usury in Medieval India," *Comparative Studies in Society and History* (The Hague), 6, 4 (1964): 399–400.

Kabīr, the capital *(pūnjī)* belongs to the *sāh;*
and you waste it all.
There will be great difficulty for you at the
time of the rendering of accounts.[83]

The relationship of the *sāh* (= *sāhu*) with the smaller merchant or peddler is invoked allegorically in the *Guru Granth Sāhib*. We have already seen how some of its verses show the *sāhu* financing the Banjāras and expecting them to buy and bring goods as will be approved by him. Arjan (d. 1606) tells of a similar relationship between the *sāhu* and *bāpārīs*, where the former clearly stands for the financier or principal and the latter for his factors or agents.[84]

Among the Banya merchants, a process of specialization led to two distinct lines of commercial activity, those of brokers (*dallāls*) and shroffs (*ṣarrāfs*, bankers and money changers). K. N. Chaudhuri notes that the institution of conducting business through brokers was unknown in south India, but elsewhere it was all-pervasive, and the Banyas dominated the profession.[85] Thevenot (1666) simply states that "everyone hath his Banian in the Indies" as a broker and that some of the brokers grew into the richest merchants in India.[86] The Banyas, on their part, had no inhibition against acting as brokers for anyone. According to Pelsaert (Agra, 1626), the Hindus acted as brokers to all the Muslim merchants. The European companies too invariably had to make use of their services.[87]

The *ṣarrāfs*, or shroffs, were practically all Hindus, and, in large part, Banyas. Evidence has yet to turn up of the existence of a single Muslim *ṣarrāf*. The *ṣarrāfs* were moneychangers, dealers in bills of exchange, deposit receivers, and insurers. "In India," says Tavernier, "a village must be very small indeed if it has not a moneychanger

---

[83] *Kabīr Granthavali*, 42.
[84] *Guru Granth Sāhib*, Nagari ed., I, 180–1.
[85] *Trading World of Asia*, 307. It seems that the point is not discussed by S. Arasaratnam in his *Merchants, Companies, and Commerce on the Coromandel Coast, 1650–1740*. "Brokers" does not appear in the index.
[86] *Indian Travels of Thevenot and Careri*, 78.
[87] Francisco Pelsaert, "Remonstrantie," trans. W. H. Moreland and P. Geyl, *Jahangir's India* (Cambridge, 1925), 78. Contrast this with K. N. Chaudhuri's view that "it was unusual for a Hindu merchant to conduct business with a Muslim" (*Trading World of Asia*, 150). It apparently escapes him that the celebrated Muslim merchant of Surat Mullā 'Abdu'l Ghafūr had Gangādās as his broker; and his grandson Muḥammad 'Alī had two brokers who were Hindus, Rājarām and Jedda Rām (Das Gupta, *Indian Merchants and the Decline of Surat*, 84). The "Moore brokers" at Surat referred to in a Surat Consultation of 1625 (*English Factories in India, 1624–29*, vol. 92) were brokers of Muslim merchants, not Muslim brokers. They could well have been, and probably were, Banyas.

called 'cheraf', who acts as banker to make remittances of money and issue letters of exchange.''[88]

The very specialized profession of *ṣarrāf* led to a separation between them and other Banya merchants. When in the 1650s the English had a dispute with the *ṣarrāf*s of Surat over the payment of insurance on the ship *Supply*, a committee of "four Banyans" (apparently, Banya merchants) appointed by the governor supported the English case, but the *ṣarrāf*s refused to accept their decision.[89] A sharper cleavage occurred in 1715 at Ahmadabad, where matters came nearly to an armed conflict between the merchants led by the *nagarseth* ("town merchant") Kapūr Chand Bhansālī and the *ṣarrāf*s led by Harī Rām, factor to Madan Gopāl, the head of the *ṣarrāf*s (then at Delhi), over the issue of an increase in a deduction called *ānth* that was made when cashing bills.[90] We thus have an example where divergent professional interests could divide the Banya caste vertically.

THE BANYAS: COMMERCIAL TECHNIQUES

The Banya usually appears as an individual merchant, broker, or banker, but the family (the Hindu joint family of modern law) often acted as a firm, with joint investments and profits. Tavernier, speaking of the brokers, gives a lively description of the family firm:

These brokers are commonly, as it were, chiefs of their families, for whom they hold all the joint property in trust to turn it to account. For that reason those qualified by years and experience are selected so that they may be able to secure benefit to all the kinsmen, being both the depositories and guardians of their goods. Every evening, when they return from business . . . the oldest of the kinsmen assemble at the house of the broker, who renders an account of what he has done during the day, and they hold counsel together as to what should be done in the future. He is especially exhorted to take care of their business, and if possible to defraud rather than be defrauded.[91]

Descriptions of individual firms are unfortunately very rare. But, to take a late example from John Malcolm, a firm of insurers at Indore, functioning before the British obtained control over the territory, was called Poornassa Maun Singh after the father; the eldest son, Kewal-

---

[88] *Travels in India*, I, 24.
[89] *English Factories in India*, 1651–54 volume, 224. See also the 1655–60 volume, 15, 62, 71, 74.
[90] *Mirāt-i Aḥmadī*, I, 410–11; see also 405–6 for more information on Kapūr Chand Bhansālī, Madan Gopāl, and Harī Rām. The *nagarseth*, says the *Mirāt*, 406, was "the head of the Hindu community." The Muslim Bohras of Ahmadabad had then a separate *seth*, or head, Mullā ʿAbdul ʿAzīz.
[91] *Travels in India*, II, 26.

jee (fl. 1801), was known for his bold ways of doing business; and his brother and "partner" in the firm, Seeta Chund, was able to show Malcolm the firm's books detailing all the old transactions.[92]

A second form of organization was the pure partnership firm, where kinship was not involved. We have already seen that the Srīmāl jewelers, Kharagsen and his son Banārasīdās, formed partnerships with men of other Banya subcastes who were unrelated to them. The terms of one such partnership *(sirkau)*[93] formed in 1611 are described in some detail. An Oswāl youth, Dharamdās, was put in partnership with Banārasīdās by his father and uncle, rich dealers in jewels (a family firm?). They advanced the partners Rs. 500 as capital *(pūnjī)*. The two partners used it to go round Agra and buy and sell jewels, keeping a daily accounts book *(rojnāma khatiāī)*. After two years, Banārasīdās wished to end the partnership. All the goods held under the partnership were then sold, and the capital of Rs. 500 was returned to Dharamdās's father. Banārasīdās had hoped to make a profit had the goods fetched more than this sum; but that was not to be. When in 1616 he terminated his partnership with Narottamdās at Jaunpur, all the assets were divided (equally?) between the two partners, the statement of settlement being made in two copies, one to be kept by each.[94]

It is doubtful whether the forms of partnership were further elaborated; for example, we have no evidence that the Banyas developed institutions similar to the joint-stock firms of the Europeans. Tapan Raychaudhuri was the first to notice four joint-stock companies of the Indian suppliers to the Dutch, formed under the Dutch company's auspices at Pulicat (Coromandel) in the 1650s and 1660s.[95] The same organization was thereafter imposed by the English on their suppliers at Madras. There have been detailed studies of these companies by Arasaratnam and Brennig.[96] Arasaratnam has now suggested that the long-held view that joint-stock companies were alien to Indian commercial practice ought to be revised in the light of our knowledge that "partnership trading" existed in India. But we also know that the public raising of capital stock and the predetermined constitution of the firm (replacing the individual contracts of partnership) that went with joint-stock were totally absent. There was, therefore, no natural

---

[92] Malcolm, *Memoir of Central India*, II, 97–98n.

[93] From *shirkat*, Arabic/Persian for "sharing, partnership."

[94] Sharma, "The *Ardha-Kathānak*," 71 and 71n, 110.

[95] *Jan Company in Coromandel, 1605–1690* (The Hague, 1962), 147–8.

[96] S. Arasaratnam has followed up his earlier studies with a discussion in *Merchants, Companies, and Commerce on the Coromandel Coast*, 239ff. Joseph Jerome Brennig, "Joint-Stock Companies of Coromandel," in *The Age of Partnership*, ed. Blair B. Kling and M. N. Pearson (Honolulu, 1979), 71–96.

transition from Indian forms of partnership to the seventeenth-century European system of joint-stock. At the same time one could agree with Arasaratnam that the joint-stock companies of the kind promoted by the Dutch and English in south India in their own interest could not be formed elsewhere in India under their aegis because of the greater independence of the merchants in, shall we say, the Banya zone.[97]

The absence of joint-stock companies did not prevent the growth of large Banya firms, whether of the individual, family, or partnership type. In such a firm the *sāhu*, or principal, had a number of factors (*bāpārī* or vāpārī). Some allegorical verses of Arjan (d. 1606), the Sikh guru, show how the *bāpārīs* had to strive to win the *sāhu's* approval all the time, deal in the proper commodities, and devote themselves wholly to his service. The distance between the *sāhu* and *bāpārī* was such that the guru exulted that in God's service

All markets (*hāt*) contain the wares of Peace, Righteousness and Happiness. The *sāh* and *bāpārī* become as of one band (*thāt*).[98]

The merchant's house, including the warehouse, was called *koṭhī*. The word occurs in this sense in the seventeenth century (Banārasīdās) and was much used in the eighteenth and nineteenth centuries. The merchant would have *gumāshta*s (Persian for "agents," "factors," or *bāpārī*s) to manage his *dukān*s ("shops"), or "factories" in the seventeenth-century English sense of the word.[99]

The merchants had factors placed at great distances inland. Pelsaert (1626) tells us that "some wealthy banians (Banyas) of Agra maintain agents in Golconda [Hyderabad] to buy diamonds and spices, which their people in Masulipatam send" to Agra. He regretted that the Dutch had no agents at Golconda to warn them of the quantities of goods being sent thence to Agra so that they could be forewarned like the Indian merchants, who received the requisite intelligence from their agencies.[100] Here, then, there is an interesting inversion of the

[97] Cf. Susil Chaudhuri, "Bengal Merchants and Commercial Organization in the Second Half of the Seventeenth Century," *Bengal: Past and Present* (1971): 201; K. N. Chaudhuri, *Trading World of Asia,* 307; and Brennig, "Joint-Stock Companies of Coromandel," 72, 93*n*.

[98] *Guru Granth Sāhib*, Nagari ed., I, 180–1, quotation on 430.

[99] Banārasīdās uses *koṭhī* for merchant's house (1641) (Sharma, "The *Ardha-Kathānak,*" 69). He left his goods at Udharan's *koṭhī* upon arrival at Agra in 1610. The *ṣarrāf*s drew bills "on their *gumāshta*s, who have their honestly-run shops (*dukān*s) in the various regions, towns and cities" (Sujān Rāi Bhandārī [1695–6], *Khulāsatu't Tawārīkh,* ed. Zafar Hasan [Delhi, 1918], 25).

[100] "A single merchant," mourns Pelsaert, commenting on this situation, "has much difficulty in dealing with such emergencies, and often neglects such warnings, to the Honourable Company's serious loss" (*Jahangir's India,* 22).

picture presented by Steensgaard of the well-informed European companies and ignorant, rumor-fed Asian peddlers.

Tavernier tells us that letters of exchange on Agra could be given from Surat, Dacca, Patna, and Banaras, and we may assume that there were many ṣarrāfs with factors at Agra and also at the other places. This is the implication too of bills being drawn on Surat from (besides Agra) Lahore, Ahmadabad, Sironj, Burhanpur, Golconda, Bijapur, and other cities. The ṣarrāfs must have had factors at Surat as well as the other places.[101] Some ṣarrāfs had branches closer together as well. In 1717 Keshav Rāi Kishanchand, whose headquarters seem to have been at Agra, discounted the Surman embassy's bills on Calcutta through his factors at Delhi, Kora, and Allahabad to the total sum of Rs. 59,000.[102]

Banya merchants of the ports similarly had factors overseas. "Banian merchants" of Surat maintained factors at Gambroon in the Persian Gulf.[103] In the Red Sea, the Banya factors were probably even more numerous, and Ashin Das Gupta has drawn a charming picture of their life there.[104] No one seems to have heeded any superstitions against crossing the sea, where profits were involved.

The conduct of trade in India was very greatly assisted by the system of brokers' services, mainly supplied, as we have seen, by the Banyas. The brokers performed all kinds of services for the merchants, from arranging the sale and purchase of goods to securing finance. Thevenot (1666) gives us a layman's view of their value, stating that the Banya brokers are

so expert in their business, that hardly any body can be without them. They give them commissions of all kinds; though it be known that they make their profit of everything, yet Men chuse rather to make use of them, than to do their business themselves; and I found often by experience, that I had what they bought for me much cheaper than what I bought myself or made my servants buy. They are of a pleasing humor, for they reject no service, whether honourable or base, and are always readie to satisfie those who employ them.[105]

We are fortunate that we have so much information about the various services supplied by brokers in the records of the English East India

---

[101] Tavernier, *Travels in India*, I, 30.

[102] C. R. Wilson, ed., *The Early Annals of the English in Bengal*, vol. 2, pt. ii, 237–8, 268, 288, 292, 297.

[103] *English Factories in India*, 1655–60 volume, 30. The English vessel *Seahorse* carried their letters to their factors.

[104] "Gujarati Merchants and the Red Sea Trade, 1700–1725," in *Age of Partnership*, 132–8.

[105] *Indian Travels of Thevenot and Careri*, 77–8.

Company. There is an adequate study of this information by A. J. Qaisar, which makes detailed treatment unnecessary here.[106]

Still more interesting techniques adopted by the Banyas were in the financial field, where the ṣarrāfs operated.[107] The ṣarrāfs' work, as indicated by the derivation of their Arabic name, was essentially to test and change money. Their skill was especially needed since, despite the uniformity of Mughal coinage, a coin always had to be expertly examined for its genuineness or metallic purity, age, and weight. This function seems to have led to the ṣarrāfs' accepting deposits of money; and there thus developed what can only be called a system of deposit banking. Sujān Rāi (1695) cited this practice as an instance of "the honesty of the people of this country," because "even when a stranger and unfamiliar person deposits hundreds of thousands in cash, for safekeeping, with the ṣarrāfs, those righteous ones repay it on demand without any evasion or delay" (my translation).[108]

A more circumstantially convincing account of deposit banking at Agra in 1645 appears in the pages of the English factory records:

Those that are great monied men in the towne, and live onely uppon interest receive from the sheroffs [ṣarrāfs] noe more than ⅜ per cent. per month. The sheroffs they dispose of itt to others [at] from 1 to 2 per cent. running some hazzard for the same, and that is their gaines. Now when a sheroff (for lucre) hath disposed of great summes to persons of qualletie att great rates, not suddenly to be call'd in to serve his occasions, then beginn his creditours (as in other partes of the world) like sheepe one to runn over the neck of another, and quite stifle his reputacion. Thus hath . . . two famous sheroffs bynn served within a moneth, one of which faileing for above three lack (300,000) of rupees, diverse men have lost great somes and others totally undone thereby; which hath caused men of late to be verie timerous of putting their monies into sheroffs hands.[109]

The alarm felt by depositors must, of course, have been a passing phase, as happens in similar situations "in other partes of the world." The normal conditions when moneyed persons kept their money with

---

[106] A. Jan Qaisar, "The Role of Brokers in Medieval India," *Indian Historical Review*, Delhi, 1, 2 (1974): 220–46.

[107] In this and the following paragraphs I have drawn heavily on my own papers: "The Currency System of the Mughal Empire," *Medieval India Quarterly*, Aligarh, 4 (1961): 3–21; "Banking in Mughal India," in *Contributions to Indian Economic History – I*, ed. Tapan Raychaudhuri (Calcutta, 1960), 1–20; "Usury in Medieval India," *Comparative Studies in Society and History* 4, 4 (1964): 393–419; and "The System of Bills of Exchange (Hundis) in the Mughal Empire," *Indian History Congress, Proceedings of the Thirty-Third Session: Muzaffarpur* (New Delhi, 1972), 290–303.

[108] *Khulāsatu't Tawārīkh*, 25.

[109] *English Factories in India*, 1642–45 volume, 303.

*ṣarrāf*s enabled the latter to gain capital, which they could employ in directly lending out or in discounting bills.

The quotations of a commercial rate of interest, or the rate (per month) the *ṣarrāf*s and merchants charged other merchants (seemingly without any barrier of caste or community), signify a fair development of commercial finance. Quotations of the rate collected from the English records offer a reasonable picture of movements of interest rates in various important commercial centers in India between the 1620s and 1660s.[110] There is a downward trend in the interest rates, a distinct fall occurring a little before or about 1650, though the rates still remained above those in England and Holland. The interest rates at Surat fell from about and above 1 percent per month to 0.5–0.75 percent; this was also the case at Ahmadabad and Agra.[111]

One major instrument of extending short-term credit, combined with a transfer of funds, was the bill of exchange, called *hundī* or *hundwī*. The *ṣarrāf*s issued *hundī*s when they actually received deposits to be repaid at some other place, and they also discounted the *hundī*s when they made a loan to be repaid elsewhere. To draw a *hundī* and have it discounted was the normal way even for a small man to raise capital, as witness Banārasīdās drawing a *hundī* for RS. 500 at Jaunpur to establish his business and purchase cloth.[112] The establishment of a standard commercial rate of interest was reflected in the similarity of the discounts on *hundī*s drawn by *ṣarrāf*s and merchants. In 1622, for instance, the *ṣarrāf*s at Ahmadabad allowed a discount of 7.25 percent on the *hundī*s they themselves drew on Burhanpur, whereas they claimed a discount of 8.5 percent on *hundī*s drawn by merchants and accepted by them.[113] Obviously, the difference of 1.25 percent reflected the *ṣarrāf*s' own service charges rather than risks arising out of the lack of creditworthiness of the merchants drawing *hundī*s.

Sujān Rāi, who marvels at the *hundī* as at deposit banking, tells us that the bill was fully salable.[114] The Indian practice was different from the European in that in India those who had discounted a *hundī* and then sold it became liable if the drawee failed to honor it.[115] It natu-

---

[110] See Irfan Habib, "Usury in Medieval India," 402–4; also Shireen Moosvi, *The Economy of the Mughal Empire, c. 1595* (Delhi, 1987), 373, who has collected some new quotations.

[111] The evidence seems to contradict K. N. Chaudhuri's assertion that "there was no long-term downward movement in interest rates in India" in the seventeenth century (*Trading World of Asia*, 159; cf. S. Moosvi, *Economy of the Mughal Empire*, 372, 374).

[112] Sharma, "The *Ardha-Kathānak*," 111.

[113] *English Factories in India*, 1622–23 volume, 68.

[114] *Khulāṣatu't Tawārīkh*, 25.

[115] *English Factories in India*, 1668–69 volume, 177.

rally made for a *hundī* being more readily accepted if it had been previously discounted by ṣarrāfs or merchants of reputation. The *hundīs* could also be insured, presumably with the ṣarrāfs.[116]

The negotiability of *hundīs* naturally made them a medium of payment and so gave rise to bill-money in the same way as in contemporary Europe. The conditions of the creation of such money are thus described in 1761:

Suppose a person having paid a fixed sum at the port of Surat to a ṣarrāf of that place brings a *hundwī,* which in Persian is called *sufta* [bill], drawn by him [the ṣarrāf] on his partner or agent at Ahmadabad; he may, if he chooses, collect cash, paying the deduction on account of *ānth* at the current rate; or, in case another person has a claim against the possessor of the *hundwī* for that sum, the latter may give it to that person, and so free himself from that obligation. Similarly, he [the new possessor] may transfer it to another, until it reaches a person against whom the drawee of the *hundwī* has claims, and who, therefore, surrendering it to the latter, relieves himself of his debt. But cash is not used throughout. (My translation)[117]

The English documents from Agra in 1652 show that the money used in actual transactions ("Cutche Ant," *kachchā-ānt*) was deemed 1 percent less in value than the bill-money ("the good exchange mony, rupees paied to the merchants, called Pucka Annt assignation," or *pakkā ānt*).[118] In other words there would be an inducement not to convert the bills into money but to use them to cancel equivalent obligations. In central India, Malcolm (1824) found that this practice of circulating "Oant, or accommodation bills" led to the rise of a "bill-currency," though when "capital" (coined money?) became easily available, it contracted.[119] Unfortunately, there is no means of knowing how much money in the seventeenth century circulated in the form of bills rather than coin.

Since the *hundīs* were usually drawn to purchase goods, the ṣarrāfs discounted them on the assumption that the goods would be transported safely to where they were to be sold and the bill honored. The next step, apparently an independent innovation in India, was for the ṣarrāfs to insure the goods. Sujān Rāi took insurance to be a praiseworthy feature of his country and noted that here "if merchants from dangers on the routes entrust their goods and merchandise and other

---

[116] When in 1647 the English at Ahmadabad discounted two bills on Thatta, they took care to insure it for 0.5 percent (ibid., 1646–50 volume, 103).

[117] *Mirāt-i Aḥmadī,* I, 411.

[118] *English Factories in India,* 1651–54 volume, 105.

[119] Malcolm, *Memoir of Central India,* II, 90–1.

property and baggage to them [the *ṣarrāfs*], the latter, taking their recompense, convey the goods to the appointed place and hand them over to the owners. In the language of these people this is called *bīma* [Hindi for "insurance"]" (my translation).[120]

One could also insure one's goods without having the *ṣarrāfs* take custody of them. The *ṣarrāfs* offered fairly modest rates for this type of insurance for goods going overland or by sea. The rates are quoted occasionally in the English records of the seventeenth century.[121] Cargo and ships were both insured. When a vessel of a Banya shipowner, Banji Revadas of Surat, was burnt, the English factors at Surat were sure that the ship had been purposely destroyed by the owner for "making his gaines here at home by the insurers."[122] Rates of insurance on cargo or ships naturally rose if the vessels were delayed or were thought to be in danger.[123]

This may be the appropriate place to mention the Indian version of respondentia and bottomry, called "awg," "avog," or "avugge" in the European records; the Indian term has not yet been satisfactorily traced. This was a form of speculative investment in a ship's cargo in which the investors lent money for its purchase. The money would be repaid if the ship carried the cargo safely to the stipulated port, the premium upon the principal naturally varying with the risk involved.[124] This method of raising capital for shipping is again mentioned in connection with Banji Revadas, who is said to have taken "a great avog upon" his ship.[125] Thus it was a technique in which the Banyas dabbled, though they might not have necessarily been its originators. Since the *ṣarrāfs* furnished insurance for cargo, and a

---

[120] *Khulāṣatu't Tawārīkh*, 25. In 1662 the English also "consulted with several sherroffes for the provision of said goods (from Agra) on Bemah or Ensurance" (*English Factories in India*, 1661–64 volume, 86).

[121] See table in Irfan Habib, "Banking in Mughal India," 16. Malcolm has very interesting observations on insurance by the Indian firms of central India, and he gives tables of insurance rates in 1795, 1800 (and later years), and 1820 for different kinds of merchandise for transport between different places (*Memoir of Central India*, II, 92–96, 97–98n., 366–9).

[122] *English Factories in India*, 1665–67 volume, 202. It was said to be "his common practice."

[123] Ibid., 1642–45 volume, 92, 161; 1651–54 volume, 177, 224.

[124] Cf. Habib in "Usury in Medieval India," 405. To the sources cited there should be added the evidence of the Armenian merchant Hovhannes, who writes of *avak* (which implies the pronunciation *avag*, with "g" as in "get") on ventures from Surat to Isfahan at 27 and 26 percent and from Surat to Basra at 20 percent during the period 1683–6 (Khachikan, "Ledger of the Merchant Hovhannes Joughayetsi," 175). In these cases the parties were all Armenians.

[125] *English Factories in India*, 1665–67 volume, 202.

speculator could presumably cushion himself against loss by insuring the whole or part of the cargo, the availability of insurance could have greatly facilitated respondentia arrangements.[126]

THEORIES OF PRECOLONIAL INDIAN COMMERCE

The foregoing study of Indian merchant communities has focused on just two such communities. I have not dealt with the Khatrīs of the Panjab, the Muslim Bohras of Gujarat, the south Indian merchants (recently studied by S. Arasaratnam), and foreign merchants, such as the Persians and Armenians. There is no doubt that a full description of commercial institutions and practices in precolonial India must come to grip with their immense variety, which has not been possible within the limited space here. Yet, the information that I have assembled is sufficiently illustrative for us to see that the precolonial commercial world of India was one of openness and competition, where separate social groups (castes) tried to establish an advantage in one sphere or another by means of inherited skills and ways of life. Such a situation led to brisk commodity exchanges and the development of a number of relatively refined commercial and financial techniques.

To the historian of an earlier generation like W. H. Moreland, these conclusions would not have seemed novel or open to much criticism.[127] To him the vulnerability of Indian commerce lay not in its structural backwardness but in the political environment, that is, in its constant constriction by the taxation and expropriations of the arbitrary, absolute despotism of the Mughal government.[128] This view has been strongly contested, however, based on evidence concerning Mughal commercial taxation and law enforcement and on the rarity of specific instances of confiscations of mercantile wealth. More recent detailed studies, like that of the merchants of Surat by Ashin Das Gupta, have also tended to reinforce skepticism about Moreland's thesis.[129]

---

[126] It will be interesting to compare our description of insured bills, risk-sharing through "avog," and insurance proper in India with Jacob Price's discussion of bills against insured cargoes, spreading of investments in shares in various ships, and, finally, marine insurance in European–American trade, which is to appear in volume 2 of this collection.

[127] See W. H. Moreland, *India at the Death of Akbar* (London, 1920), 248–50. He ranked Indian men of business in the seventeenth century as "merchants of the highest class."

[128] Ibid., 50–2, 264–5. For a similar view, advanced by B. B. Misra, see his *Indian Middle Classes* (London, 1961), 22–35.

[129] An early critique of Moreland is to be found in Brij Narain, *Indian Economic Life, Past*

A variant of Moreland's theory has now been offered by K. N. Chaudhuri, who sees a constant threat to mercantile prosperity (Hindu) from religious persecution (Muslim).[130] I have already had occasion to comment on his statement about it being unusual for Hindus to conduct business with Muslims. As a matter of fact, the brokers of Muslim merchants were invariably Hindus.[131] Chaudhuri adds that "the Surat disturbance of 1669 was far from being an isolated incident," when the entire history (relatively well illumined) of Surat tells us that in its religious genesis the disturbance was unusual. It is also surely noteworthy that the sympathies of the local Mughal officials during the incident were clearly with the Banyas and not with the *qāzī*.[132] The only important act of discrimination in the commercial sphere was when Aurangzeb (1659–1707) increased duties on goods of non-Muslim merchants to 5 percent ad valorem, while keeping them at 2.5 percent for Muslims. But even here, the higher rate was often avoided by the Hindu merchants by passing off their goods as those of Muslims.[133] All this cannot amount to any great "Islamic pressure."[134]

For quite some time now, yet another theory of the weakness of Indian (and Asian) commercial structure has been popular. This argument accepts the fact that competition, and not monopoly, was the normal background for commerce in India (and Asia). This meant that a large number of individuals with small amounts of capital ("peddlers") accounted for most of the trade. Since the "peddlers" worked perforce on faulty intelligence and could not plan controlled responses, there were violent gluts and scarcities in different markets, great price fluctuations, and therefore an enormous wastage of economic effort. These defects were rectified in the trade controlled by the European companies, which were blessed with large capital, efficient organization, and informed planning. The argument has been set out elaborately by Niels Steensgaard, who derived the concept of the peddling trade from van Leur.[135]

and Present (Lahore, 1929). My own arguments against Moreland's thesis appeared in my paper, "Potentialities of Capitalistic Development in Mughal India," *Enquiry*, Delhi, n.s., 3, 3 (Winter 1971): 47–53. Das Gupta, *Indian Merchants and the Decline of Surat*, 89–90.

[130] *Trading World of Asia*, 150–1.
[131] See n. 87.
[132] See quotations from English records in *English Factories in India*, 1668–69 volume, 192, 205.
[133] This apparently happened even more frequently when for a period of fifteen years the Muslims were exempted from the duty altogether (*Mirāt-i Aḥmadī*, I, 265, 298).
[134] K. N. Chaudhuri, *Trading World of Asia*, 150.
[135] Steensgaard, *Asian Trade Revolution of the Seventeenth Century*, 22–59.

Steensgaard's arguments have been contested by Tapan Raychau-dhuri, who denies that peddlers dominated precolonial Indian com-merce.[136] We have ourselves seen how larger merchants appear in our sources and how they control the activities of the smaller men. Even Hovhannes, the Armenian merchant, whom Steensgaard takes to be the typical peddler, was a factor operating in India and Tibet for his principals in Isfahan.[137] What place, moreover, is there in Steens-gaard's scheme for a Banya merchant like Virji Vora of Surat, who had an "estate" estimated at Rs. 8 million in the 1660s and large num-bers of factors spread all over India and overseas?[138]

Facts such as these have led Ashin Das Gupta to dilute the van Leur–Steensgaard thesis and to include even the rich merchants among peddlers, seeing them essentially as "insecure men," made so by lim-itations of information and vagaries of commerce. He sees the devel-opment of a sophisticated structure of credit and brokerage in India as an attempt "to facilitate the trade of atomized men."[139] So de-scribed, one begins to wonder how Indian or Asian trade could have been different from commerce within western or central Europe. The fact that the Red Sea, not the Cape of Good Hope, remained the main conduit for India's external trade in the seventeenth century shows that the "atomized" commerce was by no means less efficient than the trade of the Dutch and English companies (using the Cape of Good Hope route) wherever there were possibilities of free and open competition.

There has been little discussion so far, in comparative terms, of Indian commercial and financial techniques and their influence on "transaction costs." Misapprehension prevails on some elementary facts. Thus Steensgaard suggests that "trade on commission" was a specifically European practice, not "demonstrable" for Asian trade;[140] and this despite the numerous attestations to the all-pervasive nature of brokerage in Indian commerce, a field in which the Banyas had so greatly specialized.

What must, indeed, strike us as a crucial fact is the creation out of India's own commercial fabric of institutions like brokerage, deposit

---

[136] *Cambridge Economic History of India*, I, 340–2.
[137] Steensgaard, *Asian Trade Revolution of the Seventeenth Century*, 23–5.
[138] *English Factories in India*, 1661–64 volume, 308; Thevenot, *Indian Travels of Thevenot and Careri*, 22. Other information about Virji Vora is scattered in the other volumes of *English Factories in India*, where references to him can be located from the indexes.
[139] *Indian Merchants and the Decline of Surat*, 11–12. Das Gupta goes on to describe even Mullā Ghafūr, with his numerous ships, large trade, and closely knit organization, as a peddler (13).
[140] Steensgaard, *Asian Trade Revolution of the Seventeenth Century*, 42.

banking, bill-money, and insurance. These institutions did not indicate a static or stagnant state of commerce. Could it be that the European triumph over Indian (and Asian) merchants was not, then, one of size and techniques, of companies over peddlers, of joint-stock over atomized capital, of seamen over landsmen? Might it not have been more a matter of men-of-war and gun and shot, to which arithmetic and brokerage could provide no answer, whether in the earlier "Age of Partnership" or after Plassey?

CHAPTER 13

Merchants without empire: the Hokkien sojourning communities

WANG GUNGWU

CHINESE merchants have long struggled against the orthodox Confucian view that they should be at the bottom of the sociopolitical scale. The agrarian empire was established by force of arms and run by a centralized bureaucracy. This empire soon developed strict controls over the sources of mercantile wealth and thereafter kept merchant families on the defensive. The underlying principle was that such families should not be allowed to use commercial wealth to acquire political power either directly through official appointments or indirectly through high social status. And as the mandarin state evolved through the centuries, military families also were ultimately excluded from political power, except during times of dynastic crises. The mandarins, selected largely from literati with or without landed wealth, became the embodiment of imperial authority and legitimacy. Merchants could not hope to challenge such a state structure. All they could hope for was to get some of the mandarins to collaborate in the acquisition of commercial wealth and to educate some members of their families to reach literati status and help to protect their enterprises.

Behind this overall framework, however, there were countervailing trends. For the first thousand years, from the Han to the Tang dynasties (from roughly the second century B.C. to the ninth century A.D.), the major pressures against mandarin power came from military families seeking to erect feudal structures. Merchants had no place in this struggle: their lowly status placed them with the artisans, even though their skills with money in an increasingly cash-based economy made them useful agents to powerful families from time to time. After the tenth century, when no military aristocracy was possible any more

400

within China, the literati route to power was supreme and firmly established. But this opened up a different trend: it created a meritocracy in which wealth could and did play an important role, giving new encouragement to entrepreneurship and the emerging mercantile class. Thus the Sung dynasty (980–1276), and especially the Southern Sung during the twelfth and thirteenth centuries, offered opportunities to merchants to create wealth to increase the imperial revenues and, at the same time, strive for upward social mobility.[1] But the wealth was never allowed to be independent of the mandarinate. It was always contingent on its value to the court and its links with officialdom, preferably through family members who had made the transition to literati status.

It was in this context of a new role for merchants that maritime trade became important in the southeastern coastal provinces of China after the tenth century. This essay explores the nature of Chinese merchant communities through their activities overseas. Given the background of discrimination, what can we learn from those who were more daring and enterprising and who sought their wealth in areas outside mandarin control? Among the most active of them were the merchants of south Fujian, better known as the Hokkiens.[2] The first part of the essay will describe the background of their maritime activities, especially the trading conditions before the end of the sixteenth century. The second will concentrate on two of their communities: one in Manila from the 1570s and the other in Nagasaki after 1600. From their experience, it may become clear why the Chinese did not develop strong networks and organizations of the kind that emerged in Europe by the seventeenth century. The Hokkiens also provide a contrast with the merchant communities in Europe, which fared better in a variety of small contending states that needed and supported them in their overseas trade. There is also the difference between merchants barely tolerated by a centralized empire and those whose rulers and governments used them for their imperial cause. When merchants could extract favorable conditions from kings and aristocrats, they could hope eventually to gain control of the governments themselves. A mandarinate that believed that the successful state was dependent on a peaceful and prolific peasantry would question the

---

[1] Mark Elvin, *The Pattern of the Chinese Past* (Stanford, 1973), pt. 2 and chap. 14 (pt. 3).

[2] Shinba Yoshinobu, "Sodai ni okeru Fukken shonin to sono shakai keizai teki haikei" [Fukien merchants in the Sung and their socioeconomic background], *Wada Hakase koki kinen Toyoshi ronso* [Studies in oriental history in honor of the seventieth birthday of Dr. Wada] (Tokyo, 1960).

function of profit and mercantile wealth. And despised merchant communities excluded from political power could hardly expect to build merchant empires of their own.

HOKKIEN MERCHANTS

Long-distance overseas trade for the Chinese was no different than for other trading peoples. It required advanced shipping technology, large capital investment, and some degree of official protection to ensure continuity and profitability for those who specialized in it. For China, the technology for coastal trading over relatively long distances, that is, from the coasts of the Korean Peninsula down to those of Indochina and the Malay Peninsula, had been available from ancient times. We know little about private investment, but we have ample materials about the trade supported by imperial and provincial governments, either by sending their own missions overseas or by encouraging foreign merchants (official or otherwise) to come regularly to Chinese ports. By the Tang dynasty, foreign merchants were numerous enough to form communities in Guangzhou (Canton). And during the first half of the tenth century, with the establishment of independent kingdoms in the Guangdong and Fujian provinces, the Nan Han and the Min respectively, more foreign traders (many still seen as representing official missions from their rulers) frequented their ports, notably Fuzhou and Quanzhou in addition to Guangzhou. Although the two kingdoms lasted only fifty to sixty years, they laid the foundations for economic growth, notably, the opening of new lands, population increase, and the rise of local trade and industry, which made the two provinces of increasing importance to the Sung dynasty.[3]

Becoming an independent kingdom during the tenth century was a major turning point in Fujian's history. For the first time, Fujian was developed not for China but for itself. And clearly, maritime trade was essential for its future prosperity. It was no accident that Quanzhou took over from Fuzhou as the leading port. It had the better harbor, the Hokkiens had less agricultural land than the people of the Min valley to their north, and their two prefectures of Quanzhou and Zhangzhou were "frontier" territories farther from direct interference by court and provincial mandarins. Thus maritime trade began to flourish, and it grew even more rapidly when the Southern Sung trea-

---

[3] Wang Gungwu, "The Nanhai Trade," *Journal of the Malayan Branch, Royal Asiatic Society* 31/2 (1958): 1–135; Edward Schafer, *The Empire of Min* (Tokyo, 1959).

sury after 1127 enjoyed the revenues from foreign trade collected at the Maritime Trade Commission in Quanzhou.[4]

Despite its growing importance, the trade and the merchants who controlled it were never clearly described in contemporary records. The revival of Confucian orthodoxy, among other things, reaffirmed the lowly position of the merchant. Fujian chroniclers and literati were much prouder of their successes in imperial examinations, their share of high posts in the Sung court at Hangzhou, and, not least, the fact that some of the great Neo-Confucian thinkers of the time, including the greatest of them, Zhu Xi himself, were products of the province. The province's contribution to the Sung economy and to imperial finances through maritime trade and the taxes collected at its ports, in contrast, was downplayed. And as for its merchants, sailors, and their enterprises, there is only the most meager information.[5] The most extensive information we have concerns official approval and the treatment of foreign merchants.

Maritime trade depended on official support, if not sponsorship. This was particularly true at the larger ports, where trade commissioners and customs officials were posted. With official acquiescence some of the wealthy and powerful families at such ports would provide the capital for oceangoing ships and invest in their cargo. The risks were great but so were the profits when each merchant fleet returned. Lesser trading families as well as skilled artisans who produced marketable goods would also join the enterprise. In time, the successes encouraged the merchant classes in smaller ports also to invest in ships for the overseas trade. Thus, radiating out of the port of Quanzhou itself, for example, would have been a chain of minor ports like Anhai and Yuegang, which, by the following Yüan and Ming dynasties, became centers themselves for maritime trade. These lesser centers, being even farther away from official supervision, allowed their traders to act more freely and adventurously in the expanding trade. It also meant that an increasing number of coastal communities in Fujian (and to a lesser extent in Guangdong and Zhejiang) became directly involved in maritime enterprises.[6] Hence the extension of maritime skills and technology between the twelfth and fifteenth centuries, which made possible the Mongol Yüan naval in-

---

[4] Shiba Yoshinobu, *Sodai Shogyo shi kenkyu* [Commerce and society in Song China] (Tokyo, 1968); Mark Elvin has published a translation, Ann Arbor, 1970.

[5] This is most marked in the voluminous gazetteers of Fujian, for example, those of Quanzhou and Zhangzhou prefectures and those of Haicheng, Jinjiang, and Longxi counties of the Qianlong period (late eighteenth century).

[6] *Anhai Zhi* (Jinjiang, 1983); and the essays in *Yuegang yanjiu luwenji* published by the Xiamen Branch of the Fujian Historical Society, 1983.

vasions of Japan and Java toward the end of the thirteenth century and the even more extraordinary expeditions of Admiral Zheng He to the Indian Ocean at the beginning of the fifteenth. In both cases, official approval of private maritime trade paid off when the fleets and the shipbuilders and the captains and the navigators could be turned to such spectacular ventures.

The treatment of foreign trading communities living in Quanzhou and elsewhere was based on laws first devised for imperial capitals like Changan and Loyang, where foreign merchants had first come overland to China a thousand years earlier. These laws had protected the overland merchants, and they applied equally to the overseas merchants who came to the southern ports. It can also be assumed that Chinese practices were influenced by practices elsewhere in Asia, that they were modified in China with experience, and that they in turn had influenced practices elsewhere. Thus non-Chinese quarters for different foreign merchant communities were officially recognized, and they had their own formally chosen leaders, and their own community centers, markets, and places of worship.[7] Special Chinese officials and interpreters were appointed to deal with each of these quarters. Over the centuries, a pattern of rights and duties evolved in China that was probably similar in other foreign merchant communities elsewhere in Asia. In this way, Chinese merchants who aspired to trade overseas would know more or less what to expect when they went abroad and when they themselves sought to establish their own communities there. Perhaps the only difference was that the Chinese merchants who went to the ports of smaller kingdoms or fiefdoms in Southeast Asia and Japan often had the chance to negotiate with kings or nobles or powerful chiefs directly for their trading and residential rights. In contrast, foreign merchants in China were supposed to deal with commissioners sent by the court but were more likely to face lowly provincial or local Chinese officials who implemented elaborate and irksome administrative rules if they were not suitably bribed.

It is within this background that Fujian and, especially, the port of Quanzhou became the major center for foreign merchants during the thirteenth and fourteenth centuries. Fujian merchants developed their maritime skills in a relatively free, officially backed trading atmosphere. They were taxed and supervised but otherwise unrestricted. This encouraged them to set out to trade with every intention of returning after each voyage, not to stay abroad unless they really had

---

[7] Kuwabara Jitsuzo, "On P'u Shou-keng," *Memoirs of the Research Department of the Tokyo Bunko* 2 (1928): 1–79.

to, and never to remain away from home for long. If small numbers were left behind in a foreign port, they were sent there as agents for enterprises that sent ships out from China regularly, probably every year. Thus they were really sojourners temporarily residing abroad on behalf of their families or their employers. But as the trade expanded and the numbers of sojourners grew, small communities emerged, and there is evidence that they were to be found (together with some Guangdong traders) in the major ports of Champa (later part of Vietnam), Cambodia, Sumatra, and Java by this period.[8] Not surprisingly, some of the sojourners elected to settle, marrying local women and producing progeny to carry on the trading connections with China or simply to become local traders in their own right. The sojourner communities often performed valuable services for the local economy, and for that they seemed to have received favorable treatment. Unfortunately, the little evidence available is fragmentary and indirect, and no description of these merchants as communities exists.

It is also not clear whether the sojourners who returned regularly to China also married local women and left their descendants behind to become assimilated members of the local community. If they did, there would not have been settled *Chinese* merchant communities overseas. Instead, there would only have been sojourner communities, that is communities consisting of a continuous series of sojourners and providing shelters for accommodating new sets of sojourners. The first two clear references to overseas merchant communities date to early in the fifteenth century, a period when imperial policy on maritime trade had drastically changed. The change had come between the end of the Yüan (1368) and during the reign of the first Ming emperor (1368–98).[9] The new policy restricted all maritime trade to foreign tributary missions and banned overseas travel for all Chinese – hence, these two merchant communities abroad. One was on the northeast coast of Java, and the other was at Palembang (Sumatra). The former is described as Muslim, probably sinicised Muslims of foreign origin who had settled in Quanzhou (or other Chinese ports) and who had been forced by the change in Ming policy to shift their operations to Java after 1368. The latter consisted of natives of Guang-

[8] Zhou Daguan (Chou Ta-kuan), *Zhenla fengtuji,* trans. Paul Pelliot, in *Bulletin de l'Ecole Française d'Extrême-Orient* 2 (1902): 123–77; see Ch'en Cheng-hsiang, *Zhenla fengtuji yanjiu* (Hong Kong, 1975).

[9] Ma Huan, *Ying-yai Sheng-lan: The Overall Survey of the Ocean's Shores* [1433], trans. and ed. by J. V. G. Mills (Cambridge, 1970); Wang Gungwu, "Early Ming Relations with Southeast Asia: A Background Essay," in *The Chinese World Order*, ed. John K. Fairbank (Cambridge, Mass., 1968), 34–62.

dong and Fujian. They could have been descendants of Chinese so-journers who had regularly traded at Palembang, but more likely they were victims of the new Ming policy, forced to remain abroad because they had defied the trade bans and gone overseas. They were not part of a settled Chinese community but were members of armed, illegal (if not piratical) trading fleets who had seized Palembang in order to defend themselves when they found they were unable to return to China. It is likely that there were other similar communities else-where in Southeast Asia at this time: in Champa, in Siam (Ayut-thaya), on the Malay Peninsula, in the Sulu Archipelago, and on the coasts of Borneo, where there had been a thriving China trade during the fourteenth century, but no descriptions of such communities are available. The point to be made here is that a different kind of Chinese merchant community could have arisen from a sudden change of im-perial policy.

Ming policy for the first hundred years was aimed at stopping *pri-vate* overseas trade. Whatever justifiable strategic reasons the Chinese government had for this policy, the consequences for Quanzhou and Fujian merchants in this trade were calamitous. Instead of the super-vised trade that had made Quanzhou great, an elaborate machinery for registering and checking all tribute-bearing missions from west-ern, southern, and Southeast Asia was created in Guangzhou. These missions and their merchandise were then normally escorted over-land to the capital, first at Nanjing and later at Beijing, and they were showered with imperial gifts and returned overland to Guangzhou. Quanzhou and the Fujian ports were largely bypassed. Instead of foreign traders, these ports saw only imperial garrisons, who built new walled forts and manned coastal flotillas to arrest illegal ship-ping, fight off pirates (both foreign and Chinese), and prevent smug-gling. The consolation, however, was that the policy brought peace and stability to the provinces and consequently a different kind of economic growth.[10]

The policy also produced one unexpected result. The number of Chinese traders who resided abroad only temporarily was drastically cut at the end of the fourteenth century. But for those who were abroad and had failed to return to China immediately as well as those who defied the bans and continued to trade overseas and had to prolong their stay indefinitely, the policy ensured that they formed more stable communities and even settled down permanently. And as long as the bans were strictly enforced, fewer Chinese traded abroad but more of

[10] Zhu Weigan, *Fujian Shigao*, vol. 2 (Fuzhou, 1986), pt. 6, chap. 17.

those already abroad were forced to organize themselves in communities there. It was in this atmosphere that Admiral Zheng He and his navy set forth on their great voyages between 1405 and 1433. When these expeditions came to an end and it was decided never to send any more out again, they had, paradoxically, educated many more Chinese about the trading opportunities at a time when private trade was being destroyed and future generations of those who were drawn to trade privately overseas were being intimidated.

The port of Quanzhou was seriously affected by the neglect of foreign merchants and by the virtual end of Chinese overseas activity. It never regained its former greatness as a port. But the merchant classes of Fujian turned to other enterprises.[11] During the century of relative stability, their attention turned to cash crops like sugar, tea, indigo, timber, fruits, and even cotton. They produced better-quality textiles, silks, and porcelain and encouraged the development of other crafts and manufactured goods. They improved the salt and fishing industry and, in particular, developed a network of trading connections in the neighboring provinces both by land and by sea. The coastal Hokkiens (including the people in the fishing ports of Xinghua and Fuqing to the north) did not lose their skills in shipbuilding and navigation. They deepened, in fact, their experience of maritime trade up and down the whole coast of China and up the great Yangtse River into the interior of central China. They joined increasingly large and active groups of merchants in Guangdong, Zhejiang, Jiangsu, and even Anhui, to organize private trade within China. Their main strength, however, was that they were most at home at sea, because the sea provided them with their best access to all the great markets of China. They also depended most on the sea because their coastal plains were narrow and their agricultural land was limited; when their population began to grow rapidly, they were forced to turn to the sea to transport the grain they needed to buy from the grain markets of the Yangtse and Pearl river deltas. This also meant, of course, that whenever the overseas trade bans were laxly enforced or partially lifted or when local officials were prepared to turn a blind eye to Hokkien traditional maritime activity, there was never any shortage of people able and willing to reach out to markets overseas.[12]

[11] Evelyn S. Rawski, *Agricultural Change and the Peasant Economy of South China* (Cambridge, Mass., 1972).
[12] Zhang Weihua, *Mingdai Haiwai maoyi jianlun* (Shanghai, 1956); Lin Renchuan, *Mingmo Qingchu siren laishang maoyi* (Shanghai, 1987); Ng Chin-keong, "Gentry-Merchants and Peasant-Peddlers – The Response of Southern Fukienese to Offshore Trading Opportunities, 1522–66," *Journal of Nanyang University* 7 (1973–4): 161–75.

The isolationist policy of the Ming was, in fact, impossible to sustain. Its very success in curtailing lawlessness along the China coasts brought rapid economic growth and consequently also population growth. This in turn increased the pressure on coastal Chinese and, especially, the Hokkiens to look at the great profits to be made in overseas trade and seek ways to get round the trade bans. Furthermore, the prosperity of China encouraged more foreign traders to come, and more and more of them were frustrated by the pretense of being tribute-bearing missions. They too sought every possible means, with the connivance of those local officials who became increasingly tempted to condone private trade, to broaden their opportunities to trade directly with ports other than the highly bureaucratic Guangzhou, where their missions were forced to register. Chinese merchants already abroad in foreign ports were ready to help and often served as the representatives of foreign rulers or as interpreters coming to China with their missions. Others, especially the experienced but bypassed Hokkien sailors and traders, secretly went out to trade with, and perhaps even join, the small merchant communities already formed in Southeast Asian ports. Thus, despite the bans and the increased risks of trading overseas during the fifteenth century, small Chinese merchant communities abroad survived, for example, at ports like Malacca, Bantam, Brunei, and Sulu and perhaps also in the Ryukyu Islands and Kyushu. Thus, before the arrival of the Europeans, a chain of small port communities of Chinese traders was servicing a thriving trade that many people in eastern and Southeast Asia were actively seeking to expand.[13]

We have no details about these communities and what they were like. Because they were not legitimate in the eyes of China, no official accounts are available, and the Chinese sojourners themselves were either illiterate or too discreet to record anything. Their better-educated counterparts in ports in China who supported them were unable to admit publicly to their profitable involvement with this trade. Hence we begin to have a fuller picture of these communities only when first the Portuguese, then the Spanish, the Dutch, the Japanese, and finally the Chinese themselves when Ming policy was all but abandoned after 1567 left us descriptions of some of the notable ones in Faifo, Malacca, Patani, Hirado, Nagasaki, Manila, Bantam, and Batavia.[14]

---

[13] Evidence scattered throughout the Ming Veritable Records has been collected in two volumes: *Ming Shilu zhong zhi Dongnanya Shihliao,* ed. Zhao Lingyang et al. (Hong Kong, 1968, 1976).

[14] M. A. P. Melink-Roelofsz, *Asian Trade and European Influence in the Indonesian Archi-*

MANILA AND NAGASAKI

Until the end of the sixteenth century, it is doubtful whether any of the Chinese communities was more than a few hundred in number. Of course, a few hundred Chinese males who married locally and brought their children up as Chinese could quickly increase the number to thousands. But apart from Manila in the 1590s, this probably did not happen before the seventeenth century. The Chinese males were mainly sojourners, who did not plan to stay long, or if they intermarried, they allowed their children to assimilate to the indigenous people. The exception of Manila is an interesting one. Unlike the Portuguese, who had conquered well-established city-ports like Goa and Malacca and had access to rich hinterlands and technically advanced native populations, the Spanish in the Philippines settled on an undeveloped chain of islands on the frontiers of sophisticated, "oriental" civilizations. Fortunately for them in the 1560s and 1570s, the Muslims they met were weak and cut off from stronger Muslim allies by the Portuguese, and neither the Japanese nor the Chinese were interested in territory. It quickly became clear to the handful of Spanish officials, priests, and soldiers that if they wanted to defend and develop what they had, they needed to expand the China trade and, what was more, they needed Chinese ships, traders, and skilled artisans to build up Manila as a great maritime center and help speed up Spanish control of the islands. Thus they welcomed the coming of Chinese traders as no one in the region had ever welcomed them before. In less than thirty years, the Chinese population reached some ten thousand, perhaps more if the mixed-blood descendants were all counted.[15] This was the first truly large Chinese community overseas and easily the largest one in the sixteenth century.

During the seventeenth century, another large Chinese merchant community was to be found in Batavia, which eventually became much larger than that in Manila. Again, this was the result of deliberate Dutch policy, which sought to gain a total monopoly of eastern and southeastern Asia trade through making use of the Chinese trading networks already established throughout the Malay Archipelago, the Indochina coasts, and Japan. The Dutch were much stronger than the

---

pelago between 1500 and about 1630 (The Hague, 1962); Yanai Kenji, *Nagasaki* (Tokyo, 1966); Chingho A. Chen, *Historical Notes on Hôi-An (Faifo)* (Carbondale, 1974).

[15] Ch'en T'ai-min, *Chung-Fei kuan-hsi yü Fei-lü-pin Hua-ch'iao* (Hong Kong, 1985), draws fully on the rich materials translated in E. H. Blair and J. A. Robertson, *The Philippine Islands, 1493–1898*, 55 vols. (Cleveland, 1903–7). An excellent brief account is Ch'en Ching-ho, *The Chinese Community in 16th Century Philippines* (Tokyo, 1968).

Spanish and more determined to expand quickly. They welcomed Chinese cooperation and tried to woo them wherever possible away from the Portuguese and the Spanish. In that way, a Dutch-supported chain of Chinese communities grew up between Batavia and areas like the Moluccas to the east, Siam to the north, and China and Japan to the northeast. When the Portuguese were driven out of Malacca and the Moluccas and confined to Macao, the Dutch in Batavia, like the Spanish in Manila, controlled the largest Chinese communities in Southeast Asia and used them to strengthen their own maritime empires. It is no coincidence that they both also felt threatened by the numbers of Chinese attracted to their two cities, and both tried to control their Chinese very carefully. During the next 150 years, whenever the Spanish felt threatened by the Chinese in Manila, they massacred them, and in Batavia, a major bloodletting occurred in 1740. The Spanish felt specially vulnerable because their dependence on the Chinese was greater, their forces were weaker, and the homeland of the vigorous Hokkiens of Zhangzhou and Quanzhou was close by. But even with their great navies, the Dutch had to be careful to check the potential power of their Chinese allies. They could not afford to relax with large Chinese communities living in their empire, and an especially large one on their doorstep in Batavia.[16]

Two Hokkien communities, those in Manila and Nagasaki, deserve more attention here. The first is one that rose out of a dramatic demand for Chinese traders by a European power, and the other is a basically Asian development influenced by the European presence.

The story of the rise of a large Chinese community in Manila cannot be separated from Spanish policy, but it first began, on the one hand, as an extension of traditional Hokkien trade in the archipelago, reaching out from Brunei tc Sulu, and, on the other, as a response to new trading developments on the Fujian coast following the arrival of the Portuguese early in the sixteenth century. As a natural extension of their trading efforts, the Chinese established a new sea route to Luzon via Taiwan and the Babuyan Islands. This shortened the journey considerably and gave the Zhangzhou and Quanzhou people a decisive advantage over other Chinese in the Philippines trade that they never lost. Thereafter, regular voyages to specific ports in Luzon–Mindoro and in Mindanao and Sulu were normal. This new route was in no way spectacular, however, and was clearly subordinate in importance to the major trading routes to the richer ports of the west-

---

[16] Susan Abeyasekere, *Jakarta: A History* (Singapore, 1987), chap. 1, 3–47; L. Blussé, "Batavia, 1619–1740: The Rise and Fall of a Chinese Colonial Town," *Journal of Southeast Asian Studies* 12 (1981): 159–78.

ern end of the South China Sea. With the arrival of the Portuguese and the ramifications of increased trade on the China coasts, however, Hokkien trading fortunes take a surprising turn.

The Portuguese arrived at the time when the Ming trade policy had all but broken down.[17] Unofficial trade by Chinese and foreigners alike had outstripped trade through tribute. Thus when officials in Guangdong rejected the Portuguese because they were outside the tribute system and the Portuguese decided to trade anyway, using force if necessary, the impact on the Hokkiens in particular was considerable. Restless Hokkien traders were ready to seek out the Portuguese who sailed past their ports. The trade was illegal, but ineffectual officials did little to stop it. When it continued to grow and became a source of conflict and disorder with the Portuguese and their allies, some earnest imperial officials finally sought to enforce the trade bans with vigor. The uproar this created led to widespread resistance among the local Hokkien notables secretly involved in this overseas trade and among Japanese and other illegal traders. And because this coincided with virtual anarchy in Japan following a series of civil wars when many Japanese ronin were available for hire, the resistance took the form of a series of Sino-Japanese attacks on the south China coast that lasted from 1550 to 1570. Four coastal provinces were under continuous attack, especially between 1552 and 1565. Although the Ming forces eventually won, the lesson was learned, and the maritime trade bans were lifted in 1567.[18] This coincided with the arrival of the Spanish in the Philippines and was only five years before the Spanish settlement of Manila.

The prospects for a profitable relationship between these Spanish and the Hokkiens recently freed from heavy trading restrictions were good from the start. It was significant that the 150 or so Chinese whom the Spanish found in the Manila area when they first arrived were eager for the trade. This augured well for the future, and indeed the Hokkiens came in large numbers over the next three decades. As for the formation of a merchant community, which is well attested in several sources, the description in Zhang Xie's *Dongxi Yang Kao* (1617) sums it up well:

The Chinese who visit Luzon are consequently many. They often stayed on and did not return, and this was called *yadong*. They stayed together in the *Jiannei* [the Parian] to make their living, and their numbers gradually rose to several tens of thousands. One hears that some cut their hair and produced

---

[17] Chang Tien-tse, *Sino-Portuguese Trade from 1514 to 1644* (Leiden, 1934).
[18] Kwan-wai So, *Japanese Piracy in Ming China during the 16th Century* (East Lansing, 1975); also Chen Mouheng, *Mingdai Wokou Kaolue* (Beijing, 1957).

sons and grandsons there [that is, converted to Christianity or took to foreign ways, married local women, and established their families there].[19]

The Chinese settlement in Manila remained nevertheless a dependent and an uneasy one for both the Spanish and the Chinese. This was in part due to the conditions on the China coast in the aftermath of the era of "Japanese" pirates. There were several major pirate bands still harassing Chinese coastal officials, and one under Lin Feng (Limahong) sailed south to try to capture Manila in 1574–5. Lin Feng nearly succeeded and the Spanish were painfully reminded of how precarious their position still was. But they also learned something else about the Ming Empire. Ming coastal officials offered to help destroy Lin Feng's forces and were actually grateful for the Spanish success. Two groups of Ming officials visited Manila, and the second actually brought imperial approval for the Spanish to trade in China. More significantly, they showed no interest in the Chinese merchant community there. The clear message to the Spanish was that the Chinese trading abroad were really on their own and could be used to further Spanish interests in the China trade as well as their own enterprises in Southeast Asia. At the same time, as these Chinese became increasingly numerous, they had to be carefully contained in their own quarters. A special area, the Parian, was marked out for them in 1582 (this was moved several times during the next 200 years, but the principle of controlling non-Catholic Chinese remained the same). The trade in silks for silver in the 1580s had become particularly profitable, and about twenty ships were coming from Fujian each year. These numbers rose to over thirty by 1600, and three years later, the number of Chinese who chose to remain in Luzon had exceeded 25,000. In 1603 Spanish suspicion and fear of these Chinese led to a dispute that ended with most of the Chinese being killed. Of the survivors, reputedly about 500 returned to China and only 500 others remained. Hokkien gazetteers and genealogies report this tragedy with particular poignancy.[20]

Despite the many references to the Chinese in Spanish writings of this period, there are few details about how the Chinese merchant community in the Parian was organized. We are told the major traders were those selling silks and other textiles; others sold porcelain, and yet others food, furniture, tools, and personal services. Other important skills represented included tailoring and printing. But most of the Chinese opened shops and bought and sold with great success.

---

[19] Zhang Xie, *Dongxi Yang Kao* (Cheng-chung reprint, Taipei, 1962), 174.
[20] *Anhai Zhi*, 144–52, outlines some notable references to this tragedy.

Increasing numbers of them converted to Catholicism and married local women, and they were allowed to live outside the Parian. Among them and their children were found the trusted leaders who dealt with Spanish authorities on behalf of the community. Some of these trusted Chinese were even allowed to live among the Spanish within Manila fort.[21]

But it was hardly a stable Chinese community. After the 1603 massacre, the numbers were drastically reduced to about 500. Surprisingly, it did not take long for more Hokkien ships to arrive with more traders and for the numbers to rise again. Within another two decades, the total in the Philippines had reached 30,000. The policy was to allow no more than 6,000 to stay in Manila, but in practice, this had been ignored, and it is estimated that there were at least 20,000 in the Parian by 1621. Also, by this time, a clear distinction had been made between sojourning Chinese in closed areas like the Parian and converted Catholic Chinese, who were permitted to live among the "Indios" if they wanted to. And for the rest of the century, the numbers continued to fluctuate as Spanish policy changed from time to time, especially in response to the uncertainties of Chinese politics between 1620 and 1684. The Spanish learned to live with a limited number of Chinese ships arriving from China. Also, their own Chinese mestizo community had grown steadily to handle the China trade. Thus the Chinese community in Manila and elsewhere in the Philippines changed in nature. It had become divided into two related but different communities: a sojourning community and a transitional one that had become a localized community of mestizos (of part-Chinese descent), many of whom concentrated on the trade with the Chinese sojourners from their ancestral homes in Fujian, but whose descendants were on the way to becoming future Filipinos.[22]

The sojourners, the non-Catholic Chinese, were controlled by a Spanish "governor," but the Parian also had its own "headmen," who acted as intermediaries. We know nothing about how the various trades were organized. Elsewhere, one center of community life was always the temple, whether to Tian Hou, the goddess of sailors, or Guan Yu, the deity preferred by merchants, or both (often joined later by Buddha or the compassionate Guanyin). Because of the several massacres and because the Parian was moved several times, we have no relics of early temples in Manila or even any record of them having been there. The Spanish sources, on which much of our infor-

---

[21] Alfonso Felix, Jr., ed., *The Chinese in the Philippines, 1570–1770* (Manila, 1966), I, using mainly materials in Blair and Robertson, *Philippine Islands.*

[22] Edgar Wickberg, *The Chinese in Philippine Life, 1850–1898* (New Haven, 1965), 3–41.

mation depends, focus so much on the China–Mexico trade, on the Chinese threats to Spanish authority, and on the potential conversion of the Chinese to Catholicism that they do not mention what institutions the Chinese themselves used to provide solidarity or further their business efforts. It was not until the eighteenth century that secret societies, guilds, and dialect group associations became common. In any case, because the Chinese were almost all natives of Quanzhou or Zhangzhou, such organizations were probably not essential.[23]

The records suggest that the sojourners in the Parian were housed in a few streets of wooden buildings that were grouped according to the major trades or around clan, village, or county origins, with perhaps one building serving as a temple to Tian Hou and Guan Yu and small altars scattered in other buildings. The Catholic Chinese (not more than 10–15 percent of the Chinese population during the early seventeenth century), especially those who were married, lived around the churches in Binondo and neighboring suburbs. In 1687 we hear of the Gremio de Chinos de Binondo (a town council) headed by ten Chinese captains and five mestizo captains. But by the middle of the eighteenth century, the mestizos were numerous enough to have broken away from the sojourners. The impression given is certainly one where the Spanish controlled most of the population through a policy of church guidance, leaving the various groups of Chinese free to organize themselves in their own way whenever they wanted to, or to bribe the officials to allow them to do so.[24]

In sharp contrast to the community in Manila, the Chinese sojourners who went to trade in Japan at the end of the sixteenth century did not have to deal with an insecure but expansionist Western power. Instead, they could benefit from the long historical and cultural links between China and Japan. Nevertheless, these links had not been continuous or even predictable, and the traders on both sides were often victims of the variable policies of two proud imperial governments. For example, the growing trade during the Sung dynasty was cut off by the ambitions of Khubilai Khan at the end of the thirteenth century when he twice attempted to invade Japan. Later, when Ming policy confined foreign trade to tribute missions, Japan rejected the idea of a subordinate relationship, however nominal that was. And

---

[23] Temples, however, were essential. No thorough study is available on those in Manila, but Claudine Salmon and Denys Lombard, *Les Chinois de Jakarta: Temples et vie collective* (Paris, 1977), demonstrates how vital they were for Chinese communities overseas.

[24] Felix, *Chinese in the Philippines;* Wickberg, *Chinese in Philippine Life.*

Japanese pirates and smugglers at the end of the fourteenth and the beginning of the fifteenth century worsened relations to the point that it was increasingly difficult for Chinese traders to travel safely to Japan, much less to support any sojourning community there. It did not make it any easier that this was also a period when Japan was in the grips of civil war. As the various feudal lords fought bitterly to defend their territories, political anarchy made regular trading relationships impossible. All the same, the interests of the lords in Kyushu, the ports of which were closer to the southern Chinese provinces and more accessible to enterprising Chinese, did keep an unofficial trade alive. Their own ships and traders began to go beyond China and find their way to various ports of Southeast Asia. Indeed, private connections with Chinese merchants, again notably with those of south Fujian, developed further. They had become so close that when the Chinese trade bans were vigorously enforced in the middle of the sixteenth century, the Japanese and Chinese merchants who were directly affected joined forces to raid the Chinese coasts. For these raids, they used the offshore islands of Zhejiang and Fujian, but the port bases from which they organized their major attacks were in the Kyushu group of islands.[25] Many of these ports are reported to have had sojourning Chinese, but there is no evidence of a community before the seventeenth century.

It is not known how much these continuous raids on the China coast over two and a half decades satisfied commercial needs. The records emphasize the destruction of property, including cultivated fields and coastal industries, and the terrible loss of lives; and not least, they describe the very expensive efforts by leading Ming generals to crush these pirate bands and drive them back to Japan. There is little doubt that many Chinese, either individually or in small groups, escaped to Japanese ports and sojourned or settled there, and others, together with their Japanese comrades, traveled south to sojourn in various ports in Vietnam (now including Cham ports), Luzon, Patani, Bantam, and Malacca.[26] Of significance was the fact that the "Japanese" were not forgiven by the Ming. When the trading bans were lifted in 1567, the ban on trading with Japan remained in force. This meant that the Chinese sojourning in Japan could not return to China, nor could Japanese merchants trade directly with China. Thus the Hokkiens, whose enthusiasm for the illegal private trade had caused the bans to have been reinforced in the first place and whose fervent and

---

[25] Kwan-wai So, *Japanese Piracy*; Yamawaki Teijiro, *Nukeni, sakoku jitai no mitsuboeki* [The smuggling trade during the age of isolation] (Tokyo, 1965).

[26] Kawashima Genjiro, *Tokugawa shoki no Kaigai boekika* (Tokyo, 1917).

desperate pleas had led to their being relaxed in 1567, were not able to benefit where the rich Japan trade was concerned. Instead, the main beneficiaries were the Portuguese, who used their newly created.Macao base to carry the China–Japan trade both ways. And Hokkien traders had to be content to ally with and depend on Portuguese captains and join with the Portuguese in their small but successful trading and missionary centers in Japanese ports.[27]

Early in the seventeenth century, there was an excellent example of this indirect trade with Japan. The Nan'an (in Quanzhou) adventurer Zheng Zhilong, father of Koxinga (Zheng Chenggong), went to join his maternal uncle in Macao, became a Catholic convert, and accompanied the Macao fleet to Kyushu. At Hirado, he worked for the very successful Hokkien merchant Li Dan (Captain Andrea Ditties), married a Japanese wife, and when Li Dan died, took over his commercial maritime empire. Clearly, there must already have been a small Hokkien community at Hirado. Another Hokkien, named Yan Siqi, was said to have started life there as a tailor and eventually made enough of a fortune to lead his own maritime empire before Zheng Zhilong arrived. And there is evidence of other small groups of Chinese traders and adventurers at several ports in the neighborhood of Nagasaki and in Nagasaki itself.[28]

The Dutch arrived in Kyushu early in the seventeenth century, soon after the new shogun, Tokugawa Ieyasu, had reunified Japan under his control. He was quick to recognize that there were great profits in the China trade. Instead of leaving that trade to Portuguese–Dutch rivalry, he decided that Japanese merchants should recruit Chinese to help them. A new system of trading permits was introduced to cut down on the European dominance of the trade. And it was during this period that Li Dan and Zheng Zhilong built up their maritime forces and the island of Taiwan was opened up as a useful trading base by the Chinese and then by the Dutch and the Spanish. During the 1620s, the trade of Macao, Manila, Yuegang in Zhangzhou (which replaced Quanzhou as the port of the Hokkiens during the sixteenth century), Xiamen (or Amoy, which was emerging as the new Hokkien port of the seventeenth century under the influence of Zheng Zhilong), Taiwan, and Kyushu was no longer a trade for small mer-

[27] C. R. Boxer, *The Great Ship from Amacon: Annals of Macao and the Old Japan Trade, 1555–1640* (Lisbon, 1959); idem, *Fidalgos in the Far East* (The Hague, 1948); George Bryan Souza, *The Survival of Empire: Portuguese Trade and Society in China and the South China Sea, 1630–1754* (New York, 1986).

[28] J. E. Wills, Jr., "Maritime China from Wang Chih to Shih Lang: Themes in Peripheral History," in J. D. Spence and J. E. Wills, Jr., eds., *From Ming to Ch'ing: Conquest, Region, and Continuity in Seventeenth Century China* (New Haven, 1979).

chants. The arrival of the Europeans had established a new scale of long-distance trade, with their respective royal houses supporting the Portuguese and the Spanish and with official collective backing for the Dutch East India Company. The shogun's response of providing central support for Japanese merchants was a realistic one.[29] Only the Chinese – and here I refer especially to the peripheral Hokkiens in the southeast corner of a weakening Ming Empire – received no official support. Zheng Zhilong held his large maritime forces together by military and diplomatic skill, through successful trading, and, not least, by the support of his large family and his devoted Hokkien countrymen.

The situation remained fluid in Kyushu until the period of Ieyasu's grandson, when Japanese internal politics led to a full closed-door policy. Foreign relations of all kinds were ended, the Portuguese and their trading fleets were sent away, and by 1641 only one port, Nagasaki, was kept open and that only to Chinese and Dutch ships. The story of Nagasaki, the fishing village that grew in importance because of the Portuguese trading and missionary efforts of the 1570s, is a remarkable one that has often been told. The Chinese, including Chinese Catholics in the service of the Portuguese, took an active part in that development. By 1602 there is evidence of a small community of Hokkiens, and they remained the most significant group of Chinese there for the rest of the seventeenth century. It is possible to distinguish three periods of growth and decline for this small Hokkien community. The first lasted from the 1580s to 1635, when they were the strongest. During the second, from 1635 to 1688, the Hokkiens did well because they had their own naval forces, while other Chinese from Fuzhou, Ningbo, and the Yangtse delta were weakened because their home bases were more severely affected by the unrest in China between the fall of the Ming and the consolidation of Qing power. After 1688, the number of Chinese at Nagasaki declined, and the Hokkiens became much more interested in peopling Taiwan and various ports in Southeast Asia.[30]

The Tokugawa were increasingly anti-Catholic after 1600 and wanted Chinese who were willing to demonstrate that they were not Catholic. Hence the first phase of the sojourning community in Nagasaki

---

[29] Murakami Naojiro, *Boeki shijo no Hirado* [Hirado in commercial history] (Tokyo, 1917); Nagasaki shi yakusho, *Nagasaki shi shi: tsuko boeki hen, Toyo shokoku bo* [History of Nagasaki City: trade and transport, volume on eastern ocean] (Nagasaki, 1938).

[30] *Kai hentai* [Changing conditions of Chinese and barbarians], Toyo Bunko series no. 15, vol. 1 (Tokyo, 1958); Yamawaki Teijiro, *Nagasaki no Tojin boeki* [The Chinese trade of Nagasaki] (Tokyo, 1964).

was marked by an open commitment of the Chinese to Buddhism, something not expected of them elsewhere.[31] The Hokkiens were not alone here but in 1602 were the first to use a local Buddhist temple as their official meeting place. Their competitors from Jiangsu and Zhekiang went further in 1623 and established the Xingfu (or Nanking) Temple. This led the Hokkiens soon after, in 1628, to build their own, the Fuji (or Zhangzhou) Temple. And the next year, the third group, from Fuzhou, built their own, the Chongfu (or Fuzhou) Temple. In this way, they cut themselves off from the Portuguese and their Japanese and Chinese converts (including other Hokkiens converted by the Spanish in Manila) and became the favored foreign traders in Nagasaki. Later, in 1641, when the Dutch were forced to move from Hirado to Deshima, the artificial island that confined their activities at Nagasaki, it was obvious that the "Buddhist" Chinese were given favored treatment. Indeed, the Chinese were not confined to the neighborhoods of their respective temples in the town itself but were allowed to live freely among the Japanese merchant families who traded with them. However, it may be assumed that each of the three subcommunities did use their own temples as meeting places and social and welfare centers as well as places for religious activity to confirm their subethnic solidarity.[32] Unfortunately, we do not know if the temples were ever used to further their business ambitions or played any part in the successes achieved by people like Li Dan and Zheng Zhilong.

For the second period, Zheng Zhilong and his son Koxinga ensured that Hokkiens dominated whatever trade there was between Nagasaki, Xiamen, and Taiwan (and sundry other Chinese and Southeast Asian ports). More clearly than in any other period, the Zheng fleets controlled something like a maritime empire. They were helped by the Qing policy of moving coastal populations inland. This policy lasted for over twenty years (1661–81) and left the Zheng family with little competition during its declining years. During this period, the Nagasaki authorities began to supervise the Chinese more closely and took a keen interest in their social and political activities, but the Chinese were still relatively free to live among the Japanese. As for the refugees who were loyal to the Ming and escaped to Japan, they found favor by choosing to assimilate (*guihua*) and were never classified with the numerous sojourning Hokkiens. The climax came for the com-

[31] Yamamoto Noritsuna, *Nagasaki Tojin Yashiki* [The Chinese quarter of Nagasaki] (Tokyo, 1983), 146–93.
[32] Yamawaki, *Nagasaki no Tojin boeki.*

munity, however, when the Zheng "empire" collapsed and Taiwan fell in 1683 to the Qing navy and the coastal population was allowed to go to sea again. By 1687 more than 100 ships were arriving from China. Suddenly, the pressure of these numbers was seen as too great. The Nagasaki authorities decided to limit the number of ships and also to build a Chinese quarter for the Chinese. With the rounding up of all Chinese in 1689 and forcing them to live in a restricted area, like the Dutch at Deshima, a new era began.[33]

From 1688 to the middle of the nineteenth century, the Chinese in Nagasaki were confined to an enclosed and guarded "China town." This area was controlled by the Japanese, and in 1708, 96 staff were employed there, whereas 134 had been appointed to keep the Dutch in Deshima. Also, 250 staff were employed in the foreign affairs office for the Chinese, compared with 138 staff to deal with the Dutch. Among the Chinese themselves, the Hokkiens still stood out despite the fact that fewer Hokkiens looked to the Nagasaki trade in the eighteenth century. In 1708 of the 167 interpreters for various Chinese dialects, 101 of them were trained for the Quanzhou (Hokkien or Xiamen) dialect.[34]

The Hokkiens have been the focus of this essay because they were the majority of the overseas traders between the thirteenth and eighteenth centuries. They were also the most successful. They emerged as a coherent trading force on the China coast earlier than the Portuguese did on the European coast. Their earlier success was due to official support under the Sung and the Yüan emperors, just as Portuguese achievements depended on royal encouragement from the start. But when Ming imperial policy changed and official help was withdrawn after 1368, the Hokkiens persisted outside the law and survived on their own. They needed the skills of Hokkien shipbuilders and captains, the capital of wealthy clansmen who had made their fortunes in China's internal trade, and their literati relatives to speak for them and even protect some of their illegal activities. And they needed their families and village networks to provide the personnel. They also had to bribe corrupt officials at home and cooperate with foreign officials and merchants overseas. Despite all these efforts and their geographical advantages and their long-time knowledge of the

---

[33] The literature on Zheng Chenggong is now vast; see two recent collections published in China, especially *Zheng Chenggong yanjiu lunwenxuan, Xuji* (Fuzhou, 1984). On the Chinese quarter, see Yamamoto, *Nagasaki Tojin Yashiki*, 197–207.

[34] Nakamura Tadashi and Nakada Yasunao, eds., *Kiyo Gundan* [Various talks on Nagasaki] (Tokyo, 1974), 263–303.

Southeast Asian region, the Hokkiens were hard-pressed to compete with the officially sponsored and armed Portuguese.

As for the Spanish, the Hokkien advantage should have been even greater. The Philippine Islands were close by, the seas in between well-traversed, and the Hokkien merchants far more numerous than the Spanish. Furthermore, the Spanish were at the weaker end of a vast empire and restricted by hostile Portuguese and Moro shipping. The Hokkien communities in Luzon should have been able to hold their own, if not dominate political and economic affairs. But this did not happen. Instead, the Hokkiens, abandoned by Chinese officials, chose a low profile as sojourning merchants. They were helpless against Spanish imperial power and, in fact, many became instruments of Spanish expansion. On the other hand, the communities in the Philippines contributed greatly to the Chinese economy. Their successful trade brought vast amounts of silver into China and their enterprises introduced New World crops like the potato, maize, groundnuts, and tobacco, which were to transform subsistence agriculture all over their home province.[35]

The Dutch, like the Hokkiens and the Portuguese, lived on the edge of a continent and similarly faced the dangers and opportunities of the sea. Unlike the Portuguese, theirs was not a trade supported by their royal house but was backed by a chartered company. The company was organizationally modern and better adapted to the needs of an emerging bourgeois class. And unlike the Hokkiens, the Dutch had official support and legal and political protection. Their vessels, armed in the name of the Dutch East India Company, were also sanctioned by the monarch. Even in Nagasaki, when no foreign group was in control and the Chinese were theoretically equal with the Dutch, the Dutch had the advantage over the Chinese because they dealt with the shogun's officials as representatives of a foreign state. Whether the shoguns were impressed or not, the Dutch were able to continually remind them that their company had state recognition and that they negotiated on behalf of their "king." The Hokkiens could make no such claims. They could only seek the best possible arrangement that they could get, and they could get only what their hosts thought they deserved. Whether in Manila or Nagasaki, the Hokkiens could not compete with the colonists, priests, and soldiers of the Spanish Crown or with the well-armed servants of a state-supported chartered company. They were lowly provincial merchants remote from the Chinese court. They had to live by their wits, cultivate the fine art

---

[35] Rawski, *Agricultural Change*; Zhu Weigan, *Fujian Shigao*, vol. 2.

of risk taking, and, at the crunch, could count only on their family–village system and strong local Hokkien loyalties to help them through hard times.[36]

The successes and failures of the Hokkiens can be easily exaggerated. What stands out from their story in Manila and in Nagasaki is that their trading activities were greatly stimulated by the European presence and that they could, in terms of entrepreneurship and daring, do everything that the various Europeans could do. But they were helpless to produce the necessary institutional change in China to match European or even Japanese power. They were never the instruments of any effort by Ming or Qing authorities to build merchant empires; nor could they hope to get mandarin or ideological support for any innovative efforts of their own. Eventually, they had to be content to become participants, even supporting agents, in the merchant empires that their counterparts from smaller states with state-backed organizations were able to build. In such indirect ways Chinese merchant communities contributed to the growth of the world economy. The extent of that contribution will have to be the subject of future study.

[36] Ng Chin-keong, *Trade and Society: The Amoy Network on the China Coast, 1683–1735* (Singapore, 1983); Tien Ju-kang, "Causes of the Decline in China's Overseas Trade between the 15th and 18th Centuries," *Papers on Far Eastern History* 25 (1982): 31–44.

Index